Bolton 20 Years On:
the Small Firm in the 1990s

Bolton 20 Years On:
the Small Firm in the 1990s

John Stanworth and Colin Gray
Editors

Published on behalf of the Small Business Research Trust

Commissioned by National Westminster Bank

P·C·P
Paul Chapman
Publishing Ltd

Copyright © 1991, Small Business Research Trust

First published 1991

Paul Chapman Publishing Ltd
144 Liverpool Road
London
N1 1LA

British Library Cataloguing in Publication Data

Bolton 20 years on : the small firm in the 1990s.
 I. Stanworth, John, *1942–*   II. Gray, Colin
 338.6420941

 ISBN 1 85396 229 5

Typeset by Inforum Typesetting, Portsmouth
Printed and bound by The Cromwell Press, Melksham, Wilts.

A B C D E F 6 5 4 3

Contents

Foreword

In 1971, John Bolton produced his Committee of Inquiry Report on Small Firms. The 'Bolton Report', as it has been known ever since, marked a turning point in our understanding of the UK small business community.

The Research Director on the Bolton Report was Graham Bannock. John Bolton and Graham Bannock have worked tirelessly ever since (with no public recognition) to ensure that the establishment better understands small business.

By 1981 there were numerous small business organizations, both public and private. It was at this time that I, as founder of the Forum of Private Business, suggested to Graham Bannock that there was a need for an umbrella organization to bring together all the constituent parts of the small business community.

These include: the academics who research and teach small businesses; the PLCs whose customers are small businesses; the trade and professional organizations whose members are small businesses; the mixed-member business organizations whose members are big and small businesses; and the small business-only organizations, which numbered five at the time.

Graham Bannock agreed with the concept and wrote the idea into a report on small businesses for Shell. Shell and NatWest were convinced and the Small Business Research Trust started to take shape. At this time, the late Sir Charles Villiers saw the potential of the Small Business Research Trust and Graham and I were delighted when he agreed to be its Chairman.

Sir Charles worked tirelessly for the Small Business Research Trust (SBRT), talking to his enormous circle of friends and forming the Trust with NatWest, Shell and Sainsbury as the initial sponsors. This book is one of the many memorials to Sir Charles.

The Council of the Trust, representing the whole small business community (i.e. education, PLCs, trade and professionals, miscellaneous and small business owners) is the decision-making arm of the Trust, while the Trustees ensure its financial resources and direction.

The Trustees are now John Bolton, Charles Green, Professor Andrew Thomson and myself as Chairman. The Director Generals are Professor John Stanworth and Colin Gray who ensure a regular flow of academically-approved publications.

The backbone of the SBRT's work is its postal Quarterly Survey. This is now in its eighth year and provides a factual base of opinion and statistics on the progress of the small business community in the light of economic and political change.

Needless to say, the continuity from the Bolton Report to date is maintained because Graham Bannock writes the Quarterly Survey Report, which is sponsored by the National Westminster Bank, and John Bolton is a Trustee.

The next major event in the life of the SBRT was its joining forces with Europe's largest business school, The Open University (OU), based in Milton Keynes. The link between the SBRT and the OU has worked extremely well and the potential for the future is enormous.

As a result of the SBRT's standing in the small business community, it was not surprising that NatWest approached it to produce this book, *Bolton 20 Years On*, which updates the 1971 Bolton Report and brings together the multifarious strands of the small business community, showing its progress over the past 20 years.

In his original Foreword that great man, the late Sir Charles Villiers, highlighted the need for a more collaborative spirit in the UK business community. Of course, he saw this developed best in the small business community. As an example he wrote: 'The banks are the providers of much of the capital employed by small businesses. Usually, and quite wrongly, they are the last to be told of problems. The rule for banks and their customers should be "no surprises", and the idea of a code of conduct for bank relationships is a good one.'

As the Chairman of the SBRT, I will ensure that we continue to look for that collaboration, in particular with the banks and government. I dream of the day when the UK Government follows the example of the Japanese, Germans and the new President of the USA and the UK banks in this respect.

Until that day, however, the SBRT in its Open University base will strive to keep the general public informed, in particular students and all those big businesses that need to penetrate deeper into the small business community with solid factual information. This book is a fine foundation on which to build.

Stan Mendham:
Chairman,
Small Business Research Trust

Preface

The Committee of Inquiry on Small Firms, of which I had the honour to be Chairman, was appointed by Anthony Crosland, the Labour government minister, on 23 July 1969, and reported two years later, on 21 September 1971, to John Davies, his successor as President of the Board of Trade in the new Conservative government. The way in which our inquiry spanned governments of two different political complexions was to prove prophetic, for today there is all-party agreement on the need to promote the role of small firms in the economy.

1969, like 1991, was a difficult year for business generally and for many small firms in particular, but as I wrote in the preface to our report: 'It was made clear to us that the major purpose of the Inquiry was a long-term one – the collection of information on the place of small firms in a modern economy as a basis for recommendations about future policy towards them.' Twenty years later it is a source of great satisfaction to me to see that our principal recommendation, the creation of a Small Firms Division under a Minister for Small Firms, was not only implemented but has endured (albeit under a different name and a different Department of State). It is also satisfying to see that so much of the basic research we carried out recognizably remains as the basis for the large body of work outlined in this volume, which has greatly extended and at some points corrected our early efforts.

What has come to be known as the Bolton Report was, of course, a team effort. My colleagues on the committee, the late 'Ted' Robbins, Professor Brian Tew and Larry Tindale, were supported by a secretariat led by David Hartridge and a research unit directed by Graham Bannock, which included notably Professor S. J. Prais – then, as now, of the National Institute for Social and Economic Research.

The research programme included a postal questionnaire survey with responses from 3,500 firms and an extensive review of UK and international statistics carried out by the research unit. Eighteen reports on small firms in different sectors of the economy, group discussions among small businesses and various specialized topics, such as finance, were commissioned. These reports were published separately. The committee also considered a wide range of written and oral evidence, and paid brief visits to a number of overseas countries.

Of course, there have been many changes in the small firm scene since 1971: the decline of the sector, about which we were so concerned, and which we charted for the first time, has been reversed; financial facilities for small firms have been greatly extended, and an extensive training and assistance network has been built up (it is extraordinary to think that in 1971 no higher education institution offered training for small business owners: now virtually all do).

One thing has not changed. I remember a cartoon published around 1970 showing a donkey labelled 'small firms', heavily laden with boxes marked 'taxes', 'regulations', 'forms', and on top of these an animated figure with a 'Government' sash, whip and spurs, shouting, 'Faster! Faster!'. Despite the government's genuine efforts to improve things, it seems to me that it still needs to do more to reduce unnecessary burdens on business, which would do so much to contribute to economic welfare and that would enhance rather than deplete tax revenues.

This book is the work of many of the leaders of the growing army of writers and researchers on small firms that has emerged in the United Kingdom since the Bolton Committee's report. As in any free field of inquiry, there is controversy among them, but it is noteworthy that they have joined hands to produce this admirable review of present knowledge on the subject. It is to their credit – and that of the editors – that the book, intended for a wide audience, is so usable and accessible. I believe it will find a concerned readership, not only among specialists and policy-makers but also among small business owner-managers.

J. E. Bolton

Acknowledgements

The original report of the Committee of Inquiry on Small Firms – the Bolton Report – remains the single most important document of its kind ever published in Britain. Our current publication, *Bolton 20 Years On: the Small Firm in the 1990s*, is, in many ways, an extension of the original report. In keeping with its strategic importance, it contains a personal preface by John Bolton and two key chapters contributed by Graham Bannock who, it will be remembered, was Research Director on the original Bolton Report 20 years ago.

Based on an initiative by National Westminster Bank the raw planning work for the current book began with a meeting assembled in April 1991. This meeting was attended by, amongst others, Sir Charles Villiers and Stan Mendham (respectively Honorary President and Chairman of the Small Business Research Trust); David Grayson (Business in the Community); Andy Scott (CBI); Brian Jenks (Touche Ross); Mike Daley (Department of Employment); Clive Woodcock (the *Guardian*); Charles Batchelor (the *Financial Times*) plus Jane Bradford and Lyn Randall (National Westminster Bank).

Soon afterwards the detailed planning began and a team of specialist writers commissioned. These included, in addition to Graham Bannock, Colin Mason (Southampton University); Martin Binks and Christine Ennew (Nottingham University); David Kirby and Allan Gibb (Durham University Business School); Francis Chittenden (Manchester Business School); James Curran and Robert Blackburn (Kingston University); Richard Harrison (Ulster University); Elizabeth Chell (Salford University); David Storey (Warwick University) and Roger Burrows (University of Teesside).

Many other people gave help and support along the way. In addition to the three of our Trustees already mentioned – Sir Charles Villiers, Stan Mendham and John Bolton, our other Trustees – Charles Green, Andrew Thomson and Russ Wilson – were also very supportive and, of course, several members of the Small Business Research Trust's Council made helpful comments and suggestions.

Thanks are also due to the many small business owners who have taken the time over recent years to complete the Small Business Research Trust's

Quarterly Survey of Small Business in Britain questionnaires, thereby helping to build up a statistical data-base which is reported in this book.

The challenging and complex task of editing materials from a group of writers into a single unified text was accomplished to a very high standard by Les Hutton and a great deal of additional organizational work accomplished in admirable fashion by Beverley Porter-Blake. The index was compiled by Richard Raper of Indexing Specialists.

Finally, this book could never have been produced to such a high standard or so quickly without the very generous financial support of National Westminster Bank. It should be noted that any opinions expressed in this publication are not necessarily those of National Westminster Bank.

John Stanworth and Colin Gray
(Senior Editors)

1 An Economic Survey 1971–1991

The Bolton Report was not the first inquiry into the state of small business, even in the UK. Nor, of course, was it the first economic inquiry into the determinants of the size distribution of firms. It did, however, undoubtedly help to establish the groundwork for what is emerging as a significant part of the concerns of the social sciences.

Perhaps the most important contribution of the report was its use of international comparisons to raise the question of the role of small firms in economic development. These questions had been raised by economists in the nineteenth century, when large firms began to predominate, and various authors have tackled them since – notably Hoselitz (1968). At the time the Bolton Committee was appointed, however, the prevailing orthodoxy, in Britain at least, was that small firms no longer had much relevance to economic progress.

A principal finding was that, though small firms survived in large numbers, their share in economic activity was in decline, and that this decline had proceeded further and faster in the UK than elsewhere. This, the report stated, was a cause for concern:

> We believe that the health of the economy requires the birth of new enterprises in substantial numbers and the growth of some to a position from which they are able to challenge and supplant the existing leaders of industry. We fear that an economy totally dominated by large firms could not for long avoid ossification and decay . . . This 'seedbed' function, therefore, appears to be a vital contribution of the small firms sector to the long-run health of the economy. We cannot assume that the ordinary working of market forces will necessarily preserve a small firm sector large enough to perform this function in the future.

At the beginning of the report the committee devoted some space to the question of definition. A small firm was defined as one with a relatively small share of the market, one that was managed by its owners in a personalized way, and independent in the sense that it was free from outside control in decision-making. For practical purposes it was accepted that a statistical definition was necessary and that any given threshold would inevitably be arbitrary. In fact, the committee decided to use different statistical definitions for different sectors of the economy, on the grounds that what was small in one sector (for example, 200 employees in manufacturing) would be regarded as very large in another (for example, retailing, where a turnover limit of £50,000 was selected as being more appropriate). A mix of turnover and employment definitions was used, together with number of vehicles (five or less) in road transport, and the exclusion of multiples in catering. These definitions are still used for some official purposes today, adjusted to current prices to allow for inflation. The 1990 turnover threshold for retailing, for instance, had risen to £450,000.

The whole question of defining a small firm has fascinated many people, and there is at least one book solely devoted to the subject. Although this debate does raise some interesting issues, to which we return later at several points, it need not detain us here. No single definition of what constitutes a small firm can be useful for all purposes. A window cleaner with a ladder and bucket; an independent shop with two employees; a farmer with 300 acres, one employee, a tractor and other equipment; a clothing manufacturer with fifty employees; all share some common problems which are essentially different from those of a multinational company. It is not necessary to agree upon a precise threshold point at which a small business becomes a large one, to make useful generalizations about small and large firms.

At the same time the Bolton Committee's use of different definitions for different sectors greatly hampers statistical analysis. In some of the analysis below, we follow the European Commission (EC) and the Small Business Administration (SBA) in the United States in setting the limit for small firms – small and medium firms (SMEs) – at under 500 employees. However, it is important to recognize that the small firm sector embraces an enormous range of situations. We accept that on a common-sense basis, 500 is a high threshold definition, especially in non-manufacturing, and also use lower thresholds.

The EC has recently started using the term 'micro-enterprises' to include firms with fewer than ten employees. Some people prefer to exclude the self-employed without employees. There is little economic logic in this exclusion, though in some cases official statistics may omit or understate the number of firms with '0' employees and this is a major source of confusion in international comparisons. Another source of confusion in statistical comparisons is the distinction between establishments (operating or reporting units) and enterprises which are one or more establishments under common ownership. We follow the Bolton Report in using enterprise data wherever possible. Although, in manufacturing, small establishments (especially those with, say, under ten employees) are mostly independent enterprises and therefore properly referred to as small firms, this is less likely to be the case in the service sector where many more small establishments, for example, multiple retailers, are subsidiaries of large enterprises.

In the remainder of this opening chapter we describe some of the major changes in the statistical picture of small firms in the UK economy, make some international comparisons and, briefly, try to explain the dramatic changes which have taken place in the economic role of small business since the Bolton

Report. In all these spheres, the volume of research that has emerged since 1971 is so great that we have had to be highly selective. Among the important topics covered by recent research and omitted here is the role of small firms in visible and invisible exports and in innovation and technological change.

Trends in the small firms sector

We now know that even before the Bolton Report appeared, the long decline in the UK small firms sector had come to an end. This did not become apparent, however, for many years; and even now, with all the benefits of hindsight, it is by no means clear exactly when the change in trend for the sector as a whole took place.

In 1971 the committee was mainly working with data relating to the middle 1960s: the report of the 1968 Census of Production, for example, which merely showed a slowing down in the rate of decline, did not appear until the early 1970s. Even four years after the publication of the Bolton Report, Bannock (1976) was able only to write that there was no evidence of a levelling off: '[The decline] in some sectors has slowed down, but it has accelerated in others' – though he did note some indications of an increase in the small firm birth rate.

Not only were there lags in the appearance of relevant statistics, but there were no readily available comprehensive statistics on trends in the size distribution of firms in the economy as a whole, a gap which has since been partially filled by VAT statistics. To make matters worse, the substitution of annual censuses of production from 1971 onwards for the quinquennial censuses that ended in 1968 was accompanied by changes in methods which for a while cast doubt upon the apparent change in trend.

In fact, as we can now see, there was a dramatic turnaround in the trend in small firms' share in manufacturing employment in the early 1970s

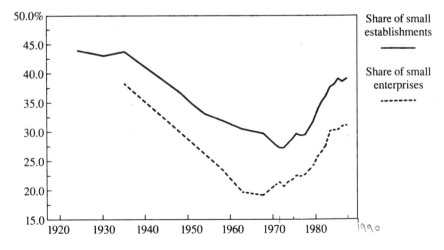

Figure 1.1   Share of small (<200 employees) establishments and enterprises in total manufacturing employment

Table 1.1   Employment in UK manufacturing

	Establishments			Enterprises		
	All establish-ments (000s employed)	Small* establish-ments (000s employed)	Small as % of total	All enterprises (000s employed)	Small* enterprises (000s employed)	Small as % of total
1924	5,115	2,257	44.1%			
1930	5,179	2,238	43.2%			
1935	5,409	2,375	43.9%	5,409	2,078	38.4%
1948	6,871	2,538	36.9%			
1951	7,382	2,576	34.9%			
1954	7,537	2,500	33.2%			
1958	7,781	2,498	32.1%	7,649	1,812	23.7%
1963	7,960	2,436	30.6%	7,846	1,543	19.7%
1968	7,826	2,339	29.9%	7,402	1,421	19.2%
1971	7,831	2,186	27.9%	7,459	1,565	21.0%
1972	7,522	2,062	27.4%	7,105	1,528	21.5%
1973	7,616	2,090	27.4%	7,268	1,506	20.7%
1974				7,406	1,592	21.5%
1975	7,467	2,160	28.9%	7,119	1,558	21.9%
1976	7,305	2,178	29.8%	6,971	1,576	22.6%
1977	7,281	2,151	29.5%	6,883	1,552	22.5%
1978	7,106	2,103	29.6%	6,642	1,516	22.8%
1979						
1980	6,495	2,069	31.9%	6,104	1,485	24.3%
1981	5,778	1,958	33.9%	5,431	1,408	25.9%
1982	5,361	1,892	35.3%	5,119	1,368	26.7%
1983	5,079	1,841	36.2%	4,859	1,351	27.8%
1984	5,059	1,912	37.8%	4,828	1,465	30.3%
1985	4,976	1,900	38.2%	4,843	1,471	30.4%
1986	4,878	1,914	39.2%	4,775	1,456	30.5%
1987	4,874	1,885	38.7%	4,673	1,455	31.1%
1988	4,932	1,933	39.2%	4,843	1,509	31.2%

Note: * <200 employees.
See Hughes (1990) for a discussion of changes in coverage of the data.
Sources: Earlier years: *Bolton Report*, Bannock (1976).
1971–1988: *Business Monitor PA1002, Census of Production*, Summary Tables, HMSO.

(Figure 1.1). Tables 1.1 and 1.2 show that (bearing in mind the changes in comparability) the trough in the small firms' employment share was reached some time between 1968 and 1973, while the number of small manufacturing enterprises reached its low slightly earlier, perhaps in 1972. By 1988, the latest

Table 1.2   Number of establishments and enterprises in UK manufacturing

	Establishments			Enterprises		
	Total establish- ments (000s)	Small* establish- ments (000s)	Large establish- ments (000s)	Total enterprises (000s)	Small* enterprises (000s)	Large enterprises (000s)
1924	163	160	3			
1930	168	164	4			
1935	148	144	4	140	136	4
1948	108	103	5			
1951	102	96	6			
1954	97	91	6			
1958	93	85	8	70	66	4
1963	90	82	8	64	60	4
1968	92	84	8	62	58	4
1971	90	83	7	75	71	3
1972	87	80	7	72	69	3
1973	94	88	7	77	74	3
1974				84	81	3
1975	104	98	6	87	83	3
1976	107	101	6	89	86	3
1977	108	102	6	90	87	3
1978	108	102	6	90	87	3
1979						
1980	109	103	6	90	87	3
1981	108	103	5	90	87	3
1982	102	98	5	85	83	2
1983	102	98	4	86	83	2
1984	136	131	4	119	117	3
1985	143	138	4	127	125	3
1986	146	142	4	130	128	3
1987	146	141	4	133	131	3
1988	148	143	5	135	133	3

Note: * <200 employees.
Sources: As Table 1.1.

year for which this series is available, the number of small enterprises in manufacturing (which had fallen by 78,000 between 1935 and 1968) seemed almost to have returned to 1935 levels. 'Seemed', because there can be little doubt that statisticians were able to identify a larger proportion of existing firms in 1988 than in 1935, but the direction and pace of the change are not in question.

Before 1979, when the VAT series became available, it is not possible to measure changes in the small business sector in the economy as a whole, and even then there are uncertainties about the number of businesses that are not registered for VAT. Careful estimates by Bannock and Daly (1990) however – see GB and P (1989a) for full details – show a massive increase in the number of SMEs, and in their share in total private sector employment, between 1979 and 1986.

Their figures show that over this period, the total number of business enterprises rose from 1.791 million to 2.471 million (1.488 million of the latter number being registered for VAT).

Of the 1986 total number of enterprises, only 12,000 had 200 or more employees and only 4,000 had 500 or more.

The share of enterprises with fewer than 500 employees increased from 57.3 to 71.3 per cent of total private sector employment between 1979 and 1986 (Table 1.3). Much of this increase was accounted for by a large increase in the number of very small firms. The number of firms, however, increased in all but two of the 1–500 size bands given in Table 1.3 (the exceptions were the 20–49 and 100–199 employee bands), and total employment increased in all but these two size bands and in the 1000 and over band, where total employment fell by almost 50 per cent. The total number of business enterprises (99.8 per cent of which, we know from VAT and self-employment data, employed fewer than 500 persons in 1986) continued to grow in the period 1987–89 and probably also in 1990.

The 4000 or so enterprises with 500 or more employees which are only 0.2 per cent of the total number of enterprises do, of course, still account for a

Table 1.3   Numbers of businesses and their employment as a percentage of the total UK, 1979–1986

	Number of firms		% of total employment	
	1979	1986	1979	1986
1–2	1,099,132	1,579,389	6.6	9.7
3–5	318,917	472,676	5.9	8.9
6–10	178,628	189,618	6.7	7.3
11–19	108,827	139,824	7.6	10.1
20–49	46,237	44,033	6.9	6.7
50–99	15,585	19,732	5.3	6.9
100–199	14,865	14,066	10.2	9.9
200–499	5,365	7,657	8.1	11.9
500–999	2,169	2,974	7.5	10.5
1,000+	1,774	892	35.3	18.2
Total	**1,791,499**	**2,470,861**	**100.0**	**100.0**

Source: GB and P (1989a).

disproportionate share of economic activity. The majority of these enterprises are quoted companies: there were about 3000 UK and foreign companies quoted on the official list and the USM in 1986. Although there is a considerable number of large, unquoted companies it is possible, as some people do, to describe the whole unincorporated and unquoted sector as the small business sector. The proportion of final output 'controlled' by large firms (500 employees and over) is much greater than their share of aggregate turnover because these firms buy in a substantial proportion of the sales value of their output from smaller firms.

According to the Bannock and Daly study, these large enterprises accounted in 1986 for 28.7 per cent of non-government employment and 29.4 per cent of the aggregate turnover of all enterprises. If we set the threshold lower, at 100 or more employees, then in 1986 the 25,600 enterprises which fell into this group (still only just over 1 per cent of all enterprises) accounted for 47.5 per cent of employment and 53.7 per cent of aggregate turnover.

The increase in the number of businesses and in employment in SMEs in the period since 1979 took place in most sectors of the UK economy, and in all regions. Over the period 1979–89, with two exceptions, there were increases in the stock of enterprises in all major sectors of the economy, ranging from 9.2 per cent in catering to 28.8 per cent in the production industries, 86.4 per cent in finance and business services, and over 100 per cent in other services (VAT statistics, Daly 1990). The two exceptions were agriculture (–0.2 per cent) and retail distribution (–2.2 per cent), though the number of businesses in wholesale distribution rose by 27.3 per cent.

The stock of businesses also increased in all eleven standard regions of the UK between 1979–89, ranging from 40 per cent in the South East, around 30 per cent in East Anglia and the South West, around 27 per cent in the Midlands and about 21 per cent in Yorkshire and Humberside, Wales, Scotland and Northern Ireland. The smallest increases were in the North West (16 per cent) and the North (19 per cent). These disparities in growth rates between the South East and the rest of the country were largely attributable to the relatively smaller stock of businesses in the service and other fast-growing areas. According to calculations by Michael Daly for 1980–87 (*British Business*, 9 June 1989), if the sectoral structure in Scotland and the South East had been the same but the growth rates for each sector were those actually experienced, the overall growth in the stock of businesses would have been the same or lower in the South East than in all other regions, other than in the West Midlands and the three northern English regions.

Since 99 per cent or more of all businesses are small, it is sufficient to look at any indicator of the total number of business enterprises to see what is happening to the size of the small business population. It can be seen from Table 1.4 that the total number of VAT-registered businesses increased in each year from 1980 to 1989. It is noteworthy that the rate of change in the stock of businesses speeded up considerably in the second half of the 1980s. These figures actually understate the growth of the business population because the number of (smaller) non-registered businesses was growing even faster. For example,

Table 1.4   Numbers of businesses registered for VAT and net change over periods year, UK 1980–89

	Stock end year (000s)	Net change (000s)	Per cent change
1980	1305	16	1.2
1981	1337	32	2.5
1982	1357	21	1.6
1983	1392	35	2.6
1984	1422	30	2.2
1985	1441	19	1.3
1986	1468	27	1.9
1987	1510	42	2.9
1988	1575	65	4.3
1989	1662	87	5.5

Source: Daly (1990).

while the VAT population increased by 14 per cent between the end of 1979 and the end of 1986, the total business population increased by 38 per cent.

Trends in self-employment and job generation

The large increase in the number of very small firms was largely attributable to the increase in the proportion of the labour force which was self-employed, almost 70 per cent of which had no employees. The number of self-employed rose from 1.906 million in June 1979 to 3.380 million in June 1990, an increase

Table 1.5   Numbers of self-employed as a percentage of the labour force – UK, selected years

1911	12.8
1921	10.1
1951	7.2
1960	7.0
1965	6.5
1970	7.4
1975	7.7
1980	7.5
1985	9.4
1990	11.7

Source: Annual Abstract of Statistics and Monthly Digest of Statistics, HMSO.

of 77 per cent. This increase restored the relative importance of self-employment to the levels of the early part of the century (Table 1.5).

By 1990 less than one-quarter of the self-employed were female, but since 1979 their number had increased by 125 per cent – compared with the increase for males of 66 per cent. In 1981, 39 per cent of the self-employed had employees, and by 1989 this proportion had fallen to 31 per cent (DoEm 1991). The increase in employment by smaller firms, however, is very much greater than that which can be attributed to the increase in the numbers of self-employed. Over the period 1979–86, the growth in the number of self-employed contributed only 49 per cent of the increase in employment in firms with fewer than 20 employees (GB and P 1989a).

It is of interest that the self-employed are a higher proportion of all in employment among ethnic minority groups (16.4 per cent) than among the white population (12.6 per cent). Well over one in five of the employed population of Indian-Pakistani and Bangladeshi ethnic origins are self-employed. The proportion of the self-employed with employees is also significantly higher (39.2 per cent) for ethnic minority groups than it is for whites (32.7 per cent). (1987–89 averages, from DoEm 1991.)

Total UK employment fell by about 500,000 between 1979 and 1986. According to the estimates made by Bannock and Daly (1990), employment in firms with 1000 or more employees fell by 3.5 million, or almost 50 per cent over the period. In firms with fewer than 1000 employees, employment increased by 3 million or 23 per cent.

One of the more interesting advances in research on small firms since the Bolton Report has been the development of techniques for measuring the contribution of firms of different sizes to net employment change. This contribution is not accurately measured by comparisons over time between the numbers employed in different size classes (as made in the previous paragraph). This is because within each employment size band, some firms are expanding their employment while others are contracting and, as a result, between any two dates some firms will have gone out of business, some new ones will have entered the bottom size band, while others will have moved up or down into different size bands.

In the late 1970s, Fothergill and Gudgin (1979) in the UK and Birch (1979) in the US published estimates of job generation using a data file of employment in individual firms at different dates. Birch's frequently quoted result – that 'small firms (those with 20 or fewer employees) generated 66 per cent of all new jobs in the US' in the period 1969–1976 – aroused great interest and considerable technical controversy. It is now clearly established that small firms have made a disproportionate contribution to job generation in at least several major countries in the 1970s and 1980s.

For the UK, a forthcoming study by Colin Gallagher will show that:

> between 1987 and 1989, firms employing fewer than twenty people created over half a million jobs, slightly more than in larger firms – even though the larger firms employed nearly twice as many people in 1987. Relative to initial employment, there

was a steep decline in performance from the very smallest firms, with fewer than five staff, to the next size band, and again from the 5–9 to the 10–19 band.

(DoEm 1991)

Gallagher's calculations suggest that the major contribution of small firms to job generation in the UK indicated by earlier studies, including his own, and the straightforward size band statistics referred to above, has continued to the end of the 1980s.

It remains difficult to say when the regrowth of the small firms sector began. We have seen that in manufacturing it began in the early 1970s; in non-manufacturing it may have begun earlier. The percentage of self-employed persons in the labour force seems to have troughed around 1965 (Table 1.5), while the crude incorporation rate increased from 1968 onwards (though the upward trend in this indicator was interrupted in 1974 and did not resume until 1980). The crude incorporation rate, as defined in the Bolton Report, is the number of new incorporations per thousand of the human population. In 1968, at 0.4 it was only one-third of the corresponding US figure of 1.2, but by 1989–90 it was 2.3 in the UK compared with 2.8 (1987) in the US. The incorporation rate is not necessarily a reliable indicator of the rate of new business formation, and can be affected by changes in company law and taxation.

Births and deaths

Much more is also known about the demography of the business population than at the time of the Bolton Report. Behind the overall changes in the size of the business stock described above lie even greater movements in and out of the business population and changes of ownership among surviving businesses.

As shown in Table 1.4, the net increase in the stock of VAT-registered businesses in 1989 was an additional 87,000 firms. This change was the product of 265,000 new registrations (15.6 per cent of the stock) and 178,000 deregistrations (10.7 per cent of the stock). However, only firms with a turnover in excess of £23,600 (1989) are obliged to register for VAT (though many register voluntarily) and large numbers of businesses below the VAT threshold are born and die each year, so that the total churning of the business population is greater than even these figures suggest.

We have implied here that VAT registrations and deregistrations are equivalent to births and deaths. But, of course, many newly registered VAT-registered firms were already in existence, trading below the required threshold for registration. And deregistrations will also not necessarily represent business deaths or failures: for example, a firm may deregister because it is sold to another registered firm or because its turnover falls below the threshold.

Bearing these qualifications in mind, it is interesting to see that the death (deregistration) rate falls sharply with size of firm, from 24 per cent in the £1–14,000 size band to around 4 per cent once over the £100,000 threshold (Table 1.6). In fact, almost 31 per cent of all deregistrations are of firms in the lowest size band (we ignore the 0 size band for reasons given in the table), and a

Table 1.6   *Registrations and deregistrations as a percentage of the stock of VAT-registered firms, by turnover size band, UK, 1980*

Turnover £000	Registrations	Deregistrations
0	14.5	13.5
1–14	15.4	24.1
15–49	14.4	12.0
50–99	11.0	7.2
100–499	8.5	4.4
500–1999	6.1	3.6
2,000+	4.9	3.8
Total	**12.1**	**10.9**

Note: The 0 size band includes firms which had not yet notified their turnover, because they had registered at the end of the year and for other reasons.
Source: Ganguly (1985).

further 38 per cent are in the next two size bands. This reflects the fact that young businesses are likely to predominate among the smallest, but it is interesting to note that the death rate is roughly stable over the larger size range from £100,000 turnover to the largest firms.

The vulnerability of businesses to failure is greatest in their earlier years. Although only some 10–11 per cent of all VAT firms deregister each year, of those formed in any year 12 per cent will 'fail' in their first year, 26 per cent within two years and 36 per cent within three years. Another way of putting these results is that about 60 per cent of all businesses deregistering do so within three years of first registration.

Both VAT registration and deregistration rates increased over the period 1980–1989, from 12.3 to 16.8 for 'births' and from 11.0 to 11.3 for 'deaths'. Only a small proportion of business deaths result in insolvencies or bankruptcies. Although the numbers increased sharply in the 1990–91 recession, in 1988 there were 15,600 insolvencies (excluding personal and non-business bankruptcies) – only about 0.6 per cent of all registered and unregistered businesses in that year. Of all closures of businesses in that year, we estimate that formal insolvencies accounted for only about 15 per cent.

This surprisingly low insolvency rate suggests that only a small proportion of VAT deregistrations represent total failures involving losses to creditors. As mentioned, some are simply dropping below the registration threshold, some will go into voluntary liquidation but many will be sold. A recent Small Business Research Trust (SBRT) survey showed that 40 per cent of small business respondents had run one or more different businesses of their own in the past. Of the previously owned businesses, 16 per cent had been liquidated, 36 per

Table 1.7   *Changes in the share of SMEs in non-primary private sector unemployment – selected countries*

	(1963 = 100)	
	1971	1985
Japan (1962 = 100)	104.3	109.0
USA	101.1 (1972)	112.9
France (1971 = 100)	100.0	112.4
Italy	96.5	105.7
Germany (1961 = 100)	95.3 (1970)	103.1 (1987)
United Kingdom	116.9 (1979)	145.6 (1986)
Switzerland (1965 = 100)	98.1 (1975)	93.0

Note: Base years for Japan and the UK are crude estimates made for the purposes of this chapter. The index numbers measure changes in the SME employment ratio. SMEs are defined as having under 500 employees, except in Germany (under 200). *Source:* Calculated from Sengenberger *et al* (1990), except for the two base years mentioned above, for Germany where the 1987 figure is from Bannock and Albach (1991), and for the UK, which includes agriculture, where the source is Bannock and Daly (1990).

cent had been sold and 20 per cent were dormant. Over one quarter of respondents who had a previous business still owned and managed that business. This implies that around 10 per cent of respondents own and manage more than one business (*Quarterly Survey of Small Business in Britain*, Vol. 5 No. 3, 1989).

International comparisons

The change in trend towards an increase in the number of SMEs and their share in employment seems to have been fairly general among the advanced countries. Even in Japan, which did not share in the secular decline in the small firms sector which took place elsewhere, there was a significant increase in the 1970s and 1980s. International comparisons of statistics on small firms are beset with difficulties, but Table 1.7 shows that among the seven countries included, only Switzerland did not see an increase in the employment share of small firms between (around) 1971 and 1985, though in most countries there was a fall in this share before the early 1970s. EC (1990) demonstrates that there was a net growth in the number of business enterprises in at least six member states between 1983 and 1986, varying from 14.6 per cent in the UK to around 6–7 per cent in Germany, France and the Netherlands, and 3 per cent in Italy.

The increase in the UK share has, however, been very much greater than elsewhere. This seems to be largely explained by the uniquely large increase in self-employment which has taken place in the UK. In fact, leaving to one side agricultural self-employment (which has been declining almost everywhere), the self-employment rate has increased in only nine out of sixteen OECD

Table 1.8   Share of SMEs in non-primary private sector GDP, selected countries, mid-1980s

Japan	1982	60
US	1982	50
FRG	1986	46
UK	1986	32

Note: Japan: under 300 employees in manufacturing, under 200 in wholesale distribution, under 50 in retail distribution; US under 500 employees; FRG and UK, turnover less than £30 million, which would correspond to an employment threshold of well under 100 employees.
For these and other reasons these estimates are not closely comparable. On a comparable basis, the US figure would probably be well below that for the FRG, though higher than the UK.
Sources: Japan: Kayutoshi Koshiro in Sengenberger *et al* (1990); US: SBA (1989) UK and FRG: Bannock and Albach (1991).

countries for which satisfactory (though still not fully comparable) data are available (DoEm 1991). While this rate increased by 65 per cent in the UK between 1979 and 1988, it remained unchanged in France, rose by 5 per cent in Germany, 7 per cent in the United States, and fell by 11 per cent in Japan. Even after the increase, however, the self-employment rate in the UK remains below the EC average and that for Japan and Australia, though it is considerably higher than in the US and Canada.

The contribution of small firms to economic activity continues to vary between countries and remains significantly lower in the UK than elsewhere. Table 1.8 brings together, from various sources, estimates of the contribution of SMEs to GDP. It can be seen that their share in the UK is approaching half that in Japan, and only around two-thirds of the German level.

Bannock and Albach (1991) show that (compared with Germany – but this is also true for comparisons with the United States and other countries) the UK SME contribution to employment and output is relatively low not because there are now fewer enterprises in Britain, but because average employment per enterprise is lower. Germany, for example, has fewer self-employed without employees, and firms in the 2–49 employee size band have an average employment of nine as against six in Britain.

Bannock and Albach conclude that the contribution of SMEs to UK private sector GDP (including agriculture) has probably increased from 24 per cent in 1963 (the Bolton estimate) to 34 per cent. It can be seen from Table 1.8 that the UK still has a long way to go to catch up.

Explaining the resurgence of small enterprises

Two important questions are raised by the reversal of the long-term decline in the numbers of small firms and their share in economic activity described in this chapter. The first question is: Why did this change take place at all? The second is: Why was the change apparently more pronounced in the UK than elsewhere?

Various answers to the first and more difficult question have been put forward. One is that technical change and the development of flexible specialization, partly stimulated by rising wealth, have altered the structure of demand and the balance of scale economies towards smaller firms. There is no doubt something in this, but it cannot explain why the shift towards small firms has occurred in both manufacturing and non-manufacturing business. The life cycle explanation – that the shift towards small firms reflects a shift towards service activities – also explains the greater share of small service businesses in the total change, but not the widespread nature of the change itself.

Changes in government policy can also be ruled out, at least as an initiator of change. It is true that the first oil crisis in the early 1970s and the ensuing steeper rise in unemployment, as well as the results of later research on job generation, focused the attention of governments around the world on the contribution to employment that small firms could make. But the upturn in small business formation in the late 1960s and early 1970s preceded these changes in policy. Most of the major policy changes in tax reform and deregulation in the 1980s, led by the UK and the United States, came later still (though the UK introduced a graduated form of corporation tax to assist small companies as early as 1973–74, a measure which the US had introduced many years earlier).

It is more probable that some macro-economic developments have acted as the initiator of the change. Historically, small business formation rates have been positively related to unemployment rates (Bannock and Doran 1984). The increase in these rates did seem to coincide in the late 1960s but, as we have seen, business birth rates actually accelerated in the latter half of the decade when unemployment was falling. This is not to say that macro-economic developments have not been relevant to the changes we have been discussing, but the relationships are clearly very complex.

Bannock and Peacock (1989) have pointed out that earlier upward and downward shifts in the share of small firms in economic activity could be explained as a necessary reaction to the excessive concentration in the economy that takes place in good times. (The share of small business in employment and output in the UK and the US went down 1910–35, up 1936–50, down 1951–70.) In other words, when the relative role of small and large firms gets out of balance, a balance which will vary according to demand technology and other factors in any given period, forces set in to readjust the relationship.

Some support for this view is to be found in the fact that much of the impetus behind the recent growth of small business has been from changes in the organizational and sub-contracting practices of large firms. Very large firms, in reaction to increased economic and competitive pressures, have been disposing of subsidiaries so as to concentrate on core activities, buying in services and production previously done in-house, and slimming down permanent workforces, not only through eliminating over-manning, but also by the increasing use of part-time and freelance employees (Bannock 1987).

Next, there is the question of the role of changes in social attitudes in explaining the general resurgence of small business. There is anecdotal evidence that these attitudes have become more favourable, and certainly it seems that UK public opinion would now like to see a still bigger role for small firms in the economy. Although no one had previously thought of canvassing the public on this issue, 3i-Investors in Industry commissioned a survey of the UK adult population early in 1991: 52 per cent of respondents believed it would be better for the British economy if there were more small companies and less reliance on big business. Only 23 per cent considered that the economy needs more big business (3i-Investors in Industry, *Quarterly Enterprise Barometer*, No. 13, February 1991).

Roger Burrows, in Curran and Blackburn (1991) has argued that the admittedly imprecise term 'enterprise culture' which the UK government has been promoting is simply a rationalization for anti-collectivist policies. Whether that is indeed the case, or whether these changes have been inevitable and necessary, it is probably true that the bulk of the electorate has not been fully committed to them. Changes of this magnitude, however, which have not been confined to the UK, must have been accompanied (and probably were preceded) by changes in social attitudes.

This brings us to the second question: Why were the changes in the small business sector greater in the UK than elsewhere? If our interpretation of the causes of the changes is correct, then the answer to this question must be that the scope for the necessary adjustment to the economic realities of the 1970s and 1980s (which included the consequences of membership of the European Community) was greater in the UK than elsewhere. As the Bolton Report established, the UK entered the last two decades with an economy more dependent upon large firms than any of its major international competitors. The ensuing adjustment has brought the UK enterprise structure closer to that of other countries but, as we have shown, there is still a long way to go. In particular, fewer manufacturing micro-businesses in the UK seem to expand upwards into the 10–499 employee size band than in other major countries.

2 Change and Continuity in Small Firm Policy since Bolton

Increasingly in the post-1945 period small firms have been seen as an important part of the competitive mechanism of the free market economy, and government intervention to support the development of the small business sector has been recognized as desirable and necessary. In many OECD countries, such as the United States, Japan and Germany, basic small business legislation was enacted in the 1950s and early 1960s (Bannock 1980). In the United Kingdom, however, an explicit small business policy only began to evolve after the publication in 1971 of the Bolton Report.

Since then successive governments in the UK have introduced a wide variety of measures designed to promote new firm formation and small firm growth (Beesley and Wilson 1982). Both the Conservative government of the day and the subsequent Labour administration acted upon a number of the Bolton Committee's recommendations in order to remove sources of unintended discrimination against small firms and to create a climate favourable to their growth. The momentum increased towards the end of the Labour administration with the appointment of a special study under Lord Lever, a senior minister, to investigate the problems of small firms and to recommend and initiate remedial action. This led to the incorporation in the budgets of 1977 and 1978 of a number of fiscal measures to assist small firms. In addition, the Labour government appointed a committee, under the chairmanship of Sir Harold Wilson, to inquire into the role of the financial institutions and the provision of funds for industry and trade; its interim report on the financing of smaller firms was published in 1979 (HMSO 1979) and a number of its recommendations have subsequently been acted upon.

The steady stream of measures to assist the small firm sector turned into a torrent on the election in 1979 of a Conservative government pledged to create a thriving private enterprise economy in which the entrepreneur would play a key role – described by Riddell (1983, p. 165) as an attempt to construct a society which is 'a cross between nineteenth century Birmingham and contemporary Hong Kong, located in Esher'. Indeed, one of the government's claims during the general election campaign of 1983 was that it had introduced 108 such measures since coming into office four years earlier, many of them intended to discriminate in favour of the small firm sector. However, since its re-election for a second and third term in office, the Conservative government has concentrated its efforts on 'repacking' and publicizing the plethora of small firms schemes available, to take account of the criticism that there was only limited awareness among the small business sector of the assistance that is on offer (as shown, for example, in a survey by the Economists Advisory Group 1983) while the sheer number of different measures was confusing to the target clientele. To this end, the government proposed in the mid-1980s to condense and simplify the 64 schemes under the remit of the Department of Trade and Industry into four groups covering investment, innovation, export and advice in an attempt to create a more 'user friendly service'. With the launch of the Enterprise Initiative in 1988, the emphasis and presentation of small firms policy changed again (see below).

Rationale for small firm policies

On the basis of the UK evidence up to the late 1960s, the Bolton Committee (1971), identified a long-term and seemingly inexorable decline in the numbers of small firms and self-employed. Contrary to those expectations, the period since the mid-1970s has seen a resurgence in this sector: self-employment has almost doubled in the past decade, and the number of firms registered for VAT has risen by almost a quarter over the same period (Department of Employment 1991; see also Chapter 1). Furthermore, there is some evidence to suggest, in the UK at least, that this resurgence in the importance of the small firm sector pre-dates the post-1979 expansion in public sector assistance and support for small business formation and development (Dunne and Hughes 1990).

Given this revitalization of the small firm sector in the UK, it is appropriate to identify the rationale for the continued existence of a public small business policy. Two primary arguments can be identified: the argument from principle, that both small and large businesses should be able to operate and compete on the same conditions; and the argument from practice, that small firms play a crucial, if not the crucial, role in economic development (Storey and Johnson 1987a).

Argument from principle

The argument from principle rests on the proposition that the small business sector remains at a comparative disadvantage to large business and without state assistance would either decline or grow less rapidly. Underlying this is the view that the free market mechanism fails to lead to an economically 'efficient' allocation of resources within society.

According to one recent review (Johnson 1990), there are four major areas of 'market failure' that might justify the development of policies designed to support and promote small-scale enterprise.

First, the existence of market failure due to monopoly provides a primary justification for state intervention: this is reflected in a wide range of policies,

including monopolies and mergers policy, competition policy and state regulation, to ensure that potential competitors are not excluded from the market.
The promotion of small business activities could also be justified as one means
of curbing the power of monopolies and ensuring that competitors reap the
benefits of the competitive process. However, it appears that in the UK a
general tolerance towards increasing concentration through merger activity is
matched by a lack of emphasis on competition policy as having any specific role
to play as part of small business policies (Bannock and Albach 1991).

Second, small firms are often at a disadvantage, because of the fixed costs
involved, *vis-à-vis* larger firms in collecting and analysing information about
market opportunities, sources of finance, government regulations and so on.
This represents a major potential competitive disadvantage for the small firm
sector that may constrain its development and thereby provide a rationale for
government intervention and support.

Third, despite the frequent identification of small firms as a fruitful source of
innovative activity in an economy, smaller businesses are less able to absorb the
risk and uncertainty, and the high initial costs which cannot be offset against
other activities within the firm, which inevitably accompany activities such as
innovation, new product development and new market development. As a
result, some of the benefits of these activities may be lost to society as a whole.

Fourth, and the subject of considerable debate in the UK (see Bannock 1980;
Binks and Vale 1990; and Chapters 4 and 6), small firms experience particular
difficulties in the capital markets relative to large firms. The existence of significant economies of scale in finance, such that the evaluation, monitoring and
control costs of making a loan to or investing in a new or small business are
much higher in relative terms than they are for a large business, combined with
higher levels of risk for the financier underlie the existence of a finance gap that
reduces small firms' access to, and raises the cost of, external finance.

Argument from practice

The argument from practice in support of small firms policies arises from the
externalities, or knock-on effects, that the development of the small firm sector
has on the rest of the economy. These benefits include the contribution of the
small firm sector to innovative activity and as a source of competition and
provider of flexibility in labour and factor markets (Brock and Evans 1989; Acs
and Audretsch 1990). However, the primary practical justification for small
firm policies throughout Europe is their role in employment creation. This
argument proceeds in a number of stages. The starting point has been that in
the crucial period of the early and mid-1980s much of Europe was experiencing
high unemployment. Furthermore, rates of new employment creation in Europe
were lower than in the United States where, following the work of Birch (1979)
and others, smaller firms were identified as playing a key role in the generation
of new employment. However, the results of these empirical studies on the
importance of the small firm in employment creation have been called into
question, and the scale of employment creation attributable to small firms *per*

se (rather than new firms) has been subjected to criticism (OECD 1985; Storey and Johnson 1987a; Sengenberger *et al* 1990). Nevertheless, 'the fact remains that most European countries have a collection of policies designed to promote the small business sector, as a way of reducing unemployment. These arguments are much more influential in justifying public small firm policies than the desirability of small firms *per se*, or that small firms prevent market inefficiencies through reducing industrial concentration' (Storey and Johnson 1987a, p. 207). Equally, as Johnson (1990) has gone on to argue, both the argument from principle and the argument from practice as summarized above do not necessarily amount to a case for a small firm policy as a separate, integrated and coherent policy area rather than as a series of 'add-ons' or adjustments to other policy areas. Despite several attempts to co-ordinate and systematize the wide range of schemes, initiatives and policies available, small firm policy in the UK still appears primarily piecemeal, designed to tackle individual identifiable examples of market failure, and non-discriminatory, in that it is aimed at the small firm sector as a whole rather than at any particular type or category of firm within the sector.

Small firm policies in Britain

Although the development of a small firm policy pre-dated the election of a Conservative government in 1979, the change in philosophy and in approach to industrial policy in general that the election victory represented stimulated a rapid expansion in the number of schemes available (Beesley and Wilson 1982). Since 1979, however, the emphasis of such policies has shifted in a number of important respects. The measures introduced in the early years of the 1980s were largely aimed at increasing the number of business start-ups: more recently the emphasis has shifted away from the promotion of start-ups (although schemes such as the Enterprise Allowance Scheme have continued) in favour of helping small firms to grow. There has also been a redirection in the scope of such measures. The schemes introduced in the early and mid-1980s were mainly concerned with removing tangible constraints on business start-up and growth – notably finance, premises and red tape and administrative burdens. More recently there has been increased emphasis on the 'software' of business support through the provision of enterprise training, advice and consultancy to equip potential and existing small firm owner-managers with the skills and knowledge needed to launch, manage and develop a successful small business.

There has been a progressive shift away from provision of small firm policies by central government towards more localized delivery through the local enterprise agency network and, more recently, the Training and Enterprise Councils (TECs). And, closely related to this last point, there has been a progressive shift away from purely public sector provision to greater private sector involvement both through job creation activities such as BSC Enterprise (Stanworth and Barker 1988) and through private sector involvement in enterprise agencies and TECs.

In the light of these changes, the present approach to small firm policy in the UK has been summarized as follows:

There are three strands in the Government's approach to small firms. First, and of most importance, the role of Government is to ensure that small firms can flourish in conditions of fair competition and to create space and incentives for enterprise by minimising taxation, regulation and red tape.

Second, the Government strongly supports and reinforces the change to more positive social attitudes towards the small business sector . . .

Third, the Government helps to fill gaps in the supply side by providing commercial services for small firms, largely to improve their access to finance, information, professional advice and training. Wherever possible, the Government's approach is provided in partnership with the private sector.

(Department of Employment 1989)

Recent developments in each of these three areas make a useful framework for discussion.

Deregulation and competition

Reduction of the administrative and legislative burdens on small firms has been an important element in the development of small firm policy in the UK in the 1980s. For the most part this has been achieved by exempting small firms from certain obligations under various pieces of legislation (for example, dismissal procedures under employment legislation and the provision of detailed financial information to the Registrar of Companies). In 1986, following a review of the administrative burdens facing small businesses (HMSO 1985), this strand of policy was developed with the establishment of an Enterprise and Deregulation Unit with the Department of Trade and Industry, with satellites in each government department. However, despite the work of this unit, new tasks have continued to be imposed with the result that there has probably been no net easing of the administrative and regulatory burden on small firms. Indeed, as Bannock and Albach (1991) have argued, the tendency in the UK has been to concentrate effort on reducing uncontentious and usually unimportant regulatory burdens, notably the burden of statistical inquiries. This was identified in the Bolton Report (1971) as a particular area of concern and machinery was established to ensure that all statistical surveys carried out by government departments were sanctioned by a central unit. However, statistical form filling is only a minor element of the regulatory/administrative burden: Bolton's estimate of 15 per cent of the man-hours in the total business paperwork burden taken up in statistical form filling may overestimate the situation in the smaller firm (Bannock and Albach 1991).

Meanwhile, the impact of public purchasing (which is made disproportionately from large firms) and taxation and regulation bear disproportionately on small firms. Although there have been few attempts to measure taxation compliance and regulatory costs (see Bannock and Peacock 1989) it is clear that small firms are placed at a disadvantage: taxation, for example, absorbs investible funds from small firms which have more restricted access to the capital markets, thereby enhancing the scale of the finance gap; there are significant economies of scale in dealing with government administrative, compliance and regulatory burdens which disproportionately disadvantage the small firm; and the effort of dealing with government's administrative requirements in the small firm generally involves the use of one of the firm's scarcest resources, the time of the owner-manager, in a way which is not common in larger organizations.

If the goal of small firms policy in the UK is, as the Department of Employment statement quoted above indicates, to ensure that small firms are not disadvantaged *vis-à-vis* larger firms, then there needs to be a more coherent and systematic investigation of the precise nature of disadvantages facing small firms in this domain as the basis for a policy thrust which genuinely seeks to restore neutrality of treatment in competition policy and in administrative and regulatory requirements. However, in seeking to achieve deregulation by, for example, freeing small firms from existing protective roles and social obligations (including those of the European Social Charter) there are potential dangers (Loveman and Sengenberger 1991). Three problems in particular can be identified. First, reducing compliance costs for small businesses, particularly in the labour market area, may save costs and enhance the flexibility of firms in the short run but are likely to lower the wage standard or other terms of employment. As a result, qualified labour (both skilled and managerial) necessary for small firms to realize their competitive advantages of producing differentiated products serving niche markets and capable of quick adjustment to market changes may be harder to attract and retain, thereby reducing rather than enhancing the competitive position of the small firm. Second, to the extent that deregulation enables small firms to operate with a lower cost strategy it may lead to complacency: competitive advantage will be sought on the basis of costs rather than on innovation, new product development or market development. Again, the initial advantage (*vis-à-vis* the present position) may not be reflected in the superior long-run performance of the sector. Third, wider cost differentials, particularly labour costs, as small firms are exempted from much of the administrative and regulatory burden in this area, may encourage large firms to increase the use of small firms as 'buffers' by increasing the volume of sub-contracting and outsourcing: while small-firm employment will grow as a result, this will be at the expense of large-firm employment and will not necessarily improve the overall level of activity in the economy (cf. Shutt and Whittington 1984).

Attitudes to small business

One of the features of the period since 1979 has been the development of a political and ideological context for understanding the revival of the small business sector and developing a policy stance towards it, to the extent that 'the discourse of the enterprise culture has become one of the major articulating principles of the age . . . the post-war years up until 1979 are characterized in terms of the creation of an anti-enterprise culture inspired by social democratic collectivism, leading to indulgency, degeneration and national demise. That-cherite policies are then presented as a painful but unavoidable "cure" leading to a quasi-spiritual rebirth of enterprise leading to widespread industriousness, regeneration and hence national recovery' (Burrows 1991a, p. 17). As Burrows (1991a; 1991b) points out, the enterprise culture has, in practice, little to do with small business, and is found only rarely among those in self-employment and small business ownership who might be expected to embody it in their everyday realities. Rather, it forms part of a larger set of cultural values which include an emphasis on the 'market', the inevitability of market-driven change and business models of the welfare state (see also Keat and Abercrombie 1991). Nevertheless, as both the launch of the DTI Enterprise Initiative and the ex-ample of policy formation in Northern Ireland demonstrate, the 'discourse of the enterprise culture' has had a significant impact on the shaping of small firm policy in the UK (Harrison and Hart 1991).

The Department of Trade and Industry White Paper of January 1988 (DTI 1988), announcing the Enterprise Initiative in Great Britain and confirming the subtitling of the DTI as 'the Department for Enterprise', clearly articulated this thinking and indicated that the encouragement of enterprise was to become one of the major goals of the government. Within Northern Ireland the equivalent Department of Economic Development reported the progress of its economic development strategy towards the end of 1987 (DED 1987). In essence, this document concentrated on the ways in which indigenous potential can be harnessed in the regeneration of a regional economy which has systematically lagged behind the performance of the national economy (Harris *et al* 1990). This new policy initiative was based on the establishment of a number of taskforces to find new and better ways of achieving economic growth in the region. In particular, the proposals included the stimulation of a more positive attitude to enterprise (by which was meant specifically self-employment and small business start-up); changing attitudes to competitiveness; encouraging export activity; exploiting the strengths of the public sector and the better targeting of public funds.

Arising out of this process the Enterprise Taskforce produced a major initia-tive in the fostering of a more positive attitude to enterprise in Northern Ire-land. This arose from the identification of the lack of an enterprising tradition in Northern Ireland (defined as the propensity of people to create jobs, for themselves and others, by engaging in and developing a legitimate activity which will earn them a living) as a major constraint on the regional economic development process. In particular, this new emphasis on enterprise in public policy is based on the identification of two major attitudinal constraints: first, 'there is a general attitude in Northern Ireland that working for oneself rather than for an established company is somehow second best'; second, 'self-employment is often seen as impractical or necessarily risky; not as legitimate or socially desirable as other employment' (DED 1987). This claim that North-ern Ireland lacks an 'enterprise culture' (inferred from the lower rates of new business formation in Northern Ireland compared with other regions (Hart

1989)) and is dominated instead by an employee, dependency culture, underlies the development of a number of new policy initiatives. In particular, an Enterprising Northern Ireland campaign was launched in July 1988 with the task of promoting and developing enterprise and the enterprise culture by adding to the current level of entrepreneurial activity, and targeting in particular perceived underdeveloped sources of enterprise ability. Funding of £350,000 was made available from the International Fund for Ireland, with further unspecified funding from LEDU, the small firm development agency in Northern Ireland. The campaign has been targeted at four main groupings: young people, women, people in employment and unemployed people. This campaign represents a major public policy initiative to stimulate economic development in an economically disadvantaged region through the stimulation of entrepreneurship and enterprise.

Although it is still too early to make a full evaluation of what will be a long term process of change in attitudes and behaviours, some evidence from a series of studies of small business start-up by one of the key groups – young people – targeted by this campaign suggests that the Thatcher notion of enterprise culture has limited acceptance (Harrison and Hart 1991). For many young people setting up in business or thinking of doing so, self-employment reflects a culture of survival rather than enterprise, with self-employment being seen as an alternative to unemployment or government scheme and many of the firms being established as marginal businesses which, while not failing, would never become business successes as commercial employment-generating firms (MacDonald and Coffield 1991). Equally, among those young people who have lived through the 'enterprise decade' there is a high degree of realism: 'young people show little indication of having become starry-eyed about the "enterprise alternative" or having been seduced by the often over-positive support for self-employment and small business ownership . . . Rather they show a down-to-earth appreciation of self-employment and its pluses and minuses which might be argued to augur better for the future of the small business in the 1990s and beyond, than any over-romantic view which understates the seriousness of the decision to opt for the enterprise alternative' (Curran and Blackburn 1989).

Supply-side deficiencies

The third major element in the UK government's approach to small firm policy has been to help rectify supply-side deficiencies and fill gaps in the provision of, in particular, finance, information, advice and training. For the most part, the approach is piecemeal: if a gap or market deficiency can be demonstrated, or if an interest group lobbies actively enough, an initiative may be developed. As a result, there is not yet a systematic approach to the diagnosis and rectification of supply-side problems as they affect the small firm sector. Reflecting the long history of the debate over the existence of a finance gap for small firms, there has been considerable government support for schemes which improve small firms' access to loan finance (through the Loan Guarantee Scheme); finance for business start-up and self-employment (through the Enterprise Allowance

Scheme); finance for investment in new technology (through, for example, the former Small Engineering Firms Investment Scheme and schemes such as the Small Firms Merit Award for Research and Technology , which support R & D in the small firm sector); and equity finance (through the Business Expansion Scheme). As is made clear elsewhere in this volume (Chapter 4 on banks; Chapter 6 on the equity gap; Chapter 8 on management training and support), these schemes have been successful to varying degrees, and small firms still face difficulties in gaining access to the capital markets on similar terms to larger firms.

However, throughout the 1980s there has been something of a shift in small firm policy, with less emphasis being given to the provision of 'hard' assistance, in the form, for example, of financial support and more emphasis being placed on the 'software' elements of business assistance information, advice and training.

Information and signposting services
One of the early policy responses to the Bolton Report was the establishment of the Small Firms Service, now operating under the Department of Employment, as the principal government-run advisory service for small businesses. Initially geared to provide information to new small firms, it was extended in 1977 to provide counselling and advice as well, through the Small Firm Counselling Service. Through a network of regional small firm centres, inquiries are dealt with primarily by telephone, with access to a computerized database of national and regional information relevant to small firms on finance, legislation and other sources of support. This has been one of the most popular government initiatives to help small firms, attracting over 300,000 inquiries in 1989/1990, and offering over 50,000 counselling sessions. More recently, of growing importance in the provision of information and advice to small firms has been the development of a network of local enterprise agencies, which seek to mobilize local resources and institutions, notably large businesses, through cash and other support (particularly through staff secondments), and more recently the Training and Enterprise Councils (TECs).

With the proliferation of this network of locally based sources of small business advice the role of the Small Firms Service has changed: it has become regarded as a source of specialist business advice to which clients can be referred. However, as one recent study has suggested (Segal Quince Wicksteed 1988), the referral process is not as good as it could be and many of the support organizations in the enterprise agency network have been less than fully aware of the Small Firms Service as a specialist resource. Furthermore, with the decision to transfer responsibility for the free telephone helpline – now known as Freefone Enterprise – to the Training and Enterprise Councils, this source of advice appears to have become less accessible to many businesses (*Financial Times*, 30 July 1991, p. 10). In particular, there have been technical difficulties with maintaining access during the transfer of responsibility from the Department of Employment. However, the problem is potentially more deep-seated. The Department of Employment has estimated that only about half of the 82

TECs in England and Wales currently provide advice lines and some of those planning such lines have delayed implementation as other activities have taken precedence in the start-up period. The result of this shift from central provision to local provision through the TECs appears to be that a single, easily recognizable point of contact is being replaced with a confusing plethora of helplines, doing little to create a coherent system of small business support (see Chapter 8 for a detailed discussion of provision, take-up and effectiveness of the small firm training and support network).

Advice and consultancy services
Increasingly, as small firm assistance has shifted from hard assistance (finance, premises) to 'soft' assistance (support for advice and training), considerable resources have been devoted to the provision of information and advice to small businesses. In the UK since 1988 there has been a progressive coincidence of small firm oriented policies and other aspects of industrial policy, such as regional policy and innovation policy.

Since 1979 the emphasis of regional industrial policy in the UK has progressively shifted towards the small firm and towards a more selective, discretionary, system (Pettigrew and Dann 1986). The changes signalled in the 1988 White Paper (DTI 1988) clearly indicate that regional industrial policy has altered in three fundamental respects. First, regional industrial policy is now largely the regionalization of national industrial and enterprise policies. Second, the Department of Trade and Industry – the department responsible for regional policy – has shifted the emphasis of its policies towards small and medium-sized firms. The Enterprise Initiative is just one manifestation of this shift. As a result, regional policy is no longer exclusively based on the attraction of industry to assisted areas; instead, the focus is on promoting indigenous development, supplemented by direct foreign investment (Wren 1990). This reflects the government's belief that the low rate of formation of new firms is one of the major underlying causes of regional and inner city problems (HMSO 1983, p. 29) and a more recent concern about growth constraints encountered by small businesses. Third, regional policy has shifted away from subsidizing the creation of employment in assisted areas towards job creation through improved competitiveness (Wren 1990).

As already noted, a key element in this new framework has been the major shift away from the provision of 'hard' assistance in the form of financial grants, sites and premises, towards 'software' assistance to enable firms to improve their management capability. Under the Consultancy Initiatives (CI) programme – the main component in the DTI's Enterprise Initiative – small and medium-sized firms can receive financial assistance towards the cost of employing independent, private sector consultants to help improve their capability in defined areas of management. In terms of small firms policy, the CI programme reflects a shift away from support for business start-ups towards assisting more established firms. In marked contrast with previous forms of regional assistance which were only available in 'assisted areas', the CI programme is available nationally, although the level of assistance is spatially differentiated, with firms in Assisted Areas and Urban Programme Areas eligible for a higher level of grant.

The CI programme was launched by the DTI in January 1988. Consultancy assistance is available in the following areas: marketing; design; quality; manufacturing systems; business planning; and financial and information systems. The scheme is intended to improve the performance of small and medium-sized enterprises (SMEs) by influencing the key non-price factors in business competitiveness through the use of outside experts.

The CI programme is available to independent firms or groups employing fewer than 500 employees. The scheme covers both manufacturing and service industries, and firms in most industries are eligible. The scheme operates throughout Great Britain, although firms in the Assisted Areas and Urban Programme Areas receive a grant that covers two-thirds of the consultancy costs compared with half in the rest of Great Britain. Assistance is provided for projects involving between five and fifteen person-days of consultancy effort, and each legally separate firm or member of a group is limited to two assisted projects. (From 1 April 1991 the scheme has been limited to one subsidized consultancy project.)

At the outset the DTI established procedures to monitor each element of the CI programme and to assess the extent to which the scheme was meeting its objectives. Based on the initial evaluation, it appears that the CI scheme has provided a concrete means for firms to address business development issues which they were already aware of, and over one-third of companies would not otherwise have proceeded with the assisted project in the absence of CI support. Although still early, most companies interviewed in the evaluation reported a significant impact of the CI scheme on business performance in terms of additional net value, reduced costs and increased employment (Segal Quince Wicksteed 1989).

Training
As part of the redirection of the scope of small firm policies in the 1980s there has been a move away from removing tangible constraints on business start-up and growth (in the areas of finance, premises and administrative burdens) towards increased emphasis on the provision of enterprise training to equip potential and existing small firm owner-managers with the skills and knowledge needed to launch, manage and develop a successful small business.

Until recently, enterprise training schemes have been the responsibility of the Training Agency (previously the Manpower Services Commission). The number of participants on the Training for Enterprise (TFE) programme has increased from 120 in 1979–80 (the programme actually began in 1977 with 32 participants) to 107,755 in 1987–88. The training budget has increased from £0.4 million in 1979–80 to £18.3 million in 1987–88, although this increase has not kept pace with the increasing numbers on the programme. As a result, unit costs have fallen from £2,009 to £268 (1986 prices) between 1983–84 and 1987–88 (National Audit Office, 1988). This reduction in per capita expenditure is reflected in the reduction in training periods and an increase in modular

Table 2.1   *BGT opportunities taken up by type of option, 1989–90*

	Option	Number of Opportunities	%
1.	Better business planning	21,577	25.6
2.	Business skills training	60,731	72.1
3.	Using consultants to manage change	1,503	1.8
4.	Joint action on skills	302	0.4
5.	Innovation in training	102	0.1
Total		**84,215**	

Source: Training Agency, unpublished statistics.

and non-residential formats (Stanworth and Stanworth 1990). The TFE programme was initially restricted to helping people involved in starting up a business (New Enterprise Programme; Graduate Enterprise Programme), but various programmes to help existing businesses have gradually been introduced (Action Learning Programme; Management Extension Programme; Private Enterprise Programme). Indeed, by 1987–88, 55 per cent of TFE places and just over 50 per cent of expenditure were for schemes to help existing businesses (National Audit Office 1988). The government has renewed its commitment to enterprise training by launching the Business Growth Training (BGT) programme in April 1989 with an annual budget of £55 million: this superseded and brought under one umbrella a number of existing and new training programmes.

BGT comprises five training programmes – termed options – which offer different kinds of assistance to businesses depending on their size, nature of activities and particular circumstances (Table 2.1) (Hillier 1989). Options 1 and 2 provide small firms with 'Business Growth Training' (Table 2.2). These options account for almost 98 per cent of the businesses funded under the

Table 2.2   *Business Skills Training*: take-up by size of firm*

Number of Employees	Percentage of Firms
1	49.1
2–5	33.4
6–20	10.7
21+	6.8

Source: Training Agency
* i.e. options 1 and 2

programme. However, as the cost of providing these options is considerably less than for the other options, they account for only around one-quarter of expenditure.

Option 1 – 'Kits for better business and training plans' – provides SMEs with a diagnostic kit in loose-leaf book form to help them to produce better business plans and identify their training needs. The kit is available in three different versions – for new businesses just starting up; established owner-managed businesses; and medium-sized 'team managed' businesses. Counselling is provided to help people work through their kits. Just over 20,000 kits were issued in the first full year of the scheme. The kits are available free-of-charge from local agents – business and training specialists such as enterprise agencies and local colleges as well as private sector firms. The local agents undertake the marketing and promotion of the kits and local workshops and counselling sessions. The kits are free but businesses pay local rates for workshop and counselling activities.

Option 2 – 'Better business skills for owner-managers' – takes over and develops several training programmes previously available under Training for Enterprise. Their objective is to help owner-managers of small businesses to improve their business skills and help produce plans for growth. The Business Skills Seminars comprise a series of one-day seminars on such subjects as tax and book-keeping and are available to any small business owner-managers who wish to improve their skills. The Growth Programmes are selective: Firmstart and the Small Business Programme provide intensive support spread over six months to new and established businesses which are judged to have growth potential. Option 2 has attracted the greatest number of participants, with just over 60,000 places taken during the first year. The various courses are subsidized by the Training Agency and are provided through appointed training providers who offer a variety of part-time and open learning programmes.

Option 3 – 'Using consultants to manage change' – is aimed at larger SMEs that are managed by a team rather than an individual. Like the DTI's Enterprise Initiative it provides financial assistance – up to half of the costs (two-thirds in Inner City Target Areas) up to a maximum of £15,000 to employ consultants to help the company devise a strategy for growth and arrange skill development and training for both the management team and staff (supervisory level and above). Just over 1500 projects have been funded in the first year of the scheme. The consultant assists with the development of better business and training plans for the whole workforce.

Option 4 – 'Tackling your skill needs jointly with other companies' – encourages SMEs operating in the same labour market to work together to improve the supply of skills by providing financial support for collaborative training projects. Just over 300 projects were commissioned under this option in the first year of the scheme. About half of the projects are managed by industrial training organizations such as Local Employer Networks, Chambers of Commerce and Industry Training Organizations and the other half directly by the Training Agency.

Option 5 – 'How to implement your own innovative training solution' – provides support to selected medium-sized firms to develop innovative training solutions that are based on their business needs. Just over 100 companies were assisted under this option in 1989–90.

With the dissolution of the Training Agency, the TECs are taking over responsibility for the training of the unemployed and young people and for the delivery of its small business programmes, including training for small business owners and managers. This shift represents 'an attempt to give the business community ownership of local training arrangements' (Department of Employment 1989) as part of the shift from public to private sector responsibility for small firm policy. As a recent review (Bennett 1990) indicates, TECs offer an opportunity to adopt a local approach to training and enterprise, introduce greater flexibility, give consumers, employers and others responsibility for the delivery of training and enterprise, and provide a local focus for the proliferation of vocational education, training and enterprise activities. Accordingly, TECs will take over responsibility for training programmes previously run by the Training Agency's area offices (such as Employment Training and the Youth Training Scheme) together with small business assistance programmes (including Small Firms Counselling) previously run by the Department of Employment. While the balance TECs strike between their general training/labour market services and specific enterprise/small business training has yet to be determined in the light of local requirements, the TECs embody most clearly two of the major shifts in small firm policy in the last decade which were identified earlier in this chapter: the shift from a centrally-managed system to one that is locally-based; and the shift from public sector responsibility to private sector involvement (with the private sector providing the majority of TEC directors). Although, as the example of the transfer of the Freefone Enterprise service to TECs discussed earlier makes clear, there are potential pitfalls in this shift of emphasis, the establishment of TECs does offer the opportunity to bring coherence and integration to the diverse range of services available to the small business, thereby breaking down the often artificial segmentation of the market by product (Enterprise Allowance Scheme, Business Growth Training, Small Firms Service and so on) rather than by customer need. If this co-ordination can be achieved, TECs offer the prospect of a move in the direction of a properly coherent and integrated small firms policy in the UK.

Impact of small firm policy

As already noted above, the resurgence of the small firm sector, from the early 1970s, pre-dates the most active period of small firm policy formulation in the UK and, in response to a range of social, economic and other factors, is likely to outlast the specifically 1980s expression of an enterprise culture (Burrows 1991b; Curran and Blackburn 1991). To date, the 'success' of particular schemes and of small firm policies as a whole has been measured largely in terms of absolute numbers: the number of participants on the Enterprise Allowance Scheme, the number of loan guarantees issued and even the total number of firms registered for VAT purposes have been cited as evidence of the success of small firm policy. The systematic evaluation of the impact of the expanding volume of assistance to the small firm sector has been identified as an important area for detailed analysis both by academic researchers and policy makers (Frank *et al* 1984; Mason and Harrison 1985). However, despite a growing number of studies of the operation of various specific measures introduced to support the small firm sector, many of which represent evaluations commissioned by the government department concerned (see Harrison and Mason (1991) and Chapter 6 of the present volume for details), there is not yet a systematic evaluation of the overall impact of the package of measures which presently constitutes small firm policy in the UK on the development of the sector. Furthermore, as Johnson (1990) has pointed out, most of these assessments (but by no means all, as evaluation procedures become more sophisticated) have not addressed the measurement of the most important success measure of all – the extent to which genuinely additional economic activity has been generated.

In many cases these studies have merely attempted to measure the direct outcome of the particular scheme under consideration. However, more sophisticated evaluations have also attempted to estimate their net benefits in order to provide a more detailed and realistic assessment of the effectiveness of the policy. This has involved deriving estimates of the displacement effect on unaided businesses by those businesses in receipt of assistance. It has also involved attempts to measure deadweight – the extent to which assistance has been made available to businesses or individuals to do what they would have done in any case – and its converse, additionality – the number of individuals starting their own business or existing firms expanding which would not have been able to do so in the absence of assistance. Indirect benefits, in the form of the additional economic activity which is created by the input demands of assisted businesses, have also been taken into account. Despite these efforts, however, it would be fair to say that the definitional and methodological problems involved in the assessment of such issues have yet to be adequately overcome.

One issue which has been relatively neglected in these policy evaluations, however, is the identification of spatial variations in the outcome (although area case studies are included in Gray and Stanworth (1986) and Segal Quince Wicksteed (1988)). Even though all of the small business support resources, with the single exception of the Consultancy Initiative, operate on a national basis with specific regional differentiation in the level of assistance, it is becoming clear that nationally available schemes to assist industry often exhibit variations between regions in both take-up rates and economic impact. For example, the South East region's share of companies receiving grants under various innovation schemes (DTI 1983), and grants under the Microprocessor Applications Project (Policy Studies Institute 1985) are substantially in excess of its proportion of the total business stock.

Similar variations in the take-up and impact of small firms support measures may also be expected. Regions vary widely in their rate of new business start-ups (Keeble 1990b; Mason and Harrison 1990; Mason 1991). These spatial variations in business start-ups are broadly in line with variations in regional entrepreneurial potential (Storey 1982; Storey and Johnston 1987b). Furthermore, there is some evidence that the subsequent post-start-up growth and performance of small firms may also vary between regions, with the South East, East Anglia and South West regions out-performing the rest of the country (Mason 1985 and 1989; Barkham 1987).

In view of these spatial variations in the dynamism of the small firm sector it has increasingly been argued that schemes to assist the small business sector will also display take-up rates which vary substantially between regions. Storey (1982, p. 195), for example, has argued that 'a policy of assisting the small . . . firm risks being regionally divisive' by conferring the greatest benefits on the most prosperous areas of the country. In similar vein Martin (1985, p. 387) has argued that policies to promote small businesses 'while not spatially discrimi- nating by intent are very much so in practice . . . [and are] inherently favouring the southern half of the country against the remainder'.

Detailed data on the regional take-up of four major initiatives introduced in the 1980s have been made available for analysis (Mason and Harrison 1985, 1986, 1989; Mason *et al* 1988; Harrison and Mason 1986). These initiatives all relate to financial assistance to small firms: the Enterprise Allowance Scheme, to help the unemployed into business; the Loan Guarantee Scheme, to encour- age bank lending; the Business Expansion Scheme, to encourage venture capital equity investment; and the Small Engineering Firms Investment Scheme, to encourage small engineering companies to invest in CAD/CAM and CNC equipment. Both the EAS and LGS are run by the Department of Employment, and the BES is administered by the Inland Revenue. SEFIS, which was admin- istered by the DTI, is the only scheme of the four no longer operating. These four schemes have involved considerable expenditure: between 1982 and 1985, for example, between £1.0 billion and £1.5 billion was channelled into the small firm sector in the UK under these four schemes (Mason and Harrison 1986). In the period 1982–88 some £585 million has been spent on EAS and £579 million on LGS (National Audit Office 1988), with over £700 million in equity capital invested under BES (Harrison and Mason 1988).

It is clear that there are considerable inter-regional differences in the take-up and impact of policy initiatives to assist the small firm sector. For each of these four initiatives there is a general tendency for the South East to record a better performance than other regions (although the take-up of EAS and LGS failure rates is exceptional). However, analysis does not support the argument that there is a simple north-south divide in the impact of small firms policy in the UK. There is, in other words, no 'natural' tendency for the peripheral regions to get less than their fair share of assistance under small firms policy initiatives, and in each of the schemes examined there is always at least one region north of the Wash-Severn axis which received more than its fair share of assistance.

However, as the discussion in Chapter 6 makes clear, in the provision of equity finance to small firms by both the private and public sectors the South East has been a beneficiary out of proportion to the region's share of the national stock of small businesses. It has also recently been argued that other forms of small firm assistance, notably the Consultancy Initiative programme, will also 'primarily . . . benefit and assist SMEs, including new firms, in the already economically buoyant regions of southern England, notwithstanding the helpful adoption of a higher rate of government grant . . . for Development and Intermediate Area firms' (Keeble 1990a, p. 70). Examination of this contention in the context of the recent shift of small firm policy to 'software' issues provides an important insight into one of the ways in which the present policy package may not be having the same impact on all parts of the small firm sector. This differential impact, which still requires substantial investigation in areas other than the regional one, represents a major potential weakness in the delivery of the policy package in the UK.

Regional variations in the take-up of the Consultancy Initiatives

In the period 13 January 1988 to 1 December 1989 there were 39,210 applications made under the CI programme, of which just over 28,000 (71.5 per cent) were approved, resulting in the commissioning of a consultancy project. Table 2.3 lists the proportion of applications and project commissions in each region. The take-up rate was assessed through the calculation of location quotients (LQs) which relate each region's proportion of the total number of applications or projects commissioned to its 'regional economic weighting' – the proportion of the total stock of businesses in Great Britain eligible to apply under the scheme. A location quotient of more than one indicates that a region contains more than its 'fair share' of applications or project commissions.

In general, northern regions and the West Midlands have higher than 'expected' proportions of applications and project commissions when compared to their share of the total stock of eligible businesses. The North East, with over 5 per cent of all applications and project commissions but only 3 per cent of the national stock of eligible businesses, has the highest application and project commission rates (LQs of 1.70 and 1.73 respectively). Other regions with higher than expected application and project commission rates are the North West, Wales, Yorkshire-Humberside and the West Midlands. With the exception of the South West, all southern regions have lower than expected proportions of applications and project commissions, with the lowest rates in Greater London (12.2 per cent of applications and 11.8 per cent of project commissions but 17.2 per cent of eligible businesses). Scotland is an anomaly as it is the only northern region which does not have a higher than expected proportion of applications (LQ = 0.99). However, because its ratio of applications to project commissions is the highest of any region it does have more than its 'fair share' of project commissions.

The higher take-up rate of the CI programme in northern regions is the opposite of the experience of the various small firm finance initiatives discussed earlier (Business Expansion Scheme, Loan Guarantee Scheme, Enterprise Allowance Scheme, Small Engineering Firms Investment Scheme). The case has been argued that supply-side factors are more important than the demand-side in explaining the higher take-up rate of these schemes in southern regions (Harrison and Mason, 1991). However, in the case of the CI programme the demand-side would appear to be more relevant in explaining regional variations in take-up

Table 2.3   Regional distribution of applications and projects commissioned under the Consultancy Initiatives[1] (13 January 1988–1 December 1989)

DTI region[1]	Applica- tions	Projects comm- issioned	Projects commissioned as a percentage of applications	Location quotients[2]	
				Applica- tions	Projects comm- issioned
	%	%	(GB = 71.5%)		
North East	5.1	5.2	72.0	1.70	1.73
North West	14.2	15.7	79.1	1.27	1.40
Yorkshire- Humberside	9.3	9.5	73.2	1.18	1.20
West Midlands	10.6	10.3	69.8	1.20	1.17
East Midlands	6.4	6.5	73.0	0.93	0 94
South West	9.4	8.3	62.6	1.04	1.03
East	8.1	7.1	62.7	0.83	0.72
Gtr London	12.2	11.8	69.2	0.71	0.69
South East: Reading	6.1	6.2	72.8	0.90	0.91
South East: Reigate	6.4	6.3	69.8	0.80	0.79
Scotland	6.8	7.9	82.7	0.99	1.14
Wales	5.5	5.3	69.4	1.26	1.20

Notes:
1 DTI regions differ from Standard Regions
   North East - Cleveland, Durham, Northumberland, Tyne and Wear
   North West - Cheshire, Lancashire, Greater Manchester, Merseyside, High Peak
   Yorkshire-Humberside - North Yorkshire, West Yorkshire, South Yorkshire, Humberside
   West Midlands - Warwickshire, Staffordshire, Shropshire, Hereford and Worcester, and the former West Midlands metropolitan county
   East Midlands - Nottinghamshire, Derbyshire (except the High Peak), Leicestershire, Lincolnshire, Northamptonshire
   East - Bedfordshire, Cambridgeshire, Essex, Hertfordshire, Norfolk, Suffolk
   South East: Reading - Berkshire, Buckinghamshire, Hampshire, Oxfordshire, Isle of Wight
   South East: Reigate - Kent, Surrey, East Sussex, West Sussex.

2   The location quotient is calculated as follows:

$$LQ_i = \frac{Cl_i}{RW_i}$$

where Cl_i = the percentage of applications/projects commissioned in region i;
        RW_i = the percentage of companies eligible for the scheme in region i.
        This was calculated for the DTI by the Business Statistics Office and involved subtracting ineligible companies (e.g. with 500 or more employees, which was imputed from company turnover) and ineligible sectors (e.g. charities, agriculture) from the stock of VAT firms in each region. This process eliminated between 1 and 2% of the VAT stock.

rates, although the supply-side plays an important indirect role by influencing the level of demand. Four supply-mediated demand-side factors can help to explain the existence of regional variations in the take-up of the CI programme.

First, the higher level of financial assistance for firms in Assisted Areas and Urban Programme Areas (most of which are in the north) may also have contributed to the higher take-up rate of the CI programme in northern regions. Second, firms in northern regions may be more aware of, and familiar with, the DTI, which is responsible for the delivery of the CI programme. The DTI has also been responsible for the delivery of regional assistance, and is responsible for the delivery of regional enterprise and innovation grants, available only to eligible small firms in the Assisted Areas. Hence, in northern regions which have, or have had, assisted area status channels of communication between businesses and the DTI regional offices are likely to be more open, and both businesses and their professional advisers are likely to have greater familiarity with the DTI, be more aware of the types of assistance that are available and be more prepared to use government assistance.

Third, awareness of the CI programme itself may be greater among SMEs in northern regions. With the exception of the first year of the scheme, when each regional office received the same budget for local promotion, both the central and regional promotion budgets have been related to the population of eligible businesses in each region. Thus, regional variations in the DTI's promotion of the scheme are likely to have been of limited significance in explaining regional differences in the take-up of the scheme. The CI programme has also been promoted by industry support organizations such as enterprise agencies, chambers of commerce and local authorities and through the consultancy industry. Some firms have become aware of the programme as a result of promotion by individual consultants (Segal Quince Wicksteed 1989). There is considerable scope for such independent promotional channels to vary spatially and so contribute to regional variations in the awareness of the scheme. This is highlighted in a previous Segal Quince Wicksteed (1988) study which noted the low take-up of the Business Improvement Scheme (BIS) in Middlesbrough. The BIS was an ERDF programme in steel, shipbuilding, textile closure areas which provided small firms with grants towards the cost of obtaining various forms of professional support, including marketing, management, financial advice and other types of consultancy. The business services industry has done much of the marketing of the scheme: Segal Quince Wicksteed (1988) ascribes Middlesbrough's low take-up to its lack of a well-developed business services sector. However, spatial variations in awareness and demand arising from private sector promotion of an initiative such as the CI programme are likely to be at the intra-regional rather than inter-regional scale.

Finally, firms in northern regions may have been encouraged to apply for the CI programme as a result of their experience of using, or awareness of, previous subsidized consultancy schemes – such as BIS (called Better Business Services [BBS] in Scotland) – which were available in designated localities within the Assisted Areas. The existence of a link between prior use of subsidized consultancy and use of the CI programme is confirmed in a non-spatial context by

Segal Quince Wicksteed (1989): they note that firms which had undertaken CI projects in disciplines that had also been covered by the Business Technology Advisory Services (BTAS) scheme showed a much greater tendency to have used subsidized (as opposed to full cost) consultancy support previously.

Regional variations in the take-up of Business Growth Training

A similar analysis of the regional impact of those elements of the options under the Training Agency's Business Growth Training specifically targeted at the start-up/small firm situation and which are predominantly used by small firms

Table 2.4   Regional variation in the take-up rate of BGT options 1, 2 and 3

Region	Option 1			Option 2			Option 3		
	No.	%	LQ[1]	No.	%	LQ	No.	%	LQ
London	1,089	5.1	0.34	8,164	13.9	0.89	157	10.4	0.67
ROSE[2]	3,714	17.2	0.86	6,422	11.0	0.52	170	11.3	0.54
South West	2,153	10.0	1.04	5,851	10.0	0.99	137	9.1	0.90
Eastern[3]	2,252	10.4	0.95	5,185	8.8	0.77	183	12.2	1.07
West Midlands	2,576	11.9	1.42	4,897	8.3	0.94	194	12.9	1.47
Yorkshire-Humberside	2,256	10.5	1.42	6,379	10.9	1.42	123	8.2	1.06
North West	2,409	11.2	1.26	9,236	15.7	1.69	171	11.4	1.23
Northern	743	3.4	0.92	3,355	5.7	1.46	81	5.4	1.38
Wales	2,003	9.3	1.79	2,426	4.1	0.76	80	5.3	0.98
Scotland	2,382	11.0	1.61	6,747	11.5	1.60	207	13.8	1.92
Head Office[4]	(986)			(2,069)			(-)		
GB Total (ex H.O.)	21,577			58,662			1,503		

Notes:

1 The location quotient is calculated as follows:

$$LQ_i = \frac{BGT_i}{VAT_i}$$

where BGT$_i$ = the percentage of projects commissioned under a BGT option in region i;

VAT$_i$ = the percentage of VAT-registered businesses in region i.

2 Rest of the South East, excluding Greater London

3 East Midlands and East Anglia

4 Projects administered by the Training Agency's Head Office. These projects have been ignored in the calculation of regional shares.

Source: Training Agency, unpublished statistics; *British Business*

confirms the general results of the above analysis of the Consultancy Initiative. As Table 2.4 shows, the take-up rate for each of the three options under examination, as with the Consultancy Initiative, exhibits a north–south contrast that is the exact reverse of many of the other small firm schemes that have been examined. In each case, with the marginal exception of the South West, southern regions contain less than their 'fair share' of assisted firms whereas the Midlands and northern regions have much higher than 'expected' proportions of assisted firms. The major exception to this is the Northern region, which has less than its fair share of BGT assisted firms in the first full year of the scheme. However, if the pilot stage of BGT option 1 is included the Northern region share rises significantly to 11.1 per cent (LQ = 2.85) of all assisted firms. The North West, Yorkshire-Humberside, Wales, Scotland and the West Midlands also have higher than expected take-up rates for option 1. At the other extreme, the take-up rate in Greater London is only one-third of its 'expected' level and only three-quarters of the expected level in the Rest of the South East (ROSE) and Eastern (that is, East Midlands and East Anglia) regions.

The North West (LQ = 1.69) and Scotland (LQ = 1.60) have the highest take-up rates under option 2. However, Wales and the West Midlands join Greater London and the ROSE and Eastern regions in containing less than their 'fair share' of assisted firms. In contrast to option 1, the take-up rate in Greater London is higher than in both the ROSE and Eastern regions.

The take-up rate under option 3 provides yet more variation on the general north–south contrast, with Scotland exhibiting the highest take-up rate. The West Midlands, Northern and North West regions also contain higher than expected proportions of assisted firms. However, Greater London and ROSE again exhibit the lowest take-up rates, along with the South West. Both the Eastern region and Wales contain approximately their 'expected' shares of assisted companies.

On the surface, and assuming that regional variations in the proportion of applications rejected by the Training Agency are not significant, it would appear that such regional variations in take-up rates are the straightforward product of regional variations in the demand for enterprise training by new firm founders and small business owner-managers. Moreover, this explanation would concur with empirical evidence on regional variations in the backgrounds, experience, confidence and commitment to training of small firm founders and owner-managers. For example, Barkham (1987) notes that new firm founders in the South East have higher levels of education qualifications and greater managerial and technical experience than their counterparts in northern regions.

It seems that the way in which the various BGT options are delivered has contributed to differences in the level of awareness among SMEs of the programme in different parts of the country which, in turn, have resulted in regional variations in the take-up rate. Based on the evidence from option 3 (Smith 1990) most firms have become aware of BGT either from the agents responsible for delivering the assistance – consultants, in the case of option 3 – or from area or regional offices of the Training Agency. Indeed, Smith (1990) comments on the growing involvement of consultants in the marketing of option 3 in order to generate projects for themselves by encouraging firms to apply for the scheme; it is the responsibility of applicants to select a consultant. Similarly, under options 1 and 2 the agents have undertaken much of the marketing. One hypothesis is that in northern regions the agents responsible for delivering the various BGT options have marketed the scheme more vigorously and as a result of superior local networks with the local and regional business community and a high level of credibility have been able to promote the scheme more efficiently, thereby raising awareness to a higher level than in the South.

The locational structure of intermediary organizations responsible for delivering assistance may also be an important factor in explaining regional variations in take-up rates (Britton 1989). In particular, where an intermediary is based at a single location rather than having a network of regional offices, this might be expected to generate a higher than expected take-up rate in the region in which it is based. In the case of option 1, the business kits were developed by the Durham Small Business Club, which acts as a national agent on behalf of the Training Agency. This accounts for the high take-up shown in the Northern region when the pilot stage data are included: the fact that BGT option 1 was developed and piloted in this region has probably subsequently depressed demand from this region.

Similarly, it can be hypothesized that the Training Agency's regional and area offices in the northern regions may have promoted the scheme more vigorously either through greater advertising and promotional efforts or because of superior networks with the local business community. The latter factor may be of particular importance: the Training Agency have adopted a relatively low-key approach to advertising BGT through the media (in marked contrast to the DTI's promotion of its Enterprise Initiative) and instead has emphasized 'face-to-face' promotion of enterprise training. It may be that the Training Agency's regional and local offices in northern regions have superior networks, perhaps as a result of a long tradition of enterprise training in these regions, and so have been able to promote the scheme more effectively than their counterparts in southern regions.

Conclusion

Storey's view – that the existence of nationally-available schemes to assist small firms 'risks being regionally divisive' (Storey 1982, p. 195) because take-up rates will be highest in southern regions – is now widely accepted as the conventional wisdom. Others (for example, Whittington 1984; Martin 1985) have made the same argument. Mason and Harrison (Mason and Harrison, 1986, 1989 and Harrison and Mason 1986) were the first to provide empirical confirmation that regional take-up rates for various schemes to provide financial assistance to small firms were generally highest in the South East region. (They did note, however, that some northern regions had higher than expected take-up rates for particular schemes, suggesting that there is no 'natural' tendency for northern regions to attract less than their 'fair share' of assistance: Harrison and Mason (1991).)

This conventional wisdom is challenged both by the above survey of the Training Agency's Business Growth Training Programme, and the study of regional take-up rates under the DTI's Enterprise Initiative Consultancy Initiatives programme. Under both schemes take-up rates have been higher in northern regions than in the south.

Explanations both for the regional pattern of take-up rates under BGT and the Consultancy Initiatives programme and for the contrast with earlier studies of the Loan Guarantee Scheme (LGS), Business Expansion Scheme (BES), Enterprise Allowance Scheme (EAS) and Small Engineering Firms Investment Scheme (SEFIS) are tentative. Storey and Johnson (1987b) have related regional variations in take-up rates to the (innate) entrepreneurial potential and business dynamism of a region as measured by Storey's (1982) entrepreneurship index, which implies that improvement will come through policy initiatives outside the small firm area itself. A contrasting suggestion is that supply-related factors – in particular the delivery mechanisms for each measure – play the central role in contributing to regional variations in the take-up rate of assistance to small firms, and this has wider significance in the context of the overall shift from public sector to private sector responsibility for small firms policy and in the light of the increased localism in the delivery of policy.

Where the delivery mechanism formally involves private sector institutions, as in the LGS (Harrison and Mason 1986) and the BES (Mason and Harrison 1989) and also in the Small Workshop Scheme (Ambler and Kennett 1985), take-up rates are highest in the South. This can be related to two factors: spatial variations in the locational distribution of such organizations, and differences between and within organizations in the promotion of the scheme across the country (Harrison and Mason 1991). However, under the BGT and the Consultancy Initiatives programme the actual assistance is delivered by independent agents although the schemes are managed by government departments or agencies – the Training Agency, and now the TECs, and the Department of Trade and Industry (DTI) respectively – and firms have to contact the regional or area offices of these organizations in order to apply for the scheme.

The higher take-up rate of Business Growth Training and the Consultancy Initiative in northern regions is, then, a function of three factors: first, the greater awareness of, and familiarity with, government agencies among SMEs in such regions on account of decades of regional policy initiatives and a decade and a half of urban policy; second, a stronger 'grantrepreneurship' tradition involving a greater readiness to seek assistance and tailor activities in order to qualify for government assistance; and, third, the superior networks of government regional/area offices and their agents in northern regions, facilitating more effective promotion of initiatives. Government plans to bring Business Growth Training along with the counselling from the Small Firms Service and the Enterprise Allowance Scheme, under the remit of the new Training and Enterprise Councils (TECs) (Tim Eggar, Employment Minister, in *Employment Gazette*, August 1990, p. 376) by altering the delivery system are likely to produce a different spatial pattern of take-up rates.

There is now evidence on the pattern of regional take-up rates of a variety of schemes to assist small firms. However, explanations for regional variations in take-up rates remain largely unresearched, and the possible existence of differential take-up and impact of small firm policy on other sub-populations of the sector has not yet been addressed. Moreover, neither government-sponsored evaluations of the effectiveness of small firms measures nor the National Audit Office (1988) evaluation of various schemes have considered regional variations in take-up rates. Attempts to explain the regional variations in take-up rates, along with studies of regional variations in the economic impact of small firms initiatives (for example, by examining whether additionality and deadweight, wastage rates and displacement effects vary between regions), and monitoring the effects of changes in the delivery system on regional take-up rates (such as the effect of TECs taking over responsibility for BGT and the EAS) must therefore remain at the top of any small firms research agenda (Mason and Harrison 1985).

3 Problems and Preoccupations

The Bolton Report was very much problem-oriented; that is to say, of its 435 pages only 82 were devoted to the section headed Economic Analysis, and the remainder given over to the problems faced by small firms and policies to deal with them. The decline in the role of small firms in the economy was largely attributed to the impact of the growth of government and to the growing importance of economies of scale in marketing and finance, rather than to technological factors or a lack of knowledge and information among owner-managers, though this last was identified as a problem by the Bolton Committee.

The key problems and issues discussed in the Bolton Report (finance and taxation, government business, monopoly policy, training and advice) are still under discussion today, and have neither been added to nor subtracted from. (There have, however, been changes in emphasis: for example, the committee devoted a whole chapter to development and planning controls which are, in general, probably no longer regarded as an issue of high priority.)

With the passage of time it is perhaps now even more obvious than it was when the committee was preparing its report that these eternal problems of small firms are an inevitable consequence of their small scale. Small business owners are acutely subject to time pressures and can easily be criticized for the lack of specialized knowledge which is available within the more elaborate management structure of the larger firm. These time pressures explain the low tolerance of small business owners for the bureaucratic burdens imposed by government. The risks faced by small firms, their exclusion from organized securities markets and their weak bargaining power *vis-à-vis* suppliers of capital, explain their concern about both taxation and financing. The same lack of bargaining power with other suppliers, and their individual weakness against larger competitors, explain their concern about monopoly policy.

The wall of problems faced by small firms is in fact so high that it seemed, at the end of the 1960s, when the Bolton Committee was taking evidence, that their role was doomed to shrink indefinitely. As we have seen in Chapter 1, this was not to be, though more recently the growth of the small business sector has again come under threat. Small firms do have considerable advantages and strengths, as the Bolton Committee recognized. High levels of motivation and flexibility, deriving from owner-management and driven more by a desire for self-expression than for short-term profitability, enable small firms to overcome their difficulties and play an important role in innovation as well as to perform economic functions which are most efficiently carried out on a small scale. Moreover, the importance is now recognized of what the committee called their 'seedbed' function, in which a few small firms – though undoubtedly in the UK too few – grow into larger firms, challenging, enlarging and changing the existing economic structure.

In this chapter we first review the problems of small firms as seen from the point of view of small business owners in their responses to the Small Business Research Trust (SBRT) *Quarterly Survey of Small Firms in Britain*. We then go on to examine the results of more recent research on two external issues – government burdens and financing – before outlining the internal problems of small firms.

The business owner's view

Since the regular SBRT surveys began in 1984, respondents have been asked to select the single 'most important problem facing your business today' from a list of thirteen items plus 'other'. The results (see Table 3.1) are expressed as the number of respondents selecting each problem as a percentage of the number responding to the survey.

Given that the percentage of respondents selecting 'other' is small (especially since the list of problems was extended by four items at the beginning of 1990), we can safely assume that the rankings cover all the important concerns of small business owners. (And a multitude of other surveys on small business problems has produced results similar to those of the SBRT surveys; see Bannock and Peacock (1989). Disaggregated analysis of the SBRT data shows that the rankings given to problems do in some instances vary systematically with size of firm and sector, but we are concerned here only with the overall picture.) It is, however, important to note that the responses indicate average perceptions of the urgency of the problems listed at the time of each survey. A decline in the percentage mentions of a problem does not, therefore, necessarily signify that the problem has diminished: it may mean only that other problems have become more pressing.

Over the period 1984–91 as a whole, finance and interest rates have come out on top in all but two of the 27 surveys. From 1990 onwards, when cost and availability of finance were distinguished as separate problems, it has been clear that it is the cost that is the more urgent issue, though this has been a period of very high interest rates.

Cashflow and payments were added to the list at the same time, and in the most recent survey a total of 42 per cent of respondents mentioned the three related issues of finance: availability, cashflow and interest rates as their most important problem.

Table 3.1   Problems experienced by respondents 1984–91

	Acc to fin	Inter-est rates	Total tax bur-den	Comp from big busi-ness	Lack of skilled empl'ees	Low t/o or lack of bus-iness	Cash flw/ pay-ments	Govt regs and pap-w'k	Short-age of mate-rial/ supplies	High rates of pay	Prems, rents & rates	Infla-tion	Other	No resp	Number of replies analysed
1984/4		17.1	15.9	12.0	5.4	15.3		12.6	1.1	4.2		3.5	10.9	1.4	3,056
1985/1		19.4	15.9	10.0	4.4	14.5		15.7	1.3	3.4		3.8	9.5	1.5	1,795
1985/2		22.1	16.1	10.8	4.3	14.3		12.5	1.3	2.4		5.0	9.1	1.5	1,181
1985/3		23.6	12.8	11.2	4.9	13.8		13.1	1.9	3.7		2.0	8.6	3.8	1,090
1985/4		24.0	16.6	11.1	5.6	15.7		10.2	0.9	2.0		2.2	9.2	2.0	1,072
1986/1		21.4	17.1	11.7	7.2	14.4		9.6	1.8	2.0		3.0	9.9	1.3	1,326
1986/2		29.9	16.3	9.1	7.3	12.6		9.9	1.2	2.2		1.7	9.4	0.6	1,052
1986/3		21.3	16.6	11.5	7.3	17.0		7.3	0.9	1.4		0.9	13.7	2.0	1,285
1986/4		25.0	17.7	11.8	7.2	14.7		6.8	1.3	1.3		1.1	10.0	3.1	1,435
1987/1		26.4	16.0	12.0	8.0	13.0		7.4	1.3	1.6		0.9	9.1	4.2	1,166
1987/2		23.7	17.7	10.7	9.6	12.0		7.6	1.5	2.6		1.0	10.3	3.3	1,746
1987/3		20.3	17.9	11.5	11.8	12.9		6.6	2.2	1.9		1.1	10.5	3.5	1,113
1987/4		18.0	21.3	12.5	11.1	13.0		6.3	1.3	1.3		1.1	9.6	4.5	977
1988/1		21.6	20.1	11.4	11.1	9.6		6.1	1.9	2.3		0.7	14.9	0.3	1,042
1988/2		19.4	15.5	14.4	12.7	10.2		8.0	2.3	1.8		1.0	13.7	1.4	933
1988/3		17.6	13.7	11.4	17.7	11.3		8.3	2.7	2.4		0.9	11.4	2.4	983
1988/4		25.5	12.5	10.4	16.9	8.7		6.0	3.3	1.3		2.8	10.6	1.9	950
1989/1*		25.1	11.2	1.2	13.2	7.2		8.4	0.4	5.9		5.5	17.4	4.7	1,523
1989/2		26.1	13.0	6.0	13.4	8.0		6.7	0.8	0.6		5.4	14.4	4.7	947
1989/3		33.5	6.0	7.0	12.9	12.2		6.2	0.5	1.6		6.5	12.2	1.5	2,236
1989/4		38.1	5.2	5.8	9.4	13.8		5.5	0.4	1.2		7.1	12.3	1.2	792
1990/1	3.0	27.5	4.2	–	5.8	15.4	13.5	6.2	0.6	3.0	9.7	3.7	4.6	2.0	1,064
1990/2	3.9	25.8	2.6	–	6.4	14.0	12.4	6.5	0.4	1.4	7.6	6.9	8.6	1.3	1,344
1990/3	3.3	28.9	4.8	3.0	5.9	15.3	15.5	3.5	0.0	2.1	4.6	4.6	5.0	1.8	1,027
1990/4	1.9	25.4	5.2	4.6	4.9	17.5	8.9	6.7	0.3	0.2	4.6	8.0	8.7	2.3	1,250
1991/1	4.0	28.6	3.5	2.7	2.9	22.2	10.7	6.1	0.5	0.9	3.5	6.6	5.0	1.3	1,239
1991/2	4.5	20.7	4.3	3.1	2.8	23.2	16.8	5.1	0.2	0.4	8.1	3.5	5.9	0.9	984

* From Survey 18 (1989/1), all figures shown in this table have been weighted to the 1988 VAT sectoral distribution.
Source: SBRT Quarterly Survey of Small Business in Britain, Vol. 7 No. 1, 1991.

The basic problem of lack of business has been quite high in the rankings, except in the boom years of the late 1980s, and most recently has come into first position with 23 per cent of mentions as continuing concern about interest rates (21 per cent) has given way to record levels of concern about the effects of the recession on sales.

Concern about the total tax burden and government regulations and paper-work, which generally ranked third and fourth in the middle 1980s with rank-ings of 16–21 per cent and 10–15 per cent respectively, seem to have been displaced by more urgent worries in the 1990s and are down to mentions of about 5 per cent for both issues. Reductions in direct taxation (though not in the total burden) probably played a part in this lessened concern, as may have making premises rent and rates a separate issue.

Lack of skilled employees was a growing problem in the 1980s and, at the height of the boom in 1988 with 17.7 per cent of mentions, actually moved finance and interest rates into second rank. The urgency of this problem has fallen to very low levels (less than 3 per cent of mentions) with the rise in unemployment and as concern about the sales outlook has grown.

Competition from big business ranked in fourth or fifth position fairly con-sistently until 1988, when high interest rates, payments and other recessionary issues began to predominate.

Inflation (which is a cumulative rather than an urgent problem) has never been mentioned as their most important problem by more than 8 per cent of respondents, and has recently been falling with the year-on-year rate for the retail price index. Shortage of materials and supplies has been of little concern (except in the first survey), rising to a peak of 3.3 per cent of mentions in 1988 and falling to insignificant levels most recently. High rates of pay have never been mentioned by more than 6 per cent and again this has declined with the 1990–1991 recession.

Government burdens

The Bolton Committee devoted a considerable amount of space in its report to the discussion of government burdens on business. This discussion focused heavily upon statistical form-filling, though the committee recognized that: 'The volume of paperwork arising from the administration of government policies dwarfs the statistics burden . . .'. The report also contained separate discussions of the paperwork burdens arising from the Industrial Training Board system, the disclosure provisions of the Companies Acts, and planning and development controls.

Twenty years on, government burdens would loom very much more import-ant in any comprehensive inquiry into the problems of small firms. There are two types of taxation, regulatory and other burdens: those which apply to all or most businesses and those which are industry-specific. The costs of these bur-dens are again of two kinds. The first are direct costs, for example the taxes paid to government which are dealt with in Chapter 5, and other costs borne by business as a consequence of regulation, such as the costs of modifying vehicles to meet safety regulations or the installation of equipment to control emissions at a factory. The second type of costs are compliance costs, for example the cost of time needed to understand the law, in dealing with the necessary paperwork and payments to legal advisers and accountants, staff training and so on.

Taxation is, of course, the largest direct government burden on business, but compliance costs are also important. When the Bolton Committee reported, there were no estimates of the scale of compliance costs, but recent calculations suggest that for business as a whole (small and large firms) they are of the order of 3–4 per cent of GDP, of which tax compliance costs alone are perhaps 60 per cent (Bannock and Peacock 1989). How large a burden this is can be best understood by comparing it with the value added contribution of the agricultural sector to GDP, which is about 1.9 per cent.

Moreover, the compliance burden is regressive – that is to say, it bears most heavily upon small firms. Several studies in the UK and other countries have shown that there are economies of scale in tax and other compliance costs, especially since in the smallest firms, much of the work may have to be carried out by the proprietor (the opportunity cost of whose time, that is to say its value in alternative use, will be relatively high) or by an outside bookkeeper or accountant. One international comparison in 1987 showed that average net compliance costs for VAT rose from well under 1 per cent for firms with a turnover of £2 million or more, to 2.5 – 8.0 per cent for firms in the £15,000 and under range (Bannock and Albach in Bannock and Peacock 1989). VAT compliance costs for very large firms in fact may be negative, in the sense that the interest earned on average tax balances and not yet paid over to the tax authorities may exceed the compliance cost. A survey of small firms commissioned by the DTI in 1985 and carried out in that year showed that VAT was mentioned as a problem by 39 per cent of respondents, employment protection by 29 per cent, statistics and local authority planning regulations by 21 per cent each, tax treatment and sick pay 14 per cent each, and health and safety 11 per cent.

Although average VAT compliance costs of, say, 1 per cent of turnover do not seem very much, it has to be remembered that these costs are only part of the total compliance burden. Costs of this order are also very large when compared with the net profit margins earned on turnover by small firms which, for incorporated businesses, are only of the order of 2–3 per cent.

The regressive nature of regulatory burdens is not restricted to tax compliance costs; rather it is a general tendency resulting from the limited nature of the administrative resources of small firms and the way in which certain fixed costs of regulation have to be borne, irrespective of the size of a business. For example, the average cost of an audit – since 1967 compulsory for all companies irrespective of size and ownership – ranges from less than 0.2 per cent of turnover for firms with a turnover of £10 million or more to 1.6 per cent for companies in the £50–99,000 size band, to over 4 per cent for companies with a turnover of under £20,000 (GB and P 1989b).

Interest in minimizing government burdens on business certainly increased considerably in the 1980s, not only in the UK but in other countries and at the European level. This reflected a greater commitment to the promotion of small business following the rise in unemployment in the early part of the decade and the results of research demonstrating the disproportionate role of small firms in employment creation (see Chapter 1).

In 1986, a central Enterprise and Deregulation Unit (EDU) was set up in the DTI with satellite units in each government department. The Commission of the European Communities also set up a central SME Task Force (now DG 23), one of the most important functions of which was to control regulatory burdens. Both these organizations took over from the United States the impact statement procedure under which new proposals for legislation had to be accompanied by an assessment of its effects upon business.

Despite these efforts, government burdens on business, though virtually impossible to measure overall, have undoubtedly continued to increase. Indeed, although the burden of statistical inquiries and other matters with which the Bolton Committee was so concerned has been curtailed, the Industrial Training Board system largely discontinued and planning and development procedures simplified, the Bolton Report was followed in the 1970s by new burdens, notably the Employment Protection Act 1975 and the introduction of VAT in 1973. The former, since largely modified, proved to have a greater psychological than practical impact on the mass of small firms, but the form which VAT took in the UK and the rigour with which it has been administered have, as we have shown and despite attempts at simplification, added considerably to burdens on small firms (burdens which are likely to increase as changes necessary for the completion of the Single Market progress). There was much other legislation in the 1970s which affected small business: for example, the Consumer Credit Act 1974.

The 1980s saw the introduction of further regulatory burdens, for example the Data Protection Act 1984, the Financial Services Act 1986, and various measures to increase the responsibilities of company directors. At the beginning of the 1990s there have already been a number of further measures which have increased burdens: for example, changes to the sick pay scheme, the widening application of British Standard 5750, and increased administrative requirements for taxation on company cars.

To list these burdens on small firms is not to deny the good intentions behind the legislation, nor to deny that some of these burdens are widely avoided, largely through ignorance. It is also true that many minor burdens have been removed or reduced and efforts made to improve communications between government and business (see DTI 1991), but any account of the state of small business in the 1990s would be seriously deficient if the complaints of business owners about the weight of government burdens were not taken broadly at their face value. As yet largely unresearched, it seems likely that their importance has hitherto been underestimated.

Finance

The preoccupation with the cost of finance among small business owners is not surprising: financial performance is the measure of success in a business, and lack of finance can threaten survival. The whole subject of small business finance is riddled with paradoxes which result from the ambiguity of small business owners' attitudes towards external sources of capital. In general, these owners wish to retain personal or family control of the business and are reluctant to sell equity even where buyers are available. At the same time, except when lack of finance threatens survival, they are reluctant to borrow because this too threatens independence. When they do borrow, they find that the cost of funds is high due to risk assessment and underlying interest rates. Matters are made more difficult by the fact that tax considerations, uncertainty and the lack of information about alternative sources of finance available to the non-specialist greatly complicate decision-making.

SME owners for the most part are inevitably unsophisticated in financial matters, but those who survive have to develop an understanding, and outside observers are often insufficiently sympathetic to the difficulties they face and to the implications of their desire for independence. For example, criticism of excessive use of high-cost sources of finance such as hire purchase and leasing often fails to take account of the simplicity and ease with which these forms of finance can be negotiated and the desire of small firms to leave bank credit lines available for emergencies. Lack of time, which may have more profitable alternative uses, can also explain the reluctance of small firm owners to collect, analyse and produce financial information for suppliers of finance.

The cost and availability of bank finance (Chapter 4), equity finance (Chapter 6) and the impact of taxation (Chapter 5) are discussed elsewhere. Here we review some of the general research findings on small business finance that have appeared since the Bolton Report.

On the whole, bank finance apart (see Chapter 4), less progress has been made in this field than in other aspects of the study of small business. Very little is still known about the financial performance and financing of unincorporated business, little more about company finance, and nothing exists in the UK, for example, comparable to the massive 'National Survey of Small Business Finance' carried out in the United States in 1988–89 by the SBA and the Federal Reserve Board. This study, conducted by interview, was able to build upon published and unpublished business accounts to expand the information available about sources and costs of finance. (The preliminary results of this 1 per cent sample of 3.5 million non-farm businesses with employees are reviewed in Bannock and Doran (1990).)

Virtually all UK studies have been based solely upon the limited information available in statutory company accounts, though there have been a few small-scale surveys, notably by the Wilson Committee. The analysis of company accounts has been greatly facilitated by the data published by the Business Statistics Office in 'Company Finance MA3' which, since 1981, has included a sample of some 500 smaller companies.

The limitations of statutory accounts are well known. In particular, for the smallest companies the freedom which owner-managers have to draw remuneration either as salary or dividends, and to fund the business by director loans rather than equity (both heavily influenced by tax considerations) greatly complicate analysis. More recently, smaller companies have not been obliged to file turnover and other information.

Some of the key features of smaller company finance revealed in recent studies, which are for the most part similar to the findings of the Bolton Report, are as follows:

1. Small firms rely to a greater extent than large firms upon debt, particularly short-term debt (they are more highly geared; see Table 3.2). However, owner's capital in small firms is understated because of the importance of

Table 3.2 *Balance sheet structure of small and medium companies compared with large companies, United Kingdom, end 1982*

Small and medium-sized companies, all industries	£ million	
Shareholders' interest	20,528	(61.6%)
Minority shareholders' interest	72	(0.2%)
Deferred taxation	1,678	(5.0%)
Long-term loans	707	(2.1%)
Short-term loans (including bank loans and overdrafts)	10,364	(31.1%)
Total capital employed	33,349	
Total debt	11,071	(33.2%)
Total shareholders' interest	20,600	(61.8%)
Large companies, all industries		
Shareholders' interest	116,780	(61.4%)
Minority shareholders' interest	9,951	(5.2%)
Deferred taxation	7,216	(3.8%)
Long-term loans	17,431	(9.2%)
Short-term loans (including bank loans and overdrafts)	38,800	(20.4%)
Total capital employed	190,178	
Total debt	56,231	(29.6%)
Total shareholders' interest	126,731	(66.6%)

Note: Large companies are defined to be those with capital employed of £4.16 million and over.
Source: Department of Trade and Industry, *Business Monitor MA3* (17th issue, final year 1982).

director loans, which may effectively be a form of equity. Fast-growing small firms are financed to an even greater extent by means of borrowed funds.

2. Small firms are more reliant upon bank finance than are large firms, particularly in non-manufacturing. Small firms also make greater use of non-bank finance such as hire purchase and factoring.

3. Trade credit (both debtors and creditors) is a larger proportion of the balance sheet total for small than for large firms, and small firms generally give more credit than they receive.

4. A lower proportion of assets in the balance sheet are fixed tangible assets in small than in larger firms.

5. Pre-tax profit as a percentage of net assets (RONA) has been considerably higher for small firms than large over the past 20 years, except in the period 1977–81. The performance of small firms is less favourable relatively, if profits are expressed as a percentage of total assets (ROTA) because of their extensive use of trade credit.

6. Margins (profit as a percentage of turnover (ROT) are much higher for large firms than for small. However, as noted, RONA is higher for small firms because they are able to generate a higher level of turnover from given assets (their turnover-net asset ratio is higher). Small firms are more labour-intensive and are forced to use capital very efficiently.

7. The dispersion of financial structure and performance of small firms about the average is greater than that for large firms. This diversity means that generalizations can be misleading. For example, although in most periods small firms in total have a larger proportion of cash in their balance sheet than large firms, and may be net depositors with the banking system, a large proportion – perhaps over 40 per cent – are net borrowers.

This summary is mainly based upon Wilson (1979), Burns and Dewhurst (1986), Hay and Morris (1984), Storey *et al* (1987), Bannock and Peacock (1989) and information supplied by 3i plc-Investors in Industry.

Internal problems

Two things stand out about the important problems mentioned by the respondents to the SBRT survey. One is that they are all issues of an immediate nature; this is of course implicit in the list provided in the questionnaire and in the phrasing of the question, which asks 'What is the most important problem facing your business today?' The other remarkable thing is that virtually all the respondents select problems that arise externally to the firm: only 0.7 to 2.2 per cent of respondents have selected internal difficulties as their most important problem since this issue was added to the list.

It is even more remarkable that small business owners should be so little concerned about internal problems when the enormous range of responsibilities which confront the owner-manager is considered. The sheer size of the range of issues involved in running a small business probably cannot be fully appreciated by anyone who has not had the practical experience of owner-management. Appendix A offers a selection of internal and external problems (prepared by Stan Mendham of the Forum of Private Business) confronting the small owner-manager. This list is capable of almost infinite expansion in detail, but it presents the essential issues that most small business owners have to deal with. To date little research seems to have been carried out in the UK on the range of responsibilities of owner-managers, how they use their time and how they cope.

It is plain that, at the outset, no business person could possibly be familiar with and expert in all these issues. This is why training and advice can be so important, but this is never sufficient. This subject has been referred to in Chapter 2 and is dealt with in some detail in Chapter 8, but here we wish to point to a central difficulty in small business owner training. The problem is that most of the course material is based upon management methods and practices developed in large firms. Small business courses do not, in general, fully take account of the fact that management problems and practices are utterly different in small business where one person is directly involved in every decision – from everyday issues such as customer inquiries, financial control and production matters, to less recurrent problems such as employee recruitment and rent reviews.

While small business courses give a grounding in basic management subjects such as book-keeping, marketing or tax administration, they do so in a static, one-dimensional form which gives the business person little or no guidance on how to divide their time between a wide range of conflicting matters, none of which he or she can fully understand without experience and many of which can spell the death of the business if neglected.

In a large business the chief executive has a number of specialists in planning, finance, production, sales, engineering and so on, all reporting to him. Each is an expert in their field. In a small business the owner has to be the generalist who can both see where the business is going and at the same time personally look after the detail. Planning for the future, which is necessary if the business is to survive, has to be squeezed into the time left after essential day-to-day matters have been dealt with. Stan Mendham gets this point across with the analogy of one of those entertainers who keeps a dozen or more plates spinning on a table: if one stops spinning it can bring the rest down. This is the position of the small business owner. By contrast, the chief executive of a large firm is conducting an orchestra – if his attention wanders momentarily there may be a false note, but the orchestra will not stop playing.

These are graphic images and raise basic questions about the nature and level of course content, teaching methods, teacher selection and entry level – questions which have hardly yet begun to be answered.

4 Banks and the Provision of Finance to Small Businesses

The small business sector has traditionally been accorded a variety of positive economic attributes, as a result of which SMEs are often seen as an engine for economic growth and efficient market adjustment.

It has been argued that they promote competition within the sectors in which they proliferate (Bolton, 1971; Wilson, 1979). Furthermore, they are thought to operate at the margin of structural change, with their entry to and exit from different sectors facilitating economic restructuring (Binks and Vale, 1990). Finally, it is suggested that their size permits operating flexibility and therefore a greater ability (if unconstrained) to respond to and benefit from changing market conditions (Binks and Coyne, 1983). These attributes, it is argued, endow small firms with the potential for rapid growth, although only a minority will ever realise this potential. For example, Hakim (1989) suggests that only a small proportion (around 10 per cent) of UK firms wish to grow rapidly and only a similar proportion of these will actually do so.

There are a number of possible explanations for the very low net result of 1 per cent. Many owner-managers choose not to expand their businesses beyond a size which they can continue to control personally. Many of those wishing to expand may be insufficiently experienced to attract external finance or may simply confront market conditions which do not justify such expansion. There is also, however, the possibility of viable growth being lost due to the limited availability of external finance. It has long been argued that small size may preclude firms from access to certain sectors of the capital markets, resulting in finance gaps (Macmillan, 1931). It is also suggested that finance gaps may arise not because of size, but because of imperfections in information flows. Where finance gaps exist, potential viable growth may be forgone.

The focus of this chapter is the availability to small firms of finance in general and of debt finance in particular. In a review of sources of finance and their role in the small business sector, Hall (1989), confirms the importance of debt as the main source of external finance available to small business in the UK. A major focus of this chapter is, therefore, on debt finance and the relationship between banks and small businesses. This analysis is set in the context of the findings of the Bolton Committee and of other related government investigations. An examination of developments in the banking sector, both in general and specifically in relation to small businesses, is followed by a discussion of patterns and trends in the provision of finance to small business from both a theoretical and an empirical perspective.

Bolton in context

The position taken by members of the Bolton Committee on the role of the banks in providing finance to small firms is clarified if we look at their contribution in the context of the contributions of previous and subsequent government 'Committees'. Although they constituted the only committee solely concerned with small firms, the timing of their research coincided with one of the most fundamental changes in the economic role of the major banks; the introduction of Competition and Credit Control. Their observations were made on the basis of evidence that referred to a financial regime that was about to change. The committee's analysis of the role of bank finance must be prefaced briefly by observations from the Macmillan Committee in 1931 and the Radcliffe Committee in 1959. Indeed, the relevant observations from these prior inquiries are acknowledged in the Bolton Report itself. It is also useful to include a summary view of the position adopted by the Wilson Committee in 1979 as an indication of the changing attitude to the financial services provided to small firms by banks.

The most significant feature to emerge from this approach is that banks changed very little in their approach to small firms in the decade after Bolton and the recognition and attempts to implement change have been largely confined to the 1980s. If a 'revolution' in bank financing of small firms is identified, it will be seen to have started in the 1980s and probably be complete by the year 2000.

The equity gap originally recognised by the Macmillan Committee, as quoted in the Bolton Report, referred to a huge funding shortfall given that it was presented in terms of 1930 prices.

> It has been represented to us that great difficulty is experienced by the smaller and medium-sized businesses in raising the capital which they may from time to time require, even when the security offered is perfectly sound. To provide adequate machinery for raising long-dated capital in amounts not sufficiently large for a public issue, i.e. amounts ranging from small sums up to say £200,000 or more, always presents difficulties.

Given the range of this finance gap, the implication is that all but a few very large firms confronted it when attempting to raise external equity finance from institutional sources. The Radcliffe Committee, reporting in 1959, argued that this gap had been largely closed by the setting up in 1945 of the Industrial and Commercial Finance Corporation (ICFC).

Despite continuing concern about certain kinds of financial provision as expressed by the Radcliffe Committee, subsequent changes in institutional provisions led the Bolton Committee to conclude (Bolton, 1971, p. 155): 'On the face of it, therefore, the flexibility of the capital market and its ability to meet new demands as they arise need no demonstration.'

The Bolton Committee cited three propositions which it felt were in need of further inquiry, given various representations made to them. These were:

(i)   that the operation of credit restrictions, and particularly of ceilings on bank lending, had particularly severe and damaging effects on small firms

(ii) that small firms have great difficulty in raising medium term finance in relatively small amounts – that is, between £5,000 and £50,000 – and that to this extent the 'Macmillan Gap', first defined in 1931, still exists

(iii) that the inability of most small firms to raise capital on the Stock Exchange is a serious disadvantage, necessitating the creation of a 'secondary market' to give them improved access to equity capital.

(Bolton, 1971, p. 150)

Given the period in which it was undertaking its research it is not surprising that the main focus upon bank lending concerned the effects of the 'credit squeeze' upon small businesses. Little attention was drawn to the question of the security or collateral provisions required of small firms since these were considered to be the acceptable norm. Although the provision of sufficient security is cited – for example, in terms of the access of small firms to invoice discounting – the main financial constraint is identified, primarily, in terms of the impact of the tax system upon the ability of firms to generate internal equity. The reliance of small firms upon the banks for external finance is acknowledged but there is very little consideration of the nature or quality of that provision.

The Wilson Committee was asked to report on the financial provisions available to small firms in response to the growing emphasis upon this sector which was emerging in the late 1970s. Its report drew specific attention to the security provisions required of small firms by the banks and the overly cautious attitude of the banks that this reflected. The first, carefully qualified indications of a potential 'debt gap' were introduced by implication, in their support for the introduction of some form of Loan Guarantee Scheme. Despite initial resistance from the main clearing banks, the subsequent introduction of an experimental scheme in 1981 was considerably oversubscribed and the problem of security provisions by small firms was acknowledged as a potential financial constraint upon their start-up and expansion. Although not referred to explicitly, the notion of a 'debt gap' confronting small firms was introduced as a natural corollary to the already well recognised 'equity gap'.

That the Bolton Committee failed to identify the debt gap is simply a reflection of the financial environment which it confronted. It is also indicative of the changing perception of the role of bank finance as a necessary prerequisite to the successful expansion of many small firms. Although many small firms succeed without recourse to bank finance, there is now a much clearer recognition of the crucial role that such provisions may represent to small firms attempting to expand and confronted by the problems of investment finance and delayed payment. A closer relationship between banks and small firms is emerging because the firms realise the need for external funding and the banks recognise the potential profitability that this provides if it is undertaken in a well informed manner. This recognition of mutual benefit is the main change in the 1990s in terms of banks and small businesses. The environment has changed fundamentally since those on the Bolton Committee undertook their research.

Developments in the banking sector

This section examines developments in the institutional background to the provision of finance to small firms from the banking sector. This entails a consideration of two specific areas. The first concerns the general developments in the banking sector from both a legislative and a managerial perspective while the second concerns specific developments in the relationship between banks and small businesses. In the last 20 years, the UK banking sector has undergone considerable change, in terms of the legislative environment in which it operates and in terms of the prevailing business philosophy. An important consequence of these developments has been a significant change in the relationship between banks and small firms.

The banking revolution?

The banking sector in the UK has traditionally been highly regulated and characterised by low levels of competition. Fiduciary responsibility dominated the conduct of business – often at the expense of the needs of the market place. This was to change dramatically in the late 1960s. The merger activity in this period produced the current structure of the four English clearing banks and (by the early 1970s) the three Scottish clearers. However, further changes were in the pipeline and these were to prove far more dramatic than the recent restructuring (Newman, 1984). Following the recommendations of the National Board for Prices and Incomes, the interest rate 'cartel' which had operated between the major banks was dismantled with the introduction, in 1971, of Competition and Credit Control. This pattern of deregulation was reinforced with the ending, in the same year, of collective agreements on bank charges and the ending of quantitative ceilings on lending.

Since the late 1960s, the general trend has been one of gradual deregulation of financial markets to encourage increased competition – the deregulation of the Stock Exchange between 1983 and 1986, opening stocks and shares dealing to the banking sector; the Building Societies Act, 1986, allowing building societies to compete more directly with banks; the Financial Services Act, 1988. At the same time as the financial markets have been deregulating, the degree of supervision of the banking sector has increased. The Banking Acts of 1979 and 1987 increased the supervisory role of the Bank of England to ensure greater protection for customers in a more competitive market place.

The competitive conditions facing the major British banks altered dramatically in the wake of Competition and Credit Control. The internationalisation of financial markets accelerated in the 1970s, with the major impulse coming from the overseas expansion of the American banks. This trend was fuelled by developments in information technology and communications which improved the efficiency and effectiveness of multinational operations. Furthermore, the traditional role of the banking sector has been placed under increased pressure by competition from non-bank institutions and an increased tendency towards disintermediation (Carey, 1989). The consequence of these developments has been a gradual re-evaluation by the banks of their approach to business and of the relative importance of their customer groups. In particular, it has encouraged the banks to develop a more market-oriented approach to the conduct of their business.

Looking back to the 1950s and 1960s, the traditional business philosophy guiding suppliers of financial services could best be described as a production/sales orientation; active marketing was largely limited to advertising and publicity (Newman, 1984). The increased competition of the 1970s and 1980s led to the development of marketing as a more integrated function within financial services organisations. Nevertheless, the role of marketing has, until recently, remained primarily tactical, in the sense that its main concern has been with developing better ways of presenting existing or slightly modified products to consumers. Increasingly however, there is evidence to suggest (Clarke *et al*, 1988) that financial services organisations and particularly banks are moving towards a strategic marketing orientation which requires that marketing take a more active role in the determination and development of overall corporate strategy. This in turn implied that it would be increasingly important to identify accurately the needs of particular groups of consumers and develop products to meet these needs (Carey, 1989). The success of such approaches would be dependent on a systematic analysis of different segments within the broad banking market, and the ability to target differentiated products to those segments.

Banks and the small business sector

The corporate sector is variously estimated to constitute about 10 per cent of the banks' customer profile and may range from new small businesses with a turnover of less than £50,000 to multi-national organisations with turnover measured in billions. Clearly a market as diverse as this will have very different banking needs and must be subdivided to allow more effective market and product targeting. The typical approach is to segment the corporate market by size. Although definitions of small, medium and large will vary across banks, a turnover of less than £1m provides a good working definition. The 'large corporates' sector (however defined), by virtue of market power and financial sophistication, is able to demand, and the banks are willing to supply, services tailored to specific needs. For smaller businesses, the same degree of customisation in service provision is not economically feasible. Nevertheless, this sector of the corporate market is growing, it is important to the banks in terms of profitability and it is likely to be an area where there is scope for increased competition, particularly from organisations pursuing a focused marketing strategy (Carey, 1989). A clear identification of the needs of this type of corporate customer and the development of appropriate products will be a key factor in retaining a strong competitive position in banking markets in the 1990s (Binks, Ennew and Reed, 1990).

If we accept that definition of small businesses as those with a turnover less than £1m then some 95 per cent of firms in the UK can be described as 'small'. This in turn implies that it is likely that a similar proportion of a bank's corporate customers will also be 'small', and their numbers are expanding. Several reasons could be put forward to explain the growth in the number of firms. In the 1950s and 1960s, the emphasis on large-scale mass production and economies of size led to the small firm sector being neglected by government and institutions since firms operating on such a scale were not envisaged as having a realistic long-term competitive future. The recession of the 1970s and the increasing trend towards product differentiation and customisation led to the small firms sector being seen as having an important role to play, not only in providing specialist products, but also as an engine for growth in an economy. This trend was reinforced by an increasingly positive government policy, which sought to encourage an enterprise culture and provided institutional support in the form of schemes such as Enterprise Allowance Scheme, Business Expansion Scheme and Loan Guarantee Scheme. Whatever the reasons for growth, the present lull occasioned by a period of unusually high interest rates and knock on multiplier effects on small businesses is likely to be temporary.

In many respects, the small business sector has been a rather neglected consumer group. Figure 4.1 presents a schematic representation of the developments in products offered to small firms and illustrates the movement from a series of 'one-off' initiatives to the development of fully integrated product ranges. The basic product range on offer to small businesses during the 1970s consisted of standard loans and overdraft facilities, with little attempt having been made to develop products specifically geared to the needs of these customers. Small businesses were not recognised as being any different from other types of business in terms of their financing needs and were not treated as such. This situation began to change towards the end of the 1970s. First, many banks were finding that competition for the business of large corporates was increasingly tight and that margins on such business were increasingly small. Similarly, the profits which derived from personal sector banking were also being squeezed. The banks began to recognise that small businesses represented a distinct market with needs that were quite different from those of other corporate customers or personal customers and, as such, they represented a new and potentially profitable market to be exploited. At the same time, the combination of a changing political climate and the establishment of the Wilson Committee brought the small firms sector to the public's (and the banks') attention. This provided the necessary stimulus for the major banks to review their policies in relation to small businesses (McKibbin and Guttman, 1986).

Initially, the banks restricted their activities to involvement in a variety of funding initiatives, particularly in inner city areas or for high technology

The Bolton Committee

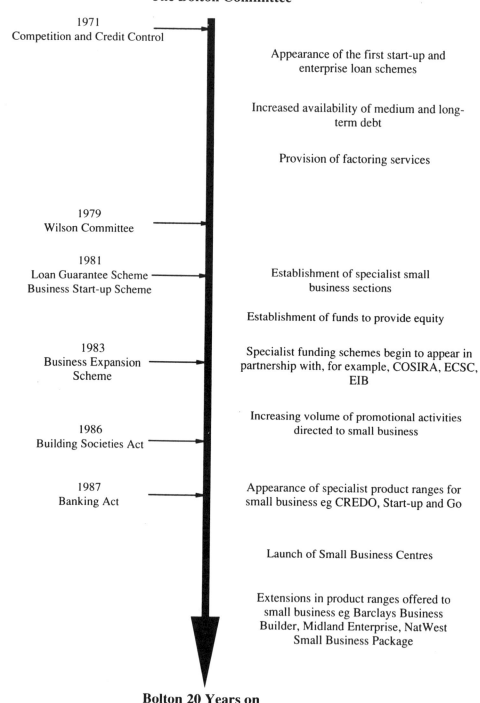

1971
Competition and Credit Control

Appearance of the first start-up and enterprise loan schemes

Increased availability of medium and long-term debt

Provision of factoring services

1979
Wilson Committee

1981
Loan Guarantee Scheme
Business Start-up Scheme

Establishment of specialist small business sections

Establishment of funds to provide equity

1983
Business Expansion
Scheme

Specialist funding schemes begin to appear in partnership with, for example, COSIRA, ECSC, EIB

Increasing volume of promotional activities directed to small business

1986
Building Societies Act

1987
Banking Act

Appearance of specialist product ranges for small business eg CREDO, Start-up and Go

Launch of Small Business Centres

Extensions in product ranges offered to small business eg Barclays Business Builder, Midland Enterprise, NatWest Small Business Package

Bolton 20 Years on

Figure 4.1   The development of banking services for small businesses

industries. As the decade progressed, the banks began much more obviously to develop integrated product ranges, including specialist business advisory schemes, to meet the needs of small business customers. Most banks now offer a start-up service in the hope that by providing help to businesses at their most difficult time, the bank will benefit in the form of long-term customer loyalty. National Westminster in particular has actively targeted this group. The range of products currently offered to small businesses includes start-up loans, free banking for a year for most start-ups, and interest bearing accounts for surplus funds. As a consequence, the bank is generally estimated to have around one third of this market.

Other banks have concentrated on the more established small businesses with a variety of investment and loan products. Increasingly, the banks are improving their advisory services for small businesses in recognition of the dependence of small businesses on their banks. The problems associated with the provision of specialist advice in every branch have generally been handled by the development of specialist advisers located at the major branches. Midland Bank operates around 340 enterprise centres throughout England and Wales providing specialist advice to small businesses. Lloyds has 342 specialist small business centres, and immediate plans to expand this to 470. Barclays has followed a similar approach through extensive retraining and by designating 330 of its branches as business centres. These business centres are probably targeted at the mid-corporates (turnover £1m–50m) rather than at the traditional small businesses. The TSB, although traditionally more concerned with its personal customer, will establish around 30 business centres under the 'Hill Samuel' title for mid-corporates but still relies on its existing branch network to service the needs of smaller corporates. National Westminster has a national network of commercial business centres offering account management for enterprises with turnovers in excess of £1m per annum and 600 major branches in key commercial locations providing the major support for small businesses.

Figure 4.1 demonstrates how banks have moved from the introduction of individual schemes to a more integrated approach in their provision of services to small businesses. Despite these initiatives, there remains concern about the relationship between banks and small businesses. The development of the UK banking system from a historical perspective and the dependence on the traditional Anglo-Saxon approach to loan evaluation have meant that the relationship between banks and small businesses developed largely on a 'hands-off' customer/supplier basis (Charkham, 1989). Consequently, many businesses not only feel some concern about the features of the service provided by their banks (interest rates, charges, term of loan), but also feel dissatisfied with the general relationship. The consequences of a relatively distant relationship between banks and the small firms centres are particularly severe in a period of recession. Banks will tend to be more wary, and re-trench in response to poor trading conditions, while small firms will often need more rather than less external finance to cover their liquidity problems.

This was clearly demonstrated in May/June 1991 when problems in the bank/small firms relationship were revealed by politicians and the media –

almost as if for the first time. In fact, the nature of the relationship between small firms and their banks and the significance in the explanation of finance gaps have been recognised for some time.

The provision of finance to small firms

Successive government-sponsored inquiries, including the Macmillan, Radcliffe, Bolton and Wilson Committees, have highlighted the problems experienced by small businesses in gaining access to debt and equity finance.

It is generally accepted that size may preclude firms from access to certain sectors of the capital markets, particularly where equity finance is concerned. The development of the venture capital market and the introduction of the Business Expansion Scheme have improved the supply of equity finance, although recent evidence suggests that the equity gap has not been eliminated (Harrison and Mason, 1990; and see Chapter 6).

It is in relation to debt, however, that the problem of access to finance may be more pressing, since debt is the most common type of external finance used by small businesses. Where small businesses experience difficulties in obtaining debt finance, potential viable growth may be forgone. If such difficulties occur with any regularity then they will severely inhibit the positive economic contribution which would be expected from the small firms sector. Difficulties in obtaining debt finance do not refer simply to the fact that some firms cannot obtain funds through the banking system. Indeed, we should not expect that all projects would automatically be financed. Genuine difficulties occur in situations in which a project which is viable and profitable at prevailing interest rates is not undertaken (or is restricted) because the firm is unable to obtain funding. However, restricted access to finance is not necessarily attributable directly to size, but is instead a result of the problems associated with the availability of information from which projects are evaluated. Such information problems are not unique to the small firms sector, but are considerably more prevalent there because of the anticipated higher costs of information collection. We focus our attention specifically on issues surrounding the provision of debt finance although the analysis may be generalised to deal with issues relating to the provision of equity finance.

The role of information

The provision of finance by a bank to a small firm can be regarded as a simple contract between the two parties in which the bank may be regarded as the principal and the small firm as the agent. In effect, the bank is requiring the firm to undertake an investment project and generate a return on behalf of the bank. In order to enter into this contract the bank will require certain information. In particular the bank must be sure that the project is an appropriate one, that the firm is capable of undertaking it, and that once the contract has been written, the firm will do what was agreed, to the best of its abilities. Under conditions of perfect and costlessly-available information, with no uncertainties regarding the state of the world which will prevail, these information requirements should not present any particular problem. In practice, banks and small firms operate in an uncertain world where information is not perfect and is often expensive to obtain. The particular problem is that the distribution of information between the parties to the contract is asymmetric. That is to say, there are certain pieces of information, having a material effect on the contract, which are available to one party but not to the other. These problems regarding information availability affect the willingness of banks to enter into contracts to supply debt and thus the amount of debt finance available to firms. In particular they can lead to the existence of debt gaps, where commercially viable projects do not obtain funding.

Information asymmetry poses two problems for the provision of debt finance. First, the bank cannot observe *ex ante* certain information which is relevant to the decision to enter into the contract – typically the actual abilities of the individuals applying for finance and the qualities of the project (adverse selection). Second, there is the risk that the small business will not perform in a manner consistent with the contract, necessitating some form of *ex post* monitoring procedure (moral hazard). Information could be collected on these attributes of the firm and the project, although the cost is likely to be prohibitively high. Even if it were available, however, the bank is likely to encounter difficulties in processing that information, thus limiting its practical usefulness.

The implications of these information asymmetries for the provision of debt finance have been evaluated from a theoretical standpoint in a number of studies. In examining capital market failure Stiglitz and Weiss (1981) identify debt gaps as a result of both adverse selection and moral hazard problems. The adverse selection effect is analogous to that observed in insurance markets and arises because borrowers have different degrees of risk attached to their projects. As interest rates rise, low-risk borrowers (although having viable projects) drop out leaving only high-risk borrowers. This is reinforced by the moral hazard problem associated with the lender's inability to monitor the project undertaken; again, it is shown that as interest rates rise the higher-risk projects will be substituted for the lower-risk projects, and there will be equilibrium credit rationing (see also Bester and Hellwig, 1989). A contrary view is expressed by de Meza and Webb (1987) who identify adverse selection in the presence of different (but unobservable) entrepreneurial abilities as leading to an oversupply of credit rather than a debt gap

While there is a need for further work to reconcile these views, common sense suggests that in practice they may not be mutually exclusive – that is to say, information asymmetries will in some situations lead to low quality projects being funded (oversupply of credit), and in others to high quality projects being denied funding (credit rationing). In particular, this result may be related to the role of collateral in bonding debt finance. Indeed, from a theoretical perspective it has been shown that the availability of sufficient collateral can counteract these problems; the low-risk borrowers who leave the market in the Stiglitz-Weiss model can signal their status by their willingness to offer appropriate levels of collateral, and the taking of collateral by the banks can provide an incentive to ensure that the firm will perform to the best of its abilities in undertaking the project (Bester, 1987). However, if collateral is in limited supply, debt gaps may still exist.

The extent of such debt gaps may be exacerbated by the presence of further information problems which may arise in relation to less costly and more objective information regarding the firm and its project. In addition to the information requirements described above, the bank's willingness to enter into a contract to provide debt finance will be affected by the information it can collect about technical aspects of the project, the financial and managerial strengths of the business, and the prospects for the industry and the market. Information about the managerial strengths of the business and its track record may be of particular significance since it may help to reduce the extent of the adverse selection and moral hazard problems. Information of this nature can be important in improving the process of loan evaluation and finance provision, but there are costs associated with the collection of such information and these costs are typically higher when dealing with smaller businesses. Even with more objective information, the problems of processing and interpretation are not eliminated, although they are likely to be less extensive than is the case with highly subjective information. In the absence of information regarding the prospects for the firm, its industry, and its markets, the risks associated with the provision of debt finance can be significantly reduced by the application of a simple capital-gearing approach to loan evaluation.

Thus, when information is costly to collect and contracts must be written with imperfect information the risks associated with the provision of debt finance can be effectively reduced by the use of a capital-gearing approach to loan evaluation, which requires 100 per cent-plus asset-backed security. The application of a capital-gearing approach will in itself create debt gaps where viable projects are accompanied by insufficient collateral, but this may be reinforced by the presence of moral hazard subsequent to the granting of any loan if formal debt-bonding arrangements are not specified. The typical solution to such problems is the employment of personal collateral, either instead of or as well as business collateral. However, a low quality project may be able to obtain funding where the bank is insufficiently well informed to judge its viability but is unwilling to refuse finance to a customer who offers more than adequate security.

With this capital-gearing approach, a debt gap may be more frequent in the case of small firms because asset-backed collateral must be valued at 'carcass value' prices to ensure the loan is realistically covered in the event of default and immediate realisation. Loans for specific items of plant and equipment will require more than the current resale price of the equipment for full collateral since the depreciation rate of the machinery will often be assumed by the bank to surpass that of the decline in loan values outstanding in the early periods of repayment. The bank should also recognise that default, resulting from specific market depression, may release considerable amounts of similar plant and equipment in a situation of depressed demand, with a consequent short-term price collapse in the second-hand market.

Small firms can experience a loan gap because they have insufficient business collateral. Alternatively, they may gain access to loan finance, but only at the cost of providing personal collateral in the form of a guarantee or house deeds. Where this refers to companies, there is a direct erosion of limited liability status and the protection it provides. This would be expected to discourage investment at the margin, given the additional personal risk it implies.

Firms that attempt to realise rapid growth potential may be more vulnerable to debt gaps because their acquisition of plant and equipment may grow faster than the value of assets which can be provided as collateral due to the impact of carcass-valuation procedures. This vulnerability will be further increased in cases where firms suffer delayed payment from customers but, due to their small size and limited market power, cannot obtain the same terms from their suppliers. There is thus a time lag between production costs and sales revenues for a given cohort of output. The faster the rate of growth the larger the amount of working capital required to cover the lag. Funding this through increased access to overdraft finance may increase the probability of a loan gap if available collateral is fully committed. Small, rapid-growth firms may therefore have a higher probability of experiencing a loan gap because their earnings potential is not considered in a capital-geared approach to loan requirements.

It is not possible to measure the viable growth which is lost due to finance gaps, but where they exist they will tend to have the greatest impact on small firms with growth potential, in part because it is here that a close relationship with suppliers of finance and a good flow of information are particularly important in order to incorporate future income prospects in the investment decision. A closer relationship, and consequently more accurate information exchange, would *ceteris paribus* increase the income-gearing element of project evaluation and reduce the loan gap. This is not a smooth process, however, since the collection of information over and above simple descriptive statistics causes a discrete and disproportionately large rise in costs to the financial institution concerned because the assessment of more qualitative aspects such as management skills is more time consuming to perform and requires a much higher level of investment in the training of those undertaking the evaluation.

In a sense, the 'banking revolution' in the UK, in terms of the supply of finance to small firms, is taking the form of a response to the problems which the finance gaps described above appear to be causing. In order to respond in an effective way, it is imperative that banks identify the nature of such problems, and the extent to which they can address these realistically. Closing the information gap may in some cases be prohibitively expensive, though we will suggest ways in which IT-based approaches may reduce these costs considerably. Given the relative paucity of market information in this area, and the severe problems involved in its collection and interpretation, this identification process is itself problematic. Indeed, another aspect of the present 'revolution' is the increasing focus of Market Information Services (MIS) on the small firm sector. The main problems which are suggested on the basis of currently available evidence can be divided into two main categories. The first of these refers to difficulties which firms claim they experience with existing financial products, and the manner in which they are delivered. The second category refers to products or delivery systems which, for whatever reason, are missing from the UK market. In the next section we will consider these two categories, and highlight the main sources of difficulty which we believe UK small firms confront, and to which banks are beginning, and will continue, to react. It is important to recognise two major qualifications when interpreting our arguments. First, in the context of existing problems, it should be noted that these have been deduced from a combination of economic theory and empirical evidence collected primarily from firms and not banks. We present selected pieces of evidence for illustrative purposes only and direct readers to original sources for a more complete and rigorous presentation. Second, in terms of the second category, when discussing conditions which have never existed in the UK it is naturally rather difficult to predict the economic impact of their introduction. Again we present some indicative evidence, but, for reasons which we will discuss further below, we believe that the actual reaction of firms to new conditions could be much greater than suggested.

Existing problems

From the theoretical analyses provided above on the main sources of finance gaps, it would be expected that those which emerge in practice be manifested by communication problems, and difficulties with the terms and conditions under which loans are provided. This is substantiated by much of the evidence collected, with a consistent focus upon bank charges, collateral requirements and poor advice. The problems of charges and advice reflect poor communications, while collateral considerations arise directly from the capital-gearing approach that banks are forced to adopt due to information asymmetries. Each of these areas will be considered in full.

Bank charges
Small firms typically express concern about bank charges for two reasons. First, there is concern about the actual level of charges which businesses incur and second there is concern about the unpredictability of those charges. The direct evidence on charges is limited, although surveys by the Forum of Private Business (Binks, Ennew and Reed, 1988, 1990) give some indication of the extent to which charges are perceived as a cause for concern by small businesses. In the 1987–88 survey, charges were identified as their major cause for concern by over 30 per cent of respondents. Of these, 34 per cent were customers of English banks and 27 per cent were customers of the Scottish banks. The customers of the English banks clearly felt that their banks were not doing enough in this respect – 27 per cent cited charges as an aspect of banks' services that could be improved. The corresponding figure for the Scottish banks was only 11 per cent.

In the 1990 survey, the level of concern about charges had dropped slightly to around 25 per cent. This reflected in part the much greater concern about interest rates at that time and possibly also some improvements in bank service

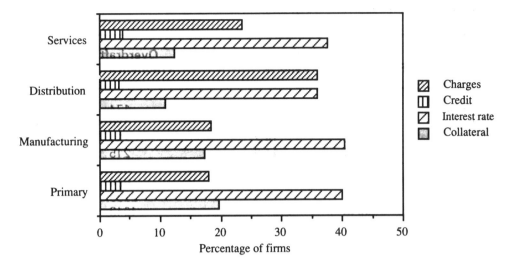

Figure 4.2   Main concern with banks by sector

including the introduction of itemised charges for some respondents. Concern about charges tends to be greater among services and retail businesses (Figure 4.2). The reliance of such businesses on services such as cash counting tends to increase their sensitivity to charges.

Collateral
Concern about collateral arises both from the amount of collateral taken (since this may affect future borrowing) and the form of collateral (because of the possible erosion of limited liability). Some initial insight into the nature of collateral requirements facing small firms can be obtained from a consideration of the evidence from the 1990 FPB survey (Binks, Ennew and Reed, 1990).

The analysis of collateral ratios presents considerable difficulty because of the extensive use of personal collateral in the form of the deeds to a house. With the rapid rise in house prices and the apparent indivisibility of this type of asset, it is likely that many firms will end up offering very large amounts of collateral for relatively small loans. Information on collateral ratios for overdraft limits and take-up is presented in Table 4.1.

These figures point to a rather bi-modal distribution, with relatively higher proportions at both very low and very high rates of coverage for overdraft limits. The average coverage for an overdraft limit is 443 per cent and for overdraft use the equivalent figure is 917 per cent. It should be noted that from the perspective of the bank it is the former figure which is of relevance since collateral will be taken with respect to the set overdraft limit rather than the firm's anticipated level of overdraft use. The collateral ratios cited for fixed term loans refer to about 800 firms and their pattern is illustrated in Table 4.2, along with aggregate security ratios for all forms of bank finance. These aggregate figures were calculated in an attempt to allow for those firms who were

Table 4.1   Security ratios on overdraft facility

	Overdraft limit		Overdraft amount	
	Frequency	**Valid %**	**Frequency**	**Valid %**
0–100%	482	24.0	174	9.6
100–150%	202	10.1	166	9.2
150–200%	285	14.2	231	12.8
200–300%	281	14.0	215	11.9
300–500%	345	17.2	354	19.6
Over 500%	411	20.5	664	36.8
Missing	2037		2239	
Total	4043		4043	
Mean	4.429		9.168	
Std deviation	2.567		22.070	
Minimum	0.12		0.00	
Maximum	100.0		400.0	

Source: *Binks, Ennew and Reed (1990)*

Table 4.2   Security ratios on loan facility

	Loans		Loans and overdrafts	
	Frequency	**Valid %**	**Frequency**	**Valid %**
0–100%	199	24.9	89	19.2
100–150%	147	18.4	82	17.7
150–200%	129	16.2	70	15.1
200–300%	132	16.5	78	16.8
300–500%	98	12.3	82	17.7
Over 500%	93	11.7	62	13.4
Missing	3245		3580	
Total	4043		4043	
Mean	3.081		2.831	
Std deviation	7.125		2.567	
Minimum	0.00		0.12	
Maximum	175		175	

Source: *Binks, Ennew and Reed (1990)*

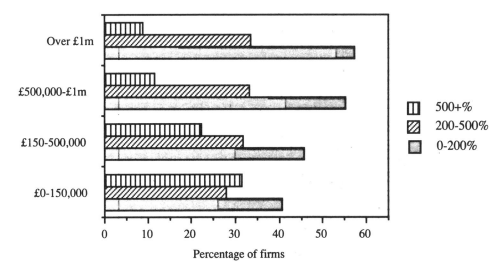

Figure 4.3   Security ratio on overdraft analysed by size of firm (annual turnover)

using the same assets as security for both an overdraft and a fixed term loan. Not surprisingly therefore, the average security ratio for all bank borrowings is rather lower than that quoted for either overdrafts or loans by themselves.

The same qualifications refer to these ratios as were made with respect to overdraft collateral ratios. It should be noted, however, that the inclusion in the calculation of the collateral ratio of personal assets such as house deeds, while introducing a distortion in the ratio itself, will be indicative of a disincentive effect as far as firms are concerned, particularly when it implies an erosion of limited liability for those which are incorporated.

When these security ratios are disaggregated it seems that small firms experience higher ratios and larger firms experience lower ratios, with this difference being significant at the 5 per cent level (Figure 4.3). It is also interesting to note that higher security ratios tend to be more common when personal assets are used, and less common in the case of business assets (possibly reflecting the 'house price' effect).

In terms of the nature of the collateral used to secure the overdraft facility, about 3,300 firms responded positively and of these 32 per cent cited personal assets as the main form of security, 25 per cent business assets, a further 25 per cent cited some personal assets and 18 per cent were not required to offer any collateral. The figures for fixed term loans were broadly similar. In terms of the collateral requirements for overdrafts and also for term loans, smaller firms tend to be over-represented in the categories which are required to provide personal collateral and also in the category where no security is required, as is shown in Figure 4.4. This reflects the balance between overdraft facilities which are too small to make collateral administratively worthwhile and those which are large enough to require security coverage, with personal assets being preferred because of the relatively low 'carcass value' of business assets.

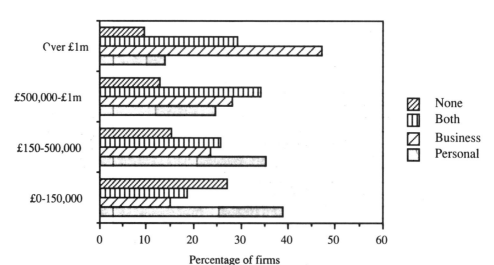

Figure 4.4   Form of collateral analysed by size of firm (annual turnover)

Furthermore, if the type of collateral is examined according to the size of the overdraft facility, then 80 per cent of the cases where no collateral is required are for overdrafts of less than £20,000. There are instances of larger unsecured overdrafts being granted, and this may indicate a slight movement towards a more forward-looking loan evaluation process. Larger firms are over-represented in the business collateral category, and less well represented in the category for no collateral requirement.

This analysis can be extended by considering how firms are affected by collateral requirements and credit availability, and there is clear evidence to suggest that manufacturing firms, fast growth firms and limited liability companies are most severely affected.

Advice
The relationship between small businesses and their banks in general and the extent to which banks understand the business environment facing their customers are of considerable importance in the context of finance gaps. These were described earlier as arising from information asymmetries. While it is clearly not possible to measure the extent of all information asymmetries, it is possible to gain some insight into the more objective elements of information asymmetry and this analysis can offer some insight into the problems which may be experienced by small firms, as well as suggesting areas in which the banks may improve their links with small businesses. Economic theory would suggest that the banks will collect available information up until the point at which the marginal benefit of the extra information is equal to the marginal cost of collecting it. However, given the market position of the banks with respect to the provision of debt finance, it is by no means clear that marginal private costs and benefits will equal marginal social costs and benefits. On the

contrary, given the limited alternatives available to small firms, the default to a capital-gearing approach may simply reflect the collection of a minimum (rather than an optimal) level of information.

To attempt to evaluate the extent and effectiveness of information flows between banks and businesses we examine particular attributes of the service provided by banks to small firms and compare their perceptions of the importance of these attributes and the quality of their provision. For each of four attributes relating to the flow of information between bank and customer – knows the business; knows industry; knows the market; gives helpful advice – respondents were asked to rank each attribute according to their assessment of its importance and the quality of its provision. Responses were received from 4000 firms from 15000 approached (the survey details are given in Binks, Ennew and Reed, 1990). The responses were analysed using simple weighting procedures (Reed, Binks and Ennew, 1990), and the following summary statistics were calculated.

The demand index is a measure of the extent to which the particular characteristic is regarded as 'important' by the firm. The measure is standardised to give an index with a maximum value of 1 and a minimum value of at least 0.

The supply index is a measure of how well the business perceives a particular characteristic as being supplied. The index is standardised to give a maximum value of 1 and a minimum value of at least –1. Given the existence of negative values in the weighting structure for the supply index, it is clear that the norm for the supply index will be lower than that for the demand index.

The attainment index is designed to reflect the extent to which there is a mismatch between what firms expect and the quality of what they receive: the higher the value, the better or closer the match.

Interpretation of the indices is complicated by the fact that the norms and the theoretical minimum values are different for each index. In order to make it easier to understand the relative importance of the indices, we have converted them to 'scores'. If an index lies above the appropriate norm then the score is calculated by the difference between the index and its norm taken as a percentage of the difference between the norm and the theoretical maximum. Similarly, if an index lies below the appropriate norm then the score is calculated by the difference between the index and its norm taken as a percentage of the difference between the norm and the theoretical minimum. In effect then, a positive score indicates that the demand (supply/attainment) index is above the norm; the nearer the score is to 100 per cent, the nearer it is to the highest level of importance (best performance/best matching) possible. Similarly, a negative score indicates that the index is below the norm; the nearer the score is to –100 per cent, the nearer it is to the lowest level of importance (worst performance/ worst matching) possible.

Using this simple approach firms' perceptions of information flows and information difficulties were examined. The national picture is summarised in Table 4.3. It is clear from the demand indices that all show positive scores. This simply indicates that the distribution of rankings is such that all characteristics tend to be regarded as relatively important. What is of relevance is the rankings

Table 4.3   *National demand, supply and attainment scores*

Attribute	Demand	Scores Supply	Attainment
Knows business	34	−7	4
Knows industry	17	−24	−12
Knows market	18	−22	−11
Gives helpful advice	32	−11	0

of the scores on the different service characteristics. It is interesting that all these characteristics have moderately low scores, and that those for knowledge of market and industry are particularly low. In interpreting these results it is important to recognise that firms and individuals do not tend to associate high levels of importance with characteristics with which they are relatively unfamiliar. Thus the lack of emphasis in relative terms upon knowledge on the part of the banks may in part reflect the fact that firms do not expect banks to exhibit a great understanding of their market or industry or business because of the traditional 'hands-off' approach which characterises their relationship.

This point is supported in that, despite the picture which emerges from the demand indices, it is quite clear that in terms of supply the main failings are attributed to these knowledge characteristics. Despite the lower relative importance associated with the knowledge-based characteristics, the attainment indices for the national picture reveal that the level of dissatisfaction here is sufficient to make these stand out as the main areas of mismatch.

Service gaps

Although the main service gaps all spring from the common source, of a lack of a relationship banking tradition, it is useful to consider each separately to highlight the extent to which change is practical, realistic or likely.

Long-term debt and special credit institutions
The long-term debt facilities with which we are concerned here are not simply categorised according to the length of term over which they apply. The products to which we refer are a result of an industrial banking tradition such as that which applies in Germany, for example. It is that background which creates an approach to lending which cannot be emulated merely by lending funds over longer terms. To understand this principle more clearly, it is useful to consider the definition of industrial banking as provided by Yao-Su Hu (1984).

There is a considerable literature which refers to the evolution of the banking system in the UK and the resultant contrasts between the nature of facilities here and those available in other countries such as Germany and Japan. While banking institutions in the UK developed primarily as deposit protecting services, those in other countries were more specifically designed to direct funds to industry. A major contrast which has emerged from these different evolutionary processes is reflected in the present role of special credit institutions and industrial banking services.

To understand how a tradition of industrial banking, or its absence, can explain some of the present disparities in banking approaches, it is necessary to define what the term conveys. One commonly accepted definition of industrial banking has been provided by Yao-Su Hu (1984, p. 17).

(i) The provision of long-term finance (long and medium-term debt, or such debt plus equity) to enterprises in the industrial and commercial sectors, in the form and combination that is most suited to their needs, as distinct from, or in addition to the provision of short-term loans of a self liquidating nature which has always been the province of commercial and merchant banking.

(ii) A sense of purpose, a perceived mission, and an institutional culture or a set of attitudes which is reflected in:
   a willingness to accept a measure of responsibility for the performance of industry: and
   an ability to understand the problems of industry, due to close relations with industry and the in-house employment of people with industrial experience and technical expertise, and therefore to accept what would be considered 'very risky' business by financiers who are ignorant of industrial realities.

It is this tradition of industrial banking which emerged in many other countries in the nineteenth century and influenced the structure of special credit institutions subsequently set up in the twentieth century. It is the absence of this tradition in the UK that may, to some extent, explain the contrast between its special credit institution, ICFC (now 3i), and those existing in other countries.

The first major difference between 3i and its foreign counterparts refers to the level of state direction, sponsorship and involvement. Both in France and Germany the special credit institutions involve an element of either state direction or sponsorship, or both. The example of 3i in the UK contrasts with this experience in that it was funded by the main clearing banks as well as the Bank of England, who instigated it. It is primarily a commercial institution and it is therefore bounded by commercial criteria in ways which do not apply in the case of the CN (Crédit Nationale) in France or the KfW (Kreditanstalt für Wiederaufbau) and IKB (Industrie Kredit Bank) in Germany.

A second major difference arises in the nature of the funding provided by these institutions. All but 3i focus primarily upon the provision of straight long-term debt. 3i (and ICFC before) typically retain convertibility equity within the funding provision, be it either directly as an equity stake, or indirectly as a facility to convert loan stock into equity at some future date,

A further source of difference between the UK facility and those operating in other countries refers to the relationship between the small credit institutions and the rest of the banking sector. Some, such as Germany, operate through the banking system because of its tradition of industrial banking, and therefore familiarity with the role which the special institutions attempt to perform. For example, the Industrie Kredit Bank of Germany has an advisory role in assisting industrial development fundings. In the case of France they operate in close conjunction with the banking institutions, but 3i in the UK is run separately from the rest of the banking system in the UK despite the history of part ownership.

Yao-Su Hu (1984, p. 18) again:

> Unlike in Germany, Japan or France, there is no mechanism whereby the institutions' funds can be made available, on a massive scale, to the industry. Nor do the major banks, the London clearing banks, have an industrial banking tradition. The result is that, in terms of final uses of the funds, household savings go mainly to finance house purchases, consumer credits, the government nationalised enterprises trailing behind all the rest.

A further observation that emerges from the UK experience is that the separatist tradition in the evolution of the banking system has caused an additional failure in the savings investment transformation process. In theory there should be a natural conversion process between those subscribers of funds who know very little of the needs of the industry to those investors of funds who are very familiar with these needs. By retaining a more separate and isolationist role from industry in the UK, the banks may be less able to provide this transformation process than are their counterparts in other countries. The role of special credit institutions refers particularly to this need. This tradition in the UK has, in a sense, frustrated the abilities of its special credit institution, 3i , to support industry to the same extent as the CN and the KfW are able to in France and Germany, because it does not have the backdrop of industrial experience in the rest of the banking system.

Since its scope is so much smaller in relative terms, 3i is not perceived as a source of influence upon the assessment and evaluation criteria conventionally adopted by the rest of the banking institutions in the UK. There is not the same educational and coercive or influential role that special institutions in other countries have performed. As a result most banks in the UK still operate for very natural and explainable reasons, on a historically traditional and restricted timetable in the assessment and evaluation of loans for investment purposes. They concentrate upon short-term viability rather than focusing upon the long-term requirements of industry for long-term restructuring and plant and equipment upgrading.

Just as the industrial banking background in countries such as Germany and France has led to the provision of many long-term debt products, so its absence in the UK has drawn frequent accusations of 'short termism'. The finance gap to which this case refers involves amounts of between £0.25m and £1m with a rate of return in the range 20–26 per cent required for projects of 10–15 years' duration. The amounts are sufficient to justify equity supplies, but the return is inadequate to cover the information and project failure costs which venture capitalists confront. The term of finance is too long for a conventional bank loan and may require elements of flexibility to match the repayment profile with that of expected returns, which the rather formal relationship between UK-style banks and firms could prohibit. Such projects would typically refer to the upgrading of capital equipment and long-term investment projects which cannot support the repayment burden involved if telescoped into a medium-term loan.

The longer-term prospects of firms requiring this type of financial product often include an increase in size as part of the project's proposal. This, and the resultant rise in demand for associated bank services, means that firms of this type are relatively attractive to institutions who are able to develop and accommodate mezzanine and other flexible financial products with a mixture of equity and debt components. It may be unrealistic to expect UK institutions to undertake the retraining required to enable them to cater for this market in the short run, although there are alternative mechanisms for acquiring the necessary expertise. Furthermore, there is no reason why the necessary change in attitudes should not be part of a medium term strategy to deal with the Single Market. At present, a number of European banks, particularly in Germany, are already well equipped to deal with this kind of product. Since the absence of a branch network would not constitute a significant barrier to entry in this particular niche, it might be expected that these banks would consider entering the UK market to supply the existing but unserviced demand.

Although estimates of the scale of problems created by this omission are difficult to provide, there is some evidence of a potential market. For example, a study undertaken in 1987, funded in part by the Department of Employment, found considerable evidence of a latent demand for a flexible long-term debt facility by larger small firms in the UK. The full effects which could emerge from the introduction of this kind of service are very difficult to predict for two main reasons. Firms naturally find it hard to assess the attractiveness of a facility of which they have no previous experience, and the extent to which others would consider using similar services, having observed its operation in practice, is also difficult to quantify. Over and above the potential demand for debt products which attempt to emulate the practices applied in other countries are other, more long term effects in terms of the educational impact which their introduction would be expected to have upon the banking sector as a whole.

Industry-specific expertise and products and the role of smaller regional banks
Industries are not distributed evenly across all regions. Some sectors are very heavily concentrated in areas with particular resource endowments, topographical characteristics or historical traditions. The cash flow characteristics and investment lead times of firms in different industries vary according to the nature of the production process and the product market. For example, firms in heavy manufacturing engineering industries exhibit very different financial problem requirements from those in the service sector. Evaluating the applications for commercial loans requires a clear perception of the constraints typically confronted by the applicant. Such expertise will usually be developed as a consequence of long-term experience in dealing with this from a particular

industry or area. In countries like Germany this tends to occur naturally because there are many regionally based banks.

Given the highly concentrated nature of the UK banking sector it is less likely for such specialisation to occur spontaneously because of the nature of the strategic development which is determined, often at a central and higher level.

Future prospects

Finance gaps, information and the banks-small firms relationship

It has been argued that the 'Anglo-Saxon' banking approach is likely to lead to the existence of finance gaps in the product range confronting UK SMEs, and that these appear to affect those SMEs with the growth potential regarded so positively by both banks and politicians. These finance gaps present opportunities for institutions that more closely fit the European investment banking tradition. Such opportunities may be strengthened, particularly in the small business segment of the market, where the apparently low degree of effective product differentiation (Binks *et al*, 1989a) has resulted in dissatisfaction with the range of services offered to these customers.

Although the major UK banks have reacted to these problems, there is still some doubt as to the adequacy of their responses. In 1988, National Westminster introduced trained small business advisers in all its high street branches; Lloyds has recently announced a £35m scheme to create 500 specialist small business centres. Barclays and Midland have both devoted substantial resources to marketing campaigns directed specifically at people who are starting or thinking of starting their own businesses. However, despite these efforts in relation to new start-ups, it is by no means clear that the UK banks have developed appropriate mechanisms for dealing with the needs of these firms when problems begin to develop at later stages.

One of the weaknesses of the approach adopted by the major banks has been the tendency to treat the small business sector in particular as a mass market – whereas there is considerable evidence to suggest that these businesses are not homogeneous. Regional and associated sectoral differences will affect financing needs (Binks *et al*, 1989b), as will attitudes to growth, the scope and nature of the business and the personality of the owners (Roach, 1989). In many cases, what such businesses require is not a single product but tailor-made advice and differentiated products to enable those firms with growth potential to realise their ambitions.

Given the present movement in most EC banks towards a comprehensive strategic review of their major markets, it is unlikely that niches with potentially high profits will be ignored. At present, the retail and large scale corporate markets appear to offer few significant opportunities to new entrants. This is not the case with the market for financial services to small and medium sized enterprises; careful segmentation, product development and targeting in this sector could offer profitable opportunities to existing suppliers or new entrants. Indeed, a number of strategic reviews among European banks have already made specific reference to the SME market in general and the UK market in particular. Banque Indosuez, for example, sees a future in servicing the needs of SMEs at a European level, including equity placements and USM listings. A similar attitude has been expressed by Dresdner Bank. Domestically, National Westminster Bank, recognising the potential importance of the SME sector from a strategic perspective, has recently announced that it is considering moving towards a system of direct equity investments for its corporate clients. Whether those banks considering the SME market (in the UK or EC-wide) will choose to enter by internal growth or acquisition is not certain, although the recent increase in mergers, takeovers and joint ventures suggests that the latter may well be the more popular route. Whilst the acquisition of UK banks by overseas banks has been restricted by the Bank of England in the past, it is difficult to envisage their ability to discriminate against other EC banks continuing after 1992. Furthermore, for UK banks such as National Westminster, moving towards a more 'bank-based' system, there are potential gains from some form of acquisition in order to be able to draw on the experience of other institutions who have operated this style of banking in relation to corporate markets.

In examining the needs of the SME sector and characteristics of the service they currently receive, it is clear that while there are some areas in which the banks have made progress in satisfying those needs there are still areas of weakness which need to be addressed. This is likely to be of particular importance given the potential attractiveness of this sector to new entrants. In evaluating marketing strategies for the SME sector in the 1990s, there are some lessons which can usefully be transferred from the banks' experience in the personal sector.

First, we can consider segmentation. The reliance on simple size or sectoral segmentation is likely to be insufficient to target accurately the needs of customers in this market. Behavioural segmentation has proven beneficial in the personal sector and the potential exists for these approaches to be transferred to the SME sector.

Second, developments in information technology are rapidly altering the process of information collection and management and delivery systems. Improvements in customer databases and systems for analysing them should enable the collection and analysis of customer information on a more systematic basis as an aid to segmentation and targeting.

Furthermore, the potential of expert systems for use in management has increased remarkably and systems for processing loan applications, for example in the personal sector, could be of benefit in dealing with the SME sector, particularly so if there are to be moves towards a more income-geared approach. It is unrealistic to expect UK banks to emulate the relationship banking approach which obtains in other countries. It is more sensible to focus on the positive aspects that such approaches create and consider how these may be generated in a different way in the UK. The most obvious outcome of close relationship banking is greatly improved communications. These lead to more accurate assessments of firms' needs, institutions' information requirements and risks. The widespread introduction of knowledge based systems by banks will enable much of this information exchange to occur without needing to develop a close relationship between lender and borrower, as a prerequisite. The use of these and other systems will enable a far higher level of transparency in the trading relationship between small firms and their banks. This in turn, will help to accelerate improvements in the other main problem areas which evidence indicates may constrain many firms.

Charges

The present trend towards itemised invoicing procedures for commercial accounts will probably be extended to provide trade credit conditions comparable to those in other industries, instead of direct deductions without warning. Firms will, therefore, be able to compare service charges between services and between institutions.

Collateral

Higher levels of communication and the perceived need to introduce financial products which include equity as well as debt components will lead to a more prospects-based income-gearing approach which will reduce pressure for personal security. If British banks are unable to implement such changes sufficiently rapidly, then it is likely that external competition will force them to accelerate.

Advice

Again, improved communications and greater devaluation of bank decision-making to regional industrial banking sectors will ensure a higher quantity of advice and therefore, greater level of trust between the two parties.

Long-term debt

There is some evidence to suggest that the opportunity provided from supplying feasible long-term debt is sufficient to attract either a private or public sector response, or both. Interest in this market is evident both from domestic supplier institutions and other European banks. All the main political parties either have plans for some form of National Investment Bank along the lines of the IKB in Germany or are considering some form of response to the growing demand for this kind of facility.

The banking revolution

We are in the midst of a banking revolution in the UK rather than having just experienced one. UK banks do not change easily due to their size. Changing attitudes is far more difficult than changing product design or even technology.

Small firms will benefit from some product changes and the introduction of new technology but the most significant benefits will be long term and reflect the combination of changing attitudes and technological expertise.

Finally, with respect to delivery systems, the personal sector has seen a number of developments in home and telebanking. The use of such approaches in the corporate sector could provide an important strategic advantage in both attracting and retaining small business customers.

Managing through recession

The recession of the early 1990s has focused attention on the quality of bank services to small firms. The pressure upon banks to change has risen at a time when lending conditions are particularly difficult. A key issue for the banks' concern is how they are to meet the needs of post-recession 'survivors' whose capital base has been eroded and who may already be heavily over-borrowed. As these firms attempt to meet rising markets through investment in stocks, plant and equipment it may be very difficult for banks to meet their requirements. Having been accused of over-lending in the mid-1980s without giving sufficient weight to the possibility and potential impact of recessionary conditions they may also be more cautious. The challenge facing the banks, therefore, is to meet the needs of business at the time when firms' capital position has been eroded, they have less to offer as collateral and the banks themselves are determined to avoid over-lending. From the above discussions the main viable solution to this problem would appear to rely upon a much more highly informed relationship between banks and their small business customers.

5 Taxation

Developments in taxation over the last two decades must be seen in the light of three separate frameworks of fiscal management: that within which the government operated in 1971; that which obtained in 1981; and the present position. There is no doubt that these changes in government policy have had a clear impact on the small business sector.

It is particularly important to include data relating to 1981 because this was a year in which the first Thatcher government was working out its monetarist policy framework. These policies, although softened a little, continue to be the basis on which economic management decisions are made (Budd 1991).

The three time periods are also comparable in terms of the economic conditions prevailing. In each case the economic background is one of recession. In 1971 the response was an expansionary budget; in 1981 it was severely deflationary, and in 1991 the Treasury intends the economic effect to be neutral. While the changes in response to similar circumstances between 1971 and 1981 reflect an underlying shift in policy, the 1991 approach may in contrast be seen as an extension of the strategy set down a decade earlier by Sir Geoffrey Howe.

The intention in 1971 was certainly to introduce an expansionary budget against a backcloth of rising unemployment and inflation, previously an unknown combination. This phenomenon became known as 'cost push inflation'. It was believed that an expansionary budget would stimulate growth in demand and push output closer to the maximum achievable rate of growth of productive potential, then estimated to be around 3 per cent per annum. This was classic demand management in the post-war tradition.

The extraordinarily tough and highly controversial 1981 budget was, by contrast, one of the boldest and most notorious in the post-war era, coming as it did in the depths of a severe recession. The objective was to continue the fight against inflation. Demand, in money terms, had in any case continued to grow resulting in higher imports and prices.

The focus of the 1981 budget was upon the Medium Term Financial Strategy (MTFS) that Sir Geoffrey had introduced a year earlier. The objective was to reduce the Public Sector Borrowing Requirement (PSBR) which had, contrary to Treasury forecasts, also continued to grow during 1980. This growth was seen as inconsistent with the government's overriding objective of reducing inflation. So the budget was designed to constrain the PSBR to £10.5 billion (from £14 billion in 1980/1) and shift the balance of the economy in favour of business and industry.

The neutral budget in 1991 continues to be consistent with this policy. A more recent innovation is the recognition of automatic stabilizers in the economy. In conditions of boom, incomes – and therefore government tax revenues – rise, enabling repayment of government debt which has a restraining effect on the economy. In times of recession, government income declines because of the lower tax take and increases in public expenditure as a result of the higher levels of unemployment. The result is a government deficit financed through a PSBR, which has an expansionist impact on the economy.

In 1991 the PSBR is approximately in balance and the fight against inflation is led by membership of the ERM with the focus of monetary policy on narrow money. The greatest uncertainty attaches to consumer spending which declined extremely rapidly at the end of 1990 at the same time as the savings ratio surged. With hindsight there may be a number of explanations for this but forecasters must remain very unsure about future developments.

In 1971 the fiscal regime in operation could hardly have been more different from the present position. Taxation rates, almost across the board, were significantly higher than at present and in addition the majority of government revenue was raised through direct, as opposed to indirect levies. Death duties and capital gains tax weighed much more heavily on the small business owner and VAT had yet to be introduced. Dividends were unearned income and so subject to a higher rate of taxation. Company profits were taxed twice, once as trading profits and then as distributions to shareholders.

The greatest similarity lay in the level of inflation, and ironically, even in 1971 the tax regime was better adjusted to coping with its impact than would now be the case (King and Wookey 1987).

Against this backcloth Bolton reviewed a wide range of taxation issues, but the committee took its brief very precisely, discarding much of the evidence presented – not because the proposals would not improve economic efficiency, but rather, because it was their brief to examine and recommend only on those matters where there was evidence of discrimination against small businesses.

The report's chapter on taxation concluded with thirteen recommendations. A measure of the vision of the committee can be gauged from the introductory paragraph which set the tone for its conclusions:

> We wish to emphasize again that what is needed is a taxation policy which will restore initiative, encourage entrepreneurial activity and improve the liquidity position of small businesses. We believe that continued reduction in taxation of personal incomes and of estates would be most likely to achieve this result. This point is not specific to small firms, however, and we therefore merely state our view for the record.
>
> (Bolton 1971, p. 229)

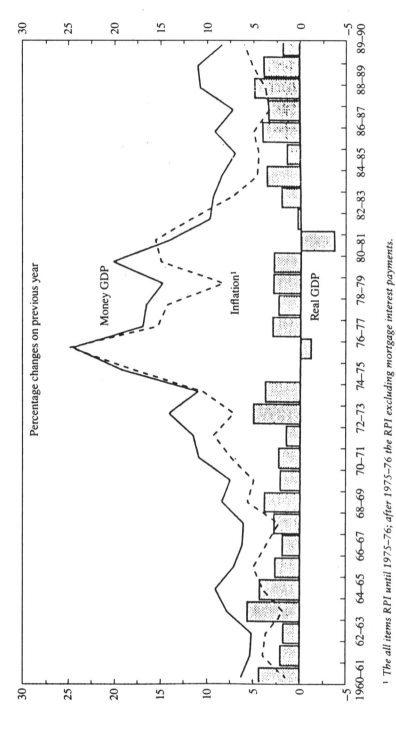

¹ The all items RPI until 1975–76; after 1975–76 the RPI excluding mortgage interest payments.
(Mortgage interest payments were included in the RPI from January 1975.)

Source: Budget Statement 1990/1

Figure 5.1   Money GDP, output and inflation

Bolton recommendations

Taking account of inflation

The first recommendation of the committee related to the impact of rising inflation on the profits and, therefore, the tax position of businesses. At the time the accountancy profession and industry were discussing ways in which historic accounts could be adjusted to reflect the real level of trading surpluses earned. In 1971 inflation was increasing rapidly and, in that year, touched its highest level since 1951 – 7 per cent. (Compound inflation for the period 1963–69 was 3.5 per cent per annum.)

Figure 5.1 shows the annual level of inflation for the period 1960–1990. While there is a remarkable similarity between the current rate of inflation in 1991 and the level experienced in 1971, the past twenty years have been dominated by soaring inflation figures which could hardly have been contemplated at the time. This is a complex and controversial issue which required several attempts by government and the accountancy profession before there was even a modest level of agreement. Even when the resulting accounting standard (SSAP 16) was finally introduced in 1980 its acceptance was far from universal. For a time many larger companies produced accounts based on the standard, but popularity declined towards the end of the 1980s, with falling levels of inflation, and it was eventually abandoned.

Bolton demonstrated the impact of inflation on the accounts of a small manufacturing company, by using an example based upon one of the research studies undertaken (Research Report 17). From this example it was concluded that accounting profits (before tax and interest) were overstated by just over 20 per cent when based only on historic cost accounting rules. The result was an increase in the effective rate of taxation on 'net economic profit less interest' from 45 per cent (the nominal rate of corporation tax) to 63 per cent. In other words, the committee concluded that inflation, running at compound rates of only 3.5 per cent, resulted in the effective rate of taxation rising by approximately 40 per cent (Table 5.1).

In reaching this conclusion the committee acknowledged that no account had been taken of the fact that under inflation the principal amount of any loans or overdrafts outstanding would be declining, thus benefiting those businesses financing part of their operations through borrowing. Historic accounting makes no adjustment for this as the full nominal rate of interest paid is charged against profits even though part (if not all) of this amount effectively recompenses the lenders for the declining capital value of their 'loans'.

Restating Table 5.1 to take account of this fact and comparing the results with similar companies today (Table 5.2) demonstrates that making this adjustment increases the funds retained in the business, after allowing for the effects of inflation, from £394 to £644. However, the inflation adjustments were still significant in 1969, and the effective rate of corporation tax on 'economic profit less interest' remained close to 60 per cent.

Standardizing the figures for 1988 makes the results, which are drawn from

Table 5.1   Adjustments for inflation to the profit and loss accounts of the average small company in manufacturing in 1969

Appropriation account	£	£
Balance before charges below		12,573
Less directors' remuneration		5,252
Less depreciation at book values		1,982
Net accounting profit (before tax and interest		5,339
Less additional provision for depreciation at current prices[1]	350	
Less stock appreciation[2]	500	
Less provision to maintain other net assets[3]	300	
Total adjustments for inflation		1,150
Net economic profit		4,189
Less taxation	2,293	
Less interest	599	
Less dividends	903	
Total appropriations		**3,795**
Retentions in the business out of the year's earnings		**£394**

Notes:
1   Assuming fixed assets (which at book values totalled £21,339) were bought on the average five years ago, and that prices have been rising at 3½ per cent a year (corresponding to the rise in the wholesale price index of manufactured products in the period 1963–69), depreciation as provided in the books will have been based on values that on average are some 17 ½ per cent (5 times 3½ per cent) too low. An additional provision has therefore been made of 17½ per cent of normal depreciation.
2   Prices of materials, etc., used in manufacturing industry rose in 1968–69 by 4 per cent a year; this proportion has been applied to the balance-sheet value of stocks (£12,681) to yield the approximate sum required to be set aside to maintain stocks constant in real terms.
3   A proportion as in 2 has been applied to the value of other net assets (totalling £7,456) comprising debtors, cash and bank balances, other current assets, *less* creditors, acceptance credits and bills payable, and current tax liabilities. It should be noted that bank overdrafts and other loans are here treated as a source of finance.
Source: Committee's Questionnaire Survey, Research Report No. 17.
The above accounts relate to incorporated businesses only, and hence differ from those quoted in Chapter 2.

two different samples, more readily comparable (Table 5.3). A number of differences are apparent. First, the committee was, in 1971, concerned about the impact of inflation on the retained profits of small companies. In 1988 these represented 35 per cent of net accounting profit compared with only 13 per cent

Table 5.2 Adjustments for inflation of the average small manufacturing company

	1969 £	1969 £	1988* £(m)	1988* £(m)
Appropriation account				
Balance before charges below		12,573		5,525
Less:				
Directors Remuneration		5,252		n/a
Depreciation at Book Values		1,982		1,437
Net Accounting Profit		5,339		4,088
(before tax and interest)				
Less:				
Additional Provision for				
Dep'n at Current Prices	350		362	
Stock Appreciation	500		71	
Provision to Maintain				
Other Net Assets	300		178	
Add Back: Decline in				
the Real Value of Loans	(250)		(213)	
Total Adjustments for				
inflation		900		398
Net Economic Profit		4,439		3,690
Less: Taxation	2,293		1,266	
Interest	599		728	
Dividends	903		271	
Total Appropriations		3,795		2,265
Retentions in the Business out of Year's Earnings		644		1,425

Note: Figures are the total for the sample of approximately 900 companies and are expressed in £ millions.
Source: (1988*) *Business Monitor MA3 Table 9 – 21st Issue Small Manufacturing Companies.* (1988 – latest year available at time of writing.)

in 1969. Ten per cent of this increase was as a result of the lower level of distributions recorded in the 1988 figures, but even after adjusting for this the level of retentions in 1988 would have been almost twice the figure observed in 1969.

Table 5.3   Adjustments for inflation of the average small manufacturing company expressed as a proportion of net accounting profit

	1969		1988	
Net accounting profit (before tax and interest) Less:		100		100
Additional provision for dep'n at current prices	7		9	
Stock appreciation	9		2	
Provision to maintain other net assets	6		4	
Add back: decline in the real value of loans	(5)		(5)	
Total adjustments for inflation		16		10
Net economic profit		84		90
Less: taxation	43		30	
interest	11		18	
dividends	17		7	
Total appropriations		71		55
Retentions In the business out of year's earnings		13		35

This significant improvement can be attributed both to the lower level of adjustments relating to inflation, down from 16 to 10 per cent, and the reduced level of appropriations which, excluding dividends, fell from 54 to 48 per cent of net accounting profits. As a result of these changes the small companies in the Business Monitor sample were much better equipped to finance their operations from internal funds than Bolton had observed in 1969.

There can be no doubt that significant progress has been made, but even so the effective rate of corporation tax for this Business Monitor sample, based upon the calculated level of net economic profit, was 33 per cent as opposed to the nominal small companies rate of 25 per cent. As a proportion this distortion is even larger than the 25 per cent increase that the committee had complained about in 1971.

Corporation tax and shortfall assessment

The second area of recommendation for the committee related to charging small limited companies at a lower rate of corporation tax than larger businesses. This recommendation was made in the light of the company taxation system introduced in 1965 which completed the separation of taxing the incorporated body from its shareholders. Prior to this date, small companies had for fiscal purposes been treated as pseudo-partnerships.

However at the same time as the introduction of a full corporate tax, special provisions, known as the close company rules, had been introduced. These provided that when companies were controlled by five or fewer people (closely held companies) special taxation rules would apply. The objective was to prevent individuals building up significant wealth within corporate bodies which would, as a result, be taxed at lower rates than the combined impact of income tax and surtax.

Without these short-fall provisions it would have been possible to build up wealth within a company and withdraw the funds by liquidating the business in an orderly fashion and distributing the assets to the shareholders. In these circumstances only capital gains tax became payable at a single fixed rate compared with income tax and surtax at the combined rate of 91.25 per cent.

At the time of the report the government was also preparing for the introduction of the imputation system of corporation tax which would alleviate the difficulty of the double taxation of profits subsequently distributed as dividends. Prior to this change, introduced in 1973, the classical system of corporation tax (still in existence in the United States) was in operation. Thus companies were taxed once on their profits and then dividends were subject to income tax.

The impact of the new rules was to establish the present structure whereby income tax deducted from dividend payments is then treated as an advance payment of corporation tax (ACT) and set off against taxation of profits in that and subsequent years.

The committee's recommendations were two-fold. First, that the rate of corporation tax applied to small companies should be lower than the rate for larger businesses. The government was, in planning the introduction of the imputation system, proposing to introduce the amended corporation tax at the rate of 50 per cent of taxable profits. The basis for Bolton's argument for a lower rate related to the added need that small businesses have to retain profits in the business, due to their relative inability to raise external funds.

The second proposal referred to the universally resented short-fall provisions mentioned above. Here the committee recommended complete abolition of this regime relating to trading income, as opposed to investment income. The government was, in any case, in the process of simplifying the definition of the 'closely held company'.

In addition, the rules for calculation of the amount of company profits which should be treated as if they had been distributed were extremely complex. The process of agreeing the amount with the Inspector of Taxes was often lengthy and full of uncertainty. The regulations, therefore, offended two out of Adam Smith's four canons of taxation, and were generally regarded as unnecessarily burdensome. Both these recommendations were, of course, implemented.

Close companies and partnerships

The committee's final proposal relating to the taxation of small limited companies has, however, yet to find favour. This related to the changes introduced in 1965 as a result of which, for tax purposes, companies finally became separated from their owners. The result was the introduction of corporation tax, replacing the previous system of taxing limited companies in a similar way to partnerships.

The Bolton Committee pointed out that from a tax point of view unincorporated businesses enjoy a number of advantages, compared with small limited companies. Individual traders may set losses in their businesses against other personal income, but the same person carrying on a trade as a one person company could not do so. And the individual trader or partner has a relatively beneficial treatment for tax purposes in the early years of business, provided the most suitable year end is chosen. This advantage is not available to limited companies.

In the opinion of the committee these differences in treatment, in addition to the difference in rates already referred to, were distorting the choice of legal structure adopted. It was felt that this was an undesirable state of affairs and that the impact of the taxation system should not influence decisions about the desirability of seeking the protection of limited liability status.

Factors of this kind are examples of the non-neutrality of the taxation system, which distorts business decisions. As a result, the committee recommended that close companies should be allowed, by unanimous decision of the shareholders, to elect to be taxed as partnerships. Appropriate safeguards would be introduced to stop companies oscillating between this and the corporation tax regime as their profits rose and declined.

This recommendation has subsequently been echoed by a number of studies, most notably the Gower Report. Although the specific suggestion that companies should be able to choose to be taxed under either income or corporation tax has yet to be implemented certain of the changes introduced in the 1981 budget sought to remove some of the distortions mentioned by the Bolton Committee (see Encouraging risk taking, below).

Pension arrangements

The next two recommendations related to the pension arrangements available to small business owners. At the time the government was in the process of improving the position of sole traders and partnerships. However, these proposals, which enabled the self-employed to obtain tax relief for contributions of up to 15 per cent of earned income or £1500, whichever was the higher, were still less advantageous than the provisions relating to employees of incorporated businesses.

In particular the regulations relating to senior employees of companies provided that tax relief could be obtained for contributions to pension schemes equivalent to 15 per cent of annual earned income or more. The committee recommended the principle should be established that the tax reliefs relating to pension provisions for the self-employed and controlling directors of close companies should be similar to those for employees and non-controlling directors. Although differences in the treatment of self-employed incomes and those of company directors and employees do still exist a significant number of changes have been introduced in this area.

Much more controversial than the alignment of pension rights between employees and the business owner was the proposal that proprietors should be given complete flexibility in the way in which their pension funds were invested. This proposal flies in the face of the powerful financial services lobby, which argues that it is imprudent to invest monies intended to provide a secure source of income for the future in what are, inevitably, relatively risky small businesses. While this argument has some force in respect of employees' pensions, presumably proprietors and controlling directors should decide for themselves the level of certainty of future income they wish to enjoy.

The committee found it incongruous that in the early years of business, due to the shortage of available resources, most small business owners find it impossible to put by substantial sums towards a pension, to such an extent that in later years the opportunity to build up a worthwhile fund is constrained. In addition it is inappropriate that when such funds are invested they should no longer be available to the business, unless borrowed at much higher rates of interest.

Bolton, therefore, recommended that proprietors and controlling directors should have complete freedom in the choice of investment for their pension funds, including the ability to plough money back into the business. Current arrangements for self-administered pension funds for companies controlled by four or fewer directors have gone some way down this route. However, there is certainly scope for significant further progress to be made in increasing flexibility in this area.

Loans

The committee next turned its attention to a recent change in taxation provisions which was seen as detrimental to the interests of the small firms sector. The Finance Act 1969 had removed general tax reliefs for loan interest paid by individuals, replacing these by a number of much more carefully defined provisions. Prior to this date, interest paid on loans to purchase shares in close companies had been generally allowable. However, the new provisions contained two substantive restrictions. First, that borrowers must have a material interest in the company and secondly, they must also be working proprietors. This had two unfortunate and potentially damaging consequences as important groups of investors were thereby excluded. Traditionally a major source of finance for small businesses has been members of the proprietors' families, and these would not normally fit both these definitions, thus placing them at a disadvantage.

In addition an appropriate means of rewarding employees and providing for continuity of management is to expand the shareholding of the business to include senior managers. Until a significant share stake had been built up they too would be excluded from obtaining tax relief for interest paid on monies raised to finance their investment.

The committee recommended that both these restrictions should be removed from the statute book. The then newly elected Conservative government promised this in their election manifesto but had not included it in their first budget. Amendments to the law were subsequently introduced, but, ironically, it was the Conservative government in 1980/1 which eventually widened the reliefs to the extent suggested by Bolton.

These recommendations completed the committee's views on income and corporation taxes.

Capital gains tax and estate duties

The committee made two clear recommendations on capital gains tax and four, some of which were substantive, on estate duties.

At the time the committee reported that certain disposals of assets, apart from straightforward sales, resulted in capital gains tax assessments. These were known as 'deemed disposals'. The major problem with these transactions was that the original owner, in disposing of the assets, faced a capital gains tax bill without having received any income from the transaction. Inevitably this presented considerable difficulties for those not having other liquid assets available to meet the tax liability.

Examples of these transactions of particular relevance to the small firms sector included the gifts of shares to relatives or to an able employee to reward them for exceptional performance. Until the Finance Act 1971 transfers of shares on the death of the proprietor were also included.

The committee concluded that the new reliefs were not sufficiently comprehensive and required extension to avoid the inappropriate burden on donors which was potentially restricting the development of the small firms sector. With hindsight it may be concluded that the resulting recommendations were somewhat half-hearted.

The proposed amendment was that in any such deemed disposal, other than of quoted shares (which are readily marketable) only 50 per cent of the gain should be charged to capital gains tax. The tax paid would then be carried forward and offset against any future gain realized from those assets. Subsequently these ideas have been enacted in a much extended form.

The second item relating to capital gains tax was linked to changes introduced in the 1965 Finance Act. These provided that no capital gains tax would be payable on the death of working business proprietors. This had the unfortunate consequence of encouraging retention of at least nominal control of businesses until death, which was certainly not the intention of the relief.

In addition, as recognized in the deliberations on pension rights, the self-employed and controlling directors were subject to less generous reliefs in respect of contributions to pension schemes. The law at that time, therefore, not only provided poorer arrangements for the provision of pension rights for business owners, but also encouraged them to retain control of their businesses long after employees would have assumed a more leisurely life-style. The committee concluded that the existing retirement relief on capital gains available to proprietors at the age of 65 or more – up to £10,000 – should be doubled. Once again these recommendations may, with hindsight, be considered to be conservative as they were subsequently enacted in a much wider form.

This was the final recommendation relating to capital gains tax. The committee concentrated the remainder of its recommendations in the area of estate duty. The first topic drew from the concessions already available for agricultural property and industrial buildings and plant and machinery. Under this heading the committee recommended that the estate duty relief of 45 per cent, introduced in 1925 to avoid the break-up of agricultural estates and extended in 1954 to manufacturing assets, should be made available to businesses in the service sector. This proposal would bring particular benefit to the small firms sector which was dominated by service based businesses.

The committee also considered that the definition of assets which attract the relief should be expanded. At the time these were restricted to agricultural and industrial buildings, and plant and machinery. It was proposed that these should be extended to include commercial buildings, goodwill, patents, certain investments, working capital and unquoted shares when they represent a controlling interest.

The basis of valuation of these items, for the purposes of relief, was to be net trading assets, including goodwill and working capital, but excluding cash and portfolio investments. It was suggested that working capital should be restricted to the average of the balance sheet amounts over the past three years, in order to ensure that the relief was not manipulated by accumulating assets shortly before death.

An example of this type of transaction which would maximize relief could be the use of cash balances to acquire trading stock. Cash was not an eligible asset, whereas trading stocks would be. Shortly after agreeing the estate duty liability it would in many cases be relatively easy to translate the stocks, through the normal trading cycle, back into cash.

A further difference existed between agricultural and business assets. The relief detailed above was available to the owner of the assets whether or not that person used them for trading purposes. Thus landlords of agricultural property were entitled to the relief. This was not the case, however, in respect of industrial land and buildings.

Clearly industrial assets were thereby discriminated against and the flow of funds restricted in favour of agricultural assets. The committee recommended that the relief should be extended so that industrial assets were treated in the same way as agricultural assets.

In making this recommendation the possibility of including commercial buildings such as shops and offices was also considered. It was acknowledged that such a change would beneficially reduce the distorting effects of the relief. However, on the basis that commercial property was a relatively profitable sector it was decided not include this amendment.

The final recommendation of the committee related to the valuation of business assets for estate duty purposes. It was recognized that for private businesses this was a difficult and uncertain process, often requiring expensive professional advice. Where there was disagreement with the Estate Duty Office the position of the executors became even less comfortable. Should the estate bear the professional costs incurred in seeking an amended valuation or simply pay the extra tax? The issue then becomes emotive in the circumstances where executors are forced to dispose of the shares in order to pay the death duties. Sadly, on this point the committee settled for a half-hearted compromise. The Inland Revenue disagreed with the suggestion that the cost of valuing the business or shares should be deducted from the value of the estate. The reasons given were a mixture of the pragmatic and the bizarre. First, it was argued that in many cases the assets had to be valued for purposes other than agreeing estate duty, a realistic comment, albeit of limited application. Secondly, they argued that death duty was a tax on the value of the estate at death and not on what the beneficiary receives. The deduction was, therefore, inappropriate.

While correctly stating the fundamental principle of a death duty as opposed to an inheritance tax (subsequently introduced n 1986) to apply it in these circumstances seems arcane to say the least and weights the power of negotiating the value heavily in favour of the tax authorities. In the face of this opposition the committee recommended that only 50 per cent of the cost of valuing the shares should be deducted from the estate. The logic is not apparent.

Changes over the past two decades – macro

Since publication of the report a significant number of changes have been introduced by successive governments, some inspired by the committee's recommendations and others by the changing political and economic climate. In looking at these changes it is perhaps appropriate to move from the general to the particular, reviewing first the general thrust of tax reform since the publication of the report.

The Bolton Committee was very strict in its approach to the brief, but recorded its views of the general thrust of taxation policy by calling for continued reduction in the levels of taxation across the board, in order to stimulate

Table 5.4   Reduction in income tax and corporation tax rates 1970/1–1990/1

	1970/1	1980/1	1990/1
Basic rate income tax	41.25	30	25
Top rate income/surtax	91.25	60	40
Corporation tax (Small co. rate where applicable)	45	40	25

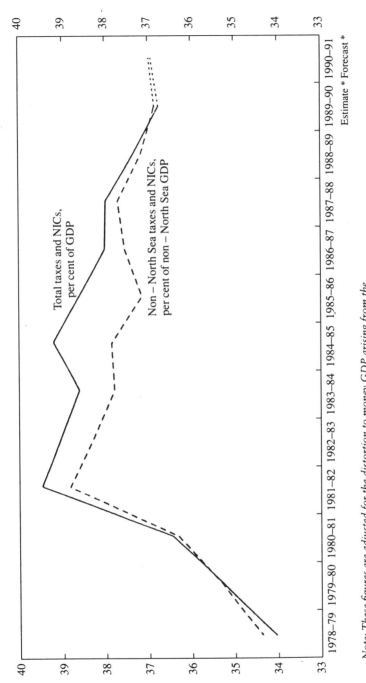

40 ⎯ ⎯ ⎯ ⎯ ⎯ ⎯ ⎯ ⎯ 40

39 ⎯ ⎯ ⎯ ⎯ ⎯ ⎯ ⎯ ⎯ 39

38 ⎯ ⎯ ⎯ ⎯ ⎯ ⎯ ⎯ ⎯ 38

37 ⎯ ⎯ ⎯ ⎯ ⎯ ⎯ ⎯ ⎯ 37

36 ⎯ ⎯ ⎯ ⎯ ⎯ ⎯ ⎯ ⎯ 36

35 ⎯ ⎯ ⎯ ⎯ ⎯ ⎯ ⎯ ⎯ 35

34 ⎯ ⎯ ⎯ ⎯ ⎯ ⎯ ⎯ ⎯ 34

33 ⎯ ⎯ ⎯ ⎯ ⎯ ⎯ ⎯ ⎯ 33

Total taxes and NICs, per cent of GDP

Non – North Sea taxes and NICs, per cent of non – North Sea GDP

1978–79 1979–80 1980–81 1981–82 1982–83 1983–84 1984–85 1985–86 1986–87 1987–88 1988–89 1989–90 1990–91

Estimate * Forecast *

Note: These figures are adjusted for the distortion to money GDP arising from the abolition of domestic rates.

Figure 5.2   Taxes and national insurance contributions

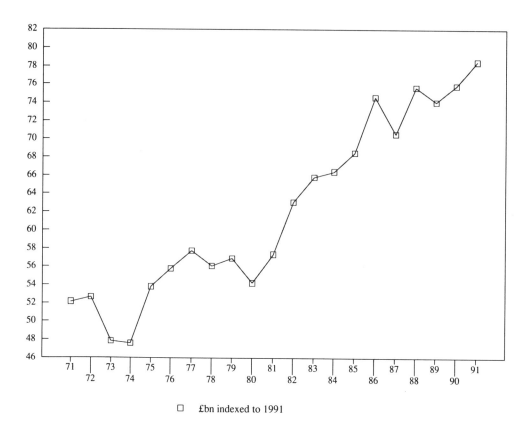

□   £bn indexed to 1991

Figure 5.3   Income tax yield 1971/1991

initiative and entrepreneurial activity. To what extent has this advice been heeded? It is generally believed that over the past decade of Thatcherism, taxation has declined – look, for example, at the reductions in income and corporation tax rates (Table 5.4). This prima facie evidence is worthy of further examination. Figure 5.2, comparing taxes as a percentage of GDP from 1978/9 to date, shows that the total tax take from the economy has not fallen as a proportion of output. Why, then, do most UK citizens believe that we now live in a low tax society when in fact there has been an increase over the last decade?

Figures 5.3–5.7 compare the government receipts year by year of five major taxes. The impact of inflation has been removed from the data which have been grossed up to 1991 prices using the retail price index.

Income tax

Over this period real GDP grew by 49 per cent. At the same time income tax receipts increased, after allowing for the effects of inflation, by just over 50 per

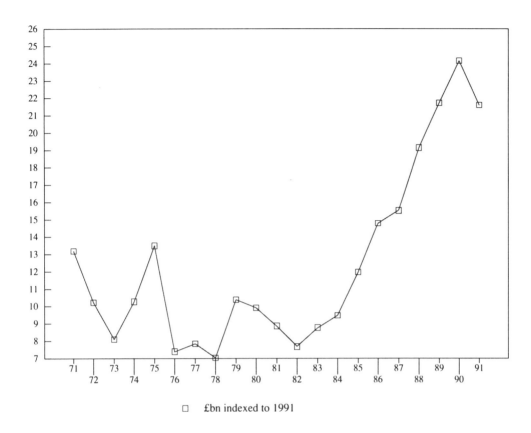

□   £bn indexed to 1991

Figure 5.4   Corporation tax yield 1971/1991

cent. Income tax has, therefore, remained a constant proportion of output, despite the reduction in higher rates.

Corporation tax

The picture here is quite different. Receipts from corporation tax, which in 1971 were only about one-quarter of the size of income tax, fell to half that level in 1978. However, once the significant changes to business taxation were introduced from 1984 onwards, reducing the levels of capital allowances and phased-out stock relief, receipts have grown very significantly, so that they are now equivalent to about 40 per cent of income tax.

Value added tax

VAT was introduced in 1973, replacing purchase tax. Receipts grew to £11 billion per year in 1975 and were then roughly stable until the standard rate

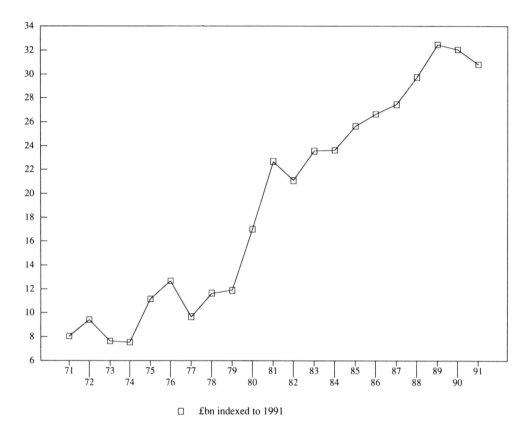

□   £bn indexed to 1991

Figure 5.5   VAT yield 1971/1991

was increased to 15 per cent in 1979. That resulted in a 50 per cent increase in revenue which, together with further amendments, has resulted in government income from this source almost trebling since that time.

Over the full period from 1971, during which time GDP has increased by 50 per cent, in real terms VAT has grown from £7 billion to £31 billion. The increase in the standard rate to 17.5 per cent introduced in the 1991 budget will, of course, result in a further significant rise in government revenue, although much of this latest increase will be used to finance the reductions in poll tax (see below).

National insurance contributions

The trend here is much less marked than for VAT or corporation tax: nonetheless, NI contributions which were equivalent to almost £19 billion in 1971 rose to £25 billion in 1978 and £35 billion in 1990/1. Recent major changes have included the widening of the NIC net to include benefits in kind, as well as

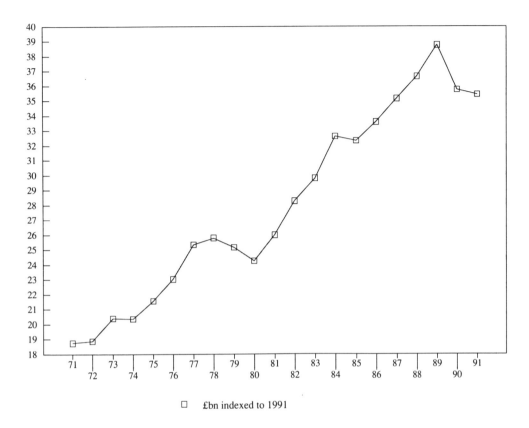

□   £bn indexed to 1991

Figure 5.6   NIC yield 1971/1991

the removal of the maximum earnings limit for employer's contributions. Across the whole period, after allowing for the impact of inflation NIC contributions have increased by 89 per cent, once again significantly faster than the rise in GDP.

Rates

A similar pattern may be observed for rates, which in real terms were yielding the equivalent of £13 billion in 1971. This figure was broadly stable until 1981/2 when it increased to £16–18 billion. Further rises to £21 billion took place in 1987/8. The announcement in the 1991 budget of the 'review of local government' and reduction in poll tax of £140 per head is set to reduce this income by some £4.5bn in 1991/2. The majority of this reduction will be financed by the increase in VAT rates mentioned above. Before adjusting for these counter-balancing adjustments, between 1971 and 1991 the yield from rates has risen, in real terms by 76 per cent: once again, about 50 per cent faster than the growth in GDP.

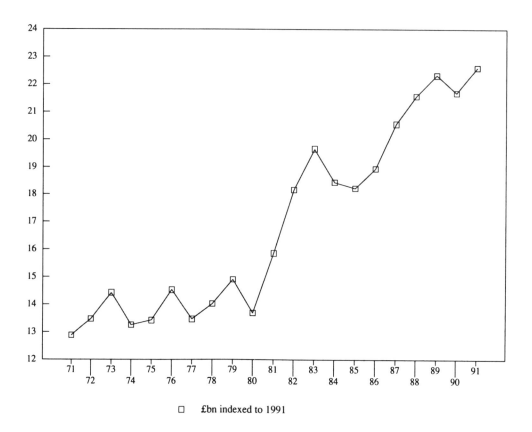

□   £bn indexed to 1991

Figure 5.7   Rates yield 1971/1991

Trends in taxation at the macro level – conclusions

Government has apparently learnt the trick that in the public's eye the rates of income and corporation taxes are the factors that influence opinion regarding the level of taxation. As individuals we appear to be much less sensitive to the level of VAT, employer's national insurance contributions and corporation tax.

There is also evidence that these traits have been particularly recognized by the Tory party, which has used them to particularly good effect in the past decade. For example, it can be seen from the figures above that the increases in indirect taxation have accelerated since the election of the current government.

These comments should not, however, be taken as overtly critical. Indirect taxation may be economically preferable to direct taxes. Where levies are based upon expenditure, such as VAT, taxpayers have much more freedom about the way in which they use their after-tax incomes. They have more choice about whether to consume or save their earnings. This is normally believed to provide greater incentives to work (for a full review of these issues see J. A. Kay 1990).

Table 5.5   Total tax revenue as percentage of GDP in the EC and other OECD countries, 1965 and 1984

	1965	1984
Belgium	30.8	46.7
Denmark	29.9	48.0
France	35.0	45.5
Germany	31.6	37.7
Greece	20.6	35.2
Ireland	26.0	39.5
Italy	27.3	41.2
Luxembourg	30.4	41.4
Netherlands	33.6	45.5
Portugal	18.4	32.0
Spain	14.7	28.4
UK	30.6	38.5
EC average[1]	29.6	41.9
Japan	18.3	27.4
Switzerland	20.7	32.2
United States	26.3	29.0
3 Non-EC states average[1]	21.8	29.5
All OECD average[1]	26.9	37.1

Note: [1] Unweighted averages
Source: OECD 1986A

So a major factor which has changed since the publication of the Bolton Report is the relationship between taxes and GDP. There has, in fact, been a significant increase in the level of taxation in the UK. It has been calculated (Bannock 1989) that this figure increased by more than 25 per cent for the period between 1965 and 1984. Even in the 1980s, the decade of enterprise, this trend has continued.

A similar pattern may be seen for all EC countries and also for those from some other parts of the world. In fact the UK fared marginally better than the EC average (Table 5.5). Total tax revenues in the EC amounted on average to almost 42 per cent of GDP in 1984 compared with under 30 per cent in 1965, an increase in the tax ratio of over 41 per cent. While the increase in the tax ratio was universal, there were considerable differences in the rate of increase between member states. The Bolton Committee's recommendations for a reduction in the overall level of taxation have not been fulfilled, but the shift to indirect taxes may be seen, both within the UK and the EC context, to have been both acceptable in scale and beneficial in terms of the increased incentives for individuals to be enterprising and work hard.

This does not apply to the increases in taxes on business, such as the significant rise in corporation tax and employer's national insurance contributions observed in the past few years. There are also strong theoretical arguments against these (Kay, 1990; Devereux, 1988) as they reduce incentives to invest or raise costs. To the extent that these continue, so the general taxation objectives of the Bolton Committee remain to be satisfied.

Taxation changes of particular relevance to small firms

A significant number of changes to the UK tax system have been introduced over the past two decades to effect this shift in emphasis. As noted, many of these changes have altered the burden of direct taxes borne by individuals. Some can be claimed to have been designed to promote self reliance and increase the rewards for enterprise, for example the improvement in the tax breaks for share option schemes, while others, particularly relating to business taxation, have had a negative effect.

Certain of the measures – such as enterprise zones – were, at the time, perceived to be particularly beneficial to small businesses. Subsequently these have proven to be of much wider appeal, attracting major retail and other developments. Broadly the changes which have been most relevant to small businesses may be categorized under five headings: developing existing small businesses; disposing of the business or passing it on; administration and collection of small business tax liabilities; encouraging risk taking; the creation of a small business infrastructure.

These are broad categories and certainly do not represent the only classification that could be used. Indeed, it is possible to argue for the inclusion of measures under different headings, or even for the same measures to be classified under more than one heading. However, it is hoped that it is a sufficiently useful framework to enable readers to develop a sense of the direction in which government taxation policies towards small businesses have moved over this period of twenty years.

The order in which the headings have been presented was determined from the timing of the budget measures introduced. Thus, for example, the earliest measures relate to the continued development of established small firms, in particular reduction of the burden of apportionment and improving the exit options of small business owners by increasing the level of relief available for subscriptions to retirement annuity funds. Both are topics on which the Bolton Committee made strong recommendations.

In order to review the number and value of these measures by category, and over time, each year's budget statement has been scrutinized and the tax changes affecting small businesses summarized by year and by classification.

The statistic taken as the measure for quantification of the change has been the estimated first full year impact of the change on government revenues. This figure has subsequently been standardized in accordance with the retail price index at April 1991.

The objective of this measure is to indicate the size of the change intended by government, as an indicator of their policy intentions at the time the budget

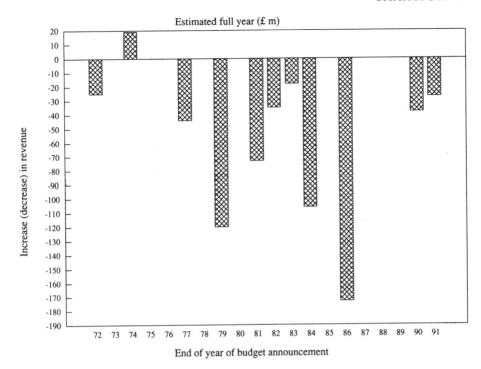

Figure 5.8   Measures to develop existing SMEs

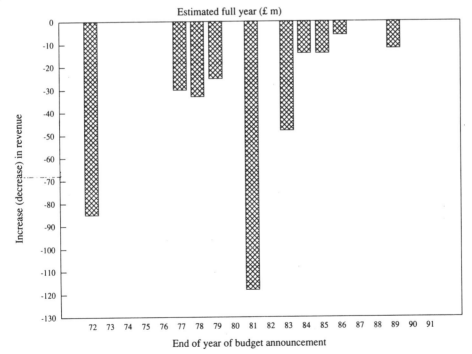

Figure 5.9   Measures to improve exit routes

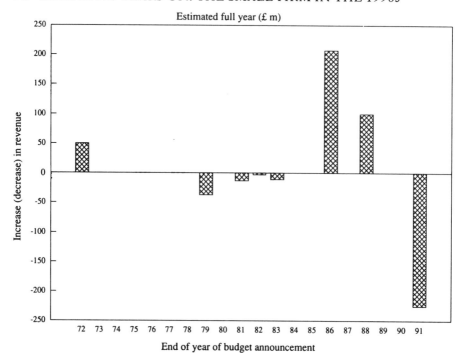

Figure 5.10   Changes in administration/collection

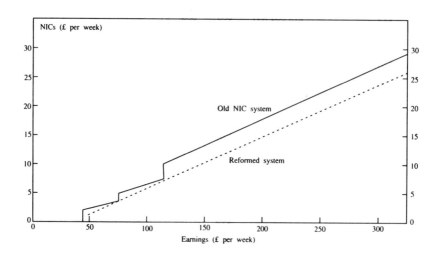

Source: Budget Statement 1989/90

Figure 5.11   Reform of employees' national insurance contributions

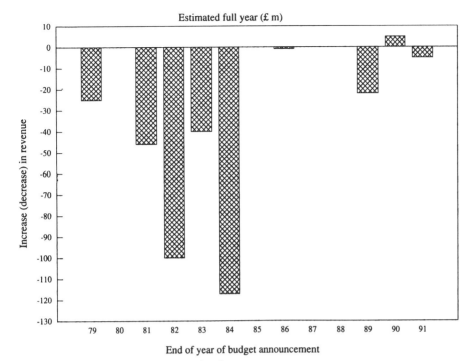

Figure 5.12   Measures to encourage risk-taking

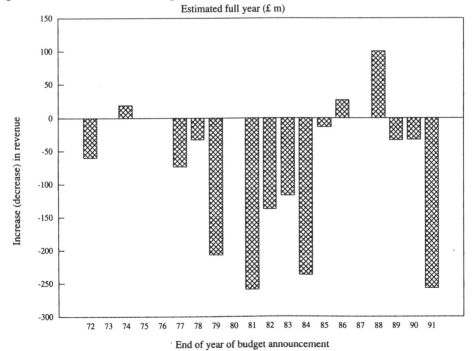

Figure 5.13   Impact of small business tax changes

was drawn up. No attempt has, therefore, been made to reconcile the antici-pated and actual impact of the change on government revenues. The measure assesses intentions not outcomes. Analysing government measures under each broad category over time provides a series of profiles (Figures 5.8, 5.9, 5.10, 5.11, 5.12, 5.13).

Developing existing small businesses

In a period of high employment of the early 1970s this was the first area to which government turned its attention. The earliest changes related to reduc-tion of the impact of close company regulations, in accordance with the recom-mendations of the committee. In fact these rules were progressively dismantled until their abolition, for trading companies, was finally announced in the 1980 budget.

A second recommendation of the committee was implemented very quickly. The small companies rate of corporation tax was introduced for 1972/3. The cost of this measure was estimated to be negligible. The bands of profits eligible for relief were initially set at £15,000, below which all profits were to be taxed at the reduced rate, and £15,000 to £25,000 for the marginal rate band.

These figures have subsequently been consistently increased to the present levels of £250,000 and £1.25m in 1991/2. Together with the reductions in the small companies rate of corporation tax down to the basic rate of income tax, it is estimated that these measures provide overall savings to small companies of some £330 million per annum.

The increase in taxation recorded in 1974 is as a result of a rise in the rate of corporation tax for all companies. This was expected to yield an extra £130 million (at 1991 prices), but only about one sixth has been estimated as attribu-table to small companies as it is known that the vast majority of corporation tax is collected from large firms. For example in 1989/90, 95 per cent of the 340,000 companies paying tax accounted for only 16 per cent of all the tax received (Inland Revenue Annual Report 1989/90).

The first year of the current administration saw a significant increase in relief for this sector. The major item in that year was the introduction of bad debt relief for VAT purposes, an issue over which debate continues. Despite further changes introduced, particularly in the 1991/2 budget, there is still little doubt that the one year delay rule before VAT can be reclaimed is extremely damag-ing to small businesses unable to take advantage of the cash accounting scheme.

The major changes introduced in the 1985/6 budget related to national insur-ance contributions. The allowance for 50 per cent of the Class 4 NIC payable on the profits of the self-employed against their income tax bills improved their comparability with employees and directors of limited companies. At the same time the reduction of flat rate Class 2 contributions payable by the same group reduced their overall NIC burden by no less than £214 million per year.

However, not all the amendments introduced over this period of time have reduced the tax burden on established small firms. For example, the changes introduced to the basis of taxation on changes in partnerships in 1985/6 closed a loophole that was being exploited with increasing regularity and increased tax revenues by £41 million per annum.

The total value of these measures in the period under review amounted to £640 million in the first full year of introduction. This category, of reliefs for established businesses, enjoyed the highest level of changes introduced by successive governments. New businesses would, of course, also benefit from the changes.

Disposing of the business or passing it on

The measures introduced under this heading fall largely into three categories, each of which the Bolton Committee identified as requiring reform: relief for retirement annuity contributions so that the self-employed were placed on an even footing with employees; improved treatment for disposal of businesses on retirement; more appropriate arrangements for the distribution of business assets at, or in contemplation of, death.

The topic of retirement annuity reliefs was addressed in the 1971 budget and subsequently in 1976, 1977, 1978, 1980, 1982 and 1983. These changes cost the Treasury the equivalent of some £290 million in a full year and raised the amount of contributions allowable for tax purposes from 10 to 17.5 per cent (more for those over 50 years of age) of net relevant earnings for the self-employed. The significant tax savings shown in Figure 5.9 for 1971/2 and 1980/1 are both largely as a result of these improved reliefs.

Differences continue to exist between the treatment of Schedule D tax payers and senior employees and directors of companies, who continue to have more flexibility in the rate of contributions which they may commit to their retirement fund. However, the wider reforms for pensions introduced in Finance (No. 2) Act 1987 have improved the flexibility and comparability of all schemes.

The second topic relates specifically to capital gains tax on disposal of businesses. This includes both roll-over relief for gifts of business assets and the introduction and subsequent improvement in relief for disposal of businesses on retirement. The former relief was introduced in 1978/9, and the latter received attention in 1978/9, 1983/4 and every year thereafter except for 1989/90. The result is that for 1991/2 retirement relief is available for business proprietors aged 55 or more (younger, if due to ill health) on 100 per cent of gains on disposal up to £150,000 and on 50 per cent of the next £450,000.

During this time other measures to improve exit routes from businesses have also been introduced. The indexation of capital gains and the amendment of certain regulations relating to companies acquiring their own shares are examples.

Finally, as proposed by Bolton, relief for transfers of business assets for the purposes of estate duty, capital transfer tax and currently inheritance tax were introduced. As proposed by the committee, business assets including working capital (but excluding cash) are now eligible for relief as are minority holdings which are taxed on 50 per cent of their value in the same way as controlling interests and the assets of unincorporated businesses. However, excepted businesses still include those dealing in land and buildings and there is no relief for professional fees incurred in negotiating asset valuations with the Inland Revenue.

Administration and collection of small business tax liabilities

This is probably the most topical area under review. It is also the only heading under which the government has increased the tax burden placed on small businesses. It is an area referred to only briefly by the committee, but which has subsequently come to prominence. It relates to the compliance costs imposed on small businesses by the taxation system. The committee, in its discussion of the planned introduction of VAT, made the comment: 'Most important for our purposes, it is envisaged that small traders would be exempted because of the disproportionate administrative costs to them of the book-keeping with VAT.'

At the time no turnover limit had been set for businesses to be exempt from the requirement to register. However, the committee expressed the wish that trade associations would vigorously represent the interests of small businesses, in determining this matter. At the time of the Bolton Report PAYE was already operating in its present form, but no discussion of the compliance costs of operating this system was undertaken. In 1971/2, the sub-contractors in the construction industry tax deduction scheme was introduced, as a measure designed to improve the collection of income tax. This was anticipated to increase revenue by some £50m per annum at 1991 prices.

Soon after publication of the report, academics were beginning to consider the differential burden placed on the smallest firms as a result of government policy requiring businesses of all sizes to operate as unpaid tax collectors. Two major studies were undertaken, the first related primarily to PAYE (Barr, James and Prest 1977) and the second to VAT (Sandford *et al* 1981). This latter study was expanded to incorporate PAYE and repeated several years later (Sandford, Godwin and Hardwick, 1989).

Table 5.6 *Analysis of compliance costs per employee in businesses classified by number of employees 1981–1982*

Number of employees	Mean compliance cost per employee (£)	Compliance cost/yield (%)
1–5	58	14.2
6–10	39	6.0
11–20	38	4.6
21–50	29	3.8
51–100	17	1.7
101–500	18	1.3
Over 500	11	0.8
Number of respondents	687	619

Note: Some respondents gave information on employment and compliance costs but not tax payments, hence the smaller number of respondents in the cost/yield column.
Source: Sandford *et al* (1989).

The startling conclusions of these studies highlighted the enormous burden faced by very small businesses. It was found that in the 1970s businesses turning over the equivalent of, at current prices, less than £100,000 per annum were faced with costs, after allowing for the cash-flow benefit of holding the taxes in their working capital cycle until paid over, equivalent to approximately 1 per cent of turnover for each tax. On a rule-of-thumb calculation these costs would be equivalent to an increase in the effective rate of tax on profits of a sole trader of approximately 15 per cent (Chittenden, Risner and McConnell 1989). In addition the costs were incurred by all businesses of that size, whether profitable or not.

In 1981/2 firms collecting less than £1000 PAYE and NIC in one year incurred costs equivalent to one-third of the tax collected. This figure fell to less than 1 per cent where the annual collection amounted to more than £250,000. The results show a similar trend when expressed in relationship to the number of people employed (Tables 5.6 and 5.7). Table 5.8 reveals that the pattern for VAT was not dissimilar. The VAT figures show that since 1977/78 there has been a substantial reduction in the level of compliance costs incurred by VAT-registered traders. The weighted mean compliance cost declined from just

Table 5.7   Analysis of compliance costs of businesses as percentage of PAYE and NI payments 1981–82

Total PAYE and NI in year	Number of respondent businesses in each category	Mean compliance cost (£)	Compliance cost/yield ratio (mean %)[1]
£1–£1,000	71	89	32.8
£1,001–£2,500	106	145	8.7
£2,501–£5,000	94	306	8.7
£5,001–£10,000	98	380	5.2
£10,001–£15,000	64	439	3.6
£15,001–£25,000	48	567	2.8
£25,001–£50,000	61	657	2.0
£50,001–£100,000	28	822	1.2
£100,001–£250,000	31	1,864	1.3
Over £250,000	18	7,818	0.7
	619		

[1] For each case, compliance cost is expressed as a percentage of annual PAYE and NI payments. These percentages are then averaged within each group.

Source: Sandford et al (1989).

under 1 per cent (0.92) in the first study to just over two-thirds of one per cent (0.69) in 1986/7. Even so the very small businesses, who have been responsible for the vast majority of new employment created over the same period, continue to shoulder a disproportionate burden.

Since the completion of this study, Customs and Excise have introduced a number of schemes to lighten the burden on very small businesses. The two most notable of these, the Cash Accounting Scheme and the Annual Accounting Scheme, were introduced in 1987/8. The first of these enables traders to pay and deduct VAT only on transactions which have been settled by the date of the return. While the Annual Accounting Scheme allows traders to pay VAT in monthly instalments based upon the expected level of turnover for the year. Any over or under payments are subsequently adjusted when a summary return is submitted at the end of the accounting year.

There is little doubt that these schemes are useful and cash accounting has been particularly popular. The simplest way of reducing the compliance burden, however, is to allow small traders to drop out of the VAT net by raising the registration threshold. The maximum turnover threshold is established by the European Community, rather than national governments. As a result it had proved impossible to raise the minimum limit by more than changes in the retail

Table 5.8   Compliance costs as a percentage of taxable turnover, 1977–78 and 1986–87 (current prices)

1977–78		1986–87	
Taxable turnover (£000s p.a.)	Compliance costs as per cent of taxable turnover (mean percentage)[1]	Taxable turnover (£000s p.a.)	Compliance costs as per cent of taxable turnover (mean percentage)[1]
0–9.9	1.64	0–20.5	1.94
10–19.9	1.23	20.5–49.9	0.78
20–49.9	0.74	50–99.9	0.52
50–99.9	0.54	100–499.9	0.42
100–999.9	0.24	500–999.9	0.26
1,000 and over	0.04	1,000–9.999.9	0.04
		10,000 and over	0.003
Overall weighted mean	0.92	Overall weighted mean	0.69

[1] For each case, compliance cost is expressed as a percentage of taxable turnover. These percentages are then averaged within each size band.
Source: Sandford et al (1989).

price index until the UK successfully lobbied the European Commission. Increased recognition of the regressive nature of compliance costs resulted in the registration threshold being raised to £35,000 (an increase of almost 40 per cent) with effect from 1 April 1991.

Nonetheless, businesses with sales of between £50,000 and £100,000 per annum incur costs in excess of 0.5 per cent of their sales. It is to be hoped that further progress will be made in this area.

Further work on the subject of administration and compliance was conducted on behalf of the Department of Trade and resulted in the publication in 1985 of a report, *Burdens on Business*. This concluded that there were a number of changes that government could make to the taxation system in order to improve the lot of small firms. In accordance with the recommendations of earlier studies (Barr, James and Prest, 1977) the PAYE system should be placed upon a non-cumulative basis. This would be a far-reaching change with wide implications for all employers and employees. But it could open the way to putting NIC and PAYE calculations side by side in the same deduction tables, which would help small employers.

Evidence from the United States is that adoption of a system which requires employees to inform their employers of the weekly amount of tax to be deducted would result in tax being collected in advance. The only draw-back of this additional relaxation is that every employee would be required to complete an annual tax return, whereas at present only a minority of PAYE employees do so.

The report's first VAT recommendation – that the registration threshold should be raised, thus releasing many very small firms from the VAT net – was implemented in the 1991 budget. There may, of course be further scope for changes as the net collection of VAT is minimal for businesses with turnover of less than £100,000. The second recommendation related to the difficulties of obtaining bad debt relief in respect of the VAT element of any transactions for which payment is not received. There have been two changes that improve the position of traders faced with this problem. The first was the introduction of the cash accounting scheme, which automatically provides for bad debt relief. In addition the 1990 budget provided that any debt more than two years old, which had been written off, could be recovered whether or not a certificate had been received from the liquidator. This period was reduced to one year in the 1991 budget. Many would argue that this relief is still far too slow in its operation, particularly in times of recession.

There was also a call for reduction in the present number of NIC rates. In the past few years more rate bands have been introduced for NIC purposes. This is to be generally welcomed as previously there was a strong disincentive for staff to break the lower NIC limit, as this triggered a step function in contributions paid which resulted in a decline in the employees' net pay. Employers were similarly penalized.

However, the amendments to NIC introduced in 1989/90 have resulted in a more graduated structure with fewer step functions, as can be seen from Figure 5.11.

Finally, the area in which there has, if anything, been a deterioration in the position of small businesses – the Statutory Sick Pay (SSP) scheme. *Burdens on*

Business called for simplification of administrative procedures, particularly relating to qualifying periods; and to allow businesses to opt out of the SSP
system where they prefer to pay sick employees at the appropriate rate without
refund. The major changes introduced, however, relate to a reduction in the
proportion of SSP which can be recovered from government. This has now
fallen to 80 per cent of the total paid – an increase in the taxation burden borne
by businesses.

As can be seen from Figure 5.10, all the significant changes in this area have
been introduced in recent years. Of particular note was the study conducted on
behalf of the government into the enforcement powers of the revenue departments, known as the 'Keith Committee' after its chairman, Lord Keith (Keith
1984). Introduction of the civil enforcement powers recommended by that
committee were announced in 1985/6 in respect of VAT and in 1987/8 with
respect to PAYE and sub-contractors tax deduction schemes.

There is no doubt that the measures have been effective in raising significant
sums of additional revenue for the government, but they have been deeply
unpopular with the businesses who, on the one hand, act as unpaid collectors
and, on the other, are heavily penalized for failing to operate the system in
accordance with the rules.

The first signs that government is coming to terms with the damage this
enforced compliance burden is inflicting on the small business community have
appeared in the past few years. The most useful changes were introduced in the
1991/2 budget with the raising of the VAT registration limit, the quarterly
payment of PAYE for an estimated 750,000 traders with monthly deductions of
less than £400, and a slight easing of the Keith Committee measures relating to
VAT.

It is to be hoped that this encouraging trend will continue, as the remaining
burden is still significant.

Encouraging risk taking

The previous section related to a topic to which the Bolton Committee gave
relatively little attention. This heading, the encouragement of enterprise, was at
the heart of its conclusions. No changes of this type, however, were introduced
until Lord Lever became responsible for small firms, towards the end of the last
Labour government. The Wilson Committee (Wilson 1979) also provided some
encouragement for these and subsequent measures.

As a result of the increasing realization that small businesses were likely to
provide the only means of reducing rising unemployment, the 1978 budget
included measures to provide relief for trading losses in new businesses under
Schedule D against employment income in the previous three years. This was a
significant change in policy and was matched, in the same year with relief
against corporation tax and capital gains tax for losses on loans extended to
traders.

This pattern was continued by the Tory party in 1980/1 and extended in
1981/2 with the introduction of the Business Start Up Scheme, the forerunner

of the Business Expansion Scheme which was announced in 1983/4 at an estimated cost of £114 million per annum at 1991 prices, £31 million per year more than its predecessor. The objective was, clearly, to improve the flow of funds into the small business sector and encourage the formation of new businesses and the expansion of existing ones by providing effective tax relief for losses in the early years of trading.

In more recent years there has been some scepticism about the nature of the funds attracted by some of these schemes and more recent changes have concentrated on tinkering rather than reform of the schemes. However, there is no doubt that the early reliefs which enabled trading losses to be offset against other forms of income improve the even-handedness of the tax system which otherwise discriminates unfairly against higher risk projects (see, for example, Domar and Musgrave, 1944).

The creation of a small business infrastructure

This heading covers tax changes relating to the development of infrastructure designed to assist and encourage small firms. There are two classifications of reliefs – those relating to physical infrastructure, such as the provision of workshop space, and those relating to the provision of advisory services, such as Enterprise Agencies.

Although Bolton did not refer to any of these under the heading of taxation, reference to such issues was made elsewhere in the report. In fact, many such initiatives were undertaken during the 1980s through government expenditure, such as the Manpower Services Commission: this section will refer only to those few which manifested themselves through tax incentives.

There was only one major item which involved a significant reduction in tax revenues. This related to 100 per cent first year allowances in respect of small industrial buildings. The scheme was introduced in 1980/1 for a period of three years at an estimated annual cost of £9 million at 1991 prices. The relief was subsequently extended in time and to cover conversion of industrial premises as well as new buildings.

The second element under this heading relates to Enterprise Agencies. Relief for contributions to these organizations was introduced in 1982/3. The cost to the exchequer was expected to be negligible.

Combined impact of tax changes

In total the reliefs discussed above amounted to approximately £1.3bn in their first full year of operation. The timing of their introduction is also of interest. Although the Labour party appointed the committee in July 1969, a relatively small number of its recommendations on taxation were implemented until the spectre of high unemployment made the creation of additional jobs a political necessity.

As a result it was the late 1970s and early 1980s in which the majority of measures were introduced. Once the Lawson boom was under way, however, enthusiasm waned and it was known that Mrs Thatcher believed that enough support had been provided to this sector, which was now required to demonstrate the required return on the government's investment. Thus between 1984/5 and 1989/90 tax changes relating purely to the small business sector were modest and largely self-balancing.

The spectre of rising unemployment in the current recession has once again encouraged a wave of reliefs. The nature of these is, however, quite different from those introduced a decade earlier. This time the emphasis is upon lightening the burden of red tape which weighs particularly heavily on the 2.5m self-employed. Cynics might argue that the boot is now on the other foot. With an election imminent, the small business sector which created a million jobs in the 1980s, mostly in very small firms, requires whichever party is to be elected to demonstrate its commitment to the sector.

Conclusions

The review conducted in this chapter has identified a number of interesting trends in the development of taxation of small businesses in the UK over the past two decades.

To a certain extent events have taken a full circle. Many of Bolton's original recommendations related to nurturing and encouraging the population of established small businesses. The early 1980s saw a significant shift, in the face of rising unemployment, towards encouraging the establishment of new firms. Subsequent experience, referred to elsewhere in this book, has shown that much of the resulting growth came in the form of very small micro businesses employing few, if any, staff. In fact a very limited proportion of all small businesses have shown any propensity to develop significantly.

With the anticipated end to the current recession in sight, if not around the corner, and the numbers of the working population declining up to the middle of the 1990s, measures designed to promote efficiency rather than to maximize employment are likely to return to the agenda. In these circumstances, public policy seems set to shift once again to the development and growth of existing businesses, rather than the sustenance of large numbers of self-employed which inevitably exhibit relatively low levels of output per person compared with their larger counterparts.

What then are the most effective fiscal policies to achieve these objectives? That there is a recognizable cycle of growth and development for small firms is now widely accepted (see for example Scott and Bruce, 1987). Some of these models show the development process as being a continuous upward curve upon which businesses travel or stall. Slightly more realistic interpretation shows that in practice most firms pass through a process of development and consolidation, back to expansion in a much more circuitous route.

Fiscal policy must, therefore, focus on the encouragement to business owners to pass through this cycle several times until their aspirations are satisfied. Possibly, from a fiscal point of view this requires two elements, not unlike Herzberg's theory of motivation in which there are hygiene factors and motivators.

In taxation the hygiene factors relate to the staggering administrative burden placed on small firms, referred to above, coupled to the attitudes towards small business owners displayed by public servants such as the Inland Revenue and VAT officers. Bannock (op. cit.) makes the point well that by delegating the collection of VAT, PAYE and NIC to business owners the civil servants involved have to a significant extent lost touch with the taxpayers. There is no doubt that from the government's point of view this has made administrative sense as public costs have been shifted on to the private sector.

However, the price that is being paid in the suppression of enterprise and distortion of the economy in favour of those businesses with the volume of transactions and, therefore, systems to cope with this burden, may be much greater than has so far been recognized.

There are a number of simple remedies which could be taken to address this position and government has thankfully begun to move in this direction by raising the VAT registration threshold and allowing businesses with very small PAYE bills to pay these quarterly, as announced in the 1991 budget. These early steps should form a basis for progressive change in these areas.

The Treasury, through the relevant departments, is now in a position to monitor the impact of these small initial changes on government revenues and the commensurate savings in the departmental administration costs, as the number of VAT-registered traders declines and the reduction in the number of PAYE payments (less any additional lost revenues when businesses become insolvent) releases staff and administrative resources.

Using this information should enable the Chancellor to continue to introduce progressive changes until the optimum balance is achieved. These changes should be supplemented by scale charge deductions which traders are authorized to make from their monthly and quarterly payments in accordance with the costs they bear. Anything less than this would seem to be little short of a dangerous distortion of the natural economic forces determining the optimum mix of sizes of businesses in the UK.

The second stage of ensuring that the hygiene factors are in place is two-fold. First, the revenue departments must once more make contact with the small business population (not just those subject to inquiry). This will require a consistent programme of re-orientation and education of staff about the nature and stresses of running small businesses and their unquestionable value to the economy.

In itself this programme should lead to further reductions in the administrative burden placed upon small businesses. A side effect should be an acceleration of the work of the Enterprise and Deregulation Unit which, it is known, faces considerable opposition within departments.

Having started the process of ensuring that the hygiene factors are moving into place, government must continue the process of sustaining and developing the motivating factors. Earlier discussion has identified the steps already taken. It is obvious that there has been a reduction in the development of this process in the most recent years. There is, of course, a limit to the tinkering that can be applied to the present systems and it may be that the laws of diminishing returns have already set in. Perhaps the time is right for a more radical approach than has been taken to date.

Since the reduction in tax relief for investment following the 1984 budget the most acceptable tax break available to smaller companies has been the self-administered pension scheme. For companies with four or fewer directors, 95 per cent of the funds can be re-invested in accordance with the wishes of the trustees. The most common route in recent years has been to purchase properties that were subsequently let to the company. Thus providing an appreciating asset for the pension fund which also receives a rental income, while the business enjoys the benefit of improved premises and a benign landlord.

There is, of course, no economic justification for this position which is overtly distortionary. In addition, with the long-run real return on property investments being somewhere in the region of 9 per cent (BZW sector report) it is possible that funds are being diverted from higher risk, but significantly higher reward businesses, into a sector offering lower returns, albeit at a lower level of risk.

While some directors would naturally prefer this combination, there can be little doubt that others will have been persuaded down this route simply because of the attractiveness of the tax breaks, which at the 25 per cent small companies rate of corporation tax or the 40 per cent top rate of income tax, would, depending upon the circumstances of the company and its owners, improve the returns by 33 and 60 per cent respectively.

Surely what is required is a taxation system that provides incentives for investments and yet is not economically distortionary. Academics are all agreed that a cash-flow base for taxation, providing automatic relief for investment is more likely to achieve the most economically efficient solution (see for example the discussion in Pointon and Sprately 1988). In addition there are positive side effects, such as neutrality to inflation and immunity to subjectiveness of accounting policies, including, for example the valuation of stocks.

Such a system is not, however, without its drawbacks. In particular, the manipulation of working capital balances over the short term could result in the sheltering of positive cash-flows in good years. This situation is not unlike the present position with the valuation of stocks under a profits base for taxation. It would not seem to be too difficult to devise adequate safeguards against widespread manipulation which would, in any case do no more than delay the payment of taxes rather than remove the liability entirely.

A more fundamental objection, however, is that it is thought likely that a cash-flow tax may prove ineffective in raising sufficient government income. In this respect small businesses provide an unusual opportunity. It is well recognized that while small firms are very many in number, their contribution to net tax revenues is proportionately smaller. This is largely due to the higher administrative costs associated with large numbers of relatively small businesses. However, in the case of small limited companies there is an added dimension as it has been shown that business owners manage their tax affairs to minimize the overall tax burden, balanced between themselves and their companies (Watson, 1990).

It is interesting to note that employees and directors taxed under Schedule E are, as a result of the change in assessment to the receipts basis in the 1989 budget, now effectively subject to taxation on cash-flow. In addition the continued computerization of tax offices is likely to enable government to change from the confusing preceding year basis for the self-employed taxed under Schedule D to assessment on a current year basis. It is known that Ministers favour this change.

At the same time the accountancy profession is reviewing its policy on the presentation of Statements of Sources and Applications of Funds. These are likely to be replaced, in the near future, by published cash-flow statements for limited companies.

Surely the time is right to introduce the cash-flow basis of taxation, initially for small, closely held limited companies. The decision would be low risk for the government, which collects relatively little tax from this source. The change would also be low risk for company owners who are able to manage their affairs so that they achieve the optimal balance between their business and personal affairs.

If the new basis of taxation proved to be particularly favourable to investment, distributions from the business and investment in pension schemes would decline and the funds would be invested within the companies. Alternatively, if the tax basis proved to be harsh, owners would continue to manage their tax affairs by withdrawing the funds or sheltering them through pension schemes. Whichever happened, government could monitor the situation and gain significant insights that would prove invaluable in shaping future taxation policy.

6 The Small Firm Equity Gap since Bolton

The majority of small firms in the United Kingdom, as elsewhere, rely on self-financing – the personal capital of the owner and his/her family and retained profits – supplemented in most cases by bank overdrafts and loans and trade credit. For example, a study of new manufacturing firms in South Hampshire (Mason, 1989) noted that in more than half of all cases the single most important source of start-up finance was one of the following: personal savings, family and friends, redundancy pay, mortgage or second mortgage on the founder's home, and previous business. Since start-up these firms have relied in roughly equal proportions on internally generated finance – namely retained profits (44 per cent) and personal savings and those of family and friends (3 per cent) – and loans from banks (23 per cent) and finance houses (21 per cent) and bank overdrafts (3 per cent). This pattern of finance is confirmed in a recent study of new firms in West Lothian by Turok and Richardson (1991): they comment that 'by far the most important source of launch capital was personal savings' (p. 80). Another Scottish study, by Reid and Jacobsen (1988) noted that only 7 per cent of firms used external equity finance at start-up.

Although external equity accounts for a small proportion of the overall finance used by small firms its availability is nevertheless of considerable significance for the vitality of the enterprise economy. For example, the financial needs of rapid-growth firms are likely to be beyond the capability of the financial resources of their founder(s) and any retained profits to meet. Similarly, technology-based firms are vulnerable to financial stress because high R & D expenditure to improve or replace existing products is required prior to new product launch at a time when profits from the existing product(s) are likely to be at a low ebb (Oakey, 1985). External sources of finance – in particular, equity finance – are therefore likely to be required by rapid-growth firms and by technology-based firms in order to fill the finance gap between investment needs and opportunities and internal resources (ACOST, 1990). However, the evidence suggests that such firms encounter difficulties in raising external equity finance despite the development of new sources of equity capital for small and medium-sized firms (SMEs) during the past decade or so. For example, a survey of small high technology firms (the majority of which were on science parks) found very little use of external equity either at start-up or subsequently and a widespread perception among the owner-managers of such firms that a shortage of equity capital exists (Monck *et al*, 1988). Turok and Richardson (1989)

Table 6.1   Owner-managers' views on the problems of raising risk capital

General comments
• 'There is a singular lack of commercial awareness of the problems/prospects of small businesses on the part of most financial institutions and a real absence of risk capital.'
• ' "Venture" capital does not seem to exist for businesses outside "blue sky" activities. "Development" capital does exist but often demands a growth rate detrimental to the long-term (five to ten years) business because of the short-term turnaround/growth in worth which the development capitalists require.'
• '... outsiders with equity finance were only interested if the investment was in a profit-making situation. In that case, we would not have been looking for more finance!'

Difficulties encountered in raising relatively small amounts of finance
• 'It is my experience that it is very difficult to raise finance in the range £80,000 to £500,000 for product development purposes. The banks seem to show no interest at all in development funding and the majority of venture capital companies are only interested in lending [*sic*] relatively large sums.'
• 'Venture capital is useless: they do not want to know if less than £500,000 is sought.'
• 'You could not get to the interview stage [with venture capital institutions] if the sum you required was less than £250,000.'

Difficulties encountered by new ventures
• 'The situation is absolutely awful for any new venture'.
• 'There appears to be no institutional funding for start-ups or young companies with no accounts, etc.'

Difficulties encountered by high-tech firms
• 'We were disappointed with the attitudes of "financiers" to high-tech. Most say no before even seeing the business plan.'

Views of the banks and venture capital funds
• 'Banks are useless – "managed" by glorified clerks authorized to lend only if 100 per cent security is available . . . sole criterion is value of one's house!'
• 'Venture funds in this country are run by young inexperienced non-technical people with blinkered views and irrelevant MBAs from Harvard. Bankers see their major role as protectors of my grannie's savings. The British Technology Group is an administrative retirement home.'

Source: Unpublished survey.

found that the proportion of growing firms that cited lack of finance as a problem was higher than for non-growing firms. These difficulties in raising external finance – both loan and equity – are perhaps best appreciated in the comments of the entrepreneurs themselves, a selection of which is given in Table 6.1.

There is a widespread perception among small firm owner-managers that there is a lack of external equity finance available – and they make limited use of such finance: on the other hand, there has been a number of significant developments in the supply of equity finance for SMEs during the past decade or so, including the creation of secondary stock markets, the emergence of a venture capital industry and various public sector initiatives.

This chapter explores that paradox.

Six decades of analysis

Concern about the difficulties encountered by small firms in raising loan and equity finance can be traced back 60 years to the Macmillan Report (HM Government, 1931). The problem to which it drew attention, subsequently termed the 'Macmillan gap', was the lack of provision for small and medium-sized businesses seeking external finance up to £200,000 – equivalent to about £4 million today – which at the time was too small to justify a flotation on the Stock Exchange. The committee identified three reasons for this situation: first, the difficulty that investors encounter in realizing their investments because of the lack of exit routes; second, the expenses incurred by investors in monitoring their investment, which encourage larger rather than smaller investments; and third, the orientation of British financial markets towards the financing of domestic and foreign trade and commerce. One of the consequences of the Macmillan Report was the formation of ICFC (now 3i) in 1945 – the first specialist development capital company in the UK – to provide long- and medium-term finance for small and medium-sized firms.

The problems encountered by small firms in raising external finance were also raised in the Radcliffe Report in 1959 which pointed to the 'danger, which is socially and economically desirable to avoid, that the growth of small firms may be impeded because they lack some of the facilities open to larger companies for obtaining capital' (HM Government, 1959, para. 932). The Bolton Committee returned to this issue in its 1971 report (HM Government, 1971). It concluded that the precise gap identified by the Macmillan Committee had been largely filled by ICFC but that small firms nevertheless, 'still suffer a number of genuine disabilities, by comparison with larger firms, in seeking finance from external sources' (para. 12.98) while in the specific case of equity finance it concluded that 'the market facing the small firm is relatively constricted' (para. 12.87).

Despite a number of government measures designed to improve the availability of finance for small firms and various institutional innovations, both of which are discussed later in this chapter, a variety of authoritative reports since Bolton have continued to highlight the existence of an equity gap. The Wilson

Committee to Review the Functioning of Financial Institutions, which issued an interim report in 1979, *The Financing of Small Firms* (HM Government, 1979), concluded that 'there are deficiencies in the availability of equity finance for small business' which was 'putting undesirable constraints on their rate of creation and growth' (p. 9). They identified three particular weaknesses. First, apart from ICFC no institutions were willing to consider investments of less than £50,000 and their preferred minimum was usually around £100,000; these amounts are equivalent to £100,000 and £200,000 respectively at today's prices. Second, and as a consequence, apart from ICFC 'there is virtually no other source to which the client seeking support of less than about £50,000 with an equity element can turn' (p. 11). The committee considered that 'it is a weakness in the system that there is no competing source of equity to offer second opinions and to pick up ICFC's inevitable mistakes' (p. 11). Third, few small firms were seeking a Stock Exchange listing because of the increasing costs and obligations of going public. This removed both a potential source of new equity and a means whereby previous investors could realize their investments.

Four authoritative reports published since 1979 have each confirmed the persistence of the equity gap. First, the initial evaluation of the Loan Guarantee Scheme – which was established as a result of a recommendation from the Wilson Committee – concluded that 'there is still a gap in the market for long-term funds (whether equity or loan) for businesses which need to raise relatively small amounts of money' (Robson Rhodes, 1984, p. 39). Second, a report by the National Economic Development Council's Committee on Finance for Industry which was published in 1986, although noting an improvement in the supply of external finance to small firms in recent years, nevertheless noted that there had been limited progress in meeting the needs of firms requiring small amounts of finance, including seed and early stage finance. It also expressed concern at the often onerous terms on which finance is made available to small firms (NEDC, 1986). Third, the report of the Advisory Council for Applied Research and Development (ACARD), *Barriers to Growth in Small Firms*, concluded that 'there is a definite equity gap, certainly in terms of the amounts that can be readily raised from external sources and, possibly, in terms of the assessment procedures that are applied by venture capitalists' (Hall, 1989, p. 55). Finally, a report by the Advisory Committee on Science and Technology (ACOST) on barriers to growth in small firms which was published in 1990 also highlighted deficiencies in the supply of equity capital for smaller, growing firms (ACOST, 1990). Specifically, it concluded that 'there is a clear need . . . for the ready availability of smaller amounts of risk capital' (p. 35). It also observed that a significant number of companies have chosen to be taken over by larger companies in order to overcome financial barriers to growth, a strategy which can be problematical.

The existence of an equity gap can be traced back through various official reports for sixty years. Each of the four major inquiries – Macmillan, Radcliffe, Bolton and Wilson – has stimulated a period of innovation in business finance by both the private and public sector, even though the financial establishment had, for the most part, denied that changes were necessary or that shortcomings existed (Bannock and Doran, 1987) which have resulted in qualitative changes in, although not the elimination of, the equity gap. The upper limit of the equity gap has been progressively reduced and is now largely encountered by new and recently established businesses and by high technology ventures. The equity gap is primarily a shortage of seed, start-up and early stage finance (Mason and Harrison, 1991a).

Finance and the small firm

The problems encountered by small firms in raising external finance arise from three sources: the nature and characteristics of the small firm; the attitudes of small firm owner-managers to equity financing; and the economics of equity capital investment.

Many of the problems experienced by small firms in gaining access to external finance arise from the nature of the small firms themselves. The general problem is that 'the smaller the firm, the larger the proportionate increase in the capital required to respond to an increase in demand, but the lower its ability to command loan and equity finance' (Binks, 1979, p. 34). Small firms generally require finance in a series of discrete jumps rather than in regular small amounts. This arises for two reasons. First, increases in the demand for a firm's products or services, especially in the early stages of its entry into the market or at the point of significantly increased market penetration, rarely occur smoothly but rather take the form of a series of discontinuous steps of considerable size relative to existing turnover. Second, increased output in response to these changes in demand will generally necessitate additional investment involving, *inter alia*, the purchase of new or additional capital equipment or a move into larger and possibly more modern premises. It should be noted that this is not just a problem encountered by small *manufacturing* firms: small service sector companies are becoming more capital intensive as a result of the acquisition of such items as microcomputers, in-vehicle telephones, photocopiers, mechanical handling, security and other devices (Bannock and Doran, 1987). Because of the indivisibility of capital, this investment will tend to be large, relative to the existing capital base. Moreover, the smaller the firm the more likely it is to be undercapitalized, using older second-hand capital equipment in old premises, and the greater the proportionate increase in its existing capital base which any new investment will represent.

As a result of these two factors, growing small firms rapidly exhaust the finance available from the private resources of the owner-manager(s) which typically take the form of personal savings, loans from family and friends and house mortgage. Moreover, small firms, particularly those in their early years of trading, are unlikely to generate sufficient (if any) retained profits to finance the significant increase in turnover and in the capital base required for expansion. Indeed, in this early period cash-flow may well be negative because of the lag between outgoings (supplies, overheads and wages) and receipts. In addition, it may be advantageous from an accounting point of view for newly established firms to make losses in the early years to offset against corporation tax later on (Binks and Coyne, 1983), while established small businesses may find that company taxation will slow down the rate at which internally generated funds can be accumulated.

Most small firms, therefore, need to raise finance from external sources in order to start and, in particular, to grow. In the vast majority of cases, however, this demand is restricted to debt finance in the form of bank overdrafts and loans. Burns and Dewhurst (1986) have noted the high and increasing gearing level of the UK's small firm sector, reflecting the low level of shareholders' funds.

Reliance on debt financing has three major consequences. First, lenders typically view small businesses – particularly new and recent start-ups – as high risk propositions, and in consequence the required ratio of security to the capital borrowed is high in order to offset this perceived high risk. A survey of new manufacturing firms in Nottingham revealed that ratios of 4:1 and 5:1 of net present asset value to liabilities is quite common; only in very rare instances did the collateral demanded merely match the value of the loan, or was the loan offered on an unsecured basis (Binks and Vale, 1984). However, most small firms have little or no acceptable security to offer, especially as capital equipment is often unacceptable as security by the banks (Binks 1979). Consequently, most owner-managers must pledge personal assets – typically their house – as security in order to raise loans. Second, the cost of loan finance, in terms of the premium over base rates and account charges, for a small firm is generally higher than for a large firm on account of higher administrative expenses relative to the size of the loan and perceived greater commercial risk. Third, the debt servicing costs of highly leveraged and under-capitalized businesses – that is, businesses incorporating a high degree of debt relative to total assets – reduces their flexibility in making investments and renders them vulnerable to high interest rates.

Nevertheless, few small firm owner-managers are prepared to consider equity finance. Many do not know what equity finance is: Dr Bernard Juby of the National Federation of Self-Employed and Small Businesses suggested on a BBC Radio 4 phone-in that if asked for a definition of 'equity' most owner-managers would reply that it was a trade union for actors. Others fail to appreciate the character of loan and equity finance and their appropriate uses and so are reluctant to surrender equity to outsiders because of the perceived loss of independence, control and freedom of action over company strategy, dilution of earnings and cost in terms of fees to professional advisers. Vickery (1989) describes this as the 'patrimonial' view in which equity is not seen as an element in the financing of the business, so much as the pillar of control and perenniality. For such businesses, long-term equity investment is regarded as financing of the last resort (Robson Rhodes, 1984).

Demand for equity finance is, therefore, limited to a small proportion of small business owner-managers who have what Vickery (1989) describes as an 'entrepreneurial' view which recognizes that there are different types of finance available, each with its own costs and advantages and that returns to financiers are the necessary compensation for obtaining the funds in the first place. They are primarily concerned to obtain the use of the resources rather than their ownership, recognizing that *de facto* managerial control is more important than financial control or ownership.

However, such firms frequently encounter difficulties in raising equity finance despite various institutional innovations in the period since the Bolton Report, and particularly during the 1980s, which were intended to increase the supply of equity finance to SMEs. This reflects two factors associated with the economics of equity capital investment. First, the administrative costs incurred by a financial institution in screening potential investee ventures and in making and monitoring an investment are relatively fixed, regardless of the size of the investment. This is reflected in the fact that many of the fees and costs are applied as fixed sums and not as percentages of amounts raised (NEDC, 1986). As a result, in general the costs of raising equity are proportionately higher the smaller the amount raised. Second, for the investor, the risks of investing in a small firm are harder to assess and the returns are more uncertain compared with investing in larger, established businesses: the probability of failure is higher and both growth prospects and exit prospects are uncertain.

Developments in the supply of equity capital

Four major developments in UK capital markets during the past twenty years are of particular note: the creation of secondary markets on the Stock Exchange, the development of a venture capital industry, tax incentives to encourage private equity investments in unquoted companies, and the establishment of local and regional public sector organizations which provide equity (and loan) investments in specific geographical areas. What are the reasons for the development of these sources of equity capital, and what impact have they had on the financing of the UK's small firm sector, and specifically on the equity gap?

Secondary markets

The Unlisted Securities Market (USM) was launched in 1980 to provide smaller companies with access to a stock market with less stringent listing requirements and lower issue costs. This was achieved by reducing the proportion of equity that had to be in public hands from 25 per cent to 10 per cent, requiring a three year instead of a five year trading record, reducing compliance costs and reducing the complex rules of behaviour and disclosure. The decision by the Stock Exchange to establish a lower tier market was a response to two factors. First, there was concern at the decline in number of companies seeking a full listing, from an annual average of 50 companies in the 1960s and early 1970s to less than half this figure during the second half of the 1970s. This was attributed to the conditions and cost of obtaining a listing, although the economic and stock market conditions of the time were also likely to have been important factors. Second, the Stock Market was concerned at the regulatory problems created by the growing interest in over-the-counter (OTC) market trading involving the use of Rule 163(2) which allowed specific dealing in unlisted shares with prior approval through the normal mechanism of the Market but without the company itself having to comply with the usual formalities beforehand. This interest had increased as a result of the publicity given to the existence of Rule 163(2) by the Stock Exchange following the evidence of several witnesses to the Wilson Committee who highlighted deficiencies in arrangements for marketing the equity of small businesses.

Despite the introduction of the USM, the number of companies trading under Rule 163(2) did not decline, in part because companies funded under the Business Expansion Scheme (discussed in detail below) – a scheme to enable tax payers to reclaim tax relief on investments in companies, subject to various restrictions – could be traded on OTC markets but not on the USM or the Official List. The Stock Market's response was to create the Third Market in 1987, a third tier market similar to the OTC but with a proper regulatory framework and the full protection of the Stock Exchange's compensation fund. However, the Third Market carried greater risk than either the USM or Official List because companies on this market were not vetted by the Stock Exchange's quotations department prior to flotation (unlike Official List and USM companies), leaving this to the sponsoring firm (which must be a member of the Stock Exchange). The Third Market was aimed at companies that were too young or too small for the main market or the USM. They only required to have a one year trading record and were not required to make a minimum amount of equity available.

The USM got off to a very fast start, with 171 companies joining in the first 30 months. These companies raised £156 million (including rights issues) for retention and a further £61 million on disposal by existing shareholders (Bank of England, 1983). During its first ten years (1980–1990) a total of 817 companies have joined (including companies which have subsequently graduated to the Official List, companies which have been taken over and companies which have gone into liquidation), raising £4.7bn, of which £1.68bn was in the form of new issues and £3.03bn from further issues. Over 400 companies were trading on the USM at the end of 1990. The companies floated on the USM have varied widely in size, profitability and sector. Originally, it was dominated by oil and gas companies, but financial and property companies and electricals and more recently service companies in the 'people business' (design, consultancy, advertising) have all increased in importance. Thus, the industrial composition of the USM is now little different from that of the Official List (Buckland and Davis, 1989). However, USM companies are smaller than those on the Official List, although relatively few have been either new or recent start-ups and many are family-owned businesses (Bannock and Doran, 1987).

The secondary markets were expected to play a pivotal role in the development of equity financing for smaller firms. Quotation of a company's shares makes it easier and usually cheaper to raise additional capital, enables existing shareholders (both those connected with the business and outside investors) to realize their investments and makes it easier, and probably cheaper, to expand by acquisition, using new shares as an alternative to internal finance or external borrowings. In addition, there are likely to be a variety of intangible benefits from the enhanced status and improved visibility of the business which accrue from USM status (Bannock and Doran, 1987).

While the USM was widely acclaimed as a great success initially, over the longer term this optimistic view of the impact of the secondary markets has not been fulfilled. One problem is that the cost of obtaining a USM listing – although much lower than for a full listing – is nevertheless quite significant. For example, Buckland and Davis (1989) indicate that the average cost of an 'introduction' – the cheapest method of entry to the USM – was about £100,000 (1985 prices), that of a 'placing' was £132,000 while an 'offer for sale' – the most expensive method on account of the advertising and underwriting fees – was £368,000. Moreover, because of the high element of fixed costs there are significant economies of scale in the issuing process (Buckland and Davis, 1989): in other words, issue costs as a percentage of the amount raised decline as the size of issue increases. Similarly, the ongoing costs of a USM listing, such as registrars' fees and the production of regular financial statements, are also fairly constant regardless of the size of company. Because of the work carried out by sponsors the cost of joining the Third Market is not significantly cheaper than the USM in absolute terms and in terms of capital raised it is much higher. Hence, in practice the USM, and to a lesser extent the Third Market, are catering for quite sizeable businesses with significantly above average returns: Buckland and Davis (1989) note that the majority of USM entrants have had profits of over £200,000 and a market capitalization of over £2.5 million. Indeed, they conclude that although the USM has provided access to firms which previously could not or would not have obtained a quotation on the Official List, USM firms are nevertheless 'generally of a size and history which could qualify them for Official List entry' (p. 136). But unlike Official List entrants, USM companies have been more likely to seek a listing in order to raise additional capital.

Another factor is that the USM has under-performed the Official List, despite bull market conditions for much of the 1980s. The USM index, which began at 100 in 1980 only rose above this value for a brief period in 1984 and between 1987 and early 1990, and by late 1990 had fallen to 68. Over the same period the FT All Share index has risen more than threefold (Jack, 1990). (However, it should be noted that the USM index does not take into account the fact that many of the successful USM companies have graduated to the Official List.) This has raised concern among many managers of USM and prospective USM companies that the market was failing to put a realistic valuation on small companies. Moreover, with the advent of a bear market since late 1987 the USM has been characterized by severe liquidity problems as a result of declining interest from market makers and investors. The volume of transactions has fallen sharply from 966,000 bargains worth £7.13 million in 1987 to 450,000 bargains worth £4.99 million in 1989. Spreads have also widened. As a result of both factors the number of new entrants to the USM has declined from over 100 per quarter in 1988 to less than 40 per quarter in 1990 (Jack, 1990).

Unlike the USM, the Third Market did not even start well. Throughout its brief existence it has failed to attract much interest from companies or investors and has been characterized by particular liquidity problems. Only 92 companies joined since it was launched, of which two transferred to the Official List and 22 moved to the USM. The closure of the Third Market was announced by the Stock Market in 1990, ostensibly as part of its reforms to conform with a European Community directive, although it was under pressure to make changes because of the market's lack of success. In effect, the Third Market 'merged' with the USM; those companies on the Third Market that met the USM's stricter entry requirements were able to join; the remainder moved to the OTC market. As part of the same changes the Stock Market announced that the trading period required to join the USM would be reduced to two years and to three years for the Official List, thereby reducing the attractions of the USM vis-à-vis the Official List. However, these changes have raised widespread concern that they have adversely affected the image of the USM both among investors and companies (Jack, 1990).

These factors have combined to renew concern about whether the Stock Market is meeting the needs of small firms. While economic conditions have clearly played some role in the USM's current problems and in the demise of the Third Market as investors have placed emphasis on 'defensive' investments, this is by no means the only factor in the declining attractiveness of secondary markets to companies, market makers and investors alike. For example, financial de-regulation has also had an effect on the level of market-making activity in less actively traded equities, such as many of those on secondary markets (Buckland and Davis, 1989). The implication is that a further reform of Stock Exchange rules is required.

A further limitation of secondary markets in the UK is that they operate exclusively as national markets. Since 1973 the (London) Stock Exchange has encompassed the activity of the regional stock exchanges. As a result, the provincial trading floors in Belfast, Bristol, Leeds, Liverpool, Newcastle and Manchester have disappeared. Prior to this amalgamation of trading there were some equities traded solely on the provincial floors, albeit relatively inactively. These were fairly small businesses which would have found it expensive to inform the wider, and largely disinterested, national investing community. Following amalgamation, companies which previously chose to be quoted only on regional floors, and those which would have made this choice in the future, had to choose between joining the national floor or not seeking a public listing. Buckland and Davis (1989, p. 122) suggest that 'there may be many potential USM entrants who have been inhibited from entry because the regional option was not available'.

The geographical centralization of equity trading depends on the elimination of regional asymmetries in the information presented and in the set of investors addressed by markets. However, if any asymmetries do exist, then a market that neglects the regionally specialized investor, or regionally specialized information, will fail to attract all potential traders. The USM encourages regional firms and investors by making it less costly to gain a national listing. Nevertheless, many firms are likely to be disadvantaged by the absence of regionally specialized trading floors; a national quotation on a secondary market is therefore a sub-optimal solution. This situation is in marked contrast to France where regional floors have survived the same kinds of centralizing pressures that the London Stock Exchange experienced. Its second tier market – the second market – is therefore available both nationally and regionally. Firms are able to choose between a regional quotation and a national one. Most French second-tier entrants have chosen to trade on a regional rather than a national market. As a result, trading on the second market has a very strong regional dimension and has done much to regenerate regionally based equity trading (Buckland and Davis, 1989). The French experience suggests that there is scope in the UK for businesses to be quoted away from London.

Birley and Westhead (1989) provide further support for the need for regional financial markets. Their study of private advertised sales of businesses in the UK indicates that 'there is a strategic loosening taking place in the corporate market-place – more businesses are being sold, and more owner-managers are choosing to exit ownership of their business . . . and more managers are becoming owners through the mechanism of management buyouts' (p. 12). However, 'the closing of the local Stock Exchanges . . . has left a vacuum: there is no regulated market for the sale of small companies at the local level' (p. 13). For most businesses the only marketplace for such deals is through newspaper advertisements, underlining the need for the establishment of a network of local, regulated financial markets. ACOST (1990) also suggest that the supply of equity finance for small and innovative businesses could be substantially increased by the development of an issuing and broking mechanism. They suggest that 'investors in this kind of company generally make their investment because they know, or think they know, something about the company concerned' (p. 40).

Venture capital

During the 1980s there was an enormous expansion in the number of venture capital funds operating in the UK. However, this has also had a limited impact on the availability of equity capital. Venture capital is generally defined as an activity by which corporate investors support entrepreneurial ventures with finance and business skills to exploit market opportunities and thus obtain long-term capital gains (Shilson, 1984). In practice, venture capital activity includes a variety of different types of financing: the provision of start-up finance, specialist portfolio investment in small unquoted companies, the provision of second and subsequent rounds of development capital for later stages of business expansion, and the financing of management buy-outs and buy-ins. All of these types of financing share a number of common features: they are equity orientated, highly selective in the choice of investee businesses to minimize risk (on a case-by-case basis, not a portfolio basis), make a medium- to long-term commitment of finance with the aim of making eventual capital gains rather than generating running income, require an identifiable exit route, and have some degree of active 'hands on' involvement in the management of the business receiving the finance in order to 'add value' to the investment. It is the latter characteristic that distinguishes venture capital from other, passive, forms of investment in business ventures (Dixon, 1989).

Before 1979 there were just over twenty venture capital funds with a total investment of £20m. These comprised the small business finance arms of the clearing banks, merchant banks (such as Charterhouse) that specialized in small business clients, some government agencies (notably the National Research and Development Corporation and the National Enterprise Board, subsequently merged and renamed the British Technology Group), and Investors in Industry, or 3i (formerly named the Industrial and Commercial Financial Corporation, or ICFC). 3i was by far the most important of these sources of small business finance. It had been established in 1945 by the Bank of England and the major clearing banks to provide long-term finance (both loan and equity) to growing firms (Clark, 1987). Hence, only part of 3i's activities can be considered as 'pure' venture capital, that is, investment in shares in small unquoted companies with the expectation of capital gain. About two-thirds of its investments are in small businesses, mostly in the form of a package of loans and equity. 'Pure' venture-type investments (by 3i Ventures) account for only around one-third of 3i's total investment activity (Clark, 1987).

However, during the 1980s an enormous expansion occurred in the number of private venture capital funds. By 1990 the British Venture Capital Association had 122 full members who had invested £1.1bn in the UK in that year, although as Cary (1991, p.7) notes, some of this expansion is simply the 're-christening' by 'many financial institutions . . . [of] . . . their traditional financing of unquoted companies as "venture capital" because this sounds better'.

These new funds are of two main types. First, many have been established by financial institutions, notably pension funds, insurance companies, merchant banks and clearing banks. These venture capital funds, in the jargon of the industry, are termed 'captives': that is, they form part of larger financial institutions through which they are also primarily funded, although they have considerable operational autonomy from their larger affiliates (Clark, 1987). Clearing bank captive funds are open-ended: they have no fixed amount of capital for investment and tend to look for part of their return in the form of continuing income rather than just from capital gains upon realization. Captive institutional funds (for example, affiliates of pension funds and insurance companies), by contrast, are usually closed-end funds. They are allocated either a fixed amount of capital for investment or a fixed proportion of the institution's total portfolio (Dixon, 1989). Second, various independent venture capital funds have been formed. They include UK subsidiaries of large US venture capital firms (for example, Alan Patricof Associates and TA Associates) and independent firms formed by venture capital managers who have 'spun-off' from established venture capital firms such as 3i. Independent venture capital organizations raise capital for investment from a variety of sources, including pension funds, insurance companies and foreign institutions. Independent funds have increased in significance during the 1980s and are now the largest category of venture capital organization, accounting for 37 per cent of the number of venture capital investments and 44 per cent of the total amount invested in the UK in 1990.

In the six years to 1990, approximately £6.2bn had been invested by UK venture capitalists, 86 per cent in the UK, 8 per cent in the US and 6 per cent elsewhere. Over this period, there has been a progressive fall in the UK share of investments and, in particular, investee companies. This is largely accounted for by a shift in investment to Continental Europe which accounted for 16 per cent of venture capital investment by value by UK institutions in 1990 compared to 3 per cent in 1988 (British Venture Capital Association, 1990; 1991).

This growth of venture capital in the UK has occurred as a result of the combination of various environmental factors which created a climate favourable to its development as well as specific supply-side and demand-side factors. First, the general climate of the 1980s has been pro-enterprise. Second, enthusiasm for venture capital in the UK was also stimulated by the growing awareness of the US venture capital industry and the spectacular success of some of the businesses that it had financed, including Tandem Computers, Federal Express, Apple Computer and LSI Logic (Dickson, 1984). A number of factors also stimulated an increase in the supply of venture capital. First, the government has taken specific measures to assist the venture capital industry. These include the indexing of capital gains tax, and the replacement of income tax liability in respect of certain share options by a capital gains tax liability, a change that helped small, fast-growing firms to attract key employees (Shilson, 1984). Developments in the UK capital markets are a second factor. As discussed in the previous section, the establishment of the Unlisted Securities Market in 1980 has provided an important means whereby venture capitalists can ultimately realize their gains and entrepreneurs can convert their 'paper' wealth to real wealth. Recent survey evidence suggests that realization of shareholders' stakes was an important consideration for many companies seeking a flotation on the USM (Binder Hamlyn, 1986; Hall and Hutchinson, 1988; Buckland and Davis, 1989). In addition, changes in company law which have allowed companies to repurchase their shares (a recommendation of the Wilson Committee) are likely to have made entrepreneurs more willing to look for outside equity because they can regain overall control at a later date and it provides investors with another 'exit route'. Third, longer-term investment became more attractive because of the prolonged bull conditions in the capital markets and the general economic optimism of the mid-1980s (Dixon, 1989). On the demand side, the key factors have been the expanding financial requirements which have stemmed from the increasing number of new business start-ups, including many in technology-related sectors, and management buy-outs during the economic recovery from the 1979–81 recession, and the growing appreciation amongst small business owners of the benefits of equity finance. As a result, the increased supply of venture capital has been matched by an increase in demand. For example, Alan Patricof Associates received over 1000 proposals in 1988 compared with 200 in 1980 (Cohen, 1989).

However, this rapid growth in venture capital activity during the 1980s (Table 6.2) has failed to fill the equity gap. Venture capital funds have been highly selective in the type of companies in which they will invest. In particular, they have been reluctant to make small investments and to invest in start-ups

Table 6.2   Venture capital investment activity in the United Kingdom

	1987	1988	1989	1990
Total amount invested (£ millions)	934	1298	1420	1106
Number of companies financed	1174	1326	1302	1221
Number of financings [1]	1208	1356	1351	1316
Average received per company (£000)	773	957	1051	840

[1] The number of financings recorded differs from the number of companies because a small number of companies have raised more than one round of venture capital finance within the year.
Source: BVCA (1990; 1991).

and early stage companies. This reflects a number of factors. First, the investment risks are likely to be higher and the exit routes less certain. Second, such companies are less likely to have a well-rounded management team with a proven track-record in managing growth and change. Third, the appraisal, arrangement and monitoring costs contain a high fixed element; hence, the costs of making a £50,000 investment are similar to those of a much larger investment. Finally, competitive pressure encourages venture capital funds to make large investments in established companies in order to maximize their scarce management resources. Thus, Cary (1991, p. 9) comments that 'as the size of the individual funds has increased so the size of the minimum investment has also risen in proportion'.

The vast majority of venture capital funds specialize in providing development capital. According the the VCR Guide to Venture Capital in the UK, only about five venture capital firms provide seed capital, about twenty provide start-up capital and about 50 provide early stage capital. By contrast, most funds provide later stage development capital and virtually all investment institutions provide funds for management buy-outs and buy-ins (Cary, 1991) (Table 6.3). The proportion of total venture capital investment accounted for by start-up and early stage finance was 27 per cent by value and 34 per cent by number of financings in 1984 (Pratt, 1990). By 1990 these figures had fallen to 12 per cent by value and 26 per cent by number (Table 6.4). Seed-corn investments account for an even smaller amount of venture capital activity. Venture capitalists invested just over £4 million in seed capital investments in 1989, a significant increase on the £1.1m invested in the previous year, but representing just 0.2 per cent of funds raised (Merchant, 1990). Not surprisingly, therefore, the venture capital industry is dominated by large investments. The average venture capital investment per round of financing has increased from less than £400,000 in 1984 to £1.05m in 1989, although this has subsequently fallen to

Table 6.3 Some structural characteristics of the UK venture capital industry[1]

	Median
Average venture capital Funds under management [2] (£m)	38
Smallest investment (£000)	155
Largest investment (£000)	2000
Average investment (£000)	600
Minimum investment [3] (£000)	175
Minimum equity stake (%)	2
Maximum equity stake (%)	49
Average equity stake (%)	25
Investment phase (% of portfolio):	
start-up	15
development	45
buy-out	23
others (rescue, etc.)	1
Take-up rates:	
(a) projects reviewed as % of those received	20
(b) investments made as % of projects reviewed	10
	% of funds
Industry preferences:	
none specified	63
technology-related [4]	24
all sectors except high-tech	4
other preferences [5]	9
Geographical preferences:	
local area (sub-regional)	6
region	10
macro-region [6]	8
UK	24
UK and overseas	40
none specified	12

Notes:
1 Based on 90 funds (excludes BES funds and organizations with government funds).
2 Includes funds already committed and available for investment.
3 A number of funds have no minimum size of investment.
4 This includes: 'high tech', biotechnology, health care/medical, software, information technology, electronics.
5 This includes: property and leisure, retail and leisure, manufacturing and manufacturing-related services.
6 Investment preferences limited to two or three (usually adjacent) specified regions.
Source: Cary (1991).

Table 6.4   Venture capital investment by stage of financing

Stage	Amount invested (% of total)				Number of financings (% of total)			
	1987	1988	1989	1990	1987	1988	1989	1990
Start-up	8	5	6	7	16	15	13	15
Early stage	5	5	9	5	11	13	25	11
Expansion	30	31	23	31	53	47	35	41
Buy-out/buy-in/ acquisition	55	56	61	52	18	21	25	26
Secondary purchase	2	3	1	5	2	4	2	7

Source: as for Table 6.2.

£840,000 in 1990 (Table 6.2). Deals of over £2 million accounted for two-thirds of the total amount invested in 1988 compared with under one-third in 1985. By contrast, financings of under £200,000 have fallen from 10 per cent of the total invested in 1985 to just 5 per cent in 1988 (Pratt, 1990). As a consequence, the modest success in closing the equity gap in the early 1980s has now been reversed (Pratt, 1990; Cary, 1991).

The declining proportion of funds invested in start-ups and early stage ventures and the increasing size of investments are both a result of the growing dominance of management buy-outs and buy-ins (MBOs and MBIs) in UK venture capital activity. MBOs/MBIs have been very attractive to UK venture capitalists for four main reasons (Mason and Harrison, 1991b). First, they have a lower risk than other types of investments, notably start-ups and early stage investments. MBOs/MBIs involve businesses that are established and profitable (or potentially profitable), the products are developed, the market is known, long-established links exist with customers and a management team, which is familiar with all aspects of the business, is in place. Second, for the same reasons, venture capitalists have to devote less time and effort to research MBOs/MBIs prior to investment and to support them afterwards. Third, because MBOs/MBIs usually involve well-established businesses in mature industries generating a comfortable and regular cash-flow they have produced the highest returns. Fourth, MBOs/MBIs offer a quicker exit route than most other types of investment. MBOs/MBIs represented 18 per cent of all venture capital investments in the UK in 1984: this had risen to 25 per cent by 1989. Over the same period the proportion of UK venture capital investment absorbed by MBOs/MBIs rose from 28 per cent to 61 per cent. Although both the number and proportion of venture capital financings accounted for by MBOs/MBIs rose slightly in 1990 a fall in the number of very large buy-outs has resulted in a fall in their share of total venture capital invested to 52 per cent (Table 6.4).

The lack of support for start-up and early stage businesses has been recognized by chief executives of major venture capital funds as the greatest failure of the industry to date (Murray, 1990). However, it seems unlikely that this situation will change over the next few years: two recent surveys of the investment preferences of venture capitalists both report that management buy-outs will continue to be the dominant form of investment over the next five years and that the limited popularity of investing seed and start-up capital will persist (Murray, 1990; *Financial Times*, 1991).

The venture capital industry has also done little to finance technology-based companies. Computer-related and electronics companies accounted for just 8 per cent of the finance invested in 1990 (compared with 30 per cent in 1984), with investments in medical, biotechnology and communications sectors accounting for a further 6 per cent of total UK venture capital investments. Venture capital investments have increasingly been oriented towards consumer-

Table 6.5   Regional distribution of UK venture capital investment

Region	% of amount invested				location quotient [1]
	1987	1988	1989	1990	
South East	57	50	48	61	1.54
East Anglia	3	3	3	5	0.87
South West	7	4	7	3	0.53
Midlands [2]	12	16	13	12	0.87
North [3]	12	18	12	11	0.66
Wales	4	2	1	1	0.39
Scotland	5	6	15	7	1.18
Northern Ireland	-	1	1	-	0.16

Notes:
1 The location quotient is calculated as follows:

$$LQ = \frac{VC\,i}{S\,i}$$

where $LQ\,i$ is the location quotient in region i
$VC\,i$ is the average percentage of total venture capital investment in region i, 1984–88
$S\,i$ is the average stock of VAT-registered businesses in each region, 1984–88
2 East and West Midlands
3 North West, Yorkshire-Humberside and the Northern region

Sources: As for Table 6.2. VAT data from *British Business*, 25 August, 1989, pp. 10–12.

related and service-sector businesses. Consumer-related activities increased their share of total venture capital financing from 23 per cent to 35 per cent between 1984 and 1990. A further 15 per cent of the amount invested in 1990 went into financial and other services.

A further concern is that despite the emergence of some elements of a regional venture capital industry in the UK which is more likely to make investments locally, in smaller tranches and in a wider range of industrial sectors than London-based organizations (Mason and Harrison, 1991b), there is still a significant north-south divide in the provision of venture capital in the UK. Throughout the 1987–90 period the South East region has accounted for over half of the amount invested by the venture capital industry (Table 6.5). When compared with its share of the total stock of UK businesses in this period (34.6 per cent), it is clear that venture capital investments have been disproportionately concentrated in the South East. In all other regions, with the sole exception of Scotland, the proportions of venture capital investment have been well below those expected on the basis of the regional proportions of the stock of UK businesses.

This spatial pattern of venture capital activity in the UK has two significant implications for regional economic development. First, promising small firms in peripheral regions of the UK are likely to encounter a lack of risk capital which will constrain their development and slow down the process of indigenously generated regional economic development. Second, many of the South East-based venture capital firms are likely to utilize nation-wide pension funds and other savings, a high proportion of which are re-invested in the South East region. Thus, the venture capital industry is contributing to a flow of investment finance from economically depressed regions in the north and west to the prosperous south.

The Business Expansion Scheme

The Business Expansion Scheme (BES) was introduced in 1983 in succession to the more restrictive Business Start-up Scheme which had been introduced two years earlier in an attempt by government to increase the flow of equity finance into small businesses by offering substantial tax breaks to investors. Under the scheme, private individuals can claim tax relief at their highest marginal rate of income tax (60 per cent until the end of the 1987–88 fiscal year, now reduced to 40 per cent) on investments in unquoted independent companies up to a maximum of £40,000 per year. To qualify, investors must be resident in the UK when the shares are issued and must not be 'connected' with the company (that is, must not own directly or indirectly more than 30 per cent of the company or be an employee, partner or paid director of the company). The relief is for investments in new, genuinely additional and full-risk ordinary capital and investors must hold their shares for at least five years. Companies qualifying under the BES must be incorporated in the UK and not be a subsidiary of, or controlled by, another company. Their shares cannot be traded on the Stock Exchange Official List or the USM for three years after their shares are issued.

Table 6.6   Total BES investment 1983/84 to 1989/90

Year	Number of companies	Total amount invested (£m)	Investments in private rented housing [1] no.	(£m)
1983/84	715	105		
1984/85	807	148		
1985/86	702	157		
1986/87	763	169		
1987/88	815	200		
sub-total [2]		779		
1988/89	2442	412	1934	362
1989/90	n/d	175 [3]		150[3]
Total	-	**1366**	-	**512**

Notes:
1 The Scheme was extended to include investment in private rented housing from 1988–89.
2 As some companies received funding in more than one year the total number of companies funded cannot be derived from the annual totals.
3 Provisional estimate.
Sources: Inland Revenue (1990); Parliamentary answer, *Weekly Hansard*, 23 July 1990, column 242.

Businesses in various financial services sectors, farming (since 1984) and heavily asset-backed companies (since 1986) are excluded from the scheme. In 1988 the scheme was extended to include private housing for rental. Also in that year a ceiling of £500,000, increased to £750,000 in 1990, was placed on investments under the BES in any individual company in any twelve-month period (with the exception of ship chartering and private housing for rent).

BES investments can be made in three ways. First, individuals can invest through specialist BES investment funds which pool investors' money in order to invest in a portfolio of companies. Second, individuals can invest in companies issuing shares directly to the public through a public offer or prospectus issue which is organized by a sponsor – usually a merchant bank, licensed securities dealer, stockbroker, venture capital house or member of FIMBRA. Finally, investors can invest directly in a company which organizes a private placing of its shares either with the assistance of a solicitor or arranged by an approved financial intermediary (see Mason *et al*, 1988 for further details of the scheme's regulations and operation).

Table 6.7   BES investments by size of financing, 1983/84 – 1987/88

Range of investment per company: lower limit, £000	number (%)	amount (%)
0	56.2	5.1
50	13.7	4.4
100	15.4	11.8
250	7.0	11.9
500	4.0	13.1
1000	3.7	53.7

Source: Inland Revenue (1990).

The government minister responsible for small firms policy at the time stated that its objectives were first, 'to encourage new and expanded activity in the small firms sector', and second, 'to encourage investment in high-risk activities, where the risk to the investor will be at least to some extent commensurate with the generous level of tax relief' (Hansard, 10 May 1984). On the surface, the initiative appears to have been extremely successful. Over £750m was invested in new equity in nearly 4000 small and medium-sized businesses through the BES between 1983–84 and 1987–88, with the amount invested rising each year (Table 6.6). Although this represents a significant addition to the pool of venture capital in the UK it has done little to close the equity gap. Certainly, a high proportion of the businesses which raised finance through the scheme have received small tranches of equity capital: 56 per cent of companies raised less than £50,000 each. However, this accounted for only 5 per cent of total investment. Conversely, 54 per cent of the amount invested was accounted for by just 4 per cent of companies which each raised over £1m under the scheme (Table 6.7). Moreover, the proportion of total investment accounted for by such large investments has risen in each year, from 30 per cent in 1983–84 to 65 per cent in 1987–88. This is reflected in the increase in the average size of investments from £147,000 in 1983–84 to £245,000 in 1987–88. Nevertheless, this is well below the average size of venture capital investment. So while the BES has provided small tranches of equity finance to a large number of businesses, only a small – and diminishing – proportion of total BES investment has been directed to this purpose.

Following the extension of the BES in the 1988 Finance Act to include residential property for letting under assured tenancy terms the scheme has now largely ceased to be a source of equity capital for the unquoted company sector. Nearly 90 per cent of the estimated £587 million raised under the BES in 1988–89 and 1989–90 has been for private-rented housing projects (Table 6.6). This reflects two factors. First, its low-risk asset-backed nature makes it particularly attractive to investors. Second, as a result of the introduction in the 1988 Finance Act of an upper limit of £500,000 on the amount that trading

Table 6.8   Regional distribution of BES investments by region, 1983/84 to 1987/88

Region	Companies		Amount invested	
	%	location quotient [1]	%	location quotient [1]
South East	49	1.44	66	1.94
East Anglia	5	1.22	6	1.46
South West	8	0.83	6	0.62
West Midlands	7	0.80	4	0.46
East Midlands	4	0.58	3	0.43
Yorkshire/Humberside	6	0.78	3	0.39
North and North West	9	0.68	5	0.38
Wales	3	0.57	3	0.57
Scotland	8	0.89	4	0.56
Northern Ireland	1	0.30	1	0.30
Total	**100**		**100**	

Note:
1 The location quotient is calculated as follows:

$$LQ = \frac{BES\,i}{S\,i}$$

where $LQ\,i$ is the location quotient in region i
            $BES\,i$ is the percentage of total BES investment in region i
            $S\,i$ is the average stock of VAT-registered businesses in each region
Source: As for Table 6.7. Source of VAT data – as for Table 6.5.

companies can raise in any twelve-month period through the BES – sub-sequently raised to £750,000 – in an attempt to channel funds to companies seeking to raise relatively small amounts of finance, it is no longer economic for trading companies to raise BES finance through prospectus issues nor for financial intermediaries to sponsor such issues. BES sponsors have therefore increasingly turned their attention to housing projects which have a maximum investment limit of £5 million.

The BES has also failed to channel significant amounts of finance to technology-based sectors. Even before its extension to include investments in private rented housing the bulk of the finance raised through the scheme has been invested in service sector businesses, often asset-backed or property-related, predominantly in the wholesale, retail, real estate and leisure sectors (Mason *et al*, 1988). BES investments have also been disproportionately concentrated in the South East region which has consistently contained about half of all investee companies. Total funds invested under the scheme are even more highly concentrated in the South East region, which attracted 66 per cent of the total amount invested between 1983–84 and 1987–88. Moreover, the South East's share of BES investments by value has increased over time, from 37 per cent in 1983–84 to 69 per cent in 1987–88. The South East and East Anglia are the only regions in which the proportion of BES investments exceeds their share

Table 6.9   Type of investment under the BES: 1983/84 to 1987/88

Year	Funds and schemes			Prospectus issues			Direct investments [1]		
	no of coys	£m	av per coy (£000)	no of coys	£m	av per coy (£000)	no of coys	£m	av per coy (£000)
1983/4	205	41.7	203	34	38.5	1132	476	24.8	52
1984/5	220	49.9	226	74	79.8	1078	513	18.2	36
1985/6	182	37.2	204	104	109.7	1055	416	10.1	24
1986/7	117	32.9	281	52	115.2	2215	576	19.9	35
1987/8	83	26.6	321	76	138.4	1821	588	26.0	44

Note:
1 Balance after subtracting data on funds and prospectus issues from Inland Revenue statistics.
Source: Updated from Harrison and Mason (1989).

of the total stock of UK businesses. Every other region has been under-represented in terms of its share of BES companies and amounts invested relative to their proportion of the UK stock of businesses (Table 6.8). Furthermore, the scheme has contributed to an outflow of finance from northern regions for re-investment in the South East (Mason *et al*, 1988; Mason and Harrison, 1989). The South East's dominance has continued following the inclusion of private rented housing in the scheme: in 1988–89 it attracted 79 per cent of the investments in private rented housing, accounting for 71 per cent of the amount invested (Inland Revenue, 1990).

The failure of the BES to contribute to the closing of the equity gap, its lack of investments in technology-based sectors and the increasingly uneven geographical distribution of investments under the scheme are all associated with a significant shift in the way in which investments have been made under the scheme in favour of prospectus issues which increased by over 250 per cent between 1983–84 and 1987–88. By 1987–88 prospectus issues accounted for 73 per cent of the amount raised under the BES (compared with 37 per cent in 1983–84) but only 10 per cent of BES investee companies (Table 6.9). The majority of prospectus issues have been large, with an average size of £1.1m in 1983–84 and around £2 million in 1987–88, and concentrated in low-risk asset-backed and property-related ventures such as wine traders, art dealers, racehorse breeders, hotels, sheltered housing and residential nursing home developments, restaurants and retailing (Mason *et al*, 1988). Prospectus issues are also overwhelmingly concentrated in the South East region. Conversely, both the amount of finance raised and the number of companies receiving finance from BES funds have declined. The proportion of finance accounted for by direct investments has also fallen sharply, from 24 per cent in 1983–84 to 14 per cent in 1987–88 (Table 6.9). Thus, as the BES has developed, so direct investment – the mode of investment most likely to contribute to the closing of the equity gap at the bottom end of the size range, and which is least over-concentrated in the South East region – has become increasingly marginalized and insignificant in terms of the proportion of finance raised under the BES (Mason *et al*, 1988; Harrison and Mason, 1989).

Local and regional sources of public sector venture capital

A further public sector response to the the continued existence of an equity gap, and especially a regional equity gap, has been the establishment of various public sector venture capital funds operating within specific geographical lim-its. These funds are of two types. First, a number of Labour-controlled local authorities, particularly those in metropolitan counties, have established en-terprise boards to invest equity and loan finance in locally-based firms. Second, regional development agencies, notably the Scottish and Welsh Development Agencies, provide a variety of forms of financial assistance, including the provi-sion of equity. Both enterprise boards and regional development agencies seek to use their investments to leverage additional private sector investment.

Enterprise boards
A number of Labour-controlled local authorities set up enterprise boards in the early 1980s to provide long-term development capital (loan and equity) for locally-based businesses in response to what was perceived as the failure of the financial institutions to supply long-term risk capital to companies with long-term commer-cial viability (Mawson and Miller, 1986). The Greater London Council (GLC), Lancashire County Council and the West Midlands, Merseyside and West York-shire Metropolitan Councils all set up enterprise councils in the 1979–1984 period. A number of other local authorities (for example, Kent County Council, South-ampton City Council, Hackney Borough Council, Lothian Regional Council) have also established economic development companies that are similar in structure but on a smaller scale than the original enterprise boards (Lawless, 1988). Enterprise boards were established as independent companies with a separate legal corporate identity but controlled by the local authority which appointed councillors as com-pany directors and received reports from the board on its activities. This structure was adopted because of the concern that local government statutes precluded local authorities from undertaking such activities. This arm's-length relationship was also thought to make boards less bureaucratic and able to respond more rapidly to particular economic situations, capable of attracting the required specialist exper-tise (such as investment appraisal) and more acceptable to the private sector (Mawson and Miller, 1986).

The abolition of the GLC and the metropolitan counties severed the legal links of four of these enterprise boards with local government. The Greater London Enterprise Board, renamed Greater London Enterprise, is now con-trolled by twelve London boroughs and the West Midlands Enterprise Board (WMEB) by all seven metropolitan district councils in the West Midlands. The West Yorkshire Enterprise Board (WYEB) has become an independent

Table 6.10   Structural characteristics of some enterprise boards

	Greater London Enterprise	Lanca-shire Enterprises plc	Lothian Enterprise Ltd	West Midlands Enterprise Board Ltd	Yorkshire Enterprise Ltd
Date of formation	1986[2]	1982	1988	1982	1982
Venture capital funds under management[1] (£m)	10.5	5.5	4.75	21	37.2
Number of investments made	31[3]	26[4]	8	56	120
Total funds invested (at cost) (£m)	9.6	5.5	0.97	15	15
Average investment (£000)	309	150	140	400	170
Mimimum investment considered (£000)	40	50	-	50	50
Minimum equity stake (%)	10	20	-	-	-
Maximum equity stake (%)	100	49	-	49	-
Average equity stake (%)	39	33.3	-	25	-
Take-up rates: (a) projects reviewed as % of those received	30	11	23	40	10
(b) investments made as % of projects reviewed	5	47	36	13	30

Notes:
1 Includes funds already committed and available for investment.
2 Originally established in 1982; re-formed in 1986.
3 1986–1989 inclusive.
4 1987–89 inclusive.
Source: Cary (1991).

company, with ex-county councillors continuing as directors, but has expanded its geographical area of operations to include the entire Yorkshire-Humberside region, being re-named Yorkshire Enterprise Ltd to reflect this change. The Merseyside Enterprise Board has also become an independent company, but five of the six Merseyside districts continue to support it (McKean and Coulson, 1987). Lancashire Enterprises Ltd (LEL) continued under the control of the county council until 1989 when it became a public company (plc) following new government restrictions on local government trading.

Enterprise boards raised their initial capital from their parent local authorities under section 137 of the 1972 Local Government Act. After the abolition of the GLC and metropolitan councils this source of funding was no longer available. However, even before abolition, enterprise boards had widened their financial base by using this public sector funding as leverage to attract additional funding from the private sector, usually in the form of syndicated investment packages, with the private sector partner taking equity or providing loan or overdraft facilities. Some enterprise boards have also raised operational funds through bank loans which have generally been secured against their property portfolio. The WMEB, which does not have a property portfolio, has attracted pension fund investment – both its parent local authority's employees' fund and general pension funds (McKean and Coulson, 1987). Ratios of non-board to board finance are 1:5 in the case of WYEB and 1:6 for LEL.

Enterprise board investments have generally taken the form of a combination of ordinary shares and preference shares, loans and, occasionally, leasing. In the case of Yorkshire Enterprise Ltd and Greater London Enterprise nearly 90 per cent of their investments have been in the form of equity or equivalent in the latest financial year for which data are available compared with 52 per cent for Lothian Enterprise Ltd and 42 per cent for the WMEB. Enterprise boards have not normally taken a majority holding (Table 6.10). For example, the WMEB normally aims to hold a maximum of 25 per cent of the ordinary share capital (McKean and Coulson, 1987). They seek ultimately to realize their investments but only when companies are able to find substitute funding and when the jobs are secure without board investment.

As a condition of receiving investment finance some boards have required companies to agree to various conditions, as set out in a planning agreement, notably relating to industrial relations conditions and practices, trade union recognition, wages and salaries, health and safety and training programmes, and specify various business and employment objectives (for example, on investment).

Making an assessment of the contribution of enterprise boards to the closing of the equity gap is complicated by the differences between boards in their philosophy, investment strategy and commercial orientation, although all of the boards have become increasingly commerical as their ties to their local author-ities have been eroded. However, with this caveat it would appear that their overall impact has been limited. First, the size of these funds is generally quite small compared with the average for the venture capital industry as a whole: of the five boards which are listed in the *VCR Guide to Venture Capital* (Cary, 1991) the largest is Yorkshire Enterprise Ltd (YEL) with £37.2 million under management (including funds already committed and available for investment), followed by WMEB with £21 million under management. The three other boards have between £5 million and £10 million under management (Greater London Enterprise, Lancashire Enterprises plc and Lothian Enterprise Ltd) (Tab-le 6.10).

Second, the larger enterprise boards in particular have tended to concentrate their investments in later stage developments and management buy-outs (Table 6.11). For example, management buy-outs account for half of the total amount invested by the WMEB and over one-third of that invested by YEL between 1986 and 1989 while later stage investments account for a further 15 per cent of the total. As a consequence, the average size of investments by enterprise

Table 6.11   Local enterprise board investments by stage of company development, 1986–89

	Greater London Enterprise		West Midlands Enterprise		Yorkshire Enterprise Ltd	
	invs	£000	invs	£000	invs	£000
Pre-start-ups	2	527	-	-	1	60
Start-ups	7	686	3	655	13	1,705
Early developments	6	2,680	3	350	23	2,119
Later developments	9	3,830	5	1,099	11	1,693
MBOs	6	1,372	11	3,194	15	4,157
Others	1	500	2	850	6	1,547
Total	31	9,595	24	6,148	69	11,281

Source: Cary (1991).

boards, while lower than that of private venture capital funds, is nevertheless either close to or above the equity gap threshold, ranging from £140,000 for Lothian Enterprise Ltd to £400,000 for WMEB (Table 6.10). These features reflect the investment strategy followed by a number of enterprise boards that has favoured investments in manufacturing and manufacturing-related sectors and in established medium-sized businesses. For example, the WMEB has primarily been concerned with filling the financial gap which has made it difficult for medium-sized manufacturing businesses to obtain development capital. The majority of its equity investments have therefore been in medium and large manufacturing firms, mainly in the key metals and foundry sectors, employing more than 50 workers. Typical situations where the WMEB has invested include: helping expansion where this was beyond the capability of existing shareholders, retained earnings or bank borrowing; financial restructuring where a company's borrowings were high in relation to its equity; management buy-outs; and mergers and takeovers which lead to increased efficiency (Marshall and Mawson, 1987). Small firms have only been eligible for assistance where they are of strategic importance to the regional economy, although it has recently established local venture capital funds to support small businesses in partnership with district councils in the region. The WYEB/YEL and MEB have followed similar investment stategies, although YEL does not follow a sectoral strategy. LEL's investments have been concentrated in smaller companies and have not been guided by any detailed economic analysis or strategy (Mawson and Miller, 1986). GLEB, in contrast, initially followed a much more radical strategy (largely abandoned following the abolition of the GLC) in which their investments – predominantly in small firms in key sectors – were designed to have wider economic, social and geographical objectives (Best, 1989).

Third, enterprise boards fund only a small proportion of the investment proposals that they receive. Their appraisal process takes into account such factors as financial structure and performance, markets and sales, products processes and production methods, personnel and industrial relations and legal and financial commitments. Those boards which operate an investment strategy which is sector based will also take the sector in which the company operates into account. Indeed, in comparison with venture capital funds, enterprise boards typically review a smaller proportion of the proposals that they receive (Table 6.10), although in most cases the proportion of proposals that are reviewed which receive investment is higher – often considerably higher – than for private venture capital funds. In the case of the WMEB, for example, it received over 1200 inquiries in its first three years of which only 57 (5 per cent) progressed to the stage of investment proposals, of which 49 (4 per cent) were subsequently approved (McKean and Coulson, 1987).

The recent Local Authority and Housing Act which restricts local authority involvement in a wide range of economic development activities has forced enterprise boards to operate independently and to become increasingly commercial in their operations (Hayton, 1989). As a result, the scope for direct local authority action to increase the supply of venture capital in the future appears to be severely circumscribed.

Regional development agencies
Regional development agencies established in Scotland and Wales in 1975 and 1976 respectively represent a further source of public sector venture capital in these regions. These agencies represent an outgrowth of a state holding company model for investment policy which was reflected nationally in the establishment of the National Enterprise Board in 1975 in 'an attempt to combine the advantages of public sector financial resources and the private sector's entrepreneurial approach to decision-making' (NEB, 1978, quoted in Grant, 1982, p. 104). Thus, while the NEB shared with private sector organizations an emphasis on commercial and financial viability, it took a longer than average view of the yield from an investment and took into account 'social considerations, notably the provision of productive employment, particularly in areas of high unemployment, and the wider national benefits and opportunities that flow from any investment.' Following the election of the Conservative government in 1979 the NEB was merged with the National Research and Development Corporation to form the British Technology Group (BTG) and its role was reduced as far as possible in the belief that the private sector would be more likely to make a success of NEB-type investments. Disposal of NEB investments to the private sector was completed in 1988. The present role of the BTG is to promote technology transfer from universities and other public sector organizations (Cary, 1991).

Despite the elimination of the NEB as a national public sector provider of venture capital, the Scottish and Welsh Development Agencies (SDA and WDA) established in the mid-1970s at least in part to replicate the function of the NEB in Scotland and Wales have continued to operate as venture capitalists. Their budgets dwarf those of the enterprise boards, although their remits are much broader. Although initially established with a view to developing a strong industrial banking function to fill the perceived equity gap in the regions, the regional development agencies rapidly acquired a much wider range of functions than the NEB, covering environmental improvement, factory building, urban renewal, industrial promotion and small business support as well as the provision of loan and equity finance. By the end of the 1970s only 8 per cent of expenditure by the SDA and WDA was accounted for by industrial investment, compared with 50 per cent on factory and industrial estate provision and over one-quarter on land renewal and environmental improvement (Cooke, 1980; 1987; Grant, 1982; Rich, 1983).

Largely on account of government pressure the operations of both agencies have become increasingly 'commercial' during the 1980s. For example, in the case of the SDA a recent government-sponsored review advocated that the investment function 'should continue to operate on a broadly commercial basis' (Industry Department for Scotland, 1987, p. 8). Other factors which have influenced this shift away from a formal interventionist approach have been the failure to achieve anything like the anticipated return on capital from the investment portfolio and the well-publicized collapse of a number of companies in which they had invested (Grant, 1982; Cooke, 1987). Both agencies now seek to play a catalytic role, identifying and investing in projects that are both commercially viable and would not otherwise be funded by the private sector, although projects must also be sufficiently attractive to encourage substantial private sector involvement alongside the agency. However, the requirement to operate in a 'commercial' manner sits uneasily with the 'development' role of each agency which involves taking a longer term view of investments than is normal for the private sector. The SDA and WDA entries in the 1991 *VCR Guide to Venture Capital* (Cary, 1991) indicate a timescale for investment realization of five to ten years and ten years respectively, compared with the typical three to seven year exit horizon of private venture capital funds.

With a combined investment portfolio of just over £100 million at cost (Cary, 1991), the investment activities of both agencies have been on a relatively significant scale: indeed, the SDA's portfolio of £73 million is larger than that of six of the eight venture capital funds based in Scotland that are listed in the *VCR Guide to Venture Capital*. Moreover, the value of the SDA's investment portfolio in the mid-1980s was one-third of that of Investors in Industry in Scotland (Industry Department for Scotland, 1987). The impact of the Scottish and Welsh Development Agencies on the supply of venture capital in their respective regions is further enhanced by their ability to achieve a leverage with their investments (1:4.9 in the case of the SDA).

The venture capital activities of the SDA and WDA are summarized in Tables 6.12 and 6.13. Over the period 1986–1989 the SDA made investments in 148 companies, with the amount invested rising from £4.2 million in 1986 to £7 million in 1988 but falling back to £6 million in 1989. Over the same period the WDA has invested in 151 companies, although the annual amount invested has fluctuated widely, between a low of £1.3 million in 1987 and a high of £4.4 million in 1988 (Table 6.12).

The pattern of investments is dominated by the start-up and early development stages. However, there are significant differences between the profile of

Table 6.12   Profile of investments by the Scottish and Welsh Development Agencies

Scottish Development Agency

Stage	1986		1987		1988		1989	
	no.	£000	no.	£000	no.	£000	no.	£000
Pre-start-ups	-	-	-	-	-	-	-	-
Start-ups	7	1,396	6	1,106	10	2,357	16	2,376
Early developments	7	1,042	12	1,261	14	1,920	9	693
Later developments	9	613	9	2,455	13	1,655	9	1,725
Management buy-outs	8	1,181	6	1,354	4	1,135	9	1,209
Others	-	-	-	-	-	-	-	-
Total	**31**	**4,232**	**33**	**6,176**	**41**	**7,067**	**43**	**6,003**

Welsh Development Agency

Stage	1986		1987		1988		1989	
	no.	£000	no.	£000	no.	£000	no.	£000
Pre-start-ups	-	-	-	-	-	-	1	7
Start-ups	21	2,493	31	767	20	2,160	15	679
Early developments	4	325	4	380	29	1,904	10	328
Later developments	-	-	-	-	-	-	5	246
Management buy-outs	1	75	2	120	5	325	2	220
Others	-	-	-	-	-	-	-	-
Total	**26**	**2,893**	**37**	**1,267**	**55**	**4,414**	**33**	**1,480**

Source: Cary (1991).

investments made by the SDA and the WDA: 58 per cent of the WDA's investments in the period were in start-ups (61 per cent by value), compared with 31 per cent in early stage investments (29 per cent by value) and 7 per cent of investments in management buy-outs. However, the proportion of investments in start-ups has declined from over 80 per cent to less than 50 per cent over the period. Investments by the SDA, by contrast, exhibit less concentration by stage of development: indeed, start-ups, early stage developments and later stage developments each account for just over one-quarter of the investments made over the period, with start-ups accounting for the largest proportion of funds invested (31 per cent). These inter-agency differences in the profile of investments made may represent different responses to different regional economic needs and patterns of investment demand as well as the particular interpretation of the remit of the agency in this type of activity. As such it re-emphasizes

Table 6.13 Profile of investments by the Scottish and Welsh Development Agencies

Scottish Development Agency: investments in the year to 31 March 1990

Stage	no.	total £000	equity £000	debt[1] £000	other £000	smallest £000	largest £000
Pre start-ups	-	-	-	-	-	-	-
Start-ups	3	635	575	60	-	85	350
Early developments	17	2205	1294	245	666	10	466
Later developments	21	1758	1316	330	112	12	313
Management buy-outs	7	1892	1725	167	-	125	313
Total	**48**	**6490**	**4910**	**802**	**778**		

Welsh Development Agency: investments in the year to 31 March 1989

Stage	no.	total £000	equity £000	debt[1] £000	other £000	smallest £000	largest £000
Pre start-ups	3	94	7	87	-	7	80
Start-ups	n/d	2544	679	1865	-	1	250
Early developments	n/d	3360	328	3032	-	1	500
Later developments	23	2094	246	1848	-	10	500
Management buy-outs	5	315	220	95	-	10	150
Total	**n/d**	**8407**	**1480**	**6927**			

1 or equivalent.
Source: Cary (1991).

the advantages of having a regionally based supply of venture capital, whether public or private sector, which can be allocated in response to regionally specific patterns of need and demand.

Both the SDA and WDA have used a combination of equity and debt financing, although there are significant differences between the agencies in the mix (Table 6.13). Of the SDA's investments in the year to 31 March 1990, three-quarters of the amount invested was in the form of equity, with almost all the remainder being loans and loan guarantees. In the case of start-ups and management buy-outs, over 90 per cent of the investment was in the form of equity. By contrast, over 80 per cent of the WDA's investments in the year to 31 March 1989 was in the form of debt finance. Equity was dominant only in management buy-outs which accounted for less than 5 per cent of the WDA's total investment by value in that year. In terms of the size of investments, irrespective of the stage of development, the WDA and SDA have made investments right across the spectrum, from £1,000 to £500,000 (Table 6.13) although the average investment size of both agencies is lower than that of the private sector venture capital industry. However, whereas the average size of investments by the SDA is £135,000 the equivalent figure for the WDA is under £50,000, reflecting the different emphasis of investment activity in terms of the stage of development funded, but as most of the WDA's smaller investments are in the form of loans the impact on the equity gap is minimal.

In contrast to the Scottish and Welsh experience, the regional development agency in Northern Ireland – the Industrial Development Board (IDB) – has had relatively little involvement in the provision of venture capital. This is despite the existence in Northern Ireland since 1976 of the Northern Ireland Development Agency (NIDA), established on the model of the NEB, SDA and WDA, with a primarily industrial banking function and a remit to set up state industries, improve and strengthen Northern Ireland firms and encourage joint ventures, acquire licences and patents and introduce these to firms in Northern Ireland (Harrison, 1990). However, as a result of strong negative experience with equity investments at the end of the 1970s, including the De Lorean sports car project (for which an aid package of over £70 million was assembled), the IDB, which took over the functions of NIDA in 1982, has not advanced equity finance to businesses except in a few rare cases. As a result, the present portfolio of £10.15 million (at cost) represents the residual holdings of equity stakes taken since 1972 (Cary, 1991). Given the experience that the SDA and WDA venture capital provision has had a catalytic effect in stimulating additional private sector venture capital investment in their regions, the failure of the IDB since 1982 to offer equity investment as part of its package of financial instruments may in part account for the fact that Northern Ireland, in relative terms, has the lowest indigenously managed supply of and utilization of venture capital in the United Kingdom.

Regional development agencies have therefore played a significant role in the provision of venture capital in Scotland, but to a lesser extent in Wales and have had virtually no impact in Northern Ireland. However, over the course of the 1980s under pressure from government both the SDA and the WDA have adopted an increasingly commercial, 'modified market' approach rather than the formal interventionist approach originally envisaged which incorporated non-financial criteria in investment decision-making. Thus, both agencies are increasingly acting like, and in some cases, duplicating, private sector funds. At the same time, both agencies are progressively reducing their commitment to venture capital provision, which is in any case a minor part of their overall portfolio of activities, as the private sector provision develops. This trend seems likely to accelerate with the merger of the SDA and the Training Agency in Scotland to create Scottish Enterprise which will be dominated by business interests.

Summary

The evidence reviewed in this section clearly shows that there has been a significant increase in the availability of equity capital in the UK during the 1980s.

Indeed, the volume of capital raised and invested by UK venture capital funds is larger than anywhere else in Europe. It has also been claimed – although also disputed (ACOST, 1990) – that by the mid-1980s the amount raised was proportionately larger than in the USA (measured in terms of the amount raised as a proportion of GDP).

At the same time, there is no doubt that the equity gap remains, even though many suppliers of risk capital claim that there is a surfeit of money available looking for sound propositions. Whereas in 1971 the Bolton Committee identified the equity gap as existing for amounts of under £250,000, however – around £1 million at today's prices – most commentators suggest that the present equity gap lies in the range £200,000 to £250,000 at 1991 prices.

This apparent paradox – the emergence of new sources of equity capital co-existing with a persistent equity gap – is easily resolved. As the ACOST (1990) report notes: 'In a well-developed capital market there will be a *spectrum* of institutional mechanisms to finance business experimentation and growth' (p. 30, emphasis added). However, the increase in the availability of equity capital since the Bolton Report has occurred across a relatively narrow spectrum. Specifically, the increase in the availability of equity capital is largely restricted to established companies seeking to raise large amounts of capital. Access to the USM is restricted to larger, growing small businesses. A large and increasing proportion of venture capital has been invested in management buy-outs and buy-ins and there has been very little investment in start-ups and early stage investments, especially in technology-based sectors, and in amounts of under £250,000. Large property-related and asset-backed ventures, and more recently rented housing schemes, have attracted the majority of funds invested through the BES. Enterprise boards and regional development agencies have also failed to fill the equity gap adequately. Hall and Lewis (1988) criticize them for failing to concentrate their investments on projects which are unable to raise finance from other sources, for seeking a normal commercial rate of return (because many have raised their funds from private institutional sources that require a commercial return), adopting a conservative investment strategy and emphasizing loan rather than equity financing.

The continued shortage of smaller amounts of equity capital, particularly for seed, start-up and early stage finance and for technology-based ventures, is therefore largely a reflection of supply-side gaps. This point is recognized by ACOST (1990) which notes that in comparison to the US there are 'two points on the capital market spectrum which are much less well-developed in the UK: namely, corporate venturing and informal networks of private venture capital investors' (p. 37). The extent to which these sources of risk capital exist in the UK is examined in the following section.

Ideas from America: corporate venturing and informal venture capital

Corporate venturing

Corporate venturing is defined by NEDC (1987, p. 1) as 'a partnership scheme between large and small companies' for the purpose of generating business development opportunities by combining the different strengths of large and small companies in the innovation process while sharing the risks. The normal process is for the large company to make a minority equity investment in the small business. The investment process can take various forms: (i) direct minority equity investment in a small company; (ii) investment via an independent venture capital fund to which the large company subscribes; (iii) investment via an internally-managed venture capital fund; (iv) investment in spin-outs of separate business activities or technologies from the large company.

The benefits of corporate venturing for the large firm are extremely varied – diversification; an opportunity to study new markets and technologies; commercialization of internally-developed technology which for various reasons (such as lack of specific expertise, insufficient market potential) it does not wish to exploit; spreading the financial burden of R & D; benefiting from the flexibility of small business; and identification of possible future acquisitions or joint venture opportunities. The advantages for small firms, apart from the provision of finance, include access to the management skills, marketing expertise and distribution networks of the large company; production and R & D support; more sophisticated financial control and advice; and increased credibility with customers, suppliers and financial institutions (Ormerod and Burns, 1988; Oakley, 1987; NEDC, 1987).

In the US corporate venturing is estimated to account for some 10 per cent of the total venture capital pool (ACOST, 1990). In the UK, by contrast, industrial corporations have accounted for an average of 5 per cent of the capital for independent venture capital funds over the 1984–1988 period, leading Pratt (1990, p. 80) to conclude that 'established companies remain . . . a relatively minor source of capital for venture capital investment'. The low level of corporate venturing activity in the UK is confirmed by the NEDC (1987) study, which estimated that only about 20 companies had engaged in corporate venturing. Moreover, most of the companies engaged in corporate venturing are subsidiaries of foreign companies. ACOST (1990, p. 38) has therefore concluded that 'corporate venturing appears to be a greatly underdeveloped aspect of the UK capital market with considerable significance for the growth prospects of smaller firms'.

Informal investment

ACOST (1990, p. 38) comments that 'a striking feature of the US capital market is the substantial but unorganized involvement of the private investor'. Informal investors – or 'business angels' – are private investors who provide risk capital directly to unquoted companies. Informal investment is the largest single source of risk capital in the US (Wetzel, 1986a; Gaston, 1989). Wetzel (1986a, p. 121) suggests that they 'finance as many as twenty times the number of firms financed by institutional venture capitalists', while 'the aggregate amount they invest is perhaps twice as big' (Wetzel, 1986b, p. 88). Gaston (1989) suggests that informal investors provide capital to over forty times the number of firms receiving investments from professional venture capital funds, and the amount of their investments almost exceeds all other sources of external equity capital for new and growing small businesses combined. Informal investors are particularly important in providing relatively small amounts of risk capital – below the amounts typically considered by institutional venture capital funds – and in providing seed and start-up finance: Freear and Wetzel (1988, p. 353) note that 'private individuals are most prominent at the early stages of a firm's development, when relatively small amounts are involved, and in those later stage financings involving under $1 million'. Thus, informal investors and venture capital funds play complementary roles.

The informal risk capital market is much less fully developed in the UK. ACOST (1990, p. 39) considers this 'to be a major gap in the spectrum of funds for smaller companies and a major contribution to barriers to their growth'. The Wilson Committee highlighted the decline in the availability of equity capital for small businesses from private investors – the so-called 'Aunt Agatha' figure, or what Bolton termed 'the rich uncle', namely wealthy relatives and family friends and local businessmen, accountants, lawyers and other professionals. The committee's interim report commented that:

> In the past it was not unusual for businessmen and other individuals to make investments in local businesses known to them, or in those of relatives. Such investments were often made on flexible terms, were often more like equity in the servicing and repayment obligations they carried, even when nominally in the form of loans, and were not always motivated entirely by hopes of a quick, or substantial return on capital. They are now becoming increasingly rare.
>
> (HM Government, 1979, pp. 12–13).

The Wilson Committee offered a number of reasons for the demise of 'Aunt Agatha'. Changes in the distribution of wealth and income since 1945 as a result of high rates of personal taxation and inheritance tax which have led to wider ownership of more modest levels of wealth appear to have increased the aversion to risk and the premium attached to liquidity. This has been accentuated by fiscal changes which have made it more difficult to realize assets in private companies. In addition there has been an expansion in institutional saving such as pensions, life assurance and other insurance linked schemes as a result of their favourable tax treatment. Over-consumption of housing has also been attractive not only because of the availability of tax relief on mortgages but also because of the tax-free capital gains resulting from the escalation of house prices.

There is growing evidence that private individuals have re-emerged during the 1980s 'as an alternative source of finance in Britain for the small company which is unable to raise money from more conventional sources' (Batchelor, 1988, p. 9). However, the nature of the private investor has changed: he (or very occasionally she) is now more likely to be a successful entrepreneur rather than a relative or family friend. The evidence is of three kinds: articles in the financial press (for example, Batchelor, 1988; 1989a; 1989b), the creation of financial match-making organizations such as Venture Capital Report (Cary, 1991) and LINC which introduce investors to small businesses seeking finance, and initial findings from the first ever study of the informal risk capital market in the UK (Mason and Harrison, 1991c; Mason *et al*, 1991).

The emergence of business angels in the UK during the 1980s seems likely to reflect the greater opportunities for wealth accumulation by entrepreneurs and senior managers in industry and commerce for whom an informal investment may be an attractive speculative investment. Until recently, high rates of taxation made it difficult for such people to accumulate sufficient amounts of disposable capital; most was either tied up in their own businesses or saved through tax-efficient institutional channels (ACOST, 1990). However, the tendency for salaries of senior employees to increase disproportionately, the increasing use of stock options offering the prospect of capital gain, cuts in the top rate of income tax, 'golden handshakes', generous early retirement incentives to senior managers made redundant, high levels of acquisition of small owner-managed companies by the corporate sector and the creation of the USM and Third Market to enable entrepreneurs to sell stakes in their companies have all contributed to an increase in the number of business people with disposable wealth. Anecdotal evidence suggests that the small business sector is often viewed as an attractive 'alternative' investment for some of this newly acquired capital (Batchelor, 1989a; Cary, 1991).

Mason and Harrison's interim findings (1991c; Mason *et al*, 1991) indicate that informal investors are almost exclusively male and most are 45 years old and over. The overwhelming majority have business backgrounds. Most informal investors are business owners, business managers and chief executives and business-related professionals (accountants, company secretaries, consultants). Moreover, most are also experienced entrepreneurs. Three-quarters of informal investors have founded at least one business (in two-thirds of cases more than one business). Many of these entrepreneurs have subsequently sold these businesses. Informal investors are well off but certainly not 'rich': their average income is just under £50,000 and their net worth (excluding principal residence) exceeds £100,000. However, relatively few have very high incomes or are millionaires.

Angels make informal risk capital investments primarily for financial reasons, notably because of the opportunity for high capital appreciation. However, non-financial motives, including the opportunity to play a role in the entrepreneurial process and the fun of making informal investments, are very important secondary investment motives for a significant proportion of angels. The key factors that they take into account when evaluating investment opportunities are the entrepreneur and the management team and the growth potential of the market.

The typical business angel is a relatively infrequent investor, investing once every 18 months on average, although a small minority are more active investors. They generally inject very small amounts of capital into the firms in which they invest – typically less than £10,000. Only a minority of angels commit more than £50,000 to a single investment. However, investments that are syndicated between a number of investors involve considerably larger amounts. The majority of business angels are minority shareholders in the companies in which they invest. Informal investors invest in virtually all industrial sectors and at all stages of company development. However, they have a strong preference for investing in companies that are located fairly close to where they live and work (typically within 100 miles). Most business angels are 'hands on' investors, playing an active role in the operations of the firms in which they invest. Most business angels are moderately patient investors and anticipate holding their investments for up to five years and in a significant minority of cases for longer. Sale to another company and stock market flotation are the most commonly anticipated exit routes.

A particularly significant finding is that most business angels in the UK want to invest more but cannot find sufficient investment opportunities that meet their investment criteria. Nearly three-quarters of the investors in our survey would have invested more in the previous three years if they had come across a greater number of suitable investment opportunities. Indeed, on average informal investors have £100,000 available for investment, compared with the average of £29,000 that they have invested during the three years prior to the survey. In aggregate, the amount available for investment is four times the aggregate amount that they have invested during the previous three years. The informal risk capital market is therefore a largely untapped source of funds for small businesses seeking venture capital.

There is as yet no evidence to indicate the size of the informal risk capital pool in the UK or its significance as a source of equity capital. A study of businesses on UK science parks, however, noted that 2 per cent of firms used private equity capital at start-up and 3 per cent had private investors as a current source of finance. This compares with 3 per cent of firms that had raised start-up finance from venture capital funds and 8 per cent of firms whose current sources of finance included venture capital (Monck *et al*, 1988). A national stratified random sample of businesses with less than 50 full-time employees found that 2 per cent of firms raised equity from private investors (Mason and Harrison, 1990). It can be inferred from the shareholding structure of a sample of small plastics manufacturing firms (Peters, 1989) that up to 5 per cent had raised finance from informal investors. Extrapolating these proportions and the amounts invested and available for investment by informal investors to the population of unquoted companies in the UK suggests that the size of the informal capital pool in the UK may be in the order of £3 billion to £5 billion – a significant sum when set against the £1.1 bn invested in the UK by the venture capital industry during 1990 (BVCA, 1991).

Conclusion

Developments in the supply of equity finance since the publication of the Bolton Report, and particularly since about 1980, have undoubtedly contributed to the closing of the equity gap. However, there is general, if not unanimous, agreement that an equity gap remains. The causes are undoubtedly a combination of demand and supply factors. Many small business owner-managers continue to reject raising external equity because of their resistance, for whatever reason, to sharing control and profits with outsiders. Others fail to appreciate both the dangers of a reliance on debt finance and the benefits of equity finance. On the supply-side, developments since Bolton have clearly mitigated the financing problems experienced by the small business sector. They have not, however, removed this constraint on small business formation and growth. Recent developments in the supply of equity finance have been largely restricted to meeting requirements of firms seeking amounts over £250,000 and so have had limited impact on companies seeking smaller amounts. It is at this level of the capital market that an equity gap continues to exist. This gap is primarily encountered by new and recent start-ups, with technology-based firms and companies in the north facing particular difficulties.

A need remains to promote new sources of finance to fill these capital gaps. The most widely canvassed proposal has been the creation of venture capital funds specializing in seed and start-up investments. For example, ACOST (1990, p. 36) has argued that 'the further development of the "seed capital" sector of the industry . . . is essential if the rate of business experimentation is to be increased to the national advantage'. This is unlikely to occur without government intervention, however, because of the economics of the appraisal and monitoring process, the very active hands-on role required and the need to make a larger number of investments in order to get a reasonable spread of risk – all of which contribute to the high costs of operating a seed capital fund. The British Venture Capital Association (BVCA) has estimated that the real cost of running a seed fund is between £150,000 and £200,000, depending upon its location, which represents an unacceptably high proportion of the funds under management (BVCA, 1989). It is difficult, therefore, for venture capital funds specializing in seed and start-up investments to operate under conventional commercial criteria.

Initiatives to change the economic structure of such funds are required to stimulate the availability of seed and start-up capital. Government has, however, been unwilling to provide financial support for a BVCA proposal to establish a dozen regional seed capital funds and some of the funds supported by the European Community's Seed Capital Initiative, which contributes towards their operating costs and the capital resources, have found it difficult to raise sufficient finance (Merchant, 1990). An alternative proposal – that the appraisal and monitoring costs incurred by seed and start-up funds could be reduced using local intermediaries such as local enterprise agencies, chambers of commerce or science park directors to undertake such functions – can be criticized on the grounds that such intermediaries might lack the necessary specialist expertise to perform this work. A further difficulty is that seed capital requires different skills to those of the remainder of the venture capital industry. The managing director of one of the few firms that specializes in seed capital investments comments that 'seed capital is rather an oddball activity. It doesn't really fit with venture capital' (*Viewpoint*, May/June 1990, p. 34). As a result, there is a shortage of venture capital executives with experience of seed capital investments. Recent local government legislation has severely curtailed the scope for local authorities to establish public sector funds specializing in seed and start-up funds.

Significant constraints exist, therefore, to limit the establishment of venture capital funds providing seed and start-up funds. Another approach is to seek ways in which corporate venturing can be stimulated. However, there has been very little growth in corporate venturing activity since the NEDC (1987) report and the associated promotional campaign, despite the establishment of a register of potential corporate investors and investment opportunities by the National Economic Development Office to promote the concept of corporate venturing. This register is run by Base International. A more promising strategy may, therefore, be to encourage the development of the informal risk capital market. Indeed, informal investors are probably the main source of equity capital for firms seeking amounts within the equity gap. However, it is a largely invisible, fragmented and unorganized market, which renders it difficult to access by small firms. Because of these market inefficiencies it is a market largely untapped by small firms.

Two steps can be taken (Mason and Harrison, 1991a).

First, there is a need to enlarge the pool of informal risk capital in the UK by making the tax treatment of equity investment in unquoted companies no less advantageous than other forms of saving in order to encourage private investors to put some of their disposable wealth into smaller companies (ACOST, 1990). The BES already provides tax incentives for personal equity investments in unquoted companies. However, as already noted, it was increasingly failing to fill the equity gap and, following its extension to include investments in private rented housing, the scheme has largely ceased to be a source of risk capital for small firms. It therefore needs to be revised along the lines suggested by Mason *et al* (1988) to ensure that after 1993, when the extension of the Scheme to include rented housing ends, it can achieve its original goal of stimulating private investments in small companies. Two changes are of particular importance. First, property-related and asset-related businesses should be excluded as they are clearly against the original spirit of the scheme and attract investors looking for low-risk tax shelters. A further refinement would be to grade the tax relief according to the type of company (for example, by age, by sector) in which the investment is made. Second, since most informal investors wish to play an active role in the companies in which they invest, the rules that exclude investors who are 'closely connected' with the company in which they invest should be relaxed. It is also important that a maximum company funding limit, originally introduced in 1988, is retained to prevent companies from using the scheme to raise amounts that are well in excess of the equity gap upper threshold and to avoid the situation whereby a large proportion of the total finance raised through the Scheme is invested in a relatively small number of companies.

Second, there is a need to mobilize the pool of informal risk capital more effectively by establishing mechanisms for bringing investors into contact with businesses seeking equity capital, and vice versa. The invisibility of informal investors, the fragmented nature of the market and the imperfect channels of communication between bona fide entrepreneurs seeking risk capital and investors seeking investment opportunities create a 'discouragement effect' –

analogous to the discouraged worker effect in labour markets – which curtails the search for equity capital by both entrepreneurs and would-be entrepreneurs and the search by would-be business angels for investment opportunities, to the detriment of economic development.

A major expansion in the number of financial match-making services would provide an efficient channel of communication to introduce potential investors to entrepreneurs seeking finance, and vice versa. Such services should be established on a regional or sub-regional basis since most investors prefer to invest in businesses located close at hand. However, all of the available evidence suggests that such services cannot be operated as a profit-making activity (Mason and Harrison, 1991c). Some form of public sector support is, therefore, likely to be required to achieve a significant increase in the amount of financial matchmaking activity in the UK which, in turn, is necessary to enable businesses to tap the available pool of informal venture capital more effectively. The justification for this support is that 'an active informal venture capital market is a pre-requisite for a vigorous enterprise economy' (ACOST, 1990, p. 41). This should be accompanied by the development of regional markets to overcome the difficulties of trading shares of small unquoted companies to facilitate the informal investment process.

7 The Small Business Owner-Manager

In the twenty years since the publication of the Bolton Report a mass of research has attempted to decipher the background determinants of small business ownership. This research has sought to discover if there are any clear characteristics shared by the owners of small businesses that distinguish them from other members of the economically active population. The general conclusion appears to be that there is no simple pattern. Rather, the evidence points towards a complex set of interrelated factors that increase or decrease the probability that an individual will become the owner of a small business.

Research on this subject comes from a number of social science disciplines, prime among which are psychology, geography and sociology. This academic division of labour is not surprising when one considers the factors likely to have an impact upon whether a person runs a small business or not – individual factors; situational or contextual factors; socio-economic background factors. These three factors interact with each other in complex ways: the attributes of a locality provide a context within which individuals with different socio-economic backgrounds and different psychological dispositions operate; psychological disposition is often a function of socio-economic background and the milieu of the locality; socio-economic background is partly conditioned by the nature of the locality and the psychological disposition of the individual concerned; and so on. However, for analytic purposes these three broad headings provide useful headings under which the existing research literature can be organized.

Characteristics of owner-managers

The idea that the small firm, owner-managed sector is heterogeneous was made explicit by the Bolton Commission of Inquiry.

> When we come to look at the human and social factors affecting [small firms] we can see that firms are, in fact, as varied and individual as the men who founded them.
>
> (Bolton, 1971, p. 22)

In describing the 'human and social characteristics' of the business owner-manager, however, Bolton emphasized their commonalities. For example, founders were likely to be both owners and managers, and supported by family; their closeness to the firm, Bolton suggests, explains their involvement, flexibility, special role in innovation and risk-taking, and their fervently guarded sense of independence. Money, it was suggested, was *not* their prime source of motivation: there is a quality of life issue; personal involvement in owning and managing one's own firm led to greater satisfaction on a number of fronts all associated with the notion of 'independence'.

Indeed, the Bolton Report distinguished owner-managers from other businessmen on this single criterion: 'the need to attain and preserve independence':

> Thus need for 'independence' sums up a wide range of highly personal gratifications provided by working for oneself and not for anybody else. It embraces many important satisfactions which running a small business provided – the personal supervision and control of staff, direct contact with customers, the opportunity to develop one's own ideas, a strong feeling of personal challenge and an almost egotistical sense of personal achievement and pride – psychological satisfactions which appeared to be much more powerful motivators than money or the possibility of large financial gains.
>
> (Bolton, 1971, p. 23)

Two difficulties are implied by this zealously guarded need for independence. First, growth of the business might affect the freedoms enjoyed by the owner-manager should he be obliged to delegate his authority to others or seek external sources of finance. Secondly, his attitude to government assistance was that it was perceived to be an undesirable intervention. 'Having rejected "the boss", respondents didn't want to suffer paternalism of Government or anyone else for that matter . . . ' (Bolton, 1971, p. 24).

Further, owner-managers were less likely to have pursued a formal education than were those holding managerial positions in large organizations. This was because owner-managers were much more likely to have followed in their father's footsteps, and that an individual's managerial role in a large organization required that they be articulate and able to muster persuasive arguments skilfully in order to win support and win the freedom to act in ways they saw fit.

Bolton singled out the craftsman for special attention. This is:

> a small and highly specialised segment of the small firm population: the independent craftsmen, who may be defined as self-employed, small scale producers of articles of high quality in a number of different, usually traditional, media. An arbitrary definition of 'the crafts' has been sanctioned by long acceptance: it includes, for example, pottery, jewellery, stone masonry, woodwork, art metalwork, calligraphy and glassware, but not, say painting, sculpture, fashion design and photography.
>
> (Bolton, 1971, p. 146)

The craftsman resents having to spend time on paperwork and administration even more than the owner-manager. Ideally he would prefer to spend all his time working with his hands and making things of beauty; the independence achieved through self-employment enables him to express his creativity in a way which working for someone else would not allow. However, his salesmanship is weak and this may present a threat to the continued viability of the business.

So although the Bolton Commission starts out by emphasizing the heterogeneity of small firm owner-managers, in large part it paints a very homogeneous picture, singling out an extreme genre that, it seems, underscores certain key characteristics of the owner-manager rather than presents an alternative type.

In 20 years of research since Bolton, how has this view of the characteristics of the owner-manager developed? Does a homogeneous view predominate? Are the same characteristics identified as being the fundamental ones? What differences, if any, have emerged and what are the implications of these in policy and research terms?

There would be little point considering this question of the nature and characteristics of business owners if it were not for the fact that such knowledge might enable us to gain a better understanding of the way in which economic, educational or other conditions might be manipulated in order to stimulate small business behaviour in a socially and economically beneficial way. We therefore have to ask the question: What stance do the economists take on this matter and in what ways have psychologists and sociologists developed useful, explanatory models of business owner characteristics and behaviour? First, though, we have to delimit business owner typologies.

Typologies of business owners

Attempts to differentiate between different types of business owner have been a preoccupation of some notable industrial sociologists. The seminal works of Collins, Moore and Unwalla (1964) and of Smith (1967) were the cornerstones of this work. Collins and his colleagues distinguished 'entrepreneurs' from 'hierarchs' who were in effect salaried managers. Smith using the same sample concentrated on the entrepreneurs which he split into 'craftsmen' and 'opportunists'.

Smith found that craftsmen came from blue-collar backgrounds, had a relatively narrow education, a good record as successful workers, and had identified in the past with plant operations rather than top management. As owner-managers they were paternalistic, utilized personal relationships in marketing, restricted their sources of finance to personal savings and money from family or friends and followed relatively rigid strategies.

In contrast, his description of opportunistic entrepreneurs was that they had middle-class backgrounds, a broader education, a variety of work experience, and a past identification with management. They were very much market-oriented, continually sought new possibilities and new opportunities. They delegated more, sought many sources of finance, were proactive and developed more innovative and diverse competitive strategies. The firms founded by opportunistic entrepreneurs experienced much higher growth rates than those of the craftsmen.

There have been a number of criticisms of this two-fold typology (Woo *et al*, 1988). Indeed, several subsequent studies indicated the existence of three 'types' which were variously labelled (see review by Hornaday, 1990), the craftsman, artisan or small business owner; the opportunist, promoter or entrepreneur; the administrator, manager or trustee. Hornaday suggests that from this a three-fold typology of small business owners might be derived.

The craftsman is a small business owner who practises a trade, craft or occupation; he 'makes the product or provides the service and enjoys doing it'.

The promoter is a small business owner whose main intention is the pursuit of personal wealth through doing 'deals', founding, growing and selling firms without regret.

The professional manager is a small business owner whose primary aim is building an organization and who attempts to maintain controlled growth and structure his firm as a 'little big business' (Hornaday, 1990, p. 29).

There are a number of detailed criticisms which may be made of this particular typology. For example, it has not been tested; the term 'craft' is being used in a particular way and not in the sense used by Bolton (1971); the term 'entrepreneur' is deliberately excluded from the model; and, the 'promoter' is represented primarily as a 'fast buck artist'. However, a more fundamental criticism is that typologies such as these are not based upon general principles, that is, they have not been developed by considering the theory of categorization.

There are several features of categorization which the seminal work of Rosch and her colleagues (Rosch *et al*, 1976) have brought to light. They are that (i) categories can be arranged hierarchically, and (ii) that things, objects, animals and so on tend to be included in or excluded from membership of a category on the basis of their resemblance to existing members of the category. For example, desks, tables and chairs are types of furniture. Roll-top desks, dining tables, coffee tables and armchairs are in turn types of desk, table or chair respectively. 'Furniture' is the all-embracing category or *superordinate category* as Rosch would term it; desks, tables and chairs are *basic level* categories, while roll-top desks, coffee tables and so on are what she termed *subordinate level* categories. Moreover, chairs tend to resemble other chairs, tables other tables and so on; people do not apply a set of rules or rigid criteria for saying a chair is a chair, or a table is a table.

How does this help us understand the variety of types of business owner? Chell and her colleagues have suggested that the term 'business owner' is on a par with the term 'furniture' – that is, it is a superordinate category (Chell *et al*, 1991). The terms promoter, professional manager and craftsman are attempts, in this case by Hornaday, to develop an exclusive set of basic level categories.

Economic psychology of entrepreneurship

What function does a business owner/entrepreneur serve in an economy? It is too easy to offer a simplistic answer to such a question when economists since the early eighteenth century have put forward differing, closely argued views (see, for example, Hebert and Link, 1988; Chell *et al*, 1991). An emerging view of particular interest is that economists have become increasingly interested in, and made shrewd observations about, the crucial characteristics that differentiate types of business owner, and in particular those that characterize the *successful* entrepreneur.

One of the earliest views was that of Cantillon (1755) who suggested that an entrepreneur engages in exchanges for profit in the face of uncertain market conditions. Here the model of the market trader or arbitrageur supplying goods and adjusting the price of these goods according to fluctuating (uncertain) market conditions is the appropriate one to consider. This model presents a useful starting point because it indicates three features of the situation facing the person engaged in business activities – making judgemental decisions in the face of uncertainty; the nature, extent and type of risk being taken; the extent to which demand might be manipulated through innovation.

Several schools of thought emerged over the next two centuries, with economists taking different positions in respect of these three issues. Others made some intriguing comments about the types and characteristics of business owner/entrepreneurs. Francis A. Walker (1840–97), for example, suggested that

> the successful conduct of business requires exceptional abilities and opportunities. Successful entrepreneurs have the power of foresight, a facility for organization and administration, unusual energy and leadership qualities which are generally in short supply.

Interestingly he distinguished four types of entrepreneur: the rarely gifted person; those with high ordered talent; those that do reasonably well in business; and the ne'er-do-wells. He identified characteristics with each type:

> The rarely gifted person has the power of foresight, is firm and resolute even in the face of disaster, and is able to motivate and lead others. Persons with a high ordered talent have a natural mastery, they are wise, prompt and resolute. Those who do reasonably well in business tend to do so through diligence rather than flair or genius, whereas the ne'er-do-wells have perhaps misidentified their vocation and, consequently, they suffer mixed fortunes. This classification conjures up a variety of images of the personality characteristics of business owners and entrepreneurs.
>
> (Chell *et al*, 1991, p. 20)

In this view, the profit accrued to the business owner/entrepreneur was the return for his/her skill, ability or talent. Other economists, notably Knight (1921) took a different view of profit; it was a consequence of economic change in conditions of uncertainty.

Several notable economists made the distinction between managing a business and behaving in an opportunistic, innovative or, what we might term, entrepreneurial way (for example, Marshall, 1920; Schumpeter, 1934). Indeed, Knight's theory of uncertainty also helps clarify the boundary between the manager and the entrepreneur. Making a judgement in conditions of uncertainty and assuming the responsibility for its correctness is the mark of an entrepreneur, not a business *manager* (and see Chapter 10).

Joseph Schumpeter's view of entrepreneurial behaviour stands in marked contrast to those of earlier theorists in that he suggested that the entrepreneur was a dynamic force whose innovative behaviour disturbed the economic equilibrium. Such innovativeness created a fundamental shift in so far as it produced 'new combinations' of factors of production. Clearly not all innovative behaviour is of this catalytic type. Binks and Vale (1990) suggest that there are three types of economic behaviour, or 'events', as they term them. Such events have implications for the nature of the opportunity open to the business owner. The concept of the 'catalytic' event is inspired by Schumpeter's concept of innovation : it stands for the 'genuinely new' instigated with 'the uncertain prospect of monopoly profits' (ibid., p. 41). The 'allocating' event occurs as a consequence of the catalytic. That is, innovation creates market opportunities which the alert business owner/entrepreneur will then exploit. The 'refining' event, however, is rather different. This concerns the optimal or efficient allocation of resources. Competitive pressures, for example, will result in attempts to increase efficiency of plant and the human resource. Endeavours to strike productivity deals or to purchase the latest technology in order to increase efficiency are instances of refining activities.

In practice, it may be difficult to identify a truly catalytic event until the impact upon the industry becomes evident. Certainly, Binks and Vale emphasize, it does not mean simply founding a 'new' business; it is a transforming process. Business owners who can engage in such activity are undoubtedly rare, but there are many more who can spot the opportunities to be exploited in the wake of such an event. Allocating and refining behaviours are more common, though the latter more so under competitive conditions (Chell *et al*, 1991).

Further consideration of contemporary approaches shows that Casson (1982) has come closest to developing a theory that combines the functional and indicative models of the entrepreneurial type. He presents the idea that an entrepreneur is someone who specializes in taking judgemental decisions about the co-ordination of scarce resources. This idea of the judgemental decision is central to Casson's idea of the entrepreneur. It is a decision 'where different individuals, sharing the same objectives and acting under similar circumstances, would make different decisions' (ibid., p. 24). They would make different decisions because they have 'different perceptions of the situation' as a result of different information or interpretation. The entrepreneur is therefore a person whose judgement differs from that of other business owners. His or her 'reward' arises from being prepared to back his or her judgement and being right. Casson defines the term 'co-ordination' as the 'beneficial reallocation of resources'; a dynamic concept intended to capture the entrepreneur as an agent of change. The qualities which enable the entrepreneur to be proficient in all aspects of decision-making are fundamental to the success of the undertaking. Such qualities – imagination and foresight – are scarce and it is the possession of them that confers an advantage.

Implicit in this analysis of entrepreneurial behaviour is the idea of a 'vision' of what the nature of the business is and where the entrepreneur wishes to take it. How clear this vision is, and how it takes shape, is perhaps a matter of some conjecture (Filion, 1990).

What is it that can be said to emerge from this very brief examination of entrepreneurial behaviour? It would appear that there is a distinct set of characteristic behaviours that determine entrepreneurial acts on the part of business owners. They may be distinguished from those behaviours which are essentially those of management. Such entrepreneurial characteristics are rare. One interpretation of this is that not all business owners are entrepreneurs; another is that business owners occasionally behave entrepreneurially – some so rarely as not to be noticed, others a great deal more frequently. The essential ingredient appears to be the ability of the entrepreneur to perceive opportunity due to his imagination and foresight. The other side of this coin is that the situation – that is, the opportunity – must also be present. The view that the entrepreneur is a dynamic force – an agent of change – is implied by the notion of his exploitation of opportunities. However, in order to do this he must manage the resources at his disposal effectively. The necessary conditions for successful business development would appear to be: the presence and perception of an opportunity, and its imaginative exploitation through skilful deployment of resources in pursuit of the realization of a vision of what the business might become.

Trait psychology

The economists have used the term 'entrepreneur' to refer to any business owner or founder. Their primary interest is the impact of entrepreneurial behaviour upon an economy. It is now clear that many economists have attempted to identify those characteristics that they believe typify entrepreneurial acts. Have the psychologists followed this lead with a systematic investigation of such entrepreneurial traits?

Neither economics nor psychology is an exact science, and the attempt to identify and 'measure' personality characteristics is fraught with difficulties. Bearing this in mind, it is perhaps not surprising that attempts to identify single 'traits' or personality characteristics of entrepreneurs have been roundly criticized – many technical problems and issues having been identified. For example:

- the lack of an agreed definition of key concepts such as 'entrepreneur' (Carsrud *et al*, 1986)
- the unhelpful separation of investigations into two divisions: small business research and entrepreneurship (Wortman, 1986)
- the equivocal nature of the findings, that is, studies of the same trait showed conflicting results (Chell and Haworth, 1990)
- the problem of external validity – that is, being able to demonstrate a link between key personality characteristics and business performance (Begley and Boyd, 1986)

- the absence of a coherent, theoretical framework or research paradigm by which means the nature of the entrepreneur could be systematically explored and a bank of information collected (Carsrud *et al.*, 1986; Chell and Haworth, 1988; Haworth, 1988)
- the variety of research tools utilized, making comparison difficult (Wortman, 1986)
- the tendency to 'reinvent the wheel' and thereby only make *apparent* progress (Sexton, 1987)
- the theoretical problems with the trait concept and the methodology for measuring traits (Chell, 1985; Hampson, 1982; Mischel, 1973; Stevenson and Sahlman, 1989)
- the need to identify constellations of personality characteristics and not simply single traits (Chell *et al*, 1991) and to relate them to criteria of business success (McClelland, 1987; Timmons *et al*, 1985)
- the need to consider the context and so develop a *social* psychological paradigm of business owner/entrepreneurial behaviour (Chell, 1985; Chell *et al*, 1991)
- the need to understand business owner/entrepreneurial behaviour in relation to their values, attitudes and goals for the business (Hornaday, 1990; STRATOS, 1990).

This list of difficulties is now long and formidable; and it might be argued that this is sufficient reason to abandon the trait approach. However, progress is being made. To view this in perpsective, it may be instructive to take a critical look at some of the studies that purport to identify entrepreneurial traits – for example, need for achievement (McClelland, 1961); risk-taking propensity (Brockhaus, 1980b); locus of control (Brockhaus, 1982; Caird, 1989, 1990); independence (Collins and Moore, 1970); innovation/creativity (Kanter, 1983).

Need for achievement
McClelland claimed that the characteristic 'need for achievement' is a fundamental characteristic of entrepreneurs. But does need for achievement drive people to become entrepreneurs (McClelland, 1961)? Or does success in business heighten the owner's achievement orientation (Brockhaus and Horwitz, 1986)? Furthermore, does achievement orientation result in higher performing businesses? McClelland and his co-workers have designed training courses to develop the achievement motive in small business owners in developing countries and have reported that the performance of their businesses has improved significantly (McClelland and Winter, 1971; Miron and McClelland, 1979).

Are entrepreneurs higher in need for achievement than say, chief executive officers (CEOs) of publicly quoted companies? In what respects are other types of business owner *not* achievement-oriented? What kinds of criteria are being used for validation purposes and are they always appropriate? For example, take the craftsperson in the sense espoused by Bolton. Such business owners perform their craft in relation to an internalized set of standards which, along with their artistic abilities, enable them to create things of beauty. Measuring the performance of their businesses in terms of economic indicators may not indicate success. Thus, an understanding of the business owner's personal values and their instrumental orientation in conducting their business affairs seems to be fundamental in order to investigate such personality constructs as achievement motivation.

Locus of control

Locus of control is another personality construct said to be associated closely with business founding. As Brockhaus and Horwitz (1986) put it: 'Individuals who cannot believe in the ability to control the environment through their actions would be reluctant to assume the risks that starting a business entails' (p. 27).

Those people who believe that they can exercise such control over their environment are said to have an *internal* locus of control, whereas people who believe that chance, fate and powerful others exercise a dominating influence over their lives are said to have an *external* locus of control (Rotter, 1966). The problem is that one can easily construct an argument to suggest that managers and CEOs could conceivably have a higher internal locus of control than the population at large (Chell *et al*, 1991). Indeed, the evidence is so conflicting that it is possible both to support the conclusion that business founders and non-founders cannot be distinguished by their locus of control scores (Brockhaus and Nord, 1979; Begley and Boyd, 1986), and that they can (Caird, 1990).

Brockhaus (1982) has reviewed the conflicting evidence, pointing out that those people with an internal locus of control are also likely to have a high need for achievement. Such a proposition in itself, however, is not linked exclusively to entrepreneurs. The study by Brockhaus and Nord (1979) demonstrated that owners of new businesses and managers did not reveal significant differences in their locus of control scores: both were internal. Brockhaus (1982) presumes that 'an internal locus-of-control is an asset to advancement in management' (p. 45). However, in a later study (Brockhaus, 1980a) he followed up the success rates of new businesses started in 1975. He found that the owners of those businesses that still existed in 1978 held more internal locus of control beliefs than those whose businesses had ceased to exist. He suggested that the internal beliefs may have resulted in more active efforts to affect outcomes of their business venture in a more positive way. Conversely the less internal business owners may have been more likely to accept less desirable outcomes as beyond their control. Clearly this argument also holds true for successful managers. He concludes that while locus of control does not distinguish entrepreneurs from managers, it may help distinguish the successful from the unsuccessful entrepreneurs.

Caird (1990) does not cite the above work of Brockhaus. She asserts that an internal locus of control differentiates entrepreneurs from managers, citing Cromie and Johns' (1983) study as evidence. A later study by Cromie and others (1990) does not support the contention that either need for achievement or internal locus of control differentiates between 'likely entrepreneurs' and managers.

It is difficult, as Chell and her colleagues have argued, to single out 'locus of control' as a distinguishing attribute of entrepreneurs. Not only does the evidence not support it, but there are also issues about how this attribute is measured and, moreover, the importance of understanding the complexities of the business context and how this affects managerial/entrepreneurial behaviour. In this regard it is useful to compare the work of Miller and Friesen (1982).

Risk-taking propensity

Economists have tended to assume that entrepreneurs pursue business undertakings in conditions of uncertainty for the sake of profit. Much has been written and debated on what is meant by 'uncertainty' (Knight, 1921; Hebert and Link, 1988) and whether, and the extent to which, risk taking is a characteristic entrepreneurial behaviour. In effect, risk-taking propensity is another contentious characteristic even among economists (cf. Schumpeter, 1934).

The usual interpretation of a risk-taker is someone who, in the context of a business venture, pursues a business idea when the probability of succeeding is low (Chell *et al*, 1991). Lay or stereotypic notions of the entrepreneur assume that he or she is typically a risk-taker. However, current thinking does not entirely agree with this idea, for Timmons *et al* (1985) following McClelland (1961) advocate that entrepreneurs take *calculated* risks. Indeed, Carland *et al* (1984), following Schumpeter (1934), suggest that risk-taking is a characteristic of business ownership and not of entrepreneurship *per se*.

The results of empirical investigation are equivocal. This may be due to differences in the way 'risk taking' was being measured and/or it may be explained by differences in the characteristics of the 'population' being sampled. Thus, if the assumption that all business owners are uniform in respect of their tendency towards risk taking is relaxed then it follows that different samples may yield contradictory findings.

The need to consider the context seems even more apparent in the case of risk taking. For example, business undertakings vary quite considerably in respect of the likely costs incurred in setting up. A person's circumstances, age, job opportunities, business experience and so on will vary. The decision to move into some form of self-employment is complex and not explained solely or even primarily in terms of risk. Once a business venture is undertaken, the options open to the individual are always constrained by the business owner's ability to spot opportunities and his or her desire to pursue them. The majority of small business owner-managers, it would seem, do not want their businesses to grow and so they rarely put themselves into a position where they must face taking decisions which involve risk.

Many researchers distinguish between entrepreneurs and small business owner-managers (Carland *et al*, 1984; Ginsberg and Buchholtz, 1989). Stevenson and Sahlman (1989), using their own terminology, refer to 'promoters' and 'trustees'. The two types are represented as occupying different ends of a spectrum characterized by entrepreneurial and administrative types of behaviours. The mark of the entrepreneur is '. . . the relentless pursuit of opportunity without regard to resources currently controlled' (Stevenson and Sahlman, 1989, p. 104).

To behave persistently in such a manner would appear to be highly risky if not reckless. Once a business has become established the owner tends to become less opportunity-driven and there is a desire to protect what has been achieved. Considerations such as the opportunity costs of making an investment or the implications of a particular strategic decision tend to be weighed more carefully and in such ways entrepreneurial behaviour gives way to administrative or managerial type behaviour (ibid.; also see Flamholtz, 1986). Moreover, many business decisions are taken on an incremental basis in an attempt to minimize risk (Quinn, 1980).

Yet another way of examining this issue of risk taking propensity is to ask from whose perspective does an action or decision appear to be risky? If entrepreneurs have a vision that they are confident they can realize, from their perspective they would not view themselves as taking risks. In other words, the subjective probability of a successful outcome is higher for them than for most external observers (for example, their bank manager or their spouse). Furthermore, for the entrepreneur the relentless pursuit of an opportunity regardless of the resources currently under their control may, from their perspective, also involve a risk minimization strategy. Some mental screening of opportunities to be pursued may already have taken place. The extent to which they are seeking to minimize risk rests on: i) information screening and assessment; ii) the ability to devise imaginative solutions to problems; iii) supreme confidence in the solution and hence the decision (Chell *et al*, 1991). Their ability to be successful thus involves a judgemental skill in order to spot a sound business opportunity in the first place. It may also necessitate persuasive skills – that is, the ability to convince others of the merits of the proposed business venture and hence to alter the perception of risk held by significant other players.

Need for independence
The Bolton Report stressed the small business owner's need for independence. This means 'the need to be your own boss'; to have escaped from the oppressive hierarchical regimes of the large organization, and to have realized a sense of purpose and self-fulfilment through the autonomy of owning and managing your own business. This idea of the independent (in Bolton's view, fiercely independent) small business owner is a view that gleans support from other studies. For example, Collins and Moore (1970) differentiated between 'administrative' and 'independent' entrepreneurs. The latter create new organizations from scratch, while the former create new organizations within or as adjuncts to existing business structures. Kets de Vries (1977) suggested that entrepreneurs are deviant or marginal characters: spurred on by adverse experiences in childhood, they become 'misfits' – unable to accept the authority of others and to 'fit into' an organization. The need for independence was thus firmly embedded into their psyches.

Cooper (1986) suggests that the motivating factors of technical entrepreneurs are the need for achievement and independence. Caird (1989), in her review of 'enterprise attributes', draws attention to the link between characteristics like independence and an internal locus of control. Interestingly, however, Hisrich (1986) cites findings from a number of research studies that indicate gender differences in the characteristic of independence of male and female entrepreneurs:

> in terms of motivation, men are often motivated by the drive to control their own destiny, to make things happen. This drive often stems from disagreements with their boss or a feeling they can run things better. In contrast, women tend to be motivated by independence and achievement arising from job frustration where they have not been allowed to perform at the level they are capable of.
>
> (Hisrich, 1986, p. 69)

Further evidence may be adduced from a study by Goffee and Scase (1985) of female business owners. In this study they discuss the instrumental nature of women's pursuit of autonomy by means of proprietorship as a strategy for dealing with oppression and subordination. From the evidence they adduce it was difficult not to draw the conclusion that for some women, at least, the desire to control and shape their own destinies was a significant motivating force.

Innovative behaviour

It is clear from what has gone before that many social scientists have singled out 'innovative behaviour' as the true mark of an entrepreneur (though not a business owner-manager). One of the problems is actually knowing what is meant by this concept. A helpful step forward is to distinguish between the related constructs 'creativity', 'innovation' and 'change' in the work context (West and Farr, 1990). To create is to 'bring something into existence . . .', so a craftsman may be very creative. To innovate is 'to bring in novelties' and so is likely to be concerned with the broader processes of change within the organization. However, while all innovations are concerned with change, not all changes are innovations (ibid.) – for example, going on short time is a change, but not an innovation, while introducing a new method of working is an innovation and a change.

Research in the field of individual innovation within independently owned businesses requires systematic, empirical investigation. What constitutes an innovation may depend on perspective – an innovation may not be absolutely new to be novel within a particular organizational context. The ability to spot and exploit opportunities may, therefore, be the mark of an entrepreneur (Stevenson and Sahlman, 1989), but not necessarily of all types of business owner. Unless such opportunities are analysed systematically the entrepreneur may not be successful (Drucker, 1985). Furthermore, some types of business owner dislike and hence resist making any changes which the introduction of innovations would bring about (Chell *et al*, 1991). Although some innovations may involve routine changes, others are radical in so far as they imply considerable organizational disruption (Zaltman *et al*, 1973).

Any elucidation of the concept of innovative activity suggests the need to consider both external and internal contexts: the external context may be defined by such macro-economic factors as the industry, technology, competitive conditions and market opportunities. The internal context, on the other hand, may be defined by the processes within the organization which enable innovation to be managed. Thus it is through the development of one's understanding of the context that it is possible to draw the conclusion that an innovation has occurred. This also means that it is necessary to determine first and foremost whether the action or behaviour or the thing produced is an example of an innovation before drawing conclusions about the implied personality characteristic of the individual to whom the innovation is attributed (cf. Amabile, 1990; Nicholson, 1990).

Limitations of the single trait line of inquiry
The idea that personality attributes may be identified without reference to the context in which the business owner is operating appears to offer only a partial analysis of their behaviour (Chell, 1985). Indeed, it is possible to identify such contexts – for example, the social, the organizational, the industry and the wider economic contexts – that are likely to influence the business owner's behaviour.

It is clear that attempts to identify single traits that characterize business owners/entrepreneurs have been of limited success. Even attempts to identify lists of personal attributes not discussed in what has gone before are open to criticism because different experts have produced different lists. For example, Timmons and his colleagues produced a list of the *ideal* attributes for successful entrepreneurship; Meredith *et al* (1982) produced a list of attributes that appeared to have been gleaned by a process of consensus among a group of experts; and McClelland (1987) derived a set of competencies.

What appears to be needed is a framework that will enable a set of key distinguishing characteristics to be identified and used for the purpose of categorizing different types of business owner. In this way sense can be made of the heterogeneous mass of business owners.

Social psychological model of business owners

The work of Chell, Haworth and Brearley (1991) attempts to address a number of these methodological issues, to develop a research paradigm and to present data in support of their conclusions. Their social psychological approach has the advantage of taking into account the context in which the individual is operating and assessing how this impacts upon their behaviour.

The primary purpose of the work was to distinguish entrepreneurs from other business owners and to assess the nature of those characteristics which typified the entrepreneur. Fundamental to their approach are: (1) the idea developed by Hampson (1982, 1988) of the trait as a categorizing concept (that is, behaviours are categorized as being typical of the trait X, whatever X may be); (2) the concept of 'prototypicality' (Rosch *et al*, 1976), that is, some behaviours are more characteristic of a trait than others; and, (3) the concept of co-occurring traits, for example, just as 'beaks' and 'feathers' tend to 'co-occur' (Hampson, 1988) so do the attributes that make up the profile of an entrepreneur (Chell *et al*, 1991).

Using a holistic method and critical-incident technique, Chell and her co-workers were able to adduce evidence in support of the following profile of the prototypical entrepreneur: opportunistic; adventurous; an ideas person; restless; high-profile image-maker; proactive; innovative; with a tendency to adopt a broad financial strategy. It was discovered further that some business owners (they were termed 'caretakers' by the research team) had none of these characteristics, and that some business owners exhibited a mix. The upshot was a hierarchically-conceived model of business owners in which the entrepreneur, the quasi-entrepreneur, the administrator and the caretaker were viewed as basic level categories of business owner.

However, in what sense (or senses) is this a *social* psychological model; how is context taken into account? Two ways were identified. First of all, the accounts of their own behaviour in response to certain critical situations given by the business owners sampled are adduced as evidence of a particular trait; the frequency and consistency of manifestations of such behaviour are also considered as crucial criteria for inclusion or exclusion from a named trait category. Secondly, two further dimensions were identified as being significant for carrying out the task of distinguishing entrepreneurs from other types of business owner. They are: growth orientation and stage of development of the business.

Growth orientation assumed that the entrepreneur desired growth and that many business owners did not. It also made possible a linkage between the personality type and some 'hard' indicators of business performance. It was, therefore, measured not only in terms of the business owner's attitude to the likely changes that would ensue if a policy of business growth and development were pursued, but also in change in the numbers employed and in the floorspace used, to indicate whether growth had in fact taken place.

Businesses vary in age and stage of their development. For example, they may only just have been set up or they may be being managed by a third or fourth-generation member of the family. It was thought important to try and build this type of feature into the model. Three stages were identified: post-start-up, established and professionally managed. They were not defined primarily by age, but rather by the degree of formality of operations and the nature of the planning procedures adopted. It was argued that it was conceivable that a business never moved from the 'established' stage as its owner wished to manage his or her business affairs on a relatively informal basis, with little by way of formal planning procedures.

The idea that the population of business owners is heterogeneous is not now in dispute. The problem is how to describe and make sense of such variety. Economists have, for some two hundred years or more, given accounts of entrepreneurial behaviour which they have distinguished from that of managers of a firm. Such behaviour is considered to be rare but may not be a permanent feature of any one business owner. Furthermore, the idea that it is possible to distinguish entrepreneurs from managers on the basis of a particular single personality trait has met with little success if not flagrant opposition (Stevenson and Sahlman, 1989). Two clear conclusions might be drawn from such work.

First, if entrepreneurs (or indeed different types of business owner) might be characterized by their personalities then there must be a constellation of such characteristics and not simply a single trait. Secondly, it would appear that many entrepreneurial or business behaviours can be best understood by reference to the situation or context in which they have occurred.

One way forward has been to develop a typology of business owners. There now appears to be a measure of agreement as to what some of these types might be (Hornaday, 1990). However, such typologies as these are not based upon general principles. In most cases no connection is made between a type and a set of personality characteristics, nor any measure of business performance or criterion of success. The most recent work of Chell *et al* (1991) attempts to redress this by adopting clear principles of categorization, linking a set of personality traits with the types and using measures of growth of the business as an indicator of performance. Further work needs to be done in order to validate this model. The categories may be refined further and a set of competencies defined that will help distinguish the more successful types of business owner from the rest.

Situational or contextual factors

The pattern of small business formation rates in the UK is reasonably clear. There is a north-south divide upon which is overlain an urban-rural difference. In the period 1980–86 the highest rates of small business formation were in the South East, South West and East Anglia. In all the other regions, with the exception of Wales, the rate was below the UK average. The lowest rates were in the most northern regions: Scotland, the North, Yorkshire-Humberside and the North West. The urban-rural dimension is a little more complex. In general, conurbations possess a markedly lower rate of small business formation than rural and semi-rural counties. There are, however, some exceptions to this general rule in that Greater London and some urban-industrial counties (for example, Lothian, Cleveland, West Glamorgan and Nottinghamshire) possess relatively high rates (Mason, 1991, pp. 74–6).

Given that the vast majority of the founders of new firms set up their businesses in the localities in which they are already living and working, it follows that the chances of becoming a small business owner will be closely related to the geographical location of an individual. But what situational or contextual factors underpin this spatial variation in propensities to move into small business ownership? Three broad and highly interdependent factors appear as important: (i) the socio-economic structure of a locality; (ii) the influence of the wider economy upon the locality; and (iii) the dominant culture of the locality.

Socio-economic structures

Research into the influence of the socio-economic structure of a locality upon patterns of small business development has concentrated on the influence of three factors upon small business formation rates: the industrial structure; the plant-size structure; and the occupational structure. Some attempts have also been made to understand the combined impacts of these three factors.

It is known that the majority of small businesses are set up in the industries in which their founders previously worked. Given that industries differ in their ease of entry due to variations in the skills and capital required it might be expected that the probability of establishing a small business will be depressed in localities dominated by industries with high barriers to entry such as chemicals, shipbuilding or aircraft manufacture. However, and perhaps surprisingly, a range of studies have concluded that the independent effect of the industrial structure of a locality has only a minor influence upon variations in new small business formation rates. Controlling for the effect of the industrial composition of a locality fails to eliminate spatial variations (Beesley and Hamilton, 1986; Burrows, 1991a, pp. 65–7; Johnson, 1983; 1986; Storey and Johnson, 1987a).

There is also some suggestion that the majority of founders of new small businesses previously worked in other small firms or in smaller divisions of larger companies (Cooper, 1973; Fothergill and Gudgin, 1982). On the positive side, it is posited that small firms provide their employees with a much more relevant experience for starting a new enterprise than large firms in terms of a greater familiarity with market conditions and close contact with an owner-manager role model. On the negative side, it is posited that large-plant-dominated localities are likely to lack suitable start-up premises (of which more below). Thus, it might be expected that small business formation rates will be low in large-plant-dominated localities and high in localities with an already significant small business population.

Unfortunately the evidence for the influence of plant-size structure on small business formation rates is ambiguous. Strong evidence in support of the hypothesis comes from the East Midlands (Fothergill and Gudgin, 1982) and the North East (Gudgin and Fothergill, 1984) where towns and cities dominated by large plants were found to possess small manufacturing business formation rates that were only one-third as high as those in other parts of the same regions. However, only a very weak association of this type has been found in East Anglia (Gould and Keeble, 1984).

The occupational class background of the owners of small businesses is now reasonably well established (and will be dealt with in some detail under the heading of socio-economic background factors below). However, the wider occupational structure of a locality will obviously have a situational and contextual influence upon the propensity towards small business ownership in that it provides a wider socio-economic milieu to various forms of economic activity. Consequently, the wider social class structure of a locality might be expected to influence the chances of an individual setting up a small business. Given that the majority of small business owners come from employer, managerial and skilled manual social class backgrounds (Curran and Burrows, 1988a, p. 25) localities rich in these social class groups might be thought more likely to generate high rates of small business formation than localities dominated by routine non-manual and semi- and unskilled manual social class groups.

Again, the empirical evidence is somewhat ambiguous on this point. Gould and Keeble (1984) identify a strong association between occupational structure and new small business formation in East Anglia, as does Whittington (1984) for the UK as a whole. However, Gudgin and Fothergill (1984) find no such link in either the East Midlands or the North East.

Although there may be some equivocation about the individual effects of the industrial, plant-size and occupational structure of a locality, the impact of these factors when they occur in combination with each other is very clear. In areas such as South Wales, West Central Scotland and North East England the combination of factors associated with the historical development of coal mining and heavy industry clearly depresses the chances of becoming a small business owner. Despite the rapid contraction of such industrial and mining complexes during the last twenty years their influence on the possibilities for small business development remains powerful (Checkland, 1981; Lloyd and Mason, 1984; Morgan and Sayer, 1985).

The influence of the wider economy

Research on the situational and contextual influence of the wider economy on variations in small business development in different localities has concentrated on three factors: the differential availability of information; the differential availability of factors of production; and differential local and regional market demand for goods and services.

The work of Sweeney (1987) suggests that information plays a crucial and underestimated role in the establishment of small businesses. Information networks tend to be local and most of the contact sources of any individual are within thirty minutes' travelling time of their homes. It therefore follows that the quality and extent of information available to a potential small business owner are largely dependent upon the wealth of the stock of knowledge in the locality: conferences, courses, exhibitions, contacts with potential customers, suppliers and other business owners, informal reading, meetings and more mundane interactions with informed and potentially like-minded individuals and organizations.

On the one hand two types of locality tend to be especially rich in such information: first, the sites of national and regional government, which often contain a concentration of information-intensive functions required to support major decision-making and policy analysis; and, second, technically progressive manufacturing regions. On the other hand two types of locality tend to be especially poor in such information: first, areas dominated by one or two sectors with 'mature' technology, high levels of concentration, external ownership and a declining level of 'best practice' – areas such as the North East and North West of England; and, second, predominantly agricultural and resource-extractive regions. However, at the current time solid empirical evidence on the role and functioning of information in the process of becoming a small business owner is lacking, and it is thus difficult to evaluate these highly suggestive ideas.

Clearly, variations in access to finance is a crucial situational and contextual factor in the process of becoming a small business owner. Although external sources of funding have become increasingly important (see Chapters 4 and 6) the overwhelming majority of businesses are still founded on the basis of the personal financial resources of the founder. Thus regional variations in per capita incomes and savings are likely to influence small business formation rates. However, given that many small business founders still raise start-up capital either by taking out a second mortgage on their home or by offering their home as collateral against a bank loan, it is likely that small business formation rates will be related to levels of owner-occupation and house prices. However, given the strong regional associations which exist between per-capita incomes and savings, propensities towards owner-occupation and house prices (Hamnett, 1989) it is very difficult to isolate which sources of finance have the greatest impact upon small business formation.

Nevertheless, despite these methodological problems, the general thrust of the above claims can be empirically substantiated. The relatively low level of owner-occupation in the North and Scotland is likely to close off access to finance to some potential small business owners in these regions, while the high house prices in the South East raise the level of personal capital available to small business founders in these areas. Whittington (1984) identifies a strong positive association between new firm formation and home ownership at the regional level in the UK, while Moyes and Westhead (1988) identify an equally strong negative association between new firm formation and local authority housing at the county level.

The availability of premises may also be associated with spatial variations in small business formation. In the UK the supply of small factory units is greatest in the South East and adjacent regions, due to the locational preferences of property developers who tend to concentrate their activities in urban areas within more prosperous regions. Consequently, public sector agencies are largely, and in some cases entirely, responsible for the supply of small factory units in remote rural areas and depressed industrial regions (Ambler and Kennett, 1985). However, and to a degree counteracting this, southern regions lack the large stock of old, redundant industrial property, often available at low rents and on short leases in the more economically depressed northern regions. Despite this, constraints on small business formation are in general greatest in areas with the highest start-up rates and least in areas with low start-up rates. This suggests that the *potential* regional differences in small business formation are even greater than those that actually take place. However, no systematic research has been carried out on this topic and the only evidence we have of 'frustrated entrepreneurship' due to lack of suitable premises is anecdotal (Ambler and Kennett, 1985).

There is also considerable spatial variation in demand for goods and services and this will clearly influence opportunities for small business development. Most small firms tend to serve a restricted geographic market and this has meant that in recent years the greatest opportunities have occurred in the more affluent areas of the country, such as the South East. However, and counteracting this tendency to a small degree, specific opportunities also clearly exist for small businesses in remoter rural and semi-rural regions. In general small firms, especially those that maintain and repair domestic and industrial equipment, can offer a faster and cheaper service to local customers than branches of major firms which tend to be based in large cities, cover a wider territory and have standard call-out and mileage charges (Economists Advisory Group, 1981).

Variability in the ownership structure and functional composition of large industry in different areas also has a considerable impact on the possibilities for small business development. Establishments that are part of multi-plant companies generally have limited freedom to source inputs independently of the overall corporate decision-making process. Local market opportunities for small businesses therefore depend to a large extent on the freedom of the region's dominant corporate units to select and use local sources of inputs. Thus, the low rate of new firm formation in the northern regions is closely associated with their relative dependence on externally owned plants with limited management functions and mass producing relatively standardized products. Conversely, large establishments in the south tend to have a greater autonomy over purchasing decisions and, as a consequence, there will be much greater market opportunities for small firms in these regions.

Variations in regional specialization are also important. Opportunities for small businesses will obviously be more limited in areas with declining industrial complexes. Clearly, the general loss of household income as a result of decline limits consumer demand, but this is also often coupled with the loss to small businesses of crucial subcontracting relationships with the previously dominant large industries. For example, the contraction of shipbuilding and heavy industry in the North East of England has led to a decline in subcontracting and component supply opportunities available to small firms (Gibb and Quince, 1980). Conversely, in rapidly expanding areas, such as Cambridge and the M4 corridor, there are likely to be considerable opportunities for small businesses to meet demand for business and consumer services as well as supplying high technology industries (Storey and Johnson, 1987b).

Dominant culture of locality

The situational and contextual influence of the general culture of a locality upon small business development is very difficult to gauge – and, certainly, the term 'enterprise culture' has been the source of much academic work of late (Burrows, 1991b; Cross and Payne, 1991; Curran and Blackburn, 1991; Goss, 1991; Hobbs, 1988; Keat and Abercrombie, 1991). However, the conclusions of this work are complex. The direction of causality between a given set of cultural values and small business activity may be two-way rather than unidirectional. Indeed, some have gone as far as to argue that any relationship between the enterprise culture and the lived experience of small business owners is largely bogus (Blanchflower and Oswald, 1991; Burrows and Curran, 1991). For these writers the rhetoric of the enterprise culture is a *post hoc* rationalization of causal influences that are material and structural rather than cultural and ideological in character.

Nevertheless, it may still be the case that localities with a propensity towards individualism and an awareness of a past history of entrepreneurial activities may provide a more conducive context for establishing a small business independently of the more structural influences already outlined. However, the empirical verification of this hypothesis remains highly problematic.

Situational and contextual factors as determinants – summary

The main factors have been summarized by Mason (1991) as follows:

> new firm formation is likely to be highest in regions and localities with the following characteristics: an industrial structure which is biased towards small, independent or autonomous, units of employment; employees who are engaged in problem-solving and have customer contact, and so possess technical and market knowledge; a concentration of technically-progressive large firms; a high awareness of past entrepreneurial actions; banks and other financial institutions that are sympathetic to the needs of small businesses; sources of help and advice available; an affluent population; and a social climate that favours individualism.
>
> (Mason, 1991, p. 99)

Socio-economic background factors

Research on the socio-economic backgrounds of the owners of small businesses *per se* is hard to come by (but for a useful recent review see Goss (1991), pp. 29–68). For the most part the data we possess tend to deal with the self-employed (see Burrows and Curran, 1989; Casey and Creigh, 1988; Dale, 1986; 1991; Goss, 1991, pp. 29–46; and Hakim, 1988 on issues of the relationship between self-employment and small business ownership) – who might or might not employ others. Thus, in most of what follows the discussion will refer to the self-employed in general (only about a third of whom employ others). Where research only refers to small business owners who employ others this will be made explicit.

In Britain in the 1980s there was an increase in self-employment from 1.9 million in 1979 (7.7 per cent of total employment) to 3.4 million in 1989 (12 per cent of total employment). There has also been a steady net rise in the number of businesses registering for VAT which, although a somewhat problematic indicator, indicates a rise in the number of small businesses.

A number of important background factors influence the propensity of an individual to become self-employed. Thus far research has tended to concentrate on six main topics: gender; age; social class background; marital status; education; and ethnicity.

Gender

In relation to gender the available research is clear. The self-employment rate for males is about twice the female rate. Meager (1989, p. 9), carrying out a secondary analysis of the 1984 Labour Force Survey, estimates an overall self-employment rate of 15.2 per cent for males and a 6.6 per cent self-employment rate for females. Curran and Burrows (1988a, p. 16), carrying out a secondary analysis using pooled data from the General Household Surveys 1979–84, estimate that for small business owners alone the ratio of men to women is over 3 to 1. Burrows (1991a, p. 61), carrying out a multivariate secondary analysis of the General Household Survey for 1985, estimates that even after controlling for class background and highest educational qualification the odds of a female being self-employed are only one-half that of a male. In short, then, the propensity to become the owner of a small business is highly influenced by gender, although this propensity tends to vary with age (see below).

However, the extent of this overall gender difference may be declining. Official estimates indicate that between 1978 and 1988 female self-employment more than doubled, while male self-employment grew by about 50 per cent (*Employment Gazette*, 1988, p. 609). These claims contradict the findings of Curran and Burrows (1988a, p. 12) who claim that between 1979–84 the ratio of men to women remained relatively stable, with men moving into self-employment at a slightly greater rate than women. However, the analysis of Meager (1989, pp. 42–3) lends considerable support to the official view that the rate for women is increasing at a faster pace than that for men.

Age

The chances of being a small business owner are also known to be closely related to age, though the relationship is far from being a clear-cut one. The self-employment rate increases strongly with age up to the 35–44 age group, then drops slightly before increasing dramatically again to peak in the post-65 age range (Meager, 1989, p. 10); see also Curran and Burrows (1988a, p. 16) in the light of the comments by Meager (1989, pp. 8–9; 54–5). Indeed, it is estimated that almost one-third of all those over 65 who are still economically active are self-employmed.

The reasons for this high rate among older members of the population are thought to be due to two main factors. First, given that many employees have no choice but to retire from work at the statutory retirement age, should such people wish to continue to work one obvious option is for them to become self-employed. Second, and probably of more importance, it is likely that the self-employed will, typically, be less well-provided for in terms of occupational pension than will their counterparts in the employed sector of the economy, and will more often be dependent purely on state pension provision. The incentive to stay in the labour force for as long as possible is, therefore, likely to be strong.

Although the broad pattern of the age distribution is similar for both men and women there is a significant variation with age in the *ratio* between male and female self-employment rates. This ratio is highest in the youngest age group (16–19) with males some five times more likely to be self-employed than females. The ratio falls through the 20s age range, until by the age range 25–34 men are less than twice as likely as women to be self-employed. The ratio rises to more than two in the 35–54 age ranges, and falls again among the oldest age groups

(Meager, 1989, p. 11). This general pattern of differential propensities towards self-employment between men and women across the life-cycle is also reported by Burrows (1991a, pp. 63–5) even after controlling for marital status.

The final notable feature of the available data on the age distribution of the self-employed is the clear indication that there exists an 'age launch window' of between about 35 and 54 for self-employment in general, and small business ownership in particular (Curran and Burrows, 1988a, p. 16). It is hypothesized that the establishment of a small business is most likely to coincide with the conjunction of a number of different conducive life-cyclical factors such as: occupational experience; access to capital (usually through home ownership, see above); and a more stable, and thus possibly more supportive domestic environment. Such an age-related dimension to such economic activity clearly mitigates against the establishment of more youthful enterprises (MacDonald and Coffield, 1991).

Social class

The social class background of small business owners is a topic that has attracted a good deal of attention. For many years most evidence suggested that, in numerical terms at least, the bulk of small business owners were drawn from families located in the lower-middle-class strata of UK society – skilled manual workers, supervisors, and routine white-collar employees, and from families already involved in some kind of small business activity (Boswell, 1973). While this pattern of distribution remains more or less uncontested at the level of simple description, the sociological interpretation of its significance has recently been called into question (Burrows, 1991a; Curran and Burrows, 1988a; Curran *et al*, 1991).

The conventional view has traditionally been that entry into small business ownership is principally a means of upward social mobility for members of the lower-middle social strata (Aldrich *et al*, 1986; Scase and Goffee, 1987). Curran and Burrows (1988a; Burrows, 1991a) do not dispute that lower-middle-class levels of UK society are important 'feeder groups' for small business ownership and self-employment. In their secondary analysis of the 1979–84 General Household Surveys they established that among small business owners just over 37 per cent originally came from skilled manual or routine white-collar class backgrounds, while just over 40 per cent of the self-employed (without any employees) came from such backgrounds. Clearly, both figures represent substantial absolute proportions. However, when one considers these figures in comparison to the class backgrounds of the rest of the employed population it becomes clear that the relative importance of these classes is not great in terms of the propensity to run a small business. Among employees some 46 per cent come from such class backgrounds. Thus, in relative terms, lower-middle-class backgrounds are *under*-represented among small business owners and the self-employed and, or so it would appear, individuals from employer/manager and professional strata are *over*-represented. As Goss in his discussion of these results puts it:

although those from skilled manual, routine white-collar and supervisory socio-economic backgrounds are numerically significant, proportionately these two groupings supply less to the small enterprise-owning strata than they do to the employee population as a whole. On the other hand, though, children of the employer/manager and professional strata are more than proportionately represented, which supports the interpretation that rather than an avenue of upward social mobility for lower social strata, small business ownership is better viewed as a 'catch net' for the downwardly mobile.

(Goss, 1991, p. 52)

Burrows (1991a, pp. 60–3) has attempted to explore the nature of this relationship in a little more detail by way of a secondary analysis of the 1985 General Household Survey. He suggests that in terms of the propensity to becoming self-employed, once one has controlled for gender and highest educational qualification, the only class background that significantly improves an individual's odds of entering self-employment is that of an employer/manager-class background. This finding strongly supports the suggestion that a significant proportion of small business owners come from small business backgrounds (Goldthorpe *et al*, 1987; Stanworth *et al*, 1989).

Goss (1991, p. 53) has recently deplored the fact that although we now possess reasonable knowledge on the class background of small business owners and the self-employed in general, we still lack data on whether different class backgrounds are associated with different forms of small business, as appears to be the case in France for example (Maya, 1987). However, this state of affairs has, at least in part, been remedied by the recent work of the ESRC Centre for Research on Small Service Sector Enterprises (Curran *et al*, 1991) which has produced some highly suggestive preliminary results on the class backgrounds of the owners of 350 service sector businesses. Given that it is estimated that over 80 per cent of all small businesses in the UK operate in what can broadly be termed the 'service sector' of the economy (Curran and Burrows, 1988a, p. 55; Burrows and Curran, 1989) inferences based upon these areas of economic activity are likely to be applicable to small business owners in general.

The research, which aims to examine a range of different aspects of service sector small enterprise activities, is based upon samples of fifty firms engaged in seven different types of activity: computer services; garage and vehicle repairs; employment, secretarial and training agencies; plant and equipment hire; advertising, marketing and design agencies; video hire and leisure businesses; and free houses, wine bars and restaurants. These firms have been sampled from five different localities each representing very contrasting economic and social structures: Guildford; Doncaster; Nottingham; North East Suffolk; and Islington in London.

The aggregate results strongly support the research findings above, which suggest a high level of inter-generational inheritance of small business related activity. However, as Goss intimates, the results also indicate a substantial degree of variation in the level of small business 'inheritance' for different kinds of enterprise. It is – very tentatively – suggested that the extent of inter-generational inheritance of small business activity is likely to be high in more 'traditional' forms of small enterprise and lower in more 'modern' forms. However, the data are not unequivocal in relation to this hypothesis and further larger-scale research is clearly required.

The data also display clear patterns of class influence in other ways. For example, people running computer services, advertising, marketing and design businesses disproportionately have fathers working in professional and managerial occupations, while those running garage and vehicle repair and plant and equipment hire businesses come disproportionately from backgrounds with fathers from routine white collar and manual occupations. Clearly then, it appears on these results that the class background of the owners of small businesses is significantly related to the type of business they are running.

The research also allows for a fuller picture of inter-generational small business activity to be deciphered than has hitherto been the case, in that it contains data on respondents fathers' *and* mothers' experiences of self-employment. In previous research it has only been possible to evaluate the social class background of fathers due, in large part, to the manner in which official data are collected (Oakley and Oakley, 1979). The results using this data on both parents reveal a quite dramatic pattern. Overall some 43.5 per cent of all the small business owners had fathers and/or mothers who had been self-employed, ranging from some 56 per cent for the owners of free houses, wine bars and restaurants down to 33.3 per cent for the owners of both advertising, marketing and design companies and computer services business. This finding thus strongly supports the contention that parental experience of self-employment in general, and small business ownership in particular, is the best single predictor of the propensity to enter into small business ownership, although this propensity will clearly differ across different types of small enterprise.

As might be expected from the research reported earlier, these initial results also indicate some regional variation in the class backgrounds of small business owners in the service sector. In summary, the data suggest that in Nottingham and North East Suffolk the opportunities for upward social mobility via small business ownership are good, in Doncaster they are slightly less favourable, and in the South East – Guildford and Islington – they are poor. The tentative hypothesis derived from these results is that the opportunities for upward social mobility into small business ownership may be related to the level of economic prosperity in the locality: the three least prosperous localities – in terms of a range of different measures – appear to offer more opportunities in this regard.

Marital status

Much is also now known about the relationship between marital status and self-employment. The self-employment rate is much lower for single people than for people in other categories. In part, of course, this simply reflects the variation in self-employment rates by age (discussed above). However, even when age is controlled for (Burrows, 1991a, p. 64; Meager, 1989, p. 12) the rate remains lower among single people than among those who are married. In this instance then, the research appears to support the received wisdom that family circumstances are an important determinant of the propensity to become self-employed.

Research on the influence of becoming widowed, divorced or separated on the propensity to become self-employed is however more ambiguous. Meager (1989, p. 13), using the 1984 Labour Force Survey, suggests that the self-employment rate among widowed, divorced or separated men is higher than it is even for married men. However, he suggests that for women the pattern is rather different. Widowed women exhibit a higher self-employment rate than any other category of women, while divorced and separated women have a lower rate compared to married women, though slightly higher than for single women. This finding therefore concurs with small-scale studies of female small business owners which have discovered relatively large numbers of widows in their samples (Goffee and Scase, 1985; Watkins and Watkins, 1984). Meager (1989, p. 13) hypothesizes two possible mechanisms by which these results may occur. First, the likely dominance of men in a high proportion of 'family businesses' means that males are more likely to 'inherit' and continue a business after divorce or separation. Second, the high rate among widowed women may be the result of women inheriting a business from a deceased husband.

These results contradict the findings of Curran and Burrows (1988a, p. 41; Burrows, 1991a, p. 64) who, using the General Household Survey, have suggested that widows do not possess a higher propensity to be self-employed than other categories of women. However, conclusive evidence on this issue is not currently available, but given that the Labour Force Survey is based upon a considerably larger sample size than is the General Household Survey (even when pooled over a number of years) or any other data source for that matter, as things currently stand the claims of Meager *et al* currently appear as the more robust scenario.

Education

Research findings on the relationship between the acquisition of various types of educational qualification and the propensity towards self-employment are very complex and not easily summarized. Burrows (1991a), for example, in his secondary analysis of the 1985 General Household Survey reports that if one uses the highest educational qualification of an individual as a measure and controls for the influence of social class background and gender then: 'compared to those with no formal qualifications those with some form of formal qualification have significantly lower odds, and those with an apprenticeship significantly higher odds of [being self-employed or a small business owner]' (Burrows, 1991a, p. 62).

These findings are broadly in line with the more detailed results reported by Meager (1989) who breaks down the highest educational qualification possessed by an individual with a greater degree of precision in his secondary analysis of the 1984 Labour Force Survey. He reports an overall rate of self-employment of 12.3 per cent for those with no qualifications, 11.3 per cent for those with GCE A-level qualifications or higher, 8.7 per cent for those with GCE O-level or the equivalent, and 6 per cent for those with CSEs below Grade 1. However, within these broad headings he presents data on more specific qualifications which display a much greater degree of variability. For example, those with degrees possess a self-employment rate of 11.8 per cent, those with just A-levels or the equivalent 13 per cent, and those with City and Guilds qualifications (which may be linked to apprenticeships of one sort or another) just under 16 per cent.

These general rates are, however, highly contingent upon gender. Very crudely, it is fair to conclude that self-employed women are generally more highly qualified than self-employed men (Meager, 1989, p. 19).

The work of the ESRC Centre for Research on Small Service Sector En-terprises (Curran *et al*, 1991), already noted above, has also recently produced results which, perhaps not surprisingly, demonstrate that the level of education-al attainment among small business owners is highly contingent upon the type of business they are running. For example, owners in possession of a degree or the equivalent constituted 41.2 per cent in computer services, almost 30 per cent in advertising, marketing and design by only 4.2 per cent in free houses, wine bars and restaurants and only 2 per cent in garages, vehicles and repairers. Some 50 per cent of owners of garages and vehicle repairers had carried out an apprenticeship of some sort, as had some 25 per cent of the owners of plant and equipment hire businesses. Businesses run by individuals with no formal qualifications of any sort also varied with type of business: in garages and vehicle repairers this constituted some 52 per cent of all owners; in plant and equipment hire 45 per cent; free houses, wine bars and restaurants 36 per cent; video and leisure outlets almost 30 per cent; employment, secretarial and train-ing companies 28.6 per cent; and in advertising, marketing and design com-panies and computer services just under 12 per cent.

As will be clear from the above, no simple conclusions can be drawn concern-ing the relationship between education and the propensity towards small busi-ness ownership. However, perhaps the following is reasonably uncontestable: the impact of education upon small business ownership is significantly medi-ated by gender; educational qualifications are highly contingent upon the sort of small business being run; apprenticeships significantly increase the odds of become self-employed (indeed, Burrows (1991a) claims that after gender and social class background it is the strongest predictor of self-employment); and the view offered by the Bolton Report (1971, pp. 8–9) that small business ownership is an important economic destination for individuals with no formal qualifications remains a reasonably valid claim.

Ethnicity

Research carried out on the influence of ethnicity upon the propensity to be-come self-employed needs to be treated with some degree of caution where it is based on national level data. The ethnic minority population in the UK is relatively small, and tends to be clustered within certain geographical areas.

This leads to relatively high sampling errors when data sources such as the Labour Force Survey (Meager, 1989) or the General Household Survey (Curran and Burrows, 1988a; 1988b) are utilized. Even given this methodological problem, however, the general conclusions of research in this area are uniform: ethnicity has a very strong influence upon the propensity to become self-employed.

Meager (1989, p. 14) suggests that compared to individuals categorized as 'white', people with a West Indian/Guyanese ethnic origin are significantly less likely to be self-employed (with a self-employment rate of about half that for whites), while people whose ethnic origin derives from the Indian sub-continent are significantly more likely to be self-employed (with a self-employment rate about twice the white rate). These findings are consistent with those found by Curran and Burrows (1988b) and reported by Ward (1991, p. 57) from other official sources. The group with the highest propensity towards self-employment, however, are those originally deriving from the Mediterranean (Curran and Burrows, 1988b).

Socio-economic background factors – summary

The various socio-economic background factors that influence who becomes a small business owner are perhaps even more complex than the situational and contextual influences reviewed earlier. No hard and fast formula for predicting who is going to establish a small business is ever likely to be forthcoming from the sociological literature. However, the above review does suggest that the following factors significantly improve the odds of an individual moving into small business ownership: that they are male; that they are either middle-aged or beyond formal retirement age; that they come from a family background within which either their mother or their father (and preferably both) were engaged in some sort of small business activity; that they are married; that they have carried out some sort of apprenticeship (or if not, that they have no formal qualifications); and finally, that they have an ethnicity which originally derives from either the Indian sub-continent or the Mediterranean.

8 Management Training and Support

The Bolton Report identified a generally low level of management in small firms and argued that this situation had contributed to the demise of the small business, since 'the development of management techniques has enabled large firms to become more efficient' (Bolton, 1971, p. 78). The report made the case for improved management information and training and picked out eight main areas in which small firms might be assisted to improve their performance – raising and using finance; costing and control information; organization and delegation; marketing; information use and retrieval; personnel management; technological change; and production scheduling and purchase control.

The report emphasized the inadequacy for small firms of the existing machinery of Industrial Training Boards and suggested that 'each training board, in consultation with the industry and the Department of Employment, should formulate an appropriate definition of the small firm in its industry and should . . . consider the possibility of providing training services on a fee-paying basis' (op. cit., p. 249).

Similarly, the report argued for an extension of advisory services to small business, in particular a network of small firms' advisory bureaux in each of the country's most important centres of industry and commerce, which would act as a referral/signposting service providing information in response to queries. With the exception of these bureaux, which should be government backed, the report suggested that, as with training, 'all management advisory services, whether in the public or the private sector, should be self-supporting, since the readiness of clients to pay and the ability of the service to survive on this basis are the only reliable indicators of their value' (op. cit., p. 138).

The report clearly, therefore, raised a number of important issues on the managerial development of small firms and introduced a set of principles for the provision of training and support services to the sector. Perhaps the most important of these were that the services provided should be a response to market demand and that the provision of management training and support to small firms should be neither free nor subsidized. In the context of management training and support, very considerable controversy exists over the adoption and implementation of these two principles. According to the report's authors, the provision of such services to industry by government would be justified only if the service is needed; if private enterprise cannot or will not provide it; if the economic benefit to the nation deriving from the services is greater than their cost; users of the service cannot or should not be expected to pay their full cost.

Essentially, the controversy exists over the distinction between 'need' and 'demand'. While from a national viewpoint the small firms sector may exhibit a 'need' for managerial training and support, that need may not be recognized by the small firms concerned and, as a consequence, may not be translated into effective demand. Likewise, those businesses recognizing the need for management development may not, by definition, be in a position to pay the full commercial costs involved. Similarly, the providers may not be able to offer the service at a price which their potential clients are able/willing to pay. A case can, therefore, be made for government support, though against this needs to be balanced the small firms' 'widespread prejudice against Government services' (op. cit., p. 141) which the report recognized also.

In pointing to the need for increased management training and support services, therefore, the report introduced a conundrum about the sort of services needed and how they might best be supplied. This debate continues, but there can be little doubt that since 1971, and particularly throughout the 1980s, the provision of training and support to small firms has increased considerably, as has the level of take-up. Even so, it would seem, and will be demonstrated later, that the adoption of training by small firms remains relatively low and the effectiveness of training as a means of arresting decline and stimulating growth and development is, as a consequence, open to question (Kirby, 1990; Stanworth and Gray, 1991).

Unfortunately, the reasons for this are unclear as 'the processes and methodologies used by owner-managers which shape and determine their perceptions of management education needs, have been a neglected area of research' (Tait, 1988). However, from the findings of previous research, it would seem that many entrepreneurs have received little or no formal education or have a poor opinion of it (Bolton, 1971; Watkins, 1983). As a consequence, they tend to be somewhat sceptical of the value of management development to their businesses and, not infrequently, reluctant to devote their time and other resources to it. Also, many are reluctant to expose the deficiencies of the firm, and themselves, to external third parties, whether in a training or a consultancy situation. Additionally, it has to be appreciated that Britain lags behind many of its competitor nations in terms of management development (Handy, 1987; Coopers and Lybrand, 1985). Unlike America, Japan and Germany, for example, there is no real tradition of management development and until recently the concept of continuous professional updating was characteristic of neither the educational system nor the world of work. Not only does it take time to change attitudes, but it requires time to ensure that the supply of management development services is appropriate to the needs of the market. Finally, it must be appreciated that not all small firms want to expand or to improve their management performance. Most commonly, small business owner-managers seek independence and autonomy rather than profits or growth (Bolton, 1971; Stanworth and Curran, 1973; Gray, 1991) and most small firms have only local horizons, a weak grasp of technological and business principles and little desire to expand (Binks and Jennings, 1986; Storey, 1986).

Clearly, all of the above is of significance to the development of an effective system of management education and support in Britain. It is in this context, therefore, that the provision of training and support services for small firms must be viewed.

The provision of training and support services

Despite the Bolton Report's recognition of the need for improved management training and advisory services for small business, the most positive outcome directly attributable to the report was the establishment in 1972–73 of a Small Firms Division within the Department of Trade and Industry (paragraph 9.27) and a network of regional Small Firms Centres providing a free general inquiry service and business counselling (paragraph 10.47). While undoubtedly several management training initiatives were developed subsequent to the publication of the report, these were piecemeal and part of no coherent strategy as the report had recommended (paragraph 14.25). Indeed, the majority of the Industrial Training Boards were abolished following an announcement made by government in November 1981. Thus, by the end of the 1970s relatively little progress had been made in terms of the provision of management training and support. Since then, and particularly since the advent, in 1979, of a Conservative government committed to the promotion of enterprise, there has developed a wide network of management training and support services specifically for small business, involving national and local government, the private sector and further and higher education. Though extensive, the range of support has inevitably appeared confused and inconsistent, in part because of the variety of apparently different initiatives and in part because of their relative impermanence. As has been observed elsewhere (Gibb, 1986, p. 175), 'the small firm support scenario in the United Kingdom is changing rapidly' – a feature that tended to characterize the development of small firm training and support services throughout the 1980s.

Training

Until 1989/90, the main thrust for training, offered through a variety of private and public sector providers, came from a semi-autonomous department of the Department of Employment variously entitled the Training Services Agency, the Manpower Services Commission, the Training Commission and the Training Agency. As Hyde (1986) has demonstrated, the evolution of a training strategy for small firms occurred in a somewhat piecemeal manner without any coherent framework and, frequently, based on individuals' perceptions rather than objective analyses of needs. As Table 8.1 demonstrates, from 1977 a variety of programmes were introduced aimed at three different groups under

Table 8.1   Training for Enterprise Programmes, by year of commencement 1977–1988

Programme title	Programme category		
	Start-up	Secondment to existing firms	Owner-manager
New Enterprise Programme	1977/78		
Small Business Course	1980/81		
Self-employment Course	1981/82		
Action Learning			1981/82
Management Extension Programme		1982/83	
Graduate Enterprise Programme	1983/84		
Graduate Gateway Programme		1984/85	
Small Business Workshop	1984/85		
Owner-manager Courses			1984/85
Firmstart	1985/86		
Business Enterprise Programme	1986/87		
Private Enterprise Programme			1986/87
Business Enterprise Programme & Graduates	1987/88		

what became termed the Training for Enterprise Programme. While the overall objective was 'to equip potential and existing entrepreneurs with the skills and knowledge required successfully to launch, manage and develop a small business . . . ' initially there was no way of running such courses, or supporting trainees, other than under the government's Training Opportunities Scheme (TOPS). This required that trainees must be unemployed and wishing to participate on a course with a view to returning to paid employment, could not have been on a previous TOPS course during the previous three years, and must have been out of full-time education for at least two years.

As a consequence, the initial emphasis in Training for Enterprise was restricted to assisting trainees to start their own businesses. Over time, the TOPS' conditions were relaxed and by 1981/82 assistance became available to existing small businesses through the Action Learning Programme, and by 1982/83 'secondees' were being used to assist existing small businesses (and help 'smuggle' training into the firms) through the Management Extension Programme. While the emphasis on start-up training continued, reinforced by the introduction in 1981/82 of the £40 per week Enterprise Allowance Scheme for those starting a new business, a gradual shift took place during the 1980s towards the development of existing businesses. During this period, also, 'many other developments were tried on a pilot basis, generally in response to ideas rather than on research' (Hyde, 1986, p. 9). Possibly it was such initiatives that contributed to the apparently fragmented and impermanent character of the Training for Enterprise Programme. By 1986, the whole programme was under review, in part to take 'account of services available to small businesses either through other Government schemes or indeed through private sector assisted schemes' (op. cit., p. 14) and in part because 'it has to be recognized that some of the products have gone through their natural life cycle and, to quote the marketing jargon, must be replaced by "new", "improved" models' (op. cit., p. 14). These new models were the Business Enterprise and Private Enterprise Programmes and the part-time variant of the New Enterprise Programme, Firmstart.

Essentially the Business Enterprise Programme (BEP) and the Private Enterprise Programme (PEP) were conceived as a combined package for start-up and business development. People wishing either to explore the self-employment option or to start a new business could participate in a seven-day BEP course before enrolling for PEP, a series of thirteen modular problem-centred seminars/workshops. These were basic accounting; computers in business; employing people; marketing overhaul; sources of finance; book-keeping; selling; financial control; computerized accounting; finding new products; sales promotion; managing change; and taxation. In designing the programmes, consideration was given to the benefit position of the unemployed with respect to Department of Health and Social Security rules and to the need to move away from full-time to part-time provision in order that participants could consider the implications of the knowledge gained for either their embryonic or existing small business. In the pre-start-up phase, as in the first year of trading (start-up), training was free. Thereafter, participants were required to make a contribution to the cost of training – normally 50 per cent.

In order to make access to information about training more readily available to small firms and others, the government also introduced, in 1986, Training Access Points, with the objective of establishing a network of 2,000 readily-accessible TAP locations within five years. At the end of January 1988 there were 137 – in libraries (22), agency offices (19), job centres (17), colleges (12), shops and supermarkets (5), careers service offices (8), advice centres (19) and other locations (35).

In September 1988 a further change took place with the Training for Enterprise Scheme being absorbed into Employment Training. In the autumn of the following year the Private Enterprise Programme was replaced by a new initiative, Business Growth Training and a series of twenty marketing, accounting and finance and general management business skills seminars – marketing your business; practical marketing; more profit . . . fast; advertising and promotion; direct marketing; personal selling skills; customer care; export marketing; book-keeping; understanding finance; accounting towards profit; accounting with computers; taxation; debt recovery and cash control; effective management; employing people; communicate for profit; time, stress and crisis management; computers in business; and negotiating skills.

Apart from the seminars, the programme offers small businesses four other options:

● free kits and expert advice to help their owners produce better business plans and identify training needs

- subsidized consultancy to help them review their business strategy and plan effective training and development for their employees
- specialist advice and financial help for projects jointly produced with other businesses to meet future skill needs
- specialist advice and financial help for innovative training projects.

Meanwhile, the Business Enterprise Programme, including a shortened and open learning version, has remained available under Employment Training. From October 1989, even more fundamental changes have taken place with the decentralization of the Training Agency's co-ordinating role through the creation of eighty-two local Training and Enterprise Councils (TECs) in England and Wales and twenty employer-led Local Enterprise Companies (LECs) in Scotland. The whole purpose of the TECs and LECs is to give the business community ownership of local training arrangements, each being required to undertake an analysis of its area to identify the needs of the local business community. TECs have three further priorities – to help ensure that the distinctive needs of the self-employed and small businesses for training, counselling and other support are met; to establish coherent arrangements for enterprise support to meet local needs; and to assist unemployed people to enter self-employment.

It is unclear how these objectives are to be met, and while the principle of local ownership of training is to be applauded, there is some concern that the TECs will lead to further fragmentation, a lack of coherence, dissipation of resources and a reduction in training provision (Batchelor, 1991).

Support services

As the provision of training for small firms has developed since the publication of the Bolton Report, so has the provision of information and advisory services. As a consequence, there now exists a diverse range of private and public sector support services intended to meet the various needs of the small business. Since 1972–73 the Small Firms Service has provided a free general inquiry service and business counselling through its various regional centres. This was a direct outcome of the Bolton Report and, for several years, was the mainstay of support for small firms. Initially established by the Department of Trade and Industry (DTI), the Small Firms Service was transferred to the Department of Employment in the mid-1980s and its counselling service is currently being transferred to the Training and Enterprise Councils. In its place, in January 1988 the DTI launched a more proactive Enterprise Initiative, intended to enhance the competitiveness of small business by providing assistance and guidance in areas such as strategic management, exports, collaborative research and technology transfer. It does this through the provision of a free Business Review (lasting for up to two days) for small firms with fewer than 500 employees to assess their problems and needs, and financial support to cover half the cost (two-thirds in Assisted and Urban Programme Areas) of engaging an approved external consultant. The purpose of the Initiative is not only to raise company performance in key areas (marketing, design, quality management, manufacturing systems, business planning and financial and information systems), but to encourage small firms to utilize third-party expertise as part of their management strategy. Other DTI initiatives are, perhaps, less well-known and publicized. They include Managing into the 90s, a programme offering information and advice on key management skills (design, quality, manufacturing, purchasing and supply); the Small Firms Merit Award for Research and Technology (SMART), an annual competition offering financial support towards the development of new technology projects with good prospects of success in firms with fewer than fifty employees; and Europe Open for Business, a campaign providing information on the Single European Market via a 24-hour telephone service, pamphlets, a database and a free quarterly newsletter. This is backed by a series of European Information Centres located, usually, in chambers of commerce throughout the country.

Similar, more localized government support is provided, usually through the economic development units of the local authority and, in Scotland and Wales, by the respective development agencies. Specialist assistance for small firms in rural areas is available, also – in England from the Rural Development Commission, the Highlands and Islands Development Board in Scotland and Mid Wales Development, the Development Board for Rural Wales. Each of these bodies has a relatively long and varied history of involvement with small business, generally dating back to the 1970s, making it difficult to identify any overall strategy and resulting in what, for the end-user, appears to be an often irrational and unfair service provision resulting from the frequent artificiality of territorial boundaries.

Apart from the increase in the extent of government support for small business, the twenty years since the publication of the Bolton Report have witnessed increasing direct and indirect private sector involvement. Indeed, the increased participation of the private sector has been a marked trend and one which might be expected to continue into the future, particularly with the formation of the TECs. Over the years, indirect support has been provided by the private sector through the sponsorship of training and other initiatives for small firms and through the secondment of staff to the various support agencies, particularly Business in the Community. This is a government-sponsored organization established in 1981 by a group of large companies with the aim of developing a network of local enterprise agencies responsible for supporting the economic needs of the local community. Each local enterprise agency is independent and services vary from one locality to another. However, like the Small Firms Service, they provide advice and counselling to small firms, usually concentrating their efforts on start-ups and very small, micro businesses. Other support from the private sector comes more directly – through, for example, company initiatives to create employment, particularly in areas where their plants are, or have been, represented (such as British Coal Enterprise and British Steel Corporation (Industry) Ltd). Increasingly, also, the professions are recognizing the importance of the small firm sector of the economy and are developing a range of specialist advisory and information services for the small business.

Table 8.2   Training for Enterprise, 1977–1990

Year	Start-up training		Training for existing businesses		Total	
	No.	(%)	No.	(%)	No.	(%)
1977–78	32	100			32	100
1979–80	120	100			120	100
1981–82	560	95	30	5	590	100
1983–84	2564	84	493	16	3057	100
1984–85	6444	82	1426	18	7870	100
1985–86	21987	78	6241	22	28228	100
1986–87	52415	78	14623	22	67038	100
1987–88	74395	69	33360	31	107755	100
1988–89*	62375	60	40959	40	103334	100
1989–90*	58532	49	61679	51	120211	100

* Including Employment Training.

Take-up of training and support services

Training

Since 1977–78, not only has the level of training increased but there have been considerable increases in the take-up of training by the small firm. Whereas only 32 small firms were in receipt of training in 1977–78, by 1989–90 something in the order of 120,000 new and existing small businesses were being trained. As Table 8.2 reveals, the growth occurred particularly in the latter half of the 1980s, especially among existing small firms, which currently outnumber new businesses. Even so, such figures suggest that the proportion of small firms in receipt of training remains small. Indeed, if the figures for 1988–89 are taken, it would appear that, among VAT-registered businesses, start-up training was received by no more than 27 per cent of new firms while training for existing businesses achieved less than a 3 per cent penetration of the total stock.

Support services

By 1981–82, some ten years after its inception, the Small Firms Service was receiving some 183,140 inquiries (that is, one for every seven VAT-registered businesses in the country). By 1989–90, the level of inquiries had risen by 75 per cent to 317,529, representing approximately one inquiry for every five VAT-registered businesses (Table 8.3). Over the same period, the take up of the Service's counselling service also showed a marked increase, from 15,758 counselling sessions in 1981–82 to 50,609 in 1989–90 – a 221 per cent increase. Even

Table 8.3 Small Firms Service: take-up of services, 1981–1990

Year	Service	
	Inquiries	Counselling
1981–82	183,140	15,758
1982–83	218,651	20,167
1983–84	290,525	25,249
1984–85	242,101	34,180
1985–86	254,752	35,114
1986–87	283,537	38,210
1987–88	266,174	39,138
1988–89	281,459	43,029
1989–90	317,529	50,609

so, this represents no more than one session for every 31 businesses registered for VAT, a figure which is of even more significance when it is appreciated that almost two-thirds (64 per cent) of the firms counselled in 1989–90 were new businesses. The pattern of take-up revealed by Table 8.3 reflects the influence of the national advertising of the service in 1983–84 and 1986–87.

Since its inception in 1988, the DTI's Enterprise Initiative has been heavily promoted via television and press advertising campaigns. The result has been that, as of March 1991, a total of 77,000 applications had been received. Of these, 68,000 business reviews had been completed and 53,500 consultancies approved. Some 27,500 consultancies had been undertaken. Even so, despite all of the promotional activity involved, the number of firms making application represents no more than 3 per cent of the total number of businesses eligible for support under the Initiative.

When the figures are broken down in more detail, it would appear that interest in the Initiative is strongest in the northern regions of the country (North East, North West and Yorkshire and Humberside) which contain 22 per cent of the firms eligible for support but provide 28 per cent of the applications, with over half of all of the total applications, nationally, coming from firms in Assisted or Urban Programme Areas. Over 90 per cent of the applications approved for assisted consultancy come from firms employing fewer than 100 people and the split between manufacturing and service firms is approximately equal. Together, the marketing and quality initiatives have accounted for over half of the 53,500 consultancies that have been approved.

Effectiveness of training and support

Training

Evaluations of the effectiveness of training have been somewhat piecemeal and, frequently, programme-specific (Atkin and Gibb, 1984; Brown, 1990; Kirby,

1984; Sym and Lewis, 1986). Possibly the most comprehensive review of the government's efforts to promote training for small firms is that undertaken by the National Audit Office in 1988. This examines the effectiveness of the Training for Enterprise Programme and reveals that between 1983–84 and 1986–87 the number of people trained increased substantially more than the increase in financial support, with the result that the unit cost of provision fell from just over £2,000 to £268. This drive to reduce unit costs and increase the volume of training available in the small business field was achieved, at least in part, by requiring existing small firms to contribute to the cost of training. Even so, as the National Audit Office recognized, 'the understandable pressure on the Training Commission to expand its business training provision rapidly carries with it the inevitable risk that the newly-developed training is introduced nationally before testing its effectiveness' (op. cit. p. 17) and there is a need to ensure 'that standards of provision are maintained; that training provision complements the advisory and counselling services of the other parts of the small firms support infrastructure; and that well-defined criteria are applied to selecting TFE providers' (op. cit. p. 3). For some time these issues have exercised the minds of those concerned to improve the performance of small firms through training, not least because, given the scepticism of many owner-managers of the value of education, ' a bad training experience can be damaging to training provision' (Kirby, 1990, p. 86). However, as the National Audit Office recognized, there is little information on either the quality of training or the competence of potential providers and there exists a need for 'research to assess the training needs of established small firms, the effectiveness of . . . training and the economic benefits likely to result from such training' (op. cit. p. 3).

Support services

Given the financial involvement of the Department of Employment in both the Small Firms Service and local enterprise agencies, the National Audit Office report of 1988 includes a review, also, of both initiatives. While it is difficult to assign, as the report recognizes, 'increases in employment, turnover and profits directly to SFS advice' (op. cit. p. 21) a report for Business in the Community (undated) suggests that:

- businesses assisted by local enterprise agencies have a superior survival rate compared with other small firms
- firms helped by local enterprise agencies are making an important contribution to job creation, with 53 per cent of the net gain in jobs coming from firms with between three and ten employees
- the help provided by the local enterprise agencies is regarded as valuable to those firms assisted, being crucial to the survival of some 29 per cent
- the most valuable forms of agency assistance are general and start-up advice, financial advice and assistance with premises.

In contrast, the National Audit Office report concludes that although the Small Firms Service is regarded as providing a quality service throughout the country, it is not significantly penetrating its potential market. At the same time, the report provides evidence of dissatisfaction with the service, noting that some 20 per cent of participants on the government's Enterprise Allowance Scheme – which provides financial assistance of £40 per week for 52 weeks to unemployed people who wish to start a new business – were not satisfied with the advice received from the service. Overall, it concludes that while the work of the local enterprise agencies and the Small Firms Service is very different 'the multiplicity of advice agencies is confusing for potential clients' (op. cit., p. 3) and there is a need 'to ensure that the network of agencies is effective and that the small-businessman or woman knows where to go for advice'.

The DTI's Enterprise Initiative has been evaluated in two reports by Segal Quince Wicksteed (1989 and 1991). These reveal that 84 per cent of the firms surveyed believed that the scheme represented value for money for their share of the costs of consultancy and that 82 per cent had already begun to implement the consultant's recommendations. In addition, some 70 per cent of the firms had experienced clear commercial benefits within a year of their consultancy project and expected to recover their costs within three years. Over half of the firms surveyed reported that they were more likely to use full-price consultancy in the future as a consequence of the Consultancy Initiatives (CI). However, the reports do urge a note of caution. While firms were generally satisfied with their consultants, the reports recognize that 'important elements of CI (the Consultancy Initiative) are the demonstration effects of the successful scheme to firms which have not previously used consultancy . . . A small number of dissatisfied clients could have a disproportionate impact on the demonstration effect . . .' (Segal Quince Wicksteed, 1991, p. 12). As with training, it is necessary to ensure the quality and standard of the consultants and to make certain that they understand, fully, their small firm clients. Small firms are very different from large organizations and it is essential that those providing consultancy to small businesses appreciate that it is not simply a difference in scale of operation.

Conclusion

Clearly, very much has been done since the publication of the Bolton Report to extend to small firms the benefits of management training and support. While many new and existing small firms have been assisted over the years, the benefits derived are, often, unclear and there is little doubt that the proportion of small firms taking advantage of the services available remains relatively low. Indeed, the proportion could well be considerably lower than that implied by the statistics, since those firms that take advantage of one service often participate in the others (that is, there is a core of small businesses that take full advantage of the various management training and support services available). It is too early to pronounce on the effectiveness of the newly formed Training and Enterprise Councils in this context but their role is critical to the extension of management training and support to the small firms sector. Gaining the involvement of the small firm will not, however, be easy and considerable consideration has already been given to ways in which small firm participation might be increased (Curran, 1988; Gibb, 1988; Kirby, 1990).

From these, and the above analysis, it would appear that the key determinants to the provision, and take-up, of management training and support for small firms are coherence and consistency; quality and relevance; and proactivity and inducement.

Small firms are reluctant to train, resulting from their scepticism of its value, their real or imagined inability to pay and their lack of time. Given this situation, policy makers and providers will have to ensure that there is some incentive for small firms to train, that programmes are perceived to be of relevance and benefit, and that they are provided at a place, pace and time appropriate to the needs of the client or clients. Whether provided via distance/open learning or the more conventional 'classroom' mode of delivery, training packages need to be more flexible than previously and tailored more closely to the specific needs of the client group, their problems and the issues of most direct relevance to their organizations. A more focused approach such as this will not only help 'sell' the benefits of training but, invariably, will assist with implementation within the company.

To facilitate such a development, and the promotion of training generally, some form of accreditation both of trainers and small firms would seem desirable. Inevitably the development of a more flexible, problem-orientated approach to training requires a different set of tutor competences than in the more traditional pedagogic situations. Under such circumstances a system of trainer/consultant training and accreditation would seem particularly relevant if good practice is to be promoted and quality assured. Equally, training and good management practice among small firms generally could be promoted further by the issuing of a certificate of management competence. Such an exercise is shrouded in controversy and would be difficult to implement but, since it was first raised by the Committee of Inquiry (Smith, 1971) numerous proposals have been put forward – a licence to trade (as promulgated by the Forum for Private Enterprise with its proposals for Commissioned and Non-Commissioned Traders), the more loosely-defined proposals of the Charter Group Initiative or a requirement on the part of funding organizations for small firms to demonstrate their managerial competence before receiving financial support. Irrespective of the precise details, some form of company accreditation would provide the incentive for small firms 'to develop managerial competence in functions which are crucial to competitive success' (Department of Trade and Industry, 1988).

Attention needs to be paid, also, to the method of promoting management training and support. Many small firms are unaware of their management deficiencies and few actively seek management training and support. This suggests that there is a need for a more proactive approach than has been evident in the past and a requirement for a more integrated and long-term service, involving the identification of needs, arrangement of company training/consultancy programmes, assistance with implementation and regular monitoring of company requirements. While Training Access Points, One Stop Business Shops (HMSO, 1988) and the Enterprise Initiative (Department of Trade and Industry, 1988) are all consistent with this, such services will need to be presented in a better, more co-ordinated and more proactive manner if management training and support is to contribute, fully, to growth and development in the small firm sector.

9 Employment and Employment Relations in the Small Enterprise

The Bolton Report devoted remarkably few of its 435 pages to discussing employment and employment relations in the small firm, despite the fact that in the industries covered by the inquiry – agriculture, horticulture, fishing and the professions were systematically excluded from its deliberations – over 30 per cent of the labour force, equivalent to about 4.4m people, worked in small firms (Bolton, 1971, pp. 33–34). On employment relations, the report stated, in a much-cited paragraph:

> In many aspects the small firm provides a better environment for the employee than is possible in most large firms. Although physical working conditions may sometimes be inferior in small firms, most people prefer to work in a small group where communication presents few problems: the employee in a small firm can more easily see the relation between what he is doing and the objectives and performance of the firm as a whole. Where management is more direct and flexible, working rules can be varied to suit the individual. Each employee is also likely to have a more varied role with a chance to participate in several kinds of work . . . No doubt mainly as a result . . . turnover of staff in small firms is very low and strikes and other kinds of industrial dispute are relatively infrequent. The fact that small firms offer lower earnings than larger firms suggests that the convenience of location and generally the non-material satisfactions of working in them more than outweigh any financial sacrifice involved.
>
> (Bolton Report, 1971, p. 21)

The rather complacent tone of this paragraph is challenged by the more complex and subtle picture of employment and employment relations in the small firm that has emerged since 1971. The radical restructuring of the UK economy that began in the 1970s and accelerated in the 1980s launches into the 1990s an economy very different from that of the Bolton era: like so much else, employment and employment relations in the small enterprise are due for reassessment.

The small enterprise labour force

The small enterprise labour force has not only become numerically and proportionately more important since the early 1970s: it has also changed greatly in character. Bannock and Daly (1990, p. 256) estimated that in 1986, for instance, firms employing fewer than 20 people accounted for about 36 per cent of all non-government employment and that this had risen from 27 per cent in 1979, a rapid change in a relatively short time period. If a more generous definition of 'small' business is adopted – say, any business employing fewer than 50 people – then the small enterprise sector was estimated to be responsible for almost half (49.5 per cent) of all non-governmental employment. The trends that produced this sharply increasing small business share of total private sector employment continued after 1986, so that by 1991 it can be taken that firms employing up to 50 were responsible for the majority of all jobs in the private sector.

Another way of putting these figures is to note the conclusions of the extensive study of job generation in the UK conducted by Gallagher and colleagues over several years (see, for example, Gallagher and Stewart, 1986; Gallagher and Doyle, 1987; Robson *et al*, 1991 and *Labour Market Quarterly Report*, 1991, p. 7). Their most recent studies, covering the period 1985–1989, indicate that most job creation took place in the smallest firms. Those employing fewer than 20 people created around 1 million jobs – that is, more than twice as many as those created by larger firms (*Labour Market Quarterly Report*, 1991, p. 7). In short, a wide range of data indicates that the small enterprise sector is now central to any assessment of both employment in the UK economy and, by implication, employment relations.

The character of employment – that is, the types of jobs and the labour force that occupies them – has also changed considerably since the Bolton Report, although to some extent these changes have been more apparent than real. (The report tended, for example, to concentrate on full-time jobs, which had the effect of under-emphasizing the importance of part-time and casual jobs. More recently, discussion has recognized the significance of non-full-time work in the labour market, and may lead people to believe that part-time and casual jobs have increased more than they have.) In the late 1960s the UK was still a major manufacturing economy, with 8.6m people employed in manufacturing, for example, in 1971 (*Annual Abstract of Statistics*, 1973, p. 131). By 1988 this total had declined to 5 million, with almost half the decline occurring after 1979 (Ball *et al*, 1989, p. 140). Conversely, the importance of services has increased greatly over the two decades. In 1969, for instance, manufacturing contributed just over a third of GDP while private services and construction contributed just over 45 per cent. By 1987 manufacturing's share of GDP had fallen to 22.8 per cent while private services and construction had risen to 54.1 per cent (Hartley and Hooper, 1990, p. 267). (A fuller picture of the importance of services in GDP is given if public services are included: in 1969 public services were responsible for a further 12.3 per cent of GDP and showed a fluctuating but overall increase thereafter to 15.1 per cent in 1987.) In employment terms, by the end of the 1980s services (including the public sector) employed 15.8m people compared with around 9.5m in 1971 (*Annual Abstract of Statistics*, 1973, p. 131; Department of Employment, 1991, p. 8).

Due to the changes in the ways in which employment statistics are compiled over the period covered, this comparison is only approximate. The differences do, however, reflect the historical shift in the importance of services.

What is noteworthy about this increased importance of services and services employment is that small firms are very strongly represented in this sector. One estimate (Curran and Burrows, 1988, p. 55) indicates that nine out of ten of *all* small businesses – that is, businesses employing between one and twenty-four people – are in services. Concentration, in other words, is lower in services than manufacturing.

The difference between the services and manufacturing sectors is maintained in the characteristics of jobs as well as the kinds of people who occupy them. For instance, services employment is characterized by high levels of part-time and casual working compared with manufacturing (Hakim, 1987, p. 551). The shift to services in the economy has also led to an increase in the proportion of the labour force working part-time. In 1971, for example, 16 per cent of all those in employment were part-time. By 1990 this had risen to almost 22 per cent (Hakim, 1987, p. 555; *Employment Gazette*, 1991, p. 176). This has produced what has been termed a 'flexible workforce', which contains mainly part-time and casual workers and which by the mid-1980s was estimated to constitute perhaps as much as a third of the whole UK workforce (Hakim, 1987, p. 551).

Another significant point in analysing changes in the labour force since 1971 is the increased importance of women. Female participation in the formal economy has risen from 37 per cent in 1971 to 43.2 per cent in 1990 (Joseph, 1983, p. 70; *Employment Gazette*, 1991, p. 182). One explanation for this is that the service sector has a higher than average level of female employment. For instance, in 1987 52 per cent of all those employed in services were women compared with 43 per cent in the economy as a whole – a proportion that increased throughout the decade. At the same time, female employment grew faster than male employment in services (Graham *et al*, 1989, p. 47). Female workers are also more than proportionately represented among the flexible labour force – about half of all women working in 1986, for instance, were in the flexible workforce (Hakim, 1987, p. 551). In short, although it is not easy to estimate the male:female proportions of the small enterprise sector labour force, it is reasonable to conclude that the sector employs a large proportion of the female labour force.

A final point which might be made, if somewhat more tentatively, is that the small enterprise labour force is likely to be markedly younger than the work-force as a whole. Evidence on the age distribution of the labour force in small firms is hard to come by but Batstone (1969, p. 13) and Curran and Stanworth (1979a, p. 431) reported significantly younger age distributions for samples of workers in small firms, albeit mainly in manufacturing. Curran and Stanworth argued that small firm employers preferred younger employees not only be-cause they were cheaper but also because they believed them to be more flexible than older workers. In this they showed the 'ageist' recruiting practices commonly found among UK employers, small and large, but small firm owners are less likely than large employers to be constrained by pressures from those who protest at such behaviour. Many of the work roles in services are, as noted above, part-time or temporary and suited to younger workers.

Overall, therefore, the labour force in the small enterprise sector is relatively distinctive – in terms of characteristics such as gender, types of work and employment contracts – and differs somewhat from the labour forces employed in larger private and public sector organizations. Care must be taken, however, to avoid over-generalization. It has been argued that the sheer diversity of the economic activities in which small firms engage makes the phrase 'the small enterprise sector' highly misleading if it is taken to mean some population of enterprises with a set of characteristics that separates them clearly from other enterprises in the economy (Burrows and Curran, 1989, p. 530). Equally, by extension, to talk of *the* small enterprise labour force is also misleading. While – as the above discussion demonstrates – it is easy to isolate certain broad attributes upon which those who work in small enterprises are likely to differ from those who work elsewhere in the economy, nevertheless those who work in smaller firms will show very considerable variation and overlap with employees in larger enterprises.

Employment relations in the small firm: early perspectives

Although the Bolton Committee did not commission or carry out any research on employer-employee relations or the small firm employment experience, the rather rosy view encapsulated in the quotation cited earlier was not based entirely on anecdote or employers' views. Early research offered conclusions consistent with the 'all-one-happy-family view' of labour relations in the small firms. The Acton Society Trust studies (1953 and 1957) and the work of Revans (1956 and 1958), for example, had concluded that the small enterprise had closer and warmer relations between employers and employees than in larger firms and that 'morale' was higher and absenteeism lower. However, these early studies were theoretically and methodologically questionable by more recent standards. Theoretically, the approach was crudely positivist: the association between organizational size and the behaviour and attitudes of those involved was seen in a straightforward fashion. Company personnel data were uncritically accepted at face value and no employee views were systematically collected. Where attempts were made to go beyond crude statistical associations, it was found necessary to bring in, in an *ad hoc* fashion, such external factors as size of town in which the enterprise was located, or other elements of the work organization not necessarily related to size. (See for example Acton Society Trust, 1953, p. 39 and 1957, pp. 11 and 26.) Overall, as with so much later research, there was a strong, if perhaps largely unconscious, managerialist perspective.

Perhaps the most influential and theoretically sophisticated of the early research was that of Ingham (1970), which emerged just prior to the Bolton

Report itself and may even have influenced the authors of the report. Ingham argued that employees tended to self-select themselves into work environments most sympathetic to their own attitude towards work. Small enterprise employees commonly had what he termed a 'non-economistic expressive orientation' to work. This placed a relatively low emphasis on economic rewards and a high emphasis on non-economic rewards such as interesting work and satisfying social relations with others in the workplace and especially superiors. This orientation might be contrasted with an 'economistic instrumental orientation' held by employees who attached overriding importance to material rewards and who were willing to sacrifice intrinsic rewards to achieve them. In Ingham's view small enterprises provided an environment most likely to meet the needs of those with non-economistic expressive orientations, and larger firms those with strong instrumental-material wants. *Ceteris paribus*, those with the former orientation would opt to work in small firms. (Ingham, 1970, Ch. 3 passim.)

While Ingham's theorizing and research offered an intellectual gloss to the more prosaic assertions of the Bolton Report, a dissenting view gradually developed – initially from theoretical doubts but then on more firmly grounded empirical evidence. For instance, Henderson and Johnson (1974) were explicitly critical of the Bolton Report in principle:

> The belief that all is well in small firms' industrial relations [asserted in the Bolton Report] seems to be based on the simple, but fallacious, reasoning that because large size and complexity of organisation can create problems, smallness and simplicity automatically eliminate them.
>
> (Henderson and Johnson, 1974, p. 28)

They went on to argue that there were obvious reasons why, *a priori*, it might be expected that employer-employee relations in the small firm might not be as smooth and happy as the Bolton Report saw them. For example, small firms were highly vulnerable economically and this could well have implications for achieving and maintaining stable employer-employee relations. Small firm owner-managers were antipathetic to a methodical and systematic approach to management: they '. . . pride themselves on their informal approach . . .' argued Henderson and Johnson (1974, p. 29), but this again may result in an unplanned, hazard-prone approach to employing others.

Empirically grounded counter views to Bolton

A more empirical challenge to the Bolton Report's view and the research published up to 1971 only began to emerge in the late 1970s. Curran and Stanworth in a series of articles (Curran and Stanworth, 1979a and b; 1981a and b) using a more sophisticated methodology and a larger sample than Ingham, found little evidence to support either early studies such as those of the Acton Society Trust or Ingham. On theoretical grounds, for example, they questioned Ingham's emphasis on the notion of self-selection, pointing out that the employment relationship involved choices by both employees *and* employers. The market relationship through which small firm owner-managers recruit and retain employees is at least as much an employer prerogative as that of employees and, indeed, the evidence (Curran and Stanworth, 1979a, p. 441) indicated that employers were highly selective about whom they wished to employ.

At the empirical level, Curran and Stanworth (1979a, pp. 435–436) found relatively little evidence of stable work orientations developing over time of the kind envisaged by the self-selection thesis. Much job changing was based upon short-term considerations or was involuntary. It may be argued that this research carried out in a locality with high employment levels in the mid-1970s, would have found higher levels of short-term or involuntary job decisions elsewhere and certainly in the much more unstable UK economy of the 1980s and early 1990s.

In a further paper (Curran and Stanworth, 1979b) it was argued that social relations within the enterprise did not accord closely with the early research or the Bolton Report's conclusions. First, different industries had different cultures which affected such relations. In printing, for example, they found less successful relations between supervisors and shop floor workers than in electronics small firms (Curran and Stanworth, 1979b, pp. 328–329). Similarly, not only did they not find the close, conflict-free, face-to-face relations between owner-managers and employees depicted in the Bolton Report, they also found that the attitudes and views of employees varied between the two industries studied. Overall, the proportion of employees who felt that relations with their employers were close was much less than would have been expected from the Bolton Report's characterization (Curran and Stanworth 1979b, pp. 329–333).

In discussions of employer-employee relations in the small enterprise, the argument is frequently made that the clear and well-documented absence of collective expressions of employee dissatisfaction with employment relationships – and especially the strike (Prais, 1978; Smith *et al*, 1979; Daniel and Millward, 1983) – is evidence of conflict-free relations in small firms (Bolton, 1971, p. 21). The absence of trade unions in small firms is often added to this argument and, again, union membership statistics support this across a wide range of industries (Daniel and Millward, 1983, p. 25).

Overt expressions of conflict of the strike variety are not, however, the only ways in which conflict in the enterprise can be expressed. In the small enterprise the strike form is less likely because the numbers sharing common interests are likely to be small and, without trade union support, collective action is much more difficult to mount. Trade unions themselves find organizing small firm employees hard work. Owner-managers' dislike of trade unions is often deep-seated, making entry into the firm difficult for unions. Each small enterprise yields relatively few members and, as some research has indicated (Curran and Stanworth, 1979a, p. 437), labour instability in small firms is higher than in large firms. This means that, having organized employees, the union may well find a few months later that the whole exercise needs to be repeated. In the 1980s, trade unions were under tremendous pressure from a changed political climate reflected in new labour legislation: survival became a major goal. Seeking to extend their penetration into the difficult small firm sector became even less of a priority.

Instead, employee conflict in the small firm is likely to be expressed in ways other than the strike. Individual forms, particularly labour turnover, are much more likely. Any persisting disagreements – between two employees, an employee and supervisor or an employee and employer – are likely to be settled by one of the parties leaving the enterprise. Where it is a clash between employee and employer, inevitably it is the employee who will leave. Conflict resulting in people leaving the firm is also likely to be more common because other forms of conflict expression are also more difficult. Slow working, persistent lateness, absenteeism or pretended sickness are all likely to be tolerated far less by the small enterprise owner-manager than by a larger enterprise. Such expressions may be less visible in a larger firm but also small firm employers will feel the impact of such practices much more acutely on output simply because each individual employee is responsible for a larger proportion of total output. Finally, the absence of a trade union also means a lower likelihood of an employee having a representative who can speak on behalf of employees who feel unable or unwilling to speak on their own behalf.

Conflict expression can take a wide variety of forms and employees in different economic contexts have different conflict strategies at their disposal. A similar point was made by Newby (1977) in analysing paternalistic relationships in the economy and the community. Such relations are or were common in rural communities where authority relations between superiors and their subordinates stem from beliefs supposedly shared by all involved. These beliefs stress personal relations, mutual obligation and the importance of a stable social order embodied in immutable traditions.

As Newby pointed out, such relations are often seen as best exemplified in traditional landowner-village community relations, but they are also sometimes seen, in less-pure forms, in industrial and urban settings, including the small enterprise. But, he argued, the persistence of such relations may not so much reflect the commitment of employees to the kind of conflict-free, all-one-happy-family view of the enterprise but rather a pragmatic acceptance of the *status quo* where there is a perceived lack of alternatives. In other words, where few alternatives yielding superior rewards and relations are seen by employees, they tailor their responses to the situation. An analysis along these lines might well be extended beyond the small enterprise to a much wider cross-section of the economy in the UK of the 1980s and early 1990s.

Three recent perspectives

Three main weaknesses are evident in the discussion of employment relations in the small enterprise that stemmed from the Bolton Report and the critique it provoked.

The first was that, like the report itself, much of the later writing over-emphasized the small firm in manufacturing. Ingham (1970) and Curran and Stanworth (1979a and b; 1981a and b) concentrated solely on employees in manufacturing firms whereas, as noted above, most small firms and most small firm employees are in services.

This was compounded by a second weakness – the inability of theorists and researchers to encompass the sheer variety of employment contexts in which small firms are found. This led to over-generalization even when researchers were careful to claim that their findings applied only to the kinds of small firm employer-employee relations studied.

The third research weakness – which extends back beyond Bolton to the very earliest studies – was the inability to focus on day-to-day relations within the enterprise. Secondary data on absenteeism levels, employers' statements of their attitudes and behaviour towards their employees and interviews with employees themselves – all provide valuable data. But secondary data rarely reveal the meanings context which the statistics signify and human beings often offer views and accounts of their actions that do not correspond with what actually happens in everyday situations.

Three post-1980 studies illustrate the ways in which more-recent theorizing and research have coped with the above weaknesses and continued to develop a more subtle and credible picture of employer-employee relations in the small enterprise.

The process of industrial relations in small firms

The first study is that of Scott *et al* (1989). This attempts to meet many of the weaknesses of previous research and takes the debate on employment relations in the small firm forward in a number of areas.

The research design involved interviewing almost 400 owner-managers of small firms in both manufacturing and services and conducting more-detailed case studies of 30 firms (which allowed the researchers to gather employee views, although the number of employees interviewed is not given). The prime focus of the study was seen as investigating the day-to-day industrial relations practices of small firms. In other words, the research sought to avoid some of the major weaknesses of earlier work by investigating a range of small enterprises in different sectors of the economy and gathering information from both employers and employees and especially by looking at the *process* of industrial relations rather than producing a snapshot picture from one-off interviews with those involved.

Many of the findings represent a continuity and confirmation of previous research. For instance, the notion of prior orientations as important in determining employee self-selection into small firm employment again receives little support. Industrial sub-cultural differences were also found to be pronounced, with employers' and workers' attitudes, as well as their relations, varying considerably. Labour instability was also common and high, though again it varied considerably with economic sector. Overt disputes were found to be relatively rare but employers also displayed high levels of dissatisfaction with the employees they recruited – finding people with the 'right' attitudes, skills and behaviour, and then retaining them, appeared to be a permanent headache for a high proportion of employers.

Scott *et al* (1989, p. 42) point out that much of the discussion of small firm industrial relations has been implicitly premised on theorizing and research about these relations in large firms. Small firms are then evaluated by these benchmarks, and offering evidence of their departure from the norms of large firm industrial relations patterns is seen as sufficient in explaining the distinctive characteristics of small enterprise employer-employee relations. Scott *et al* argue that what is required for a more adequate interpretation is a positive analysis of *why* employer-employee relations in the small firm take the patterns found.

The central theme of the interpretation offered by Scott *et al* is that '. . . personal relations *through process* become "industrial" relations issues' (p. 42) (emphasis in the original). Particularism is a common feature of small firm social relations. People and especially owner-managers in their assessment of employees, see each other person-to-person within a framework of what is termed 'informal routinization'.

When asked about labour relations, the conventional reply from owner-managers was that there were few problems – everybody gets along with everybody else, with perhaps the occasional problem. This 'occasional problem' is often explained in personal terms, as the result of an employee with the 'wrong attitudes', someone who 'did not fit in' or was 'a trouble-maker'. In other words, what might be seen as industrial relations issues in other contexts – resulting, for example, from employees having different views from their employers or inconsistencies of managerial practice or organizational and work arrangements – are not perceived as such by employers. Employers have a strongly unitarist view of the enterprise and relations between themselves and employees. The firm is their creation and sustained through their investment and hard efforts, which gives them the right to define its aims and how they will be achieved. Without the owner-managers' investment and hard work there would be no jobs for anybody. Disagreement with management, therefore, is illegitimate except under very unusual circumstances.

Control within the enterprise is informal and personal. For instance, one owner-manager in Scott *et al*'s sample '. . . laid great emphasis on the fact that he did not require his workers to "clock in" ' (Scott *et al*, 1989, p. 43), but as one of the employees pointed out, the owner-manager could see at a glance if anybody was late. Informal controls of these kinds may be much more effective than the formal controls typical of the larger firm where individuals can often escape the more bureaucratic monitoring of their performances because they are only one of a large number.

Employees' attitudes differed both by industry and type of work. Thus, technical and scientific employees in high-tech firms displayed the same careerist attitudes as their counterparts in larger firms: working in a small firm was often seen as a career stage, an opportunity to acquire particular kinds of skills for later stages but if possible with no sacrifice of earnings since earnings were regarded as public recognition of career progress achieved. For employees in traditional sectors, on the other hand – in both manufacturing and services – entry into employment in small firms was often precipitated not by any positive career plan but by unemployment and some informal connection with the firm. Involvement in the job was often instrumental and balanced against the available alternatives, although as Scott *et al* point out, 'The power of inertia and routine should not be underestimated' (1989, p. 40). These employees were not usually energetically seeking alternatives but rather keeping an eye on the market and willing to take advantage of an opportunity should it be presented – for example, as the result of another employer poaching employees.

Relationships within the enterprise are always problematical, argue Scott *et al*, because any crisis in relations due, for example, to poor worker performance or the need to redefine work practices to meet new market demands, may require employer sanctions and the explicit demonstration of inequalities of power. Employers are often understandably reluctant to do this, since it can damage employer-employee relations beyond repair. Sometimes, for example, employers will approach the troublesome employee indirectly through another employee who will be asked to 'have a word' with him or her. The intermediary may be the person who originally recommended the problem employee, or somebody who gets on well with them. Delays in using formal sanctions often mean that when the employer feels there is no alternative to dismissal, the latter is enforced quickly without formal warnings. One result is that small firm owner-managers are disproportionately involved in industrial tribunal proceedings (Dickens *et al*, 1984).

This somewhat abbreviated account of Scott *et al*'s study nevertheless provides a sufficiently full picture to demonstrate the range and depth of the analysis. The study undoubtedly takes the interpretation of employer-employee relations in the small enterprise a good deal further, building on earlier work. It is not, however, without its weaknesses. For instance, the simple two-fold division into manufacturing and services giving broadly equal weight to both is misleading because it fails to acknowledge the greater numerical importance of services small firms. In turn, this leads to an underestimation both of the variety of employer-employee relations settings in services and the special characteristics of services work. For instance, much service employment involves routine direct contact with the customer, with production and consumption occurring simultaneously. This makes it more difficult for the employer to control output quality and employee performance than, for example, in manufacturing, where inspection can usually be performed before the product reaches the customer.

Much service work also involves what has been called 'emotional labour' (Hochschild, 1983; Filby 1990; Kitching *et al*, 1990). This involves the use of facial and bodily displays, the deliberate use of emotion-invoking strategies, including sexual varieties, to elicit particular customer responses and satisfactions. Again, this dimension of work role performance is generally absent in manufacturing but in services its presence must add to the problems of employer control and industrial relations. Finally, as Kitching (1991, p. 73) points out, despite their declared attempt to offer a more balanced view, the approach of Scott *et al* still favours employers' strategies for controlling the labour process and employee performance. Much less attention is given to exploring how employees influence the wage-effort bargain and employers' performance. One reason for this might be that although the authors stress the importance of observing the process of industrial relations within the enterprise, the case study approach used involved visiting each firm on only three occasions for what must have been relatively short periods. The absence of trade unions means that collective attempts to influence employers are relatively rare, but there is no reason to believe that employees are devoid of bargaining strategies of a more individual kind.

Structural economic forces and small firm industrial relations

The second more-recent study which illustrates the development of recent research on small firm employment relations is that of Rainnie (1989). One problem of virtually all previous work is its pervasive dualism – almost inevitably, small firms are distinguished from large firms with each contrasted with the other implicitly or explicitly. This means that, all too often, the small firm sector is seen as somehow apart from the rest of the economy and isolated from it. One common form of this dualism in the past was to see the small enterprise as part of some out-moded traditional economy doomed to wither away under the pressures from a dominant modern economy of large-scale enterprises. More recently, however, a range of re-structuring theories has emerged, seeking to interpret the massive structural changes in the UK and other advanced industrial economies over the last fifteen years, and these have given the small enterprise a higher profile as part of a new economy (see, for example, Piore and Sabel, 1984; Allen and Massey, 1988; Murray, 1989).

In this new economy, small firms are seen as playing a necessary though generally secondary role. For example, in the core-periphery thesis offered by Atkinson (1985) and Atkinson and Gregory (1986) it is argued that the dominance of large-scale mass production firms of the 'Fordist' era – roughly 1910–1975 – is increasingly disappearing to be replaced by a 'flexible firms' economy. In this there are 'restructured' large firms which have shed what is regarded as their non-core activities, such as transport, cleaning, catering and security, by sub-contracting them to outside suppliers. In addition, these newer firms develop 'flexible labour forces' consisting of permanent 'core' workers and peripheral employees hired and discarded as required for particular needs. The periphery of this new economy is populated largely by small firms and the self-employed.

One criticism made of this and similar theories is that, apart from the highly questionable notion that small firms are mainly or inevitably peripheral to the main development of the economy (thus neglecting the fact that in many sectors such as electronics and computing, it is small firms which are often at the leading edge of the economy), the small enterprise itself is a 'black box' (Curran, 1990). Little attention is given to those who run or are employed in small firms or how small firms function as economic units or how these aspects are linked to the role the small enterprise occupies in the wider economy.

Rainnie (1989) seeks to offer not only a more adequate answer to the question of how the small firm is integrated into the economy than the various core-periphery, 'Post-Fordist' and 'flexible economy' theses but, more importantly for the concerns of this chapter, on how differing patterns of integration affect industrial relations within the small firm. In other words, he tries to dissolve the false dualism of so many earlier views and show how industrial relations in the small enterprise is not simply a matter of interpersonal relations between owner-managers and their employees.

Rainnie argues that, historically, industrial economies have never developed evenly and smoothly. There has never been a single, clear path of economic development but rather several lines of development co-existing at any one time so that overall development is uneven in the economy with all kinds of cross-linkages – contradictory and mutually supporting – at any one time. This allows a wide range of forms of organization to exist alongside each other. Old and seemingly outdated systems of production continue to function quite successfully in an economy with other allegedly highly efficient, state-of-the-art production systems.

From time to time, periods of high uncertainty emerge when rapidly changing technology and especially markets are unpredictable. The period from the early 1970s onwards is one such period and one response, from larger businesses especially, has been to fragment their activities into smaller units, either smaller entirely owned plants or through sub-contracting to independent outsiders, many of whom will be small businesses. This allows larger enterprises to operate much more flexibly and thus respond more quickly and effectively to unstable external conditions. Labour costs are also lowered since smaller firms offer lower levels of rewards and trade union power is reduced. These processes, it should be stressed, are not only found in the UK but in many other advanced industrial societies including the US, Italy and most recently are emerging in Eastern bloc countries. Japan has had this kind of economy for several decades already.

From this overall thesis, Rainnie (1989, p. 85) derives a four-fold typology of relations between small firms and the wider economy. (As he makes clear (1989, pp. 84–6) he is here developing the earlier three-fold approach of Shutt and Whittington (1984), who offered a similar overall thesis.)

(i)   Dependent – where small firms serve the needs of larger firms, for instance, as sub-contractors with their survival and success entirely linked to large firm strategies and decisions.
(ii) Competitive dependent – where small firms compete with larger firms but only succeed by the intense exploitation of labour and equipment.
(iii) Old independent – small firms operating in niche markets unlikely to be bothered by larger firms because these markets offer few opportunities for making large profits.
(iv) New independent – small firms operating in new or developing markets but likely to receive the acquisitive attention of larger firms should a market flourish.

Rainnie goes on to argue that internal social relations within the small firm and the labour process are determined largely by the position the firm occupies in the above typology. He illustrates the point by case studies of small firms in the clothing and printing industries. The clothing manufacturing industry is a prime example of a 'dependent' relationship. Most clothing firms are small, entry into the industry is cheap and the technology is simple. The customers for the small firms' output are mainly large high street retailers epitomized by Marks and Spencer with its 600-plus suppliers. Intense competition among high street clothing retailers means that prices to suppliers are shaved to the minimum: suppliers, in turn, are forced to minimize their costs (including labour costs) and run their machinery hard. Since their raw materials – textiles – also come mainly from large firms, they are again squeezed by powerful suppliers.

In short, Rainnie is arguing that clothing manufacture, the classic 'sweat-shop' small firm industry with its reputation for low wages, poor conditions and autocratic management, is a reflection of the position of these firms in the wider economy. Their industrial relations patterns can only be understood by reference to these external conditions. Small firm social relations may be highly personalized but they are even more fundamentally conditioned by the position of the firm in the economy.

Small clothing firms are contrasted with small firms in printing. Though very much a small firm industry, printing is much more diverse in terms of technology and products than clothing firms: the main emphasis in Rainnie's account, however, is on the small, local jobbing printer engaged in producing relatively small quantities of 'bespoke' output for other businesses and individual consumers. Larger printing firms are not interested in this market because there are few advantages of scale. For several decades, small firms in general printing were fair approximations to the 'old independent' type and industrial relations patterns reflected this with relatively well organized employees and employers able to cope with organized labour through their local market advantages.

However, small jobbing printers are highly dependent on other businesses for demand for their output and the severe recession of the early 1980s and early 1990s (particularly the former) produced acute competition among existing firms and from new sources such as in-house printing, 'instant' printers and print substitutes such as electronics-based information systems. New technology in the industry added further to the disruption of traditional patterns in the industry.

On the employee side of the industrial relations equation in small printing firms, new technology fragmented and destroyed traditional skills. Many firms no longer use trained printers, weakening trade union organization. Other firms have emerged that specialize in techniques of printing that use only a limited range of skills. On the employer side, many owner-managers have not had a long career in the industry as in the past when progression from crafts-man to owner-manager was common. Instead, many new owner-managers are much more market-oriented than production or craft-oriented (see also Goss, 1991, pp. 80–81). The result is that social and industrial relations patterns in the industry have been undergoing radical changes over the last decade or so.

Rainnie's argument is largely successful in defeating the previous tendency in the discussion of small enterprise industrial relations towards implicitly seeing the firm existing in a vacuum. He shows how small enterprise employer-employee relations might well be highly contingent upon how the small enterprise relates to the wider economy. He also attempts to take into account variations in this relationship and how these impact on social relations inside the enterprise. But, again, the analysis has some obvious weaknesses. Employers' perspectives are seen in an over-determined way as strict outcomes of external forces rather than the activities of real people. The question may be asked whether employers and small firms are really so constrained by their external environments? Many would argue that national and local economies are much less closely integrated than this thesis implies – certainly many owner-managers do not see themselves in this way (Curran, 1987; Scott *et al*, 1989, p. 9). Finally, the empirical support for the thesis draws upon a very narrow range of small firm activities – two main kinds only, clothing manufacture and printing – and, even more regrettably, is again confined to manufacturing. To what extent does the thesis apply to the great majority of small enterprises not in manufacturing?

Relating employer and employee strategies to each other

The third and final example of the ways in which the study of employer-employee relations in the small firm have developed in the 20 years since the Bolton Report is the work of Goss (1986 and 1991). As argued above, a weakness of the Bolton Report's view of industrial relations in the small enterprise was its one-dimensional character. Not only did it present an over-harmonious view but implied that this was common across the whole range of small firm environments regardless of the sector of the economy. Equally, it might be argued that Rainnie's choice of a 'sweatshop' industry, clothing manufacture, and printing, a highly unionized industry with a history of employer-employee struggles, was also misleading. Not all small firms are 'sweatshops' by any means and few economic sectors where small firms predominate are highly unionized. Scott *et al* did strive to cover a wide range of economic sectors and drew some differences between the sectors but this was at a very general level, comparing, for example, 'traditional manufacturing' with 'high-tech services' or 'high-tech manufacture' with 'traditional services'.

   Goss (1991, p. 71) notes that much of the research since Bolton undermines the harmony view, since it shows that small enterprise employees do not differ fundamentally from large firm workers in terms of their attitudes, and labour turnover levels in small firms do not indicate any great attachment to the firm or employer. Yet union membership and overt dispute levels *are* lower in small firms generally than elsewhere in the economy. There is also variation across the small enterprise population and Goss argues that this may best be explained by a close analysis of the ways in which employers exercise control over employees and the labour process – which is known to be subject to wide variation – and the ability of employees to '. . . individually or collectively . . . resist the exercise of proprietorial prerogative' (Goss, 1991, p. 63). Employers may, for instance, be heavily dependent upon employees where the latter are highly skilled and scarce. Under these conditions, proprietorial prerogative will be exercised only with great care by employers. Employers, in other words, will adopt modes of control that take into account employees' expectations and bargaining power.

Using a similar approach to that of Rainnie discussed above, Goss offers a typology of owner-manager controls which reflect employee bargaining resources:

(i) Fraternalism. This control strategy will be common where there is a high level of employer dependence on employees who provide skills and other inputs crucial to the success of the business. One example of this situation is small construction firms where the owner-manager is essentially *primus inter pares*, working alongside employees whose skills differ from the owner-manager's but are just as essential to the successful completion of the firm's work.

The employer negotiates with rather than controls employees and there is a strong egalitarian ethos. Similar arrangements are common in small profession- al service enterprises or 'partnerships', and in high-tech firms in relation to highly skilled employees. The harmonious relations commonly found in these situations is not simply a reflection of the personalities of those involved or good person-to-person relations but an outcome of the particular circum- stances in which employers and employees find themselves.

(ii) Paternalism. This occurs where the employers' dependence on employees is less than under fraternalism and also where employee power is lower. Dif- ferentiation between employer and employee is marked, but there is also a cultivation of subordinates' identification with their superiors. The relationship has been very clearly analysed by Newby (1977) in his study of farming. The social and economic differences between the large landowner/farmers and em- ployees were very marked. Ordinary workers were not only highly dependent on employers for their livelihoods – there were few alternative forms of employ- ment in the area – but also for the roof over their heads. Employees were unable to see how this situation could ever change: it had always been like this and always would be. Yet the farmers needed commitment and skill from the em- ployees. Livestock, machinery and the land itself are all valuable assets and much of the employee's work was not supervised directly. Paternalism as a control strategy tries to secure employee identification with the employer's aims by strong personal relations and mutual duties and obligations extending beyond work to life more generally. Employers will, for example, undertake duties in the wider community backing their efforts with resources. In short, wages may be low, but the individual employer cannot be blamed since the consideration and kindness extended to employees and others clearly refute any responsibility the farmer might have for these poor rewards. Paternalistic con- trol is likely to be effective only where the employment relationship is isolated from the wider economy.

(iii) Benevolent autocracy. Here the employers' control is based more on simple positional power – that is, their role as employer. They are not powerful enough to achieve paternalistic relations but neither are employees so depend- ent that they cannot assert a measure of independence. The closeness of the links between employers and employees is emphasized but only within the employment relationship: there is no extending of the relationship beyond the workplace. A balance is achieved, therefore, between a necessary particularism and impersonal market forces. This produces a relationship in which for much of the time the people involved accept the imbalance of power between employer and employee as a fact of life rather than as a basis for struggle or negotiation. But, equally, relations are relatively informal and friendly, with first names used much of the time and people treated as individuals, but relations are ring-fenced by the enterprise boundaries. Both employers and employees are aware of the realities and limits of their relations.

(iv) Sweating. Here employer power is dominant and employee power weak. Employers can replace employees easily and therefore have no incentive to develop relations much beyond a narrow market relationship. Labour costs are more critical than labour stability or trustworthiness. Here Goss's account closely parallels Rainnie's discussion of the small clothing manufacturer. Employers are at the mercy of the unpredictable market, demanding rush orders, cancelling long-term orders where consumer taste changes, and competition between firms is fierce.

As Goss argues, the value of his typology is that it allows some of the complexities of small firm employer-employee relations to be brought out in a systematic fashion. Further, it attempts to bring both employer and employee attitudes, actions and strategies into the analysis. This brings employees in particular into the analysis as players, as proactive contributors to the enterprise and its social relations, something which previous research has largely failed to do with any conviction. It also gets away from both the 'all-is-harmony' and 'all-is-evil' views of small firm employer-employee relations and offers good reasons why such relations may be largely independent of the personal qualities and personal relations of those involved in the small enterprise since, as in many other spheres of life, the people in question are often coping with forces and constraints beyond their control.

Again, there are clear weaknesses to be noted in the approach. The likely distribution of small enterprises between the four types is almost certainly highly uneven with the third, benevolent autocracy, containing the great majority of firms. This means that further categorization would be required if a more adequate analysis is to be produced. Moreover, it might well be that more than one type of relationship will exist in the same firm at the same time. For example, fraternalistic relations may dominate between employer and highly skilled workers but other kinds – benevolent autocracy or even sweating – may dominate in the employer's relations with other employees in the firm. Relations and their bases may also be unstable over time due to changes in the bargaining powers and strategies of employers and employees. And, finally, the examples of work environment upon which Goss bases the typology cover the building industry, high-technology industries, agriculture and printing with virtually no attention to service sector enterprises. (The printing industry holds a curious fascination for small business researchers and particularly those interested in industrial relations: besides Goss, for whom printing provides the most detailed industrial sector example in his theorizing and research, it will be noted that Rainnie, 1989, and Curran and Stanworth, 1979a and b and 1981a and b, give the same sector prominence in their analysis.)

Conclusions

The understanding of employer-employee relations in the small enterprise has developed greatly over the last twenty years, as researchers have offered an increasingly complex and subtle analysis of how employers' labour strategies are patterned and how employees in small firms react to their employment circumstances.

The three contemporary contributions to theorizing and research on small firm employment relations selected for detailed discussion – Scott *et al* (1989), Rainnie (1989) and Goss (1991) – were chosen because they bring out key aspects of the processes involved. Scott *et al* seek to focus on the *process* of employer-employee relations within the enterprise and to go beyond employer and employee statements of what they believe and what they say happens. Rainnie opens up the issue of the way in which the small firm's role in the wider economy can determine relations between those within the enterprise. Goss indicates how the variety of owner-manager labour management strategies and employee behaviours may be put within a wider, systematic framework. Although there is overlap between the three sets of concerns, each contribution has also widened the range of issues addressed to produce a fuller picture. Overall, they (and other contributions over the last twenty years) have produced an immeasurably more convincing and thought-provoking account of employment relations in the small firm than existed in 1971.

It remains the case, however, that too little attention is given to employment and employment relations in the small firm's functioning. Compared, for example, with the immense literature devoted to entrepreneurs and entrepreneurship and the management of the small business, those employed in small firms and their relations with owner-managers, still arguably receive much less research effort. One reason for this is that the owner-manager/entrepreneur is often equated with the enterprise as if nobody else were involved. Another reason for this neglect is that conventional industrial relations studies are still anchored in the large enterprise, focusing centrally on large enterprise employment relations, trade unions and large-scale conflict expression so that the small enterprise is almost ignored.

Now that small firms, defined as firms employing less than 100 people, are almost certainly responsible for over half of all employment in the private sector, the neglect of employer-employee relations in such firms becomes increasingly reprehensible in policy and research terms. The nature of the work process in smaller enterprises and the precise ways in which employer and employee construct their mutual relations and sustain them in order to produce a major proportion of the nation's output, must be understood if training policies, employment and industrial relations laws are to be effective in meeting the needs of firms, employees and the economy.

Conventional industrial relations studies also need a fundamental reorientation. They grew up in the 'Fordist' economy of the early and middle decades of this century, an economy dominated by large mass production firms and heavy industry with labour forces and employers highly organized in powerful trade unions and employers' associations. Governments felt unable to govern without consulting the key bodies and representatives of this 'fifth estate' of the realm (Taylor, 1978). In the economy that emerged in the 1980s, large units have become less important in employment terms. Small firms are much more important numerically in the UK economy and many larger firms have fragmented their activities through the use of smaller establishments and sub-contracting. The fifth estate has also lost much of its force. A smaller proportion of the labour force belongs to trade unions, labour and industrial relations legislation has reduced the power of unions and decentralized bargaining has reduced the importance of employers' associations as collective bargaining bodies.

What the above changes mean is that the small enterprise and its employer-employee relations patterns have not only become more important in terms of the proportions of the workforce they affect but, in many ways, they point towards what might be termed 'the new industrial relations' of the new UK economy. In these new industrial relations, national collective negotiations and bargaining are much less important. Employees and employers are much more frequently involved in one-to-one relations and the critical industrial relations processes have descended several levels from the national to the local to the particular employer and the particular employee.

It has been argued in the popular press and elsewhere that the above changes are producing a new anarchism in employment relations in the UK economy. For instance, it is suggested that the drift away from national wage and salary bargaining produces a disorganized bargaining process. This is also alleged to contribute to a leap-frogging in rewards which added greatly to the severe inflationary pressure seen in the late 1980s and government difficulties in dealing with it effectively. By implication, this analysis is sometimes extended to suggest that employment relations themselves are becoming anarchic – employers can hire and fire at will, unilaterally tear up employment contracts and employees' bargaining power dissolves.

While it would be wrong to suggest that employer bargaining power has not increased over the last decade or so, or that some employers have not used their power to reduce employee reward levels and introduce tough, demanding work requirements, this is not the whole story. The developing body of theorizing and research on the small enterprise – particularly the kinds highlighted in this chapter – indicates that the sweatshop or equivalent is far from common. People have to get along with each other to maintain productive relations over time and may construct these relations in a wide variety of ways subject to external constraints. Moreover, these relations are also far from anarchic. On the contrary, they are patterned in particular ways which researchers have slowly been revealing. In other words, theorizing and research on the small firm have much to contribute to the understanding of employment and industrial relations much more generally. Only a few years ago, it was possible to argue that small firm researchers were overly influenced by conventional industrial relations studies based on the large firm (Rainnie and Scott, 1986, pp. 47–48). The small firm's employment relations were judged by the norm of what happened in large firms. Now it is possible to see how this situation may well be reversed with theorizing and insights from small business research offering a key contribution to the fundamental rethinking of conventional industrial relations studies required to understand employment in Britain in the 1990s.

Of course, the above should not be taken to suggest that little remains to be understood in small firm employment relations. For instance, the neglect of small firms in services, where by far the majority of small firms are located, remains a serious weakness. The distinctive characteristics of the small enterprise sector labour force have already been emphasized – the high proportions of part-time, female and younger workers, for example – and research designs investigating employer-employee relations need to recognize these characteristics much more explicitly. Or again, the process of employment relations as it happens in the day-to-day life of the enterprise remains largely unknown because of the sheer difficulty of devising methodologically satisfactory ways of observing what actually happens, especially over relatively long time periods – say, two to three years. It is necessary to extend this observation over such periods not just to collect more detailed accounts but to observe what happens over the kind of business cycle now experienced by the UK economy. Much of the current and previous research relies too much on a 'snapshot' of what is happening at a single point in the cycle.

10 Managers and Management within Small Firms

One of the most frequently quoted aspects of the Bolton Report (1971) was its conceptual definition of a small business – legally independent; with a small market share; and owned and managed by the same individual or group of individuals. The last of these characteristics is now open to challenge, both as to generality and relevance. While the very smallest firms *do* combine ownership and management within the same individual, this is not the case once the firm grows beyond a very small scale. At some point, probably in the range of ten to twenty employees in many industrial sectors (and obviously varying from one sector to another) individuals have to be appointed whose task is, at least partly, to be responsible for the management of others. Since these are often not owners of the firm the concurrence of ownership with management as envisaged by Bolton begins to disappear. A business with between one and two hundred employees in the manufacturing sector is regarded by the Bolton statistical definition as a small firm. Such a firm, however, is likely to have a cadre of non-owning managers who are likely to considerably outnumber the owner or owners.

Despite the power of this simple observation it is striking to consider the extent to which the concept of 'owner-manager' dominates the small firm literature. Probably the best illustration of this is the authoritative review by Curran (1986) of research in the fifteen years following the publication of the Bolton Report. In Curran's review there are many references to 'owner managers' yet not a single reference to 'non-owner managers'. This reflects the emphasis of small firm researchers and our consequent ignorance of the role and significance of small firm managers who are not owners. It is only in very recent times – that is, since the Curran review – that the role of the small firm non-owning manager has come to be recognized at all. This may reflect the changing emphasis in research and policy towards smaller firms, in the UK. In the last few years there has been a greater concern with faster growing small firms where non-owning managers are of greater importance.

According to Bannock and Daly (1990) there are 2,459,000 businesses in the UK with fewer than 200 workers, but of these only 78,000, or three per cent, have between 20 and 199 employees. That 3 per cent provides the focus of this chapter, which derives in large part from an ESRC-sponsored programme of research on Industrial Competitiveness (Managerial Labour Markets, ESRC Grant No. 20230022).

Non-owning managers: what do we know already?

This section begins by reviewing some of the relevant strategic and organizational literature that relates directly to the performance of smaller firms. In undertaking this review it is worth stressing the point that a small firm is not simply a scaled-down version of a large firm (Storey *et al*, 1987). It is clear that the strategic and organizational issues facing the small young firm are fundamentally different from those facing the larger firm. Nowhere is this point made more graphically than by Penrose (1959) who says: 'the differences in the administrative structure of the very small and the very large firm are so great that in many ways it is hard to see that the two species are of the same genus . . . we cannot define a caterpillar and then use the same definition for a butterfly' (p. 19).

To contextualize any review of the role of non-owner managers in small firms requires us to anchor the discussion initially in the more familiar territory of the owner manager. This focuses upon two main issues. First, the personal and socio-economic characteristics of the founders of small firms and their motivations for starting the business; second, and most important in the current context, their styles of management, forms of internal organization and relationships with their employees.

The owner manager

Strategic, behavioural and organizational literature on the smaller firm, where it is in any way related to firm performance, examines only the owner or owners. Lafuente and Salas (1989) describe a familiar form with their typology set out in Figure 10.1.

In their categorization of entrepreneurs, Lafuente and Salas suggest there are three, not necessarily independent, dimensions. The first dimension consists of the personal background characteristics of the individual, such as gender, education, age and parental occupation. The second is work experience in terms of whether they worked in a large or small firm, the industry in which they worked and whether or not they had managerial experience. A third dimension is a

Figure 10.1   Small firm performance in the traditional owner-manager typology

set of behavioural and motivational characteristics, such as their attitudes to risk and whether or not they were unemployed. From these characteristics, a number of typologies of entrepreneurs have been formulated and related both to the probability of an individual becoming an entrepreneur and to their 'success' once in business. There are a number of reviews of this literature such as Storey (1982), Bragard *et al* (1985), Chell (1985) and Lafuente and Salas (1989).

These studies reach broadly similar conclusions – that there are differences in the performance of small firms that are related to the characteristics of the owner. For example, most studies show the education level of the founder to be broadly correlated with firm performance, except perhaps among those with the highest academic qualifications (Bragard *et al*, 1985). It also appears to be the case that managerial experience, employment within the same industry, and observation of market opportunities are also positively related to 'success' (Monck *et al*, 1988).

Non-owner managers and small firm performance

It is not the purpose of this chapter to provide a comprehensive review of the role of small firm founders and firm performance. Its intention is to shift the debate away from the extensive literature cited above – in which the founder(s) or owner(s), *per se*, are viewed as the sole managerial resource – and towards the question of how that/those individual(s) manage the process of growth through the employment of non-owner managers. An examination of the strategy and organizational literature on smaller firms where it relates to firm performance determines the extent to which the issue has been addressed.

Small firm strategy is examined by Feeser and Willard (1990) who conclude from their study of high technology firms that the most basic strategic question of 'what market(s) should we enter with what product(s)?' has to be answered correctly to ensure success. As they put it, 'the experimental "cut and try, learn as you go" approach does not pay off in the early years'.

Covin and Slevin (1989), argue that organizational structure and strategic posture need to be very different for small firms to operate successfully in hostile, compared with benign environments (markets). In many senses their findings reflect the Structure Conduct Performance paradigm favoured by economists since it suggests the clear importance in hostile, highly competitive markets of organizational flexibility and a willingness to undertake risky projects and exercise market leadership. In a more benign environment, the successful smaller firm places an emphasis upon formality and rules within the organization. In its strategic behaviour in the market place the successful firm in the benign environment is more likely to follow than to lead the introduction of new products, preferring to make modest alterations to existing lines.

Even these studies, while they have examined strategy and organization in small fast-growing firms, did not address the issue of implementing strategic decisions, and the impact that this could have on performance. A key element in the implementation of decisions is to be able to assemble managerial expertise for this purpose. In most cases this will consist of a team of non-owning

managers. Where these issues have been addressed it has been by those researchers undertaking case study type work, rather than by those using a more
aggregate approach.

The study by Grieve Smith and Fleck (1987), using a case study approach to
examining business strategies in small high technology firms in Cambridge, UK
illustrates the point well. Referring to one company they say:

> A major factor in Domino's success seems to have been that the founder was con-
> scious from the start of the need to bring in people with business or manufacturing
> experience to complement the technical expertise on which the company was based.

They continue:

> Of concern to many companies was the establishing and keeping of an experienced
> management team. Many of the newer companies such as IQ Bio, Domino and Eicon
> had recognized a need to complement their founder's technical skills and to appoint
> experienced managing directors and management specialists from large companies.
> *This awareness, coupled with the willingness of professional managers to join a small
> company, may be one of the crucial conditions for long term success* [our emphasis].

Grieve Smith and Fleck then go on to point out that the small firm can have
difficulty recruiting such managerial skills, since it cannot offer as high salaries
and cannot provide such a clear career path as the manager could expect in a
large company. Their Cambridge cases highlight several other important issues:
for example they refer to the founder at Domino being conscious, *at the start*,
of the need to bring in external managers. They also refer to the need to appoint
these individuals *from large companies*, presumably on the grounds that the
intention is to grow the company from small to large. Finally, they also refer to
the need to bring in managers with different skills to those already in the firm
'to complement the expertise on which the company was based'. This suggests
that the founder of the firm has some concept of a balanced managerial team.

Similar issues were raised by the Advisory Committee on Science and Technology (ACOST) in its work on barriers to growth in small firms. It says:

> From our case studies it is apparent that growth creates major management and
> organizational problems. The principal dimensions of this relate to the need to
> develop a balanced managerial team which combines appropriate marketing, finan-
> cial and technical skills; and the need to create an organizational structure which
> supports an appropriate delegation of decision making.

There are, however, many forms of small firm (young/old, high-tech/low-tech,
independent/large firm subsidiary), each operating in a wide variety of economic environments. There are also many different ways of organizing the operations of any particular small firm and an even wider variety of small firm
owners and managers with varying motivations and expectations. It would,
therefore, be extremely unwise to generalize on the basis of findings for small
high-technology firms alone.

In the UK there have been very few studies concerned exclusively with the
recruitment, retention or careers of managers in the small firm sector. A study

by Deeks (1972) of managers in the furniture industry found that small firm managers were likely to be younger than those in larger firms. It also found that they were more likely to have moved companies than large firm managers: Deeks found that almost one-third of non-shareholding managers had worked for more than six companies during their career, compared with studies of larger firms where less than 7 per cent of managers had worked for six firms or more. Thirdly, Deeks found that there were major differences in the levels of educational attainment between large and small firm managers. Less than 1 per cent of managers in the (small firm) furniture industry were graduates, whereas other broadly comparable studies of managers in large firms showed that between 19 per cent and 43 per cent of managers had degrees.

The more recent findings of Nicholson and West (1988) are also supportive of some significant differences between managers in small and large firms. They find:

> Managers in small organizations have made the greatest number of employer changes and upward status moves . . . this finding is easily explained. The larger the organization the greater the opportunities for internal movement, therefore people in small organization are more likely to come to their present position from outside.
>
> (Nicholson and West, 1988, p. 61)

Nicholson and West also find that:

> Twice as many managers moved to smaller sized organizations as moved to larger sized organizations, before finding established career positions in smaller organizations where their talents can find more expressive scope.
>
> (ibid. p. 64)

There are, however, some doubts about the extent to which the Nicholson and West data on managers in smaller firms refer to owners, and the extent to which they refer to individuals who are managers, but without an ownership stake in the firm. The authors specifically include self-employed small business owners in their sampling frame, although their work histories and backgrounds may differ somewhat from that of the small firm manager.

There is also some evidence provided by Handy *et al* (1988) in their international review of the education, development and training of managers that:

> Smaller companies are different. In no country do they take the same long-term view of management development, nor are they prepared to spend the time and the money on any form of training which does not have an almost immediate payoff.

Finally, two studies (Stanworth and Curran, 1973, and Watkins, 1983) have examined the attitudes of owners of small businesses to managerial and professional employees. The main findings were that owners were often reluctant to delegate responsibilities to newcomers either because they wished to retain control or because they were fearful that these professional employees would start up in business in competition with them if they were allowed to develop their skills. Also, attempts by newcomers to reorganize work practices frequently led to friction with their employers, who often saw this as a clear criticism of their management skills. Cultural differences between owners and professionals also had the potential to create frictions and endanger growth because:

> Functional experts are often cosmopolitans, whose commitment to their professional skills may override their commitment to any particular firm. In the extreme case, their current employer is regarded merely as a stepping stone in their career, to be rejected when further possibilities for career advancement occur elsewhere. Unless the owner-manager can master this new situation by delegating authority to specialists (thus relinquishing an element of personal independence), integrating his longer-standing managers with his new specialists, and coping with the occasional loss of specialists, a quest for growth may be transformed into a battle for survival.
>
> (Stanworth and Curran, 1973, p. 159)

To summarize, it would appear that there is a significant lacuna in our knowledge about small firm non-owning managers, certainly in comparison with our knowledge of large firm managers. We know the group is important in facilitating the growth of some small companies, but we remain ignorant about the backgrounds and motivations of this group. We are also unaware of how these individuals come to be in post in these firms and about their roles in relation to those of owner managers. The remainder of this chapter is given to a research attempt to provide some insight into these questions.

The data

A sample of non-owning managers in small firms had first to be derived by researchers. The purpose in deriving the data was to assess the contribution of owners and non-owner managers in the growth of smaller firms. It was deemed that this could not be satisfactorily conducted by the much-favoured postal survey. Face-to-face interviews were conducted with managers and owners in their places of work.

Researchers began by defining a 'fast-growth small firm', which they took to be one which began life as an independent firm and became quoted on the Unlisted Securities Market (USM) within ten years of starting to trade.

To make a comparison with a more conventional small firm, they chose to specify a 'match' firm. By this was meant that the 'match' firm was similar to the 'fast-growth' firm in four respects: it was of the same age, it traded within the same sector, it was located (or initially began) in the same region and it was independently owned at start-up. Hence if there was an initially independent eight-year-old marketing consultancy which reached the USM and which was located in London, then a 'match' would be sought. This also had to be a London-based marketing firm which was between five and ten years old and which was independently owned at start-up. This is referred to as 'one-for-one matching'. In all cases the 'fast-growth' firm outperforms the 'match' firm in the sense of being larger for a given age.

The purpose in choosing this sampling methodology was to minimize the (between sample) impact of four key variables known to affect performance –

firm age, location, ownership and sector. In essence, since all these four key factors are being held constant, performance differences between the two groups of firms are more likely to reflect differences in management and internal organization. A full description of the sampling procedure is available from David Storey, Warwick University, but for present purposes the following brief description should suffice. In December 1987 there were 605 companies which had been quoted on the Market since its inception in 1980. Of those, 125 were independent firms that had reached the Market within ten years of start-up and so were eligible for the survey. In practice researchers interviewed and were able to obtain a 'match' for forty-nine of these.

At the time of the interview the median age of both the fast-growth and the match firms was thirteen years. The median employment size of the fast-growth firms was 250 employees and the median employment of the match firms was twenty-four employees. In the following two years, fast-growth firms were expecting to grow by 40 per cent, whereas match firms were expecting to grow by 28 per cent.

It can be seen, therefore, that the sampling procedure has been highly successful in achieving its objectives. Two groups of firms of similar ages, with similar geographical distributions and operating in the same sectors have been derived. The firms differ to the extent that firms in one group are more than ten times larger than those in another.

In deriving this sample it should, of course, be pointed out that obtaining a USM listing within ten years of start-up is not the only criterion of growth of a young business. Other criteria could have been chosen but this criterion had two advantages: first, that all firms achieving this status were indeed fast growers and, secondly, that information about them was plentiful.

Finally, there may be a tendency in the reader's mind to infer that the match firms are slow-growing small firms. This is not the case. To have survived for thirteen years and to have a median employment of twenty-five employees means they would be well within the upper quartile of business starts. The sampling frame is, therefore, comparing the truly exceptionally performing group of firms – the 'fast growers' – with a well above average, but not truly exceptional group of firms – the 'match' firms.

The small firm manager

In this section we describe the results of interviews with those individuals who are currently non-owner managers in the fast-growth and match firms. In the subsequent text, for ease of exposition, we shall refer to fast-growth firms as USM.

Some basic characteristics

Table 10.1 shows that of the 107 managers interviewed, fifty-five were in USM companies and fifty-two were in match companies. These managers were employed in the forty-nine USM companies and the forty-nine match companies,

Table 10.1   Personal characteristics of the small firm manager

	USM	Match
Number of respondents	55	52
Age, in years, at time of survey	37	38
No. of males	48 (87%)	41 (79%)
No. of females	7 (13%)	11 (21%)
No. with degree or chartered qualification	30 (55%)	22 (42%)
No. with no qualification	2 (4%)	5 (10%)
Per cent of respondents reporting directly to top person in organization	75	86

so that in six USM companies and three match companies two managers were interviewed.

The mean and median ages of both groups were approximately the same – thirty-seven years for the USM managers and thirty-eight years for the match managers. Both groups contain primarily male managers, although females are slightly more likely to be found among the match group.

The sample of managers interviewed are extremely senior in their organization, with at least three-quarters of them reporting directly to the top person in that organization. In the context of the smaller firm the top person in the organization for the match firms is generally the owner, and the person who is interviewed here is normally the most senior manager, who may also be a director of the company. The person interviewed either does not own any shares at all in the business or, mainly in the case of USM managers, owns only a very small proportion. In no case is the interviewee a significant shareholder.

The manager's career

This section briefly examines the career patterns of managers in smaller firms, again making a distinction between those currently employed in USM companies and those in match firms.

The purpose is to examine the extent to which, within the managerial labour market, there are different career patterns between USM and match managers. Specifically, are match managers more likely to have spent their managerial career in small firms, or with the same small firm? And when they move from one firm to another, do they tend to stay within the same sector? Finally, at what stage in their career did they obtain managerial responsibilities?

The most basic information on the size of their employer in their previous job is presented in Table 10.2. It shows that 54 per cent of match managers compared with only 23 per cent of USM managers were previously employed in a

Table 10.2   Size of employer in prior jobs

Size of firm	Prior job				Second prior job			
	USM		Match		USM		Match	
	No.	(%)	No.	(%)	No.	(%)	No.	(%)
< 100 workers	12	(23)	26	(54)	20	(40)	17	(37)
100–500	19	(36)	7	(15)	8	(16)	6	(13)
501–2000	10	(20)	6	(12)	8	(16)	6	(13)
> 2000 workers	11	(21)	9	(19)	14	(28)	17	(37)
Total	52	(100)	48	(100)	50	(100)	46	(100)

firm with fewer than 100 workers, suggesting that match managers are more likely to have had a 'small firm background'.

We must recognize, however, that managers may be transferred to a different job within the same company. In many cases this constitutes promotion (called 'inspiralling' by Nicholson and West) but not in all instances. It is therefore appropriate to make a distinction between where the manager changes employer, and where there is a change of job with the same employer.

The results of this distinction (Table 10.3) show that only 2 per cent of match managers have stayed with their current employer in their last three jobs, compared with 18 per cent of USM managers. This is not, in any way, a surprising result since the match firms in the sample have far fewer managerial posts than the USM firms.

Table 10.3   Changes of employer

	USM		Match	
	No.	%	No.	%
With same employer for last three jobs	10	18	1	2
New employer in current job, same employer in jobs 2 and 3	5	9	2	4
Same employer in current job as in job 2, different employer in job 3	12	22	12	23
Different employer in last three jobs	23	42	27	52
No answers/not had three jobs	5	9	10	19
Total	55	100	52	100

Table 10.4   *Size of employer in previous job*

	USM				Match			
	Same		Different		Same		Different	
	No.	%	No.	%	No.	%	No.	%
< 100 workers	8	40	4	14	10	90	12	46
100–500	12	60	6	21	1	10	5	19
501–2000			8	29			5	19
2000+ workers			10	36			4	15
Total	**20**	**100**	**28**	**100**	**11**	**100**	**26**	**100**

To some extent this serves to explain the differences between current USM and match managers in terms of the size of their previous employer. This is shown in Table 10.4, which makes it clear that current USM managers are much more likely to have joined their current employer from a large firm, than is the case for the current match managers. Thus out of the forty-eight USM managers about whom there is full information, twenty transferred from another job with the same organization. Of the twenty-eight who joined from an outside organization, eighteen or 64 per cent were formerly employed in a firm with more than 500 workers. This contrasts with only 34 per cent of current match managers who joined their current employer from a firm employing more than 500 workers. This clearly demonstrates that current match managers are more likely to move employers to reach their current position, and also that they are more likely to have worked previously in another small firm.

While this difference exists between sizes of firm, it is also important to examine whether the manager remains in broadly the same trade sector or whether a move from one employer to another is also a move to another trade.

Table 10.5 examines the four instances where a manager changed employer with a view to examining whether that change of employer also resulted in a change in the sector of business in which the manager worked. It is assumed that, where the manager stayed with the same employer, there was no change in the sector in which the individual worked. Although this may not necessarily be the case for the USM companies, a number of which are split into divisions and operate in several sectors, it is a justifiable assumption for the match companies. In order not to overstate any differences between the two groups of firms, the research therefore only examined employer changes for sectoral moves, rather than all job changes.

Table 10.5 Sectoral differences in prior job among those changing employers

	USM		Match	
	Same sector	Diff. sector	Same sector	Diff. sector
Changed employer from current to prior: same employer prior to prior 2	0	5	0	1
Changed employer from prior to prior2; same employer prior to current	4	8	7	5
Three different employers; prior to current	7	15	17	10
Three different employers; prior2 to prior	9	14	8	17
Total	**20**	**42**	**32**	**33**

Table 10.5 examines the four possible employer changes. The first row takes those managers who have changed their employer between their current job, and their last job, but who in the job prior to their last job – called prior2 job – had the same employer. It shows those who changed sectors, and those who merely moved to another firm in the same sector when they moved between their current and their prior employer. The second row of the table takes those managers who have the same employer in their current job as in their prior job but who, in their prior2 job had a different employer. The numbers show those who, in that move, changed sectors and those who remained within the same sector.

The final two rows of the table show the moves made by those managers who have had three different employers in their last three jobs – that is, those who have made two moves. The third row of the table shows the move between their current and their prior employer, and the final row shows their move from their prior2 to their prior employer.

In total, Table 10.5 identifies sixty-two managerial moves involving a change of employer for the current USM managers, and sixty-five changes of employer involving current match managers. It appears that the USM manager is more likely, when changing employer, also to move into a different trade or sector than is the case for the match manager. Thus 67 per cent of current USM managers change sector when they change employer, compared with only 51 per cent of current match managers.

This finding is confirmed in the next section where the responses of owners are reported, in relation to the characteristics of those managers whom they choose to employ.

The management team

In the early days of a business, the key founder will play the central role in developing a management team, deciding when new expertise is required and in ensuring that appropriate people get hired. In this section we examine the nature of the expertise within the managerial team, how it grows as the business develops and how these functions differ between the USM and the match firms. This information derives primarily from interviews with the key founder.

Six areas of business expertise are identified – production; finance; marketing; personnel; R & D; and general management. Each owner respondent was asked to assess the extent of that expertise both when the business started, and as the business is today. Respondents were given five options: considerable, good, moderate, some and none. Table 10.6 shows the results of these responses in two ways. The first is to construct a scoring system under which four points are given for the 'considerable' answer, three for the 'good' answer, two for the 'moderate', one for the 'some' and none for the 'none' answer. This is shown in the Score columns.

A second way of presenting the answers is to be concerned only with those firms which regarded themselves as having considerable expertise in that functional area. The % Consid columns show the percentage of all respondents who regarded their firm as having considerable expertise in the particular functional area.

If we examine the left hand side of Table 10.6, which shows the key founder's perception of the expertise of the management team at start-up, it is clear that both USM and match companies are broadly similar. For both groups the areas in which expertise is judged to be highest, according to the score column, is in production, followed by marketing and general management. For both groups, finance occupies an intermediate position, with personnel and R & D achieving the lowest.

A broadly similar picture is derived by looking at the percentage of firms that regarded their expertise in the functional area as being considerable. For both

Table 10.6   Expertise within the business

	Start-up				Current			
	USM		**Match**		**USM**		**Match**	
	Score	% Consid.	Score	% Consid.	Score	% Consid.	Score	% Consid.
Production	2.09	24	2.11	22	3.61	71	3.30	54
Finance	1.63	13	1.64	7	3.63	65	3.18	36
Marketing	1.84	16	1.95	27	3.33	56	2.89	42
Personnel	1.42	7	1.93	7	2.62	18	2.75	18
R & D	1.52	11	1.03	9	2.89	43	1.91	11
General management	1.96	16	1.88	12	3.37	50	2.93	27

USM and match companies, marketing, production and general management scored highest. The lowest scores were in personnel and R & D, with finance occupying an intermediate position. The perhaps somewhat surprising result is that, among the match companies 27 per cent of companies felt they had considerable expertise in marketing at start-up. This was considerably higher than the 16 per cent of USM companies that felt they had considerable marketing expertise at start-up and is, in fact, higher than any other functional area for either the USM or the match group.

The differences in the relative ranking of functional expertise do vary somewhat according to the measures used. This demonstrates the important point that in some functional areas there is a considerable spread of levels of perceived expertise, whereas in other instances the replies are more heavily concentrated. It is for this reason that the two measures are presented.

The right hand side of the table shows the self-assessed expertise of the management team in the six functional areas in the business as it is today. The key points to note are that, not surprisingly, the perceived level of expertise in all the areas, for both groups, has improved significantly since start-up. Less obviously, while there were few differences between the scores of the USM and match companies at start-up, currently the USM companies comfortably outscore the match in all functional areas with the exception of personnel. Even in this functional area, 18 per cent of respondents from both groups regarded themselves as having considerable current expertise.

There is a major change, since start-up, in the rankings of some of the functional areas. The most important of these is the perceived increase in expertise in finance, particularly for USM, but also to a considerable extent for the match companies. For USM companies the finance function currently scores highest, although a higher proportion of USM respondents regarded their company as having considerable expertise in production.

It seems likely that increased perceived finance expertise among USM firms has come about through the experience of being quoted on the Market. Nevertheless the fact that a similar, if less spectacular, growth has occurred amongst match companies suggests that finance expertise is rarely present when the business begins. It is not clear to what extent this reflects the proportion of managers in the population at large who regard accountants as the answer.

Among the other functional areas, relative expertise rankings do not appear to have changed significantly for either the USM or the match firms. Thus production expertise is regarded as being of leading or prime importance for both groups, as at start-up, with marketing and general management also in high ranking positions. As at start-up, neither personnel nor R & D is regarded as a function in which expertise is great.

There is, however, one significant caveat to that statement with regard to R & D. Almost one-quarter of both USM and match firms did not regard R & D as a relevant area of management, because they did not undertake any. This is by far the highest non-response area of the six functions. Taking account of this differential response rate, 43 per cent of those USM firms undertaking some form of R & D thought that they had considerable expertise in this area, compared with only 11 per cent of the match firms undertaking some form of R & D. This is by far the biggest difference in perceived functional expertise in the businesses as they are today. It is also important to notice that at start-up considerable R & D expertise was assessed to be in 9 per cent of match and 11 per cent of USM companies. Currently, however, the percentage of match companies with considerable expertise in R & D has risen only to 11 per cent, compared with 43 per cent of USM companies undertaking R & D. This represents a major change since the business was established.

Assembling the managerial team

In the above section the research shows that, for all the six functions identified, the self-assessed level of managerial expertise in the business today is consider-ably higher than when the business began.

This section examines the ways in which that managerial expertise has been assembled. It was assumed that there were three prime ways in which this expertise could be developed. First the owners themselves could make it their responsibility to develop the function. This was called 'developed by start-up team'. A second way is that new individuals can be added to the management team, either as part owners or as salaried managers. These individuals can either be recruited from outside the company, or they can be promoted from a non-managerial position within the company. There are other possibilities which do not fall clearly into any of these categories, and respondents were asked to identify such cases, but they occurred so infrequently that they are ignored in the subsequent analysis.

Each respondent was then asked, for each of the six identified functional areas, to identify whether new managerial expertise was accumulated by the original owners, by the recruitment of outsiders or by in-house promotion. Clearly it is possible that, in some functional areas, more than a single mode could be used, but in Table 10.7 the only responses which are tabulated are where a single mode is specified.

The responses documented in Table 10.7 are very revealing. Overall there is a much greater likelihood of the USM company recruiting outside managers, whereas the match company owners are much more likely to take over and develop the particular functional area. The Total row of Table 10.7 shows that only about two-thirds of USM company respondents, compared with match, identified areas which the original owners developed as their managerial area. Conversely only about two-thirds of match, compared with USM, companies identified a function as being one in which outsiders made the prime contribu-tion. Both USM and match companies, overall, seemed to rely equally on in-house promotion.

There are also several interesting differences between functional areas. It will be recalled from the previous section that the major functional area in which companies felt there had been a major improvement in their managerial ex-pertise was in the field of finance. This was particularly true for the USM companies.

Table 10.7   Assembling the managerial team

Expertise/ background	Developed by start-up team				Recruitment of outsiders				Promoted in-house			
	USM		Match		USM		Match		USM		Match	
	No.	%	No.	%	No.	%	No.	%	No.	%	No.	%
Production	3	8	10	15	2	3	4	10	8	26	4	14
Finance	4	10	10	15	26	39	19	45	1	3	3	11
Marketing	9	22	14	20	15	23	7	16	4	13	5	18
Personnel	11	28	16	23	11	17	5	12	9	29	6	21
R & D	4	10	8	12	6	9	3	7	5	16	3	11
General management	9	22	10	15	6	9	4	10	4	13	7	25
Total	**40**	**100**	**68**	**100**	**66**	**100**	**42**	**100**	**31**	**100**	**28**	**100**

An examination of Table 10.7 shows that this increased expertise has been accumulated primarily through the recruitment of outsiders. In some ways this might be predicted for USM companies since all Market entrants would be expected to have a professionally-qualified finance director with an appropriate background at the time of application for membership. It is therefore interesting that the dependence upon outsiders for the improvement of financial expertise is even clearer in the case of the match companies. It provides further support for the view that rarely is high-level financial expertise in place when the company begins and that, above all other areas of expertise, it is obtained through external recruitment.

There is a clear contrast between finance on the one hand, and both personnel and general management on the other. In the case of personnel it will be recalled from Table 10.6 that, for the USM companies, this was a function in which they felt their expertise was lowest of all six identified, both at start-up and currently. For match firms the personnel function was one in which they felt their expertise was lowest, with the exception of R & D.

Table 10.7 shows that, in contrast to finance, personnel managerial expertise tended to be accumulated either by the promotion of a person from a non-managerial position, or by the key owner/individual becoming responsible for this function. It suggests that, in total contrast to finance, rarely is a fully trained professional manager recruited from outside, but that firms tend to make do in this area. It is this that goes a long way towards explaining the low scores in the personnel expertise area.

Table 10.6 also showed that self-assessed general management expertise fell in relative terms for the USM companies and stayed broadly similar for the match firms. Table 10.7 shows that the characteristic of managerial

Table 10.8   Qualities sought from new managerial appointments

Qualities	First two appointments				Last two appointments			
	USM No.	%	Match No.	%	USM No.	%	Match No.	%
1. Personal skills	39	29	31	19	25	18	36	28
2. Experience/knowledge	30	22	37	23	56	40	33	26
3. Formal qualifs/excellence/ expertise	46	34	37	23	37	26	23	18
4. Personal qualities	20	15	57	35	22	16	35	28
Total	**135**	**100**	**162**	**100**	**140**	**100**	**127**	**100**

appointments in this area is that they tend, as with personnel, to be internal promotions rather than recruitment of external professionals.

Managerial qualities

The previous section showed that the way in which the managerial team was assembled varied between functional areas. We now turn to the question of how, in practice, those individuals became members of the team.

The procedure used is to report the responses of key founder/owners to questions about the first two and last two managers/directors appointed. The first concern is not with the functional expertise that the new individual brings, but rather with the particular qualities sought by the key founder/owner in recruiting that individual to the team. As before, the key distinction is between USM and match firms.

The answers are segmented in two ways. First we are seeking to investigate whether the qualities sought by the USM key individual/owner differ from those of the match counterpart. Our second concern is whether the qualities sought from the first two managers/directors which the business employed in its early days differ from those employed in more recent times.

Owner respondents were allowed to respond in a totally open-ended way to the question of the qualities which they were seeking from the individual managers/directors in these posts. In Table 10.8 the possible responses are condensed into four major quality types.

The first group is called personal skills, where these refer specifically to the personality of the manager/director. It includes cases where respondents have placed emphasis upon 'flair', 'get-up-and-go', 'personal empathy', 'strong personality', 'public presence', 'ability to get things done', when talking about their managerial appointments. The skills are deemed to be inherent within the individual's personality, but are positively related to their ability to do a job with some flair or style.

Those responses that emphasize the personal skills of managers/directors need to be distinguished from instances where owner respondents emphasized the experience and knowledge needed for the post. In this group are included instances where respondents emphasized 'business experience', 'proven track record', 'organizational experience', 'knowledge of clients or market', 'experience in key functional area', required by managers/directors in this post. Here the respondent generally required the manager/director to have a fairly narrow range of skills tightly focused upon the particular requirements of the particular business. The point was often stressed that the expertise was in a particular field, and it was only obtained through experience of working in the industry. Key owners/individuals would frequently comment that the manager needed to have specific knowledge of 'my customers/industry'. In many respects these may be considered the more mundane qualities associated with narrow experience.

A third, and very different, group of responses refers to the need for formal qualifications/technical excellence/expertise. Here respondents refer to 'the right qualifications', 'exceptional technical ability', 'outstanding creativity'. In other words there was less of an emphasis upon job-specific knowledge and experience that can only be gained from working in the industry, and much more emphasis upon the type of wider concepts of excellence associated with formal academic and professional qualifications or exceptional talent of some form. It is probably reasonable to refer to 'talents' as being associated with the high-flyer type of individual.

The fourth grouping is called personal qualities and needs to be distinguished from the first group called personal skills. The latter are very positive characteristics such as those of flair, strength of character and so on. The responses placed in the 'personal qualities' category, however, tend to be more neutral, such as 'compatible with organization', 'loyalty, commitment and diligence', 'trustworthy, reliable, punctual', 'supportive attitude' or even 'young and cheap'. In other words the emphasis here is less on an ability to do a job with flair and more on an ability to fit in with the ends of the organization.

Given the way in which the categorization has taken place, it would be expected that the USM firms would place more emphasis on the types of positive qualities in items 1 and 3, with match firms placing more emphasis on 2 and 4.

Some support for these hypotheses is provided from an examination of responses to questions about the qualities sought from the first two managers/directors employed in the business. For these appointments, with which the key owner/individual generally had a central responsibility, 63 per cent of all responses by USM key owners/individuals fell into categories 1 and 3. This compares with only 42 per cent of match firms.

Matters are, however, less clear cut when the last two managerial appointments are considered. As predicted, the USM companies appear to continue to place considerably more emphasis upon formal qualifications – item 3 – than the match firms. Equally, the match firms continue to place more emphasis on personal qualities – such as fitting in with the organization – than the USM firms. The change since start-up is that the USM company in its recent managerial recruitment seems now to place much greater emphasis on the relatively narrow concept of experience – item 2 – and significantly less upon personal skills – item 1 – such as flair and dynamism.

The most likely explanation for this change is that there has also been a change in both the seniority and functions of the managers/directors employed. In its early days the company with aspirations for rapid growth is seeking to recruit individuals with the type of flair, drive and ability necessary to achieve these high ambitions. The managers, recruited by the key owner/individuals are likely to closely resemble the owner in the sense of being entrepreneurial. In more recent years, however, as the company has grown there will be an increasing need for relatively narrow specialist knowledge and this is reflected in the greater emphasis placed upon this characteristic.

Conclusions

This chapter has attempted to add to the relatively modest knowledge available about non-owning managers in smaller firms. It has pointed to the fact that the Bolton Committee, and much of the subsequent research, has assumed that ownership and management in smaller firms are in the hands of the same individual. We have pointed out, however, that once firms grow beyond a minimum size of about twenty workers, then professional, but non-owning managers are appointed.

These individuals are frequently acknowledged to be a crucial resource in the subsequent development of the business. Yet despite this recognition the non-owning manager in a small firm has not been, until now, the subject of detailed scrutiny.

We have distinguished between those non-owning managers in small firms that have grown exceptionally fast and other small firms showing above average, but not spectacular, rates of growth. Our purpose has been to identify whether there are differences in the managerial teams assembled by these two different types of firms.

Results suggest that there are some quite sharp differences between the managers employed in the fast-growing firms, compared with managers in match firms.

In examining the careers of such managers we show that managers in the fast-growth firms are much more likely to have had a background in a large firm environment than is the case for match managers. We also show that those managers currently employed in fast-growth firms are more likely to have stayed with their current employer in their last two jobs than is the case for the match manager. Finally we show that managers currently in fast-growth firms are much more likely, when they change jobs, to move to a firm in a different sector, than is the case for match managers.

We have also examined managerial team-building within smaller firms and shown that in an examination of functional specialisms businesses are generally initiated by those with a production, marketing and general management background. They are much more rarely begun by those with a background in finance. Expertise in this functional area almost always seems to be brought into the company once the business has been established for a few years and by the appointment, from outside, of a qualified individual. This contrasts most clearly with, for example, the personnel function where a qualified person is rarely appointed from outside. Instead the function tends to be performed either by the founders themselves or by somebody being appointed internally from a non-managerial position.

There does appear to be some evidence that the types of individuals who are sought to occupy non-owning managerial positions in the early stages of a company's life influence the development of the business. It would appear that the individuals sought by companies that were subsequently to grow rapidly differ according to their personal skills and formal qualifications. When asked to recall the qualities which they sought in their first two managerial appointments, owners of fast-growth companies placed considerable emphasis on the personal skills and formal qualifications of their managers. On the other hand, match firm owners appeared to emphasize a number of more neutral personal qualities such as 'being compatible with the organization', loyalty, trustworthiness or 'having a supportive attitude'.

Particularly in this final area there is always the risk of ex-post rationalization on the parts of owners. Our purpose, therefore, has not been to present a definitive statement on the creation and evolution of managerial teams in the small firm sector. To do this in a wholly satisfactory way would require longitudinal studies over real time with smaller companies. The current results, however, do provide an interesting insight into some important and under-researched issues.

11 Some Factors Influencing the Future of Small Scale Enterprise in the UK

In its references to the future of the smaller business, the Bolton Committee was decidedly sceptical:

> The *contribution* of the small firm to national output and employment is declining in the long term not only in this country but in all the other developed countries . . . The *number* of small firms in existence in the United Kingdom is also decreasing . . . Behind these statistics lie a number of factors which amount to an increasingly hostile environment for the small firm. Indeed, we have found it extremely difficult to identify any factors working strongly in favour of the small firm.
>
> (Bolton, 1971, p. 75: emphasis in the original)

In contrast, one of the most significant economic and political events of the last ten years has been the revival of the smaller business within the UK (see Chapter 1) – although over-optimism must be guarded against: for example, the impact of new technology small firms on employment generation and the number of people entering home-working have been vastly over-estimated by some analysts (for discussion, see Stanworth and Stanworth, 1991).

In 1979 just less than 2 million people were self-employed (8 per cent of the total employed workforce) a figure which had risen to over three and a quarter million by 1990 or 12 per cent of the total labour force (Department of Employment, 1991a and b; *Employment Gazette*, 1991a). Similarly, as we observed in Chapter 9, it has been estimated that by 1986 firms employing less than 20 people employed 36 per cent of the private sector labour force compared with 27 per cent in 1979 (Bannock and Daly, 1990).

The growth in importance in output and employment terms was set against a background of rapid socio-economic change which undoubtedly shaped the nature and composition of smaller firms. This was the decade of the longest period of Conservative Party governance since the 1950s, with a manifesto pledge to roll back the frontiers of the state through privatization, deregulation and competitive tendering and the reduction of the power of organized labour. Concurrently, there was a wide array of measures to encourage the budding 'entrepreneur' (Department of Employment, 1991a; Department of Trade and Industry, 1988; and see Chapter 8).

These political decisions were given force by the activities of the large-scale corporate sector, which underwent massive restructuring, part of which was a fragmenting of its activities in response to economic pressures. The extent to which small firms benefited from restructuring is debatable (Pollert, 1988), but a consensus appears to be emerging that this had some impact on the performance of smaller businesses, even though this differs considerably between sectors.

Economic growth in this period vacillated tremendously, from a low of –2.3 per cent to high of 4.7 per cent in 1987 (OECD, 1989) but this was sandwiched between two recessions, one at the beginning of the 1980s the other at the beginning of the 1990s. The revival of small firms in this period seemed un-affected by the recession of the early 1980s although that of the early 1990s appears to be having some impact through closures and the slowing down in the growth of the registered self-employed. However, the extent to which this a longer-term, paradigmatic shift or a mere blip in the inexorable trend towards the concentration in ownership, as discussed by some analysts (Allen, 1988), is worthy of investigation.

This chapter, therefore, aims to assess the future of the smaller business, taking into account a range of socio-economic and political factors. In the trade-off between scope and depth in any investigation, to facilitate depth of analysis not all *known* factors will be covered. The agenda in this chapter is determined by the issues of the day, some of which may decline in importance as the decade passes. Less predictable is the importance of the significant 'un-foreseen events' that have wrought havoc on previous predictions in the last twenty years – the deflationary and inflationary effects of the quadrupling of oil prices in the mid-1970s; the impact of the Falklands/Malvinas and Gulf wars; and the liberalization of Eastern Europe.

The chapter begins by taking an overall look at the nature of restructuring within the UK economy, over the last decade or so, with an emphasis on the new role of small-scale capital. It then moves on to discuss the performance and trends of the economy as a whole, focusing on the projected changes in the labour force and the relationship between unemployment and entry in to self-employment. There is an industrial sector dimension to this inquiry. Nine out of ten small firms are located in the service sector, so any investigation into the future of the small business requires an assessment of the employment, demand and ownership trends within these industrial sectors. One key factor governing the performance of smaller businesses is the institutional and political environment within which they have to operate. The 1980s could be described as the halcyon decade for small business support from government. It is critical to ask to what extent such support will continue into the 1990s and what sort of opportunities and threats will changes in the institutional environment, par-ticularly through the Single European Market, bring to smaller firms? The final section of the chapter examines the extent to which there is a new enterprise culture in Britain, based on the premise that if the shift towards small scale activities is to have any longevity then it must be as a result of the desire of people to start and run their own business rather than be employees within the corporate sector. No projections are made without qualification but from the factors taken into account in this analysis, the new role that small businesses have assumed of late will be tested as we enter the next century.

Restructuring of the economy and the role of small firms

To appreciate the future role of small scale enterprise in the UK economy, it is essential to understand its contemporary role and importance. This is not, however, a straightforward undertaking, not least because of the heterogeneity of small firms. There is also some difficulty of relating what existing empirical evidence we have to the variety of models of the economy. This is put more critically by Rainnie:

> Despite the burgeoning amount of published material concerned with the small firm, the vast majority remains prescriptive, descriptive, lacking in critical edge and devoid of analytical weight. The result is that stereotypes abound . . . and analysis seems to be incapable of separating the short run effects of recession from the long run effects of restructuring on the small business form.
>
> (Rainnie, 1991, p. 1)

Following the rationalization central to the restructuring of the 1980s, there exists a range of theories on the current role of small firms in the economy. What is common to all is that the economy of the 1990s is more fragmented and more service-sector-orientated than that of a decade ago. There has been a decline in 'Fordism' as the single most dominant form of production and a rise in 'post-Fordism' or 'Neo-Fordism' (Figure 11.1). (For a more detailed discussion of what is meant by 'Fordism', see Meegan, 1988 and Clarke, 1990.)

Fordism	Post-Fordism
Slow innovation	Fast innovation
Dedicated production technology	Flexible production technology
Mass production of homogeneous products	Small batch production of differentiated products
Mass marketing	Niche marketing
Large inventories	Low inventories
Vertical and horizontal integration	Vertical and horizontal disintegration
Mechanistic organization	Organic organization

Source: Curran and Blackburn (1990: Table 11.4)

Figure 11.1   Key features of the Fordist and post-Fordist models of production

Some social scientists are arguing that we are entering a period of 'disorganized capitalism', within which small firms may benefit from the fragmentation of culture, consumption and production (Lash and Urry, 1987). This fragmentation means that there has been a breaking down of the methods, organization and location of production and service activities, which has affected the role of small-scale activities in the economy. However, there consensus ends. The reorganization of the economy in the 1980s left in its wake a trail of social scientists attempting to explain new forms of production and distribution:

> There is some debate about the origin and nature of the restructuring taking place and the continuing role of small enterprise within this process. Nor have analysts found it easy to characterize the restructuring: different writers have used different terms and emphasized different aspects of the processes involved.
>
> (Curran and Blackburn, 1991, p. 168)

In a sense, analysts are attempting to understand what is essentially a moving target. In spite of a plethora of new 'models' of the economy our understanding of what is occurring remains partial. However, in order to illuminate the various ramifications of different models of the economy, for the longevity of the revival of small-scale enterprise, attention will be concentrated on two main schools of thought.

At one end of the spectrum is the 'regulationist school' the essence of which is the 'crisis' of 'Fordist' methods of production, distribution and consumption (see Figure 11.1) that has led to *some* fragmentation of economic activities by large corporations (Aglietta, 1979). The revival of small-scale economic activities is a result of the need to fragment production in order to reassert control over labour and the labour process, the need to minimize innovation risk, and to mitigate the impact of demand fluctuations (see, for example, Shutt and Whittington, 1987). According to this paradigm, the main forces shaping the economy remain in the hands of large organizations, such as multinationals. The apparent shift towards small-scale capital, measured by employment and new firm formation, is a result of the decisions of large scale capital rather than a new era of entrepreneurship.

In contrast, the 'institutionalist' school stresses the inability of mass production techniques to cope with increasingly differentiated and individualistic patterns of consumption and stresses the growth of 'flexible specialization' as the emerging basis for production (Piore and Sabel, 1984; Hirst and Zeitlin, 1989; Sabel, 1989). This model has three main characteristics: a new flexible manufacturing technology which reduces fixed costs; a renewed craft tradition which provides workers with more autonomy over decisions; and the disintegration of 'mass' markets, including the resurgence of regional economies. This model also emphasizes the notion of 'industrial districts' of which there are various definitions including:

> The industrial district is essentially a territorial system of small and medium sized firms producing a group of commodities whose products are processes which can be split into different phases.
>
> (Goodman, *et al*, 1989, p. 21)

	Flexible specialization model	Fragmentation model
Market types	Niche, fragmented	Sub-contracted, vertically disintegrated
Relations with large firms	Independent, inter-dependent	Dependent
Role of small firms/ self-employed in economy	Central	Peripheral

Source: Based on Curran and Blackburn (1991, p. 170)

Figure 11.2   Emerging patterns of flexibility

The term is used extensively by Marshall (1961) but also used widely in studies of certain regions of Italy (Goodman *et al*, 1989).

This method of industrial organization is suited to the rapidly changing markets of the late twentieth century:

> In the new unstable and uncertain environment, it is important for organizations to be able to respond quickly and flexibly as market conditions change: and it is argued that systems of inter-connected specialized firms, drawing upon multi-purpose tools, new information and communications technologies, polyvalent workers and craft traditions, are best able to respond economically and efficiently to such volatile conditions.
>
> (Amin and Robins, 1990, p. 3)

The implications of the 'fragmentation' and the 'flexible specialization' models of the economy for independent business may be summarized schematically (Figure 11.2). In short, the flexible specialization model elevates the smaller business into a central position in the economy while the fragmentation model tends to give it a more peripheral role, in a dualistic industrial structure. A dualistic industrial structure and flexible form of production are not necessarily new forms of industrial organization (see Rainnie, 1991).

Evidence for both models is survey-based and remains incomplete, and there is debate about the appropriateness of either to the UK economy.

The bulk of the evidence for the flexible specialization model derives from the industrial districts of Emilia-Romagna (Goodman *et al*, 1989; Brusco and Sabel, 1981) although even in relation to Italy its significance has been questioned recently (Amin, 1989). For the UK, however, there is little evidence that this is the emerging dominant form of production.

Support for the fragmentation model in manufacturing within the UK economy remains confined to specific sectors because of the variety of sub-contract relationships and their implications for the distribution of power between contractor and supplier. Major contributions from Rainnie (1989) on the clothing sector and earlier from Friedman (1977) on the motor industry indicated in depth the uneven power relationship between client and supplier in sub-contracting relationships. Yet these examples have clearly existed for decades now, and more recent evidence has shown both that the growth in sub-contracting in the 1980s is not as widespread as predicted and that the nature of the contract 'power' relationship may be more even.

A study of the UK white goods industry found that there have been organizational changes but:

> ... these have been far from homogeneous ... Levels of sub-contracting within the sector have, in general, not shown any tendency to grow and have, in the case of many of the more innovative manufacturers, declined as certain core activities are brought back in-house or on-site.
>
> (Milne, 1991, p. 248)

With regard to a change in the *nature* of contract relations, there is some evidence of a mixture of the two models of the economy. Imrie and Morris found that the relationship between clients and suppliers tends to take a collaborative rather than dependent basis with an emphasis on 'preferred supplier status' (PSS):

> PSS is a situation whereby corporations give preferential treatment to a specific group of contractors and attempt to develop a long term relationship with them on a basis of trust.
>
> (Imrie and Morris, 1988, p. 8)

The move towards more selective suppliers, a greater involvement of the supplier in the design and development of components and just-in-time delivery is supported by a study of sub-contracting by Japanese firms in Britain (Sako, 1989).

Elsewhere a study of British and French engineering (Lorenz, 1989) revealed that sub-contracting in French firms was more developed than in Britain, again augmenting the view that sub-contracting in Britain is of less significance than in other parts of Western Europe. However, in relation to the nature of sub-contract relations, Lorenz again reinforces the trend towards co-operation rather than dependency:

> The existence of a moral contract, the importance of loyalty and the need for mutual trust ... [which] ... reflects a growing perception of the mutual dependency that exists between client and sub-contractor.
>
> (Lorenz, 1989, p. 124)

One variant of the fragmentation thesis is the 'flexible firm' model (NEDO, 1986), which identifies the functional and numerical labour requirements of large firms in certain sectors. One aspect of this is the role of self-employed labour as a peripheral form of activity in the economy. However, as pointed out elsewhere, although flexible working practices were widespread:

. . . they did not cut very deeply in most of the firms, and therefore the outcome was more likely to be marginal . . . than a purposeful and strategic thrust to achieve flexibility.

(Atkinson and Meager, 1986, p. 26)

On the whole there is insufficient evidence to suggest that the revival of small scale enterprise is mainly a result of a rise in the putting-out of manufacturing work by large firms. Some studies of the UK manufacturing sector in fact suggest a relatively under-developed contracting-out system compared with Japan (Trevor and Christie, 1988; NEDO 1991). It has also been pointed out that this is not a new form of production organization (Pollert, 1988; Pahl, 1984). In relation to service sector work, however, the story is different.

Possibly one methodological weakness of the fragmentation and flexible specialization polarities is their oversimplification of independent business activities. Some small businesses both perform contract work, based on overflow work from larger businesses and also undertake the production or supply of their own designed products thus transcending any rigid categorizations. Even the type of sub-contract work can differ. Some types of contracts may include autonomy over specification or design and thus resemble off-the-shelf purchases (see Blackburn, 1991; Rainnie, 1991). Moreover, research on contracting is set predominantly in manufacturing which is inappropriate for studying its significance for small firms, the bulk of which are in the service sector.

In summary, because of the perpetual re-organization of production activities and the debate over the role of small firms within the latest economic forms, it is difficult to predict the future role of small manufacturing firms with any precision and confidence. On the one hand, it could be argued that both the flexible specialization and fragmentation models combine processes that indicate the continued numerical importance of smaller businesses well into the next decade. If the ability of small business owners to have autonomy is an issue, however, then clearly those having characteristics common to the flexible specialization model are more able to determine their own fate. Those firms having more in common with the fragmentation model will be more dependent on the decisions of the corporate sector. The latest trend towards preferential suppliers and emphasis on them meeting an assured quality may spell trouble for those smaller firms fitting the flexible firm model, if they cannot afford to meet the training, capital equipment and infrastructure concomitant with the new standards. However, there are few indications that large firms are reversing their strategies of the last decade and the contract work that does exist will continue well into the 1990s. What can be stated is that small firms now occupy a much more central role in the UK economy and this position should provide them with opportunities well into the next century.

Small firms in the service sector

There is a strong sectoral bias in the small business population which needs to be considered in any assessment of its future. Nine out of ten of those firms

Table 11.1 *Distribution of self-employed by industrial sector 1989 and per cent change 1981 and 1989*

Sector	1989 (000s)	1981–89 % Change
Agriculture, forestry, fishing	243	2.0
Metal goods, engineering, vehicles	83	81.1
Other production industries	199	101.2
Construction	722	88.7
Distribution, hotels, catering, of which:	824	19.3
Retail distribution	488	
Hotels and catering	175	
Transport and communication	162	64.7
Banking, finance, insurance etc., of which:	372	100.6
Business services	282	
Other services	576	101.9
All services	1,934	
All manufacturing	280	
All industries and services	3,182	57.3

Source notes: 1989 absolute figures derived from Daly (1991), *Employment Gazette* (1991, March, p. 161).
Per cent change figures based on a different series. Data kindly provided by Michael Daly, Department of Employment.

employing between one and twenty-four people are in the services and construction sectors (Curran and Burrows, 1988, p. 55) and self-employment is concentrated in distribution, hotels and repairs; construction; and other services (Table 11.1). The future of the smaller business is, therefore, inextricably bound up with the performance and structural changes within this sector.

Past trends show that the rate of growth of self-employment is integral to the shift towards services in the economy. For example, between 1977 and 1987 the 53 per cent growth in services sector self-employment mirrored the growth in the services sector as a whole (Graham *et al*, 1989). Thus, self-employment in services has only been able to maintain its position relative to the total size of the services sector labour force, a fact reflected in the United States (Steinmetz and Wright, 1989).

One explanation of this growth is that as the economy becomes wealthier service sector functions such as health care for the elderly or eating out may enter the private or formal economy. The structural change in consumption helps small businesses because of the relatively low barriers to entry and localized nature of service sector activity. One characteristic of many service sector goods is that consumption often takes place at the point of purchase, and

Table 11.2   VAT registration net changes by sector 1980–1989

Sector	Net change 1980–1989	Stock end-1989
Agriculture	–0.2	176.1
Production	28.8	155.8
Construction	46.1	264.4
Transport	30.4	72.7
Wholesale	27.3	122.0
Retail	–2.2	263.0
Finance etc.	86.4	147.2
Catering	9.2	128.4
Motor trades	18.4	80.1
Other services	100.5	252.7
All industries	29.0	1,662.3

Source: Employment Gazette (1990, November, pp. 558–559).

distribution therefore often needs to be localized, favouring smaller outlets. Both series of data in Table 11.1 and Table 11.2 show the rise in self-employment and firm formation amongst 'consumer services'.

There has also been a rise in small business activity among 'producer services'. A more detailed disaggregation of *Labour Force Survey* results shows that the biggest increases in self-employment were in 'other services', 'banking, finance etc.' (Table 11.1). (Daly, 1991, p. 119.) This picture of growth is augmented by UK VAT data for the same period, which reveal that the biggest growth sectors (as a proportion of registrations in 1980) included finance, property and professional services and other services (Table 11.2).

Explanations of the rise in small businesses among 'producer services' are in their early stages. One approach is to link these with the fragmentation approach discussed earlier. This emphasizes the transfer of jobs from manufacturing to services as the corporate sector externalizes labour-intensive parts of service activities to the competitive small firm sector (Wood, 1988). These activities include both 'professional, managerial, commercial and technical consultancy activities' and manual activities such as 'building maintenance, equipment service and repair, catering, cleaning, printing, packaging, security, delivery and transportation' (Wood, 1988, p. 98). This view stresses that small firms are in essence a dependent stratum:

> In spite of some evidence for the resurgence of the competitive small firm sector, especially in support services, . . . the dominant position of corporate priorities and decision-making is unlikely to be challenged by current trends.
>
> (Wood, 1988, p. 99)

The *Employers' Labour Use Strategies Survey* – a survey of 877 firms – provides some evidence on the sub-contracting of services (Wood and Smith,

1989). Twenty-six per cent of establishments were using self-employed person-nel compared with only 18 per cent four years earlier and there was evidence of a substitution of employees by self-employed staff. More significantly, there was evidence of a growth in the contracting-out of service work, although unfortunately the authors fail to indicate whether those firms receiving con-tracts were small independents or large contractors, of which there is a growing number (see below). Other studies have also suggested that there has been a growth in service sector contract work from both manufacturing (Imrie and Morris, 1988; Marginson *et al*, 1988; Marshall, 1989) and services itself (Hirschhorn, 1988).

This view is to some extent disputed by Graham *et al* (1989), who relate the growth in services to a wealthier economy. They argue that those sectors that have seen the largest absolute growth in self-employment (distribution; bank-ing, finance, insurance; other services) are not likely to have benefited from contracting out: 'contracting out is unlikely to have been responsible for more than a minor proportion of the employment growth of 2.4 million' (Graham *et al*, 1989, p. 50).

However, this view does not coincide with evidence cited earlier and cannot be readily accepted. The fragmentation of large corporations' non-core ac-tivities has undoubtedly affected positively the growth of producer service small firms. Thus it is misleading to assume that all smaller businesses are in com-mand of their own fate and much depends on their competitive advantage over the in-house capacity of larger corporations.

It is necessary to answer two key questions when assessing the future of small scale activities. First, to what extent can those small firms supplying consumer markets continue to prosper? Second, how permanent are the new relations between large and small firms and what future ownership structures are likely to emerge in the next decade? One possibility is that as the shift towards services slows down and the size of the service sector stabilizes, the concentra-tion of ownership may take place.

In consumer services there has been a slowing down of new business forma-tion (Table 11.2), not only because of the recession of the late 1980s and early 1990s but also because of some restructuring of ownership and the introduc-tion of new legal forms. In retailing, a sector heavily populated by small busi-nesses and the self-employed, the concentration of ownership which has been taking place since the Bolton Report is likely to continue. Retailing has also undergone a revolution in its location with the development of out of town shopping:

> In the 1980s the retail trade was characterised by an increasing polarisation between the large and small operator. As the big stores got bigger and tended to move into larger retail developments on the edge of town, so the smaller operators were squeezed out of the market. This led to a major realignment amongst the smaller companies, which, unable to compete with the giants across the board, had to compete on the basis of specialisation or convenience.
>
> (Keynote Report, 1990a, p. 2)

Small independents are also faced with rising entry costs and the introduction of new technology through electronic point of sale systems reducing labour costs and improving stock control at the expense of higher fixed costs. Small businesses may not be able to reap the benefits of this because they may not have a sufficient turnover to spread the fixed costs of such systems. Furthermore, the rapid expansion of franchising in the retail sector, such as in convenience stores, cigarettes, news and tobacco and fast food, will also erode the truly independent business. Franchising provides the franchisee a licence to use a proven business format, giving them an advantage over independents. Although it is difficult to count the number of franchises exactly, one estimate is that their number doubled between 1984 and 1988 to 16,000 employing over 180,000 (The NatWest/British Franchise Association Survey, 1988, p. 6) and every indication is that their numbers will continue to rise throughout the next decade or so (Felstead, 1991).

However, in some other sectors, such as restaurants, the independent small businesses will continue to expand because of their strong niche advantage associated with a fragmentation of consumption culture. The 'post-modernist' thesis suggests that there is a fragmentation of culture in society. This has strong positive implications for smaller businesses, which benefit from non-standardization and niche markets, although large firms may be able to provide niche products and services to a limited extent. However, the extent to which 'post-modernism' is occurring remains debatable (Curran and Blackburn, 1991, pp. 182–184). Some studies are suggesting, for example, a homogenization of culture in leisure, which would benefit mass provision (Henley Centre for Forecasting, 1991).

The picture for the future of 'producer services' smaller firms is also mixed. The less optimistic thesis seems to suggest that there will be a growth in concentration of ownership to match that which took place in manufacturing in the 1950s and 1960s. Rather than provide vague generalizations, two sectors, once dominated by smaller businesses, may be examined to clarify the processes taking place.

Much has been said about the contracting-out of cleaning services from both the public and private sectors and this is sometimes linked with a growth in independent contractors (Keynote, 1990b). However, after a spate of acquisition activity, contract cleaning in the UK is now dominated by two large multinationals. It is estimated that there were around 5,000 individual firms in 1990, of which approximately 1,200 comprised three or more staff, the larger firms employing up to 1,400 people, the smallest being husband and wife operations (Keynote, 1990b). One of the motivations behind the concentration of ownership in this sector was the need for successful firms in the South East to find offices elsewhere in order to penetrate new markets.

In the financial services market also, there has been a concentration of ownership. However, in certain niches the independent sector continues such as in single-office estate agents, although their future is not assured. In a survey of independent estate agents, the response to the question: 'Is there a future for the independent estate agent?' seemed to be that there would be a growing dualistic structure, with the medium-sized independent of five to ten offices facing extinction. Those independents which are likely to survive will be those of one or two offices with owners who can provide a reputable personal service, have knowledge of the local area, a well trained staff, strong local contacts, aggressive marketing and some sort of niche or specialization such as agricultural property (Hallet, 1990).

In summary, the last decade has seen a growth in small-scale economic activity in both 'consumer' and 'producer' services. The causes of this growth are complex but after a brief review there is no certainty that this growth will continue into the twenty-first century, not least because of the slow down in the shift towards services (Rajan, 1987). Concern has been expressed over the growing concentration of ownership in producer services. The dominance of smaller businesses in consumer markets will very much depend on the pace of the homogenization of culture and there are indications that this will not take place in the next decade or so.

Changing demographic and economic conditions

This section will focus on the likely demographic changes and the implications of growth rate of the economy to the year 2000. Any changes in the demographic profile of the labour supply will inevitably have implications for small scale enterprise, first as employers of labour and, second, on the supply of potential new business owners. There is also the need to evaluate what may be occurring at the macro-economic level in terms of the growth in GNP and how this will affect entry to business ownership.

Changes in the composition of the labour force

A recent announcement (*Employment Gazette*, 1991b), based on certain assumptions, suggests the major expected changes in the labour force to 2001 may be summarized as follows:

> The labour force will be bigger than that at present by 675,000. This represents a slowing down of the growth compared with the previous decade . . . Almost all of the projected net-increase is among women who are expected to make up 45 per cent of the labour force by 2001 . . . The labour force in 2001 will be older than in 1990, with a fall of over one million aged under 25 and a rise in those aged 25–54.
>
> (*Employment Gazette*, 1991b)

These projected changes will have different implications for small businesses as employers and for entry into business ownership. Changes in the labour force composition represent a constraint on the future growth of smaller businesses. Research has shown that small businesses tend to employ younger, less qualified and female staff when compared with the corporate sector (Storey and Johnson, 1987). The projected fall of over 1 million in the under-25s cohort entering the labour market will undoubtedly cause problems for smaller businesses.

The root of the problem likely to be faced by small businesses is based on the finding that they: 'tend to offer inferior employment packages, in terms of wages, fringe benefits, job security and other conditions of employment, compared with larger firms' (Johnson, 1991, p. 95). Recruitment shortages will be particularly acute for specialist staff in management, professional and technical roles where small firms have to compete directly with large firms. Such shortages were experienced by small businesses in the late 1980s compared with the mid-1980s. As Johnson comments, the labour market can change rapidly: 'In other words, the extent of recruitment difficulty amongst smaller businesses appears to have almost doubled over this three year period, during which time unemployment had declined and there had been relatively rapid economic growth' (Johnson, 1991, p. 98).

Others have even found evidence of large firms poaching staff from smaller businesses (Bannock and Stanworth, 1990) about which small firms can do little because they tend to be disadvantaged in terms of the reward packages they can afford.

Since smaller firms tend to employ a higher than average proportion of females (Curran *et al*, 1991a; Atkinson *et al*, 1991), one redeeming feature of the projected labour supply patterns for small firms is the continued growth in the female labour force. Of the increase in the civilian labour force of 3,259,000 since 1971, almost 90 per cent have been women. Although the growth in the labour force will slow down to the year 2000, the proportionate growth in female employment will continue. However, although small firms employ a disproportionate amount of women and therefore the projections appear to be beneficial for small firms, the fact that they will increase as a proportion of the labour force to 2000 does not necessarily leave room for complacency among smaller employers.

Again the responses and recruitment strategies of large firms have to be considered. In response to the changes in the composition of the labour force, it is the corporate sector which has been most innovative. Large firms and the public sector have introduced job packages to attract female labour and older workers. These initiatives have included more flexible working hours, job sharing career-break schemes and crèche facilities (see Stanworth and Stanworth, 1991, p. 221). This point must be kept in perspective – these schemes are not very widespread and those that do exist attract a great deal of publicity. Small firms, on the other hand, have shown few initiatives, probably because of their high fixed costs. Older people could be suitable labour for smaller businesses but the latter need to overcome the ageism found in surveys of the 1970s and 1980s (Naylor, 1988).

The changes in the labour force outlined above will, however, have very different implications for the supply of potential business owners. Research suggests that there is a distinctive 'age launch window' for small business ownership with the bulk of new business owners tending to be in their thirties (Curran and Burrows, 1988 and see Chapter 7). Labour force projections show that this age group will increase in the next decade: 'There will be a 3.7 per cent growth in the 25 to 44 age group . . . the male labour force in the 25 to 44 age group will peak in the mid-1990s whereas the female labour force will continue to rise gradually throughout the decade' (*Employment Gazette*, 1991b, p. 271).

Thus, there will be a growth in the age group from which small business owners have come in the past. Between 1981 and 1989 female self-employment increased by 81 per cent and male self-employment increased by 50 per cent (Daly, 1991). At first sight, the employment projection data suggests that female entry into female small business ownership will continue to rise relative to males. However, caution needs to be exercised as the relationship between numbers in the age launch window and entry into self-employment is not a straightforward statistical one. Much depends on what employers can offer to females and this age group and, as already discussed, the corporate sector has introduced some initiatives to attract the female labour force which may displace their entry into business ownership. As pointed out by Allen and Truman, the future of female business ownership is tied in with wider factors such as the ability to break down occupational barriers and the level of social provision (Allen and Truman, 1991).

There is some uncertainty to the inflows into the labour force. Although immigration is currently minimal compared with the late 1950s and early 1960s, there are possible changes which may affect the composition of the labour force. For example, there may be a rise in immigration from Hong Kong following its 'realignment' with the People's Republic of China. Certain ethnic minorities have a higher than average propensity to run a business than UK nationals (see Ward, 1991, and Chapter 7), and it would be expected that should there be immigration from Hong Kong there will be a small rise in the number of people self-employed.

Changes within the composition of the UK labour force will also have implications for the rate of entry into small business ownership. For example, a rationalization of the armed forces following any relaxing of international conflict will increase the number of potential entrepreneurs in the labour market. The proposed reduction in the numbers employed in the armed services in the early 1990s will cause a rise in the entry into new business activities, especially if they enter a depressed labour market, bringing with them skills and severance pay.

On the relationship between changing economic conditions and the rate and type of small business formation

The relationship between new firm formation rates and the level of economic activity at the macro level has excited debate among academics, policy makers and their advisers. Historically, entry into self-employment has been associated with recession (Foreman-Peck, 1985) and econometricians have in general found a positive relationship between the rate of unemployment and entry into business ownership. For example, the decline and rise in self-employment in eight OECD countries have been seen as counter-cyclical:

> The revival of self-employment roughly coincides with a period of economic stress beginning in the mid-1970s, characterized by slow economic growth . . . rising levels

of unemployment and part-time employment, and the spread of various forms of contingent and substandard employment.

(Bogenhold and Staber, 1991, p. 227)

Results of studies in the United Kingdom tend to support the positive relationship between unemployment and firm formation (Hamilton, 1989; Johnson *et al*, 1988) although there are some exceptions (Binks and Jennings, 1986; Blanchflower and Oswald, 1990). In studying this relationship over the 1966–1986 period Johnson reported that: 'these results suggest that self-employment is positively and significantly correlated with the rate of unemployment . . .' (Johnson, 1991, p. 92).

The statistical association has been given causality through surveys of the employment histories of people entering business ownership. 'Recession push' has been cited as one of the salient factors determining the decision to enter business ownership in the 1980s although the issues are complex and debatable (for discussion see Meager, 1991, ch. 7). Those entering self-employment from unemployment may not have been 'involuntary' entrants. As pointed out by Hakim, unemployment or redundancy may have been the catalyst necessary to the starting of a business (Hakim, 1989). In addition, redundancy packages would provide some capital to start a business. The provision of government incentives such as the Enterprise Allowance Scheme and the flow of cheap secondhand-equipment from companies suffering from a recession may have also helped (Binks and Jennings, 1986).

Although results from surveys give some credence to the 'recession push' thesis as one of the factors behind the revival of the smaller business in the past twenty years, more-recent evidence has shown a breakdown in the straightforward relationship between unemployment and net new firm formation. Studies in the USA (Steinmetz and Wright, 1989) and in the UK (Johnson *et al*, 1988) highlight this point:

> It does appear to be the case that over the latter half of the 1980s, whilst registered unemployment has declined from over 3 million to less than 2 million, growth in the number of self-employed people and in the rate of new business registrations has continued at the pace of the early 1980s.

(Johnson, 1991, p. 93)

Thus, the association between unemployment and small business activity appears unstable over time. Exploratory research on the relationship between unemployment and entry into self-employment shows two distinct patterns, one a positive relationship the other a negative relationship, but more needs to be done to understand the reasons behind this pattern.

This causes some difficulty for any assessment of economic growth on future small business trends: but first it is necessary to consider medium term economic forecasts for the UK economy. In general, economic forecasters are predicting a continuation of the severe recession faced by the economy in the early 1990s. Although levels of pessimism differ, no forecaster predicts a complete recovery of the economy in the medium term. For example, the London Business School predicts an increase in unemployment after 1992 (LBS, 1991);

the National Institute for Economic and Social Research forecasts a long and deep recession with continued unemployment (Marsh, 1991); and the National Westminster Bank also suggests that unemployment will stay high after the current recession (Brummer, 1991). Of course, these models are built using certain assumptions, but the main implication is that when the economy does pick up, much of the new activity will involve 'jobless growth'.

In the light of these forecasts, some implications for smaller business may be suggested. First, the projections that any upturn in the economy will feature jobless growth will mean that the impetus to become self-employed or start a business because of the lack of attractive employee jobs will continue in the 1990s. However, when the level of economic activity recovers enough to produce a growth in labour demand, there will inevitably be a negative impact on new business formation. The extent of this effect depends on the ability of employers to provide attractive employee packages and thus take on would-be new business owners.

Second, the level of unemployment and economic growth will also add a qualitative dimension to the stock of smaller businesses. It may be postulated that an increase in economic activity will discourage the formation of more marginal businesses which are started, say, because of few other employment opportunities or, alternatively, a growth in the size of smaller firms because of the need to employ others.

Third, those small businesses that already exist should benefit from an expansion in economic activity. As indicated earlier, the economy is much more fragmented than it was twenty years ago and any upturn in demand will therefore reinforce new economic and ownership structures. An increase in the demand for goods and services will affect the smaller businesses directly through their sales in the service sector (as in the consumer-led boom of the mid-1980s) and through any 'post-Fordist' links (flexible firm or flexible specialization variants) with larger manufacturing firms.

In summary, whether the 1990s is a decade of slow or rapid economic growth, smaller scale activities will benefit but in different ways. Slow economic growth will have a positive effect on the numerical expansion in small businesses. Alternatively, a faster growth in demand in the economy will have a positive 'knock-on' effect to small firms, strengthening the new economic structures established in the last twenty years. Caution does need to be stressed, however, on this optimistic view in reaction to the nature and depth of any recession. While smaller firms have shown some resilience to recessionary conditions – which in fact may have 'pushed' some people into founding a business – if a recession is very deep then this will lead to rise in company insolvencies, reducing the number of small businesses. Thus, in a very severe recession small businesses will suffer, as in the early 1990s, and we will see a negative relationship between the rate of unemployment and new firm formation.

Changing institutional and political environment

This section will examine and speculate on the changing institutional environment within which small firms will operate in the 1990s. The Europe of the

1990s is very different from that of the 1980s, especially with the breaking up of centrally-planned economies in Eastern Europe. Small business ownership in the latter is small (ILO, 1990) but will undoubtedly rise as the decade progresses. However, attention in this section will focus on the more direct effects of the European Community and the UK legislative environment.

The European dimension

In 1992 the twelve member states of the European Community will adopt legislation to facilitate the free movement of capital, labour and goods and services within the community. Much has been written about the impact of '1992' on smaller businesses but it will be argued that, on closer inspection, although the effects are complicated to evaluate it will have only a minor impact into the next century. One problem is that of data deficiencies. As pointed out by Curran (1990) there are substantial differences between member states in the proportion of small businesses in their economies, primarily because of their very different industrial structures. Nor have differing methods, efficiency of data collection and definitions of the small firm helped the community to achieve consistency in its economic data.

The fact that the single market opens up 340 million consumers has been interpreted by some as a strong advantage for all, including smaller businesses. The Cecchini Report argued that the main losers from the pre-1992 tariff barriers were small and medium-sized businesses (SMEs). This was based on the findings of a survey of 11,000 businesses in six major member states (Cecchini, 1988). For smaller and medium-sized businesses (that is, up to 250 employees) customs costs per consignment of exports could be 30 to 45 per cent higher than for larger firms (Cecchini, 1988, p. 9). Thus, the removal of tariff and non-tariff barriers would disproportionately benefit SMEs involved in exporting.

While not disputing the logic of this argument, its significance in real terms is overstated quite simply because the bulk of smaller businesses do not export. A survey of small firms in all economic sectors in the UK in 1987, for example, found that 94 per cent did not export and only 4 per cent exported more than 10 per cent of their output (Storey and Johnson, 1987). Similarly, in a survey of 350 firms in seven service sectors in 1989–1990, only 3.7 per cent were exporting more than 10 per cent of their activities abroad (Curran *et al*, 1991a). In a study of retailing post-1992, one analysis concluded:

> the removal of physical, technical and fiscal barriers within the EC . . . will not remove the important cultural and socio-economic barriers which will remain important determinants of expansion strategy, Indeed, it would not be reasonable to expect 1992 to create an homogeneous market, but it remains clear that the problems uppermost in retailers' minds are based on an appreciation of the issues raised by regional diversity.
>
> (Alexander, 1990, p.186)

These findings reinforce the view that since nine out of ten small firms are in the service sector and their sales are attuned to local markets, culture and tastes, the only conclusion one can reach is that, in the medium-term at least, '1992' will have little impact on the trading patterns of small firms. Perhaps on mainland Europe there will be more cross-border sales because of closer proximity.

Another possible way in which smaller firms will be affected is through the indirect impact of cross-border mergers. There was a rise in acquisition and merger activity in the late 1980s and early 1990s:

> There has been a steady increase in mergers and acquisitions in Europe since 1985 . . . As 1992 approaches the increase in mergers, joint ventures and strategic alliances is likely to be sustained and will probably accelerate. This will have inevitable effects on SMEs – because of both the changes to the market place and the reduction in the number of big companies to be served.
>
> (Economist Intelligence Unit, 1990, p. 90)

Although this merger activity is taking place among larger firms, small firms may be affected by a rationalization of the purchasing activities of the new transnational organizations. For example, it may be hypothesized that a trans-European company may seek to source its components from lower unit cost nations within the community which will be detrimental to UK suppliers. This would be reinforced by the legislative impact of the adoption of BS5750 (see below).

Differing financial markets may also affect the performance of small businesses' activities within different member states. An analysis of the different banking traditions in the European Community has shown that British small firms are operating at a disadvantage (Binks, 1991). Among the weaknesses of the UK banking system is the way in which a firm is assessed for lending, British banks tending to calculate the value of a firm's assets, continental banks the earning potential of the firm. Binks argues that this will particularly affect larger small firms who will be at a disadvantage to their counterparts elsewhere in the European Community and therefore will be constrained from expansion. As a result, this could mean that the latter could be better placed to penetrate the British market than British firms to penetrate European markets.

In summary, the impact of '1992' on smaller businesses is complicated, although it has been argued here that overall the impact will not be central to the activities of smaller businesses in the 1990s. This view should not be taken as a signal for complacency, however, and the impact of '1992' will increase as time elapses and there will obviously be sectoral differences.

The UK dimension

The introduction of quality standards within the UK illustrates the negative aspects of the harmonization of product and service provision and the implications if these are introduced from the European tier of government. The introduction of British Standard BS5750 has been having, it has been alleged, an adverse effect on very small firms. The aim of the standard is to ensure that every aspect of a firm's business – from the switchboard operation through to the control of raw materials – meets a minimum quality standard. However, it is expensive to introduce and involves a complete overhaul of a company's administration. As a result of being unable to find the extra resources needed to meet the new standards, smaller businesses, and especially the self-employed, may suffer because larger firms are starting to insist that their suppliers conform to the standard (Batchelor, 1991).

The political composition of the government also needs to be considered. The 1980s saw a period of uninterrupted Conservative governance which aimed to support small-scale enterprise covering three broad areas: finance; legislation and administration; and information and advice (Department of Trade and Industry, 1988; Goss, 1991, ch. 7). Since 1979 it has been estimated that there have been well over 200 policy measures to support small businesses, which for example between 1980 and 1985 cost the exchequer £1 billion (Edmonds, 1986). These measures have undoubtedly had a positive impact on the number of small businesses. For example, by March 1991 over 550,000 unemployed people had benefited from the Enterprise Allowance Scheme (EAS) and the survival rate of EAS businesses trading after three years was 65 per cent. The Loan Guarantee Scheme, introduced in 1981, had over 27,000 applicants, totalling lending of over £880 million by 1990 (Department of Employment, 1991a, pp. 18–19). If there was a continuation of Conservative Party governance well into the 1990s, support for small firms would continue. The nature of the support may, however, change and already there are some indications – for example the closure of the Co-operative Development Agency – that this policy may be rationalized, and that there may be a move away from 'blanket support'. Elsewhere it has been argued that 'already there are some indications that small firm policies are less central to the government's thinking' (Curran and Blackburn, 1991, p. 179).

While the commitment of the Conservative Party towards small-scale activity has been well demonstrated in the 1980s, the policy of the Labour Party is less easy to determine. In the late 1970s, the Labour Party did not have a specific small firms policy and stressed a 'corporatist' approach to running the economy. For some the re-introduction of corporatism is seen as the death knell for small-scale activities (Bannock, 1991). However, the last Labour government often had policies which had implications for small scale activities. In 1977, it appointed the Wilson Committee to inquire into the role of the financial institutions and the provision of funds for industry, including small firms. Local authorities controlled by Labour often supported local purchasing strategies and the Greater London Council (GLC) through the Greater London Enterprise Board supported the promotion of small firms particularly in the clothing and furniture sectors (Rainnie, 1991).

More recently, however, the Labour Party has come round to recognize the significance of smaller businesses in the economy. With regard to skills a more recent policy document states: 'The special problems of small businesses will be recognized and they will be encouraged instead to establish training consortia with other companies' (Labour Party, 1991, p. 7).

Later the document becomes more explicit in the support: 'Our economic policy and industrial strategy will . . . continue to help small firms get going.

But the core of our approach will be to improve support for growing firms . . . We will facilitate the establishment of small businesses by women, . . . [and] small businesses established by the ethnic minorities' (Labour Party, 1991, p. 11).

The 1980s may well have represented a high point of support for small scale activities (Burrows and Curran, 1991, p. 21) although there is some question about the effectiveness of these policies (Goss, 1991, ch. 7). More recently, there has been a minor convergence in the small business policies of the Conservative and Labour Parties and it seems that whatever the political composition of government in the 1990s, smaller businesses will continue to be viewed favourably. However, the expense of supporting small firms, the fact that many of the initiatives in the 1980s were one-off changes which could not be repeated, the recent acceptance in some policy circles of a move towards selectivity and the likelihood of a swing away from free market policies, can only lead to the conclusion that there will be a contraction in the amount of support from government. Any changes in legislation must, however, be kept in perspective. Surveys have shown time and time again that, given the meagre proportion of small businesses that receive any support, what is of importance is the level of aggregate demand for goods and services produced by smaller businesses which will be affected by general macro-economic polices (for example, Curran *et al*, 1991a; Atkinson *et al*, 1990) or industry specific policies.

The 1990s: a new enterprise culture?

One of the most debatable dimensions of social change in the 1980s is the extent to which there was an emergence of an 'enterprise culture'. This is of significance when analysing the future patterns of employment, because it may be argued that working for oneself could be one of many manifestations of the label. Causality between culture and economic structure is very complex and difficult to identify:

> So far there have been few attempts to understand the affiliation between the reality of the restructuring process as it has, in actuality implicated the prime moral subjects of the discourse – the petty bourgeoisie – and the wider rhetoric of the enterprise culture.
>
> (Burrows and Curran, 1991, p. 10)

The links between the two must be addressed in the context of this chapter because, as suggested elsewhere: 'If the revival of small firms is to be a long-term trend, then it must have its roots in the aspirations and economic beliefs of the population' (Curran and Blackburn, 1991, p. 179).

To what extent, for example, have younger people accepted the central elements of the 'enterprise culture' as manifested in a desire to run their own business? Or, alternatively, to what extent have new business owners entered this employment option because of few other opportunities rather than a positive desire to run a business? Two problems emerge: defining the concept and measuring its acceptance by the population.

It has been suggested that there are a number of different 'enterprise cultures' depending on the perspective taken (Ritchie, 1991). It often '. . . appears as a free floating articulating principle of our times, when in reality it is being manoeuvred by powerful interests pushing disparate claims over it' (Ritchie, 1991, p. 17).

Ritchie argues that there is a need to put the different uses of the term into a framework to assist the analysis of the concept. He distinguishes between several discourses of the enterprise culture including subject, believer, sceptic and analyst (Ritchie, 1991). 'Believer-driven' versions argue that there is a new 'enterprise spirit' which has been one of the driving forces behind restructuring as advocated strongly by government over the past decade. These versions embody rewards for hard work and individualism, are anti-collectivist and pro-self-help. We are essentially concerned with the 'subject' – that is, the small business owner – and the extent to which 'believer-driven' versions are accepted by them.

Yet there is no consensus on whether there has been a ready acceptance of an enterprise culture in contemporary Britain and its significance in the social and economic restructuring of the 1980s is difficult to determine. Some writers argue that rather than being an explanatory or causal factor in this restructuring, the 'enterprise culture' has become one way of explaining the restructuring – as argued by Burrows (1991):

> The enterprise culture is thus a discourse which provides a wide ranging semiotic rationale for the present restructuring (p. 5) [and] . . . has thus been a contingent rather than a necessary feature of the present restructuring of Britain and its survival is by no means guaranteed.

(Burrows, 1991b, p. 10)

As a result, Burrows argues that any decline in the enterprise culture in the 1990s might be expected to have little effect on petty capitalism (Burrows, 1991).

These issues are not easily resolved. Culture cannot be quantified or measured easily and we have to rely on surveys that elicit explicit views on the enterprise culture or life and career aspirations of the whole population or ask existing business owners about their motivations for running their own business.

There are problems also over gathering suitable data with a satisfactory time series element, and this renders it difficult to make an evaluation of changes over time. The British Social Attitudes Survey (Blanchflower and Oswald, 1990) allows some time series comparison between 1983 and 1989 on the attitudes of adult members of the population to the 'enterprise culture'. It finds that there is little evidence that the self-employed are more likely to have suffered from unemployment (as confirmed by Labour Force Surveys) or '. . . that unemployment provides a spur towards enterprise' (Blanchflower and Oswald, 1990, p. 130). It also 'examine[s] the hypothesis that an enterprise culture has flourished in Britain since 1983' (Blanchflower and Oswald, 1990, p. 133) by asking employees if they had seriously considered self-employment. The results show that:

There is no evidence at all here of any increase in the *desire* among employees for self-employment. Thus, between 15 and 17 per cent of employees in each year said that they had seriously considered self-employment.

(Blanchflower and Oswald, 1990, p. 134: emphasis in the original)

However, because the positive relationship between unemployment and entry into self-employment broke down in the late 1980s, the authors suggest that this may be a result of a new entrepreneurial spirit amongst the population, although this remains speculative.

More-explicit surveys of the population on the enterprise culture have been undertaken despite the methodological problems of defining the concept. Bannock has developed an 'enterprise barometer' since 1988 which involves asking directors of 3i companies the question 'Do you agree or disagree that there is a new enterprise culture in this country?' (1991, p. 28). In January 1988 the percentage balance was 79 per cent, in January 1989 72 per cent, and in September 1990 it had fallen to 42 per cent (1991, p. 28). These results are associated with the recession of the early 1990s, although an identical question to the general population finds no change in the same time period at a low of 32 per cent. Obviously, such surveys are problematic: the question may be leading and the short-term fluctuations in the views of industrialists tend to suggest that it is more about business confidence than any deep-rooted cultural change.

Focusing more specifically on small business owners themselves does not resolve many issues as surveys tend to show little affinity with believer-driven versions of the enterprise culture. Research into the attitudes of the self-employed compared with employees in 1985 found 'no evidence of any fundamental differences between employees and the self-employed in the basic *work ethic*' (Hakim, 1988, p. 435).

Nor has there been any evidence from surveys of small business owners that there has been a revival in business ownership as a result of an acceptance of believer-driven versions of the enterprise culture:

As has often been demonstrated (Curran, 1986, 1987; Curran and Burrows, 1987; Hakim, 1988; Ritchie, 1991) those directly involved in small scale economic activities do not utilize such cultural sets to interpret their experiences or guide their behaviour to any marked extent.

(Burrows and Curran, 1991, p. 20)

A qualitative analysis of 140 small, service-sector business owners confirms this view (Curran *et al*, 1991b). When asked what the enterprise culture meant to them, a third said that the phrase meant little or nothing and felt unable to discuss it further. Of the two-thirds who were able to talk about the notion, there were wide-ranging opinions – some ascribing it to politicians, others linking it with 'yuppie' culture of the 1980s – but in general '. . . a large proportion felt it did not have very much to do with them or their businesses' (Curran *et al*, 1991b, p. 32).

People have entered small-scale enterprise in the 1980s for many differing factors (Meager, 1991). It appears that the 'believer-driven' versions of the enterprise culture may have highlighted self-employment and business ownership as acceptable forms of work whereas previously they may have been absent from the population's occupational horizons.

A central element to the future of small business is the desire of the younger working population to start a business. An analysis of the demographic changes in the working population early revealed that there would be no downturn in the numbers in the 'age launch window' throughout the 1990s. This does not, however, guarantee a continued flow in business ownership, as much depends on the attractiveness of this employment option. Younger people – those who were at their most impressionable in the 1980s – may be expected to display a positive attitude to the enterprise culture as manifested by a desire to enter business ownership. Organizations such as 'Livewire' have claimed that there has been a growth in young enterprise: 'The rise of the enterprise culture has created an environment in which young people can explore the potential for taking their futures into their own hands' (Project North East, 1989, p. ii). One problem with such surveys is that they tend to take place in a strong 'pro-enterprise' context. Other surveys have found a more restrained impact of the enterprise culture on younger people. In a survey of over 800 sixth formers, Curran and Blackburn (1990) found that just under 25 per cent thought it likely that they would run a business of their own eventually, which almost reflected the proportion of parents of the sample who were small business owners or self-employed. Elsewhere, MacDonald and Coffield (1991) highlight the struggle of young business owners in an economically depressed area and find a culture of survival rather than a spirit of enterprise as the main motivating forces for running a business.

On the positive side, however, is the impact of 'inter-generational inheritance' which will increase the numbers of new business owners in the 1990s. The strong positive relationship between parents and their offspring who run a business has been well documented (Curran and Burrows, 1988; Goldthorpe, 1987; Stanworth et al, 1989). This has received support when looking at the employment intentions of young people. Curran and Blackburn (1990) found a strong positive association between those young people who wanted to run a business and parents who owned a business. The larger number of small business owners in the 1980s will therefore have a positive impact on the numbers entering this employment option in the 1990s because of this 'inter-generational effect'.

Conclusion

This chapter has examined some of the socio-economic changes that are likely to affect smaller businesses in the next decade or so. The changes in the economy in the last decade have been rapid and deep. The economy is more service-sector-oriented and more fragmented than it has been in the past. As a result, small firms have taken on a more central role, although there is some debate about the exact nature of this position – some suggesting that smaller firms are servicing larger firms, others that through a re-organization of production and cultural changes they are exerting more independence. Much of the discussion surrounding new economic structures and flexible specialization remains to be proven with respect to the UK economy.

However, one of the major reasons for the growth in small business activity in the 1980s has been the rise in the service sector. Small firms have an advantage over large firms in services because they are geographically dispersed, can serve local market needs and are embedded in local culture. A continued shift towards services in the economy will therefore benefit small-scale activities. However, a number of concerns may be voiced for the future. The move towards services can be seen as a 'once and for all' change and will not continue into the next decade: thus numerically there will be fewer opportunities for small businesses. Moreover, as the service sector matures, larger firms will begin to penetrate the traditional domain of smaller businesses. The concentration of ownership in both consumer and producer services is already taking place and this poses a major threat to the independent business sector. New legal forms, such as retail franchising, also threaten the truly independent sector. The dominance of the small business in this sector is ultimately, however, dependent on the continuance of the heterogeneity of culture.

Changes in the composition of the labour force will also affect the future of the small business. An analysis of demographic changes reveals that there will be no demographic downturn in the number of people in the 'age launch window' for small business ownership. In contrast, small employers will face difficulties as the number of younger people entering the labour market falls. In any tight labour markets, smaller businesses will suffer because they are unable to compete with the corporate sector in terms of employment rewards.

The level of aggregate demand and economic growth rate will also affect small firms. Some argue that one of the main reasons behind the revival of smaller businesses in the 1980s has been the recessionary conditions at the beginning and end of the decade. However, it has been difficult to disentangle the impact of recession from the general restructuring discussed earlier. Nor is there a straightforward relationship between unemployment and entry into small business ownership, which renders problematic any interpretation of economic forecasts for the level of small business activity. However, two alternatives may be considered. If economic growth is slow and unemployment continues to stay at around 2 million, it is argued here that numerically the level of small business activity will grow because of too few *employee* opportunities. This must be qualified by the depth of any recessionary conditions: a severe recession will undoubtedly reverse this direction.

On the other hand, if the economy experiences rapid growth into the next century, small-scale capital will flourish because of the new fragmented structures that have emerged in the last decade, and particularly between large firms and small service-sector firms. Caution must be exercised here also. If small businesses cannot compete in the labour market for employees or if employee rewards in the corporate sector are attractive enough to deter potential and existing business owners, the small business sector will be constrained in its growth rate, although the quality of existing businesses will be augmented. The implication for small employers is that they must adopt new recruitment and retention strategies to meet changes in the supply of labour. For example, they must look to new sources of labour, including older people, that they have tended to ignore in the past.

Changes in the institutional and political environment will also affect small business activity but to a lesser extent than the economic forces above. The Single European Market will introduce legislative changes and may lead to an internationalization of markets. Most notably, one immediate result is the introduction of a quality standard, BS5750, which may lead to a rationalization of suppliers to large firms. However, in general, the short term effects of a Single European Market are expected to be minimal because of the cultural diversity between member states.

The 1980s were without doubt the decade in which small business activity received an unprecedented amount of state support through a variety of financial, legislative and information measures. It has been argued in this chapter that any diminution in this support – the most likely possibility – will affect small businesses to only a minor extent. Three main reasons are proffered for this stance. First, although large efforts were made to benefit small businesses, only a minor proportion of small firms received any aid. Second, a good deal of support was for new start-ups rather than the small business population as a whole – for example, the Enterprise Allowance Scheme increased the number of small businesses although their overall impact has been difficult to evaluate in terms of their additionality and displacement effects. Finally, general macro-economic policies often swamp more targeted small business polices, as illustrated by small business owners' criticisms of the use of interest rate policy as the main instrument of government policy in the 1980s.

The final dimension to the factors under consideration in this chapter is that of the enterprise culture. If the British population have adopted an enterprise culture, it could be argued that one occupational aspect of this is business ownership. However, it has been argued that the concept is difficult to define, difficult to measure and even when these issues are overcome or ignored, there is little evidence that there has been a radical break in cultural values. What is more important is the 'inter-generational' impact of business owners on their offspring. The larger number of small business owners in the 1980s will have a positive impact on the numbers entering business ownership through this 'inter-generational effect'.

In short, this chapter has investigated a range of socio-economic factors likely to be faced by small-scale enterprise through the next decade. The issues faced are complex and it is far from straightforward to interpret aggregate trends for small businesses. However, the analysis has shown that on balance the new importance that small-scale economic activity has achieved in the UK is likely to be tested over the next decade.

References

Chapter 1

Bannock, G. (1976) *The Smaller Business in Britain and Germany*, Wilton House.

Bannock, G. (1981) *The Economics of Small Firms*, Basil Blackwell.

Bannock, G. (1987) *Britain in the 1980s: Enterprise Reborn?*, 3i-Investors In Industry.

Bannock, G. and Albach, H. (1991) *Small Business Policy in Europe*, Anglo-German Foundation.

Bannock, G and Daly, M. (1990) Size distribution of UK firms, *Employment Gazette*, May 1990.

Bannock, G. and Doran, A. (1987) *Going Public*, Paul Chapman Publishing.

Bannock, G. and Doran, A. (1990) *Business Banking in the 1990s*, Lafferty Publications.

Bannock, G. and Peacock, A. (1989) *Governments and Small Business*, Paul Chapman Publishing.

Birch, D. L. (1979) *The Job Generation Process*, MIT.

Burns, P. and Dewhurst, J. (eds.) (1986) *Small Business in Europe*, Macmillan.

Curran J. and Blackburn, R. (eds.) (1991) *Paths of Enterprise: the Future of Small Business*, Routledge.

Daly, M. (1990) The 1980s – a decade of growth in enterprise, *Employment Gazette*, November 1990.

DoEm (1991) *Small firms in Britain 1991*, HMSO.

DTI (1985) *Burdens on Business*, HMSO.

DTI (1991) *Cutting Red Tape for Business*, HMSO.

EC (1990) *Enterprises in the European Community*, Commission of the European Communities.

Fothergill, E. and Gudgin, G. (1979) *The Job Generation Process in Britain*, Centre for Environmental Studies.

Ganguly, P. (1985) *UK Small Business Statistics and International Comparisons*, Paul Chapman Publishing.

GB and P (1989a) *Small Business Statistics: a Feasibility Study for the Department of Employment*, Graham Bannock & Partners Ltd., December 1989.

GB and P (1989b) *Small Business Perspective*, Graham Bannock & Partners Ltd., December 1989.

Hay, D. A. and Morris, D. J. (1984) *Unquoted Companies*, Macmillan.

Hoselitz, B. F. (1968), *The Role of Small Business in Economic Growth*, Monton, Paris.

Hughes, A. (1990) *Industrial Concentration and the Small Business Sector in the UK: the 1980s in Historical Perspective*, Working Paper No. 5, SBRC, University of Cambridge.

SBA (1989) *The State of Small Business*, US Government Printing Office.

Sengenberger, W. *et al* (eds.) (1990) *The Re-emergence of Small Enterprises*, International Institute for Labour Studies.

Storey, D. *et al* (1987) *The Performance of Small Firms*, Croom Helm.

Wilson, H. (1979) *The Financing of Small Firms*, Report of the Committee to Review the Functioning of Financial Institutions, HMSO Cmnd 7503.

Chapter 2

Acs, Z. J. and Audretsch, D. B. (1990) *Innovation and Small Firms*, MIT Press, Cambridge, Mass.

Ambler, S. and Kennett, S. (1985), *The Small Workshops Scheme: a Review of the Impact of the Scheme and an Assessment of the Current Market Position for Small Workshops*, HMSO, London.

Bannock, G. (1980), *The Economics of Small Firms*, Basil Blackwell, Oxford.

Bannock, G. and Albach, H. (1991) *Small Business Policy in Europe: Britain, Germany and the European Commission*, Anglo-German Foundation, London.

Bannock, G. and Peacock, A. (1989) *Governments and Small Business*, Paul Chapman, London.

Barkham, R. (1987) Regional variations in new business size, financial structure and founder characteristics: survey results. *University of Reading Discussion Paper in Urban and Regional Economics*, Series C, No. 32.

Beesley, M. and Wilson, P. (1982) Government aid to the small firm since Bolton. In J. Stanworth *et al* (eds.) *Perspectives on a Decade of Small Business Research*, Gower, Aldershot.

Bennett, R. J. (1990) (ed.) Training and Enterprise Councils (TEC) and Vocational Education and Training (VET), *Regional Studies*, 24, 65–82.

Binks, M. and Vale, P. (1990) *Entrepreneurship and Economic Change*, McGraw Hill, London.

Birch, D. (1979) *The Job Generation Process*, MIT Program on Neighborhood and Regional Change, March.

Britton, J. N. H. (1989) Innovation policies for small firms, *Regional Studies*, 23, 167–73.

Brock, W. A. and Evans, D. S. (1989) Small business economics, *Small Business Economics*, 1, 7–20.

Burrows, R. (1991a) The discourse of the enterprise culture and the restructuring of Britain. In J. Curran and R. A. Blackburn (eds.) *Paths of Enterprise*, Routledge, London.

Burrows, R. (1991b) (ed.) *Deciphering the Enterprise Culture*, Routledge, London.

Curran, J. and Blackburn, R. A. (1989) Young people and enterprise: a national survey. *Kingston Business School Occasional Paper No. 11*.

Curran, J. and Blackburn, R. A. (1991) (eds.) *Paths of Enterprise: the Future of the Small Business*, Routledge, London.

Department of Economic Development (1987) *Building a Stronger Economy: the Pathfinder Process*, Department of Economic Development for Northern Ireland, Belfast.

Department of Employment (1989) *Small Firms in Britain*, Department of Employment, London.

Department of Employment (1991) *Small Firms in Britain 1991*, HMSO, London.

Department of Trade and Industry (1983) *Regional Industrial Policy: Some Economic Issues*, DTI, London.

Department of Trade and Industry (1988) *DTI – The Department for Enterprise*, Cmnd. 278, HMSO, London.

Dunne, P. and Hughes, A. (1990) Small businesses: an analysis of recent trends in their relative importance and growth performance in the UK with some European comparisons. *University of Cambridge Small Business Research Centre Working Paper No. 1.*

Economist Advisory Group (1983) *The Small Firm Survivors*, Shell UK Limited, London.

Frank, C. E. J., Miall, R. H. C. and Rees, R. D. (1984) Issues in small firms, research of relevance to policy-making. *Regional Studies* 18, 257–266.

Gray, C. and Stanworth, J. (1986) *Allowing for Enterprise: a Qualitative Assessment of the Enterprise Allowance Scheme*, Small Business Research Trust, London.

HMSO (1971) Bolton Report (1971) *Report of the Committee of Inquiry on Small Firms*, chaired by J. E. Bolton, Cmnd. 4811, HMSO, London.

HMSO (1979) Wilson, H. (1979) *The Financing of Small Firms*, Report of the Committee to Review the Functioning of Financial Institutions, HMSO Cmnd 7503.

HMSO (1983) *Regional Industrial Development*, Cmnd. 9111, HMSO, London.

HMSO (1985) *Lifting the Burden*, London.

Harris, R. I. D., Jefferson, C. W. and Spencer, J. E. (1990) (eds.) *The Northern Ireland Economy: a Comparative Study in the Economic Development of a Peripheral Region*, Longman, London.

Harrison, R. T. and Hart, M. (1991) Encouraging enterprise in Northern Ireland: constraints and opportunities. *IBAR – Journal of Irish Business and Administrative Research*, 13.

Harrison, R. T. and Mason, C. M. (1986) The regional impact of the small firms loan guarantee scheme in the United Kingdom, *Regional Studies*, 20, 535–550.

Harrison, R. T. and Mason, C. M. (1988) Risk finance, the equity gap and new venture formation in the United Kingdom: the impact of the Business Expansion Scheme. In B. Kirchoff *et al* (eds.) *Frontiers of Entrepreneurship Research 1988*, Babson College, Wellesley, Mass.

Harrison, R. T. and Mason, C. M. (1991) Regional variations in the take-up and impact of small firms policy in the United Kingdom: analysis and future prospects. In R. T. Harrison and M. Hart (eds.) *Spatial Policy in a Divided Nation*, Jessica Kingsley, London.

Hart, M. (1989) Entrepreneurship in Ireland: a comparative study of the Republic of Ireland and Northern Ireland, *Entrepreneurship and Regional Development*, 1, 129–141.

Hillier, R. (1989) Making training a key factor in business performance, *Employment Gazette*, May, 219–224.

Johnson, S. (1990) Small firm policies – an agenda for the 1990s. Paper to the Thirteenth Small Firms Policy and Research Conference, Harrogate, November 1990.

Keat, R. and Abercrombie, N. (1991) *Enterprise Culture*, Routledge, London.

Keeble, D. E. (1990a) New firms and regional economic development: experiences and impacts in the 1980s. In G. Cameron *et al* (eds.) *Cambridge Regional Economic Review*, pp. 62–71.

Keeble, D. E. (1990b) Small firms, new firms and uneven regional development in the United Kingdom, *Area* 22, 234–245.

Leslie Hays Consultants Ltd. (1990) *Evaluation of Regional Enterprise Grants*, HMSO, London.

Loveman, G. and Sengenberger, W. (1991) The reemergence of small scale production: an international comparison, *Small Business Economics*, 3, 138.

MacDonald R. and Coffield, F. (1991) *Risky business? – Youth and the Enterprise Culture*, Falmer Press, Brighton.

Martin, R. (1985) Monetarism masquerading as regional policy? The Government's new system of regional aid, *Regional Studies*, 19, 379–388.

Mason, C. M. (1985) The geography of 'successful' small firms in the United Kingdom *Environment and Planning A*, 17, 1499–1513.

Mason, C. M. (1989) Explaining recent trends in new firm formation in the UK: some evidence from South Hampshire, *Regional Studies*, 23, 331–346.

Mason, C. M. (1991) Spatial variations in enterprise: the geography of new firm formation. In R. Burrows (ed.) *Deciphering the Enterprise Culture*, Routledge, London.

Mason, C. M. and Harrison, R. T. (1985) The geography of small firms: towards a research agenda. *Progress in Human Geography*, 9, 1–37.

Mason, C. M. and Harrison, R. T. (1986) The regional impact of public policy towards small firms in the United Kingdom. In D. Keeble and E. Wever (eds.) *New Firms and Regional Development in Europe*, Croom Helm, Beckenham.

Mason, C. M. and Harrison, R. T. (1990) Small firms – phoenix from the ashes? In D. A. Pinder (ed.) *Challenge and Change in Western Europe*, Belhaven Press, London.

Mason, C. M., Harrison, J. and Harrison, R. T. (1988) *Closing the Equity Gap? An assessment of the Business Expansion Scheme*, Small Business Research Trust, London.

National Audit Office (1988) *Department of Employment/Training Commission: Assistance to Small Firms*, HMSO, London.

OECD (1985) Employment in small and large firms: where have the jobs come from? *OECD Employment Outlook*, September, 64–82.

Pettigrew, P. and Dann, S. (1986) Streamlining regional industrial aid? *Regional Studies*, 20, 182–184.

Policy Studies Institute (1985) *Promoting Innovation: Microelectronics Applications Project*, PSI, London.

Riddell, P. (1983) *The Thatcher Government*, Martin Robertson, Oxford.

Segal Quince Wicksteed (1988) *Encouraging Small Business Start-up and Growth*, HMSO, London.

Segal Quince Wicksteed (1989) *Evaluation of the Consultancy Initiatives*, HMSO, London.

Sengenberger, W., Loveman, G. and Piore, M. (1990) *The Re-emergence of Small Enterprises: Industrial Restructuring in Industrialized Countries* International Institute for Labour Studies, Geneva.

Shutt, J. and Whittington, R. (1989) Large firm strategies and the rise of small units: the illusion of small firm job generation, *University of Manchester School of Geography Working Paper 15*.

Smith, C. (1990) *Business Growth Training (B.G.T.): An Evaluation of Option 3 Lead Projects*, Training Agency, Sheffield.

Stanworth, J. and Barker, G. (1988) *Stimulating Enterprise*, Small Business Research Trust, London.

Stanworth, J. and Stanworth, C. (1990) Small firms policy and its regional implications in Britain, *Piccola Impressa/Small Business*, 1, 89–110.

Storey, D. (1982) *Enterpreneurship and the New Firm*, Croom Helm, Beckenham.

Storey, D. and Johnson, S. (1987a) *Job Generation and Labour Market Change*, Macmillan, London.

Storey, D. and Johnson, S. (1987b) Regional variations in entrepreneurship in the UK, *Scottish Journal of Political Economy*, 34, 161–173.

Whittington, R. C. (1984) Regional bias in new firm formation in the UK, *Regional Studies*, 18, 237–256.

Wren, C. (1990) Regional policy in the 1990s, *National Westminster Bank Quarterly Review*, November, 52–64.

Chapter 3

Bannock, G. and Doran, A. (1990) *Business Banking in the 1990s*, Lafferty Publications.

Bannock, G. and Peacock, A. (1989) *Governments and Small Business*, Paul Chapman Publishing.

Burns, P. and Dewhurst, J. (eds.) (1986) *Small Business in Europe*, Macmillan.

DTI (1991) *Cutting Red Tape for Business*, HMSO.

Hay, D. A. and Morris, D. J. (1984) *Unquoted Companies*, Macmillan.

SBA (1989) *The State of Small Business*, US Government Printing Office.

Storey, D. *et al* (1987) *The Performance of Small Firms*, Croom Helm.

Wilson, H. (1979) *The Financing of Small Firms*, Report of the Committee to Review the Functioning of Financial Institutions, HMSO Cmnd 7503.

Chapter 4

Bester, H. (1987) 'The Role of Collateral in Credit Markets with Imperfect Information', *European Economic Review*, Vol. 31(4) pp. 887–899.

Bester, H. and Hellwig, M. (1989) 'Moral Hazard and Equilibrium Credit Rationing: an Overview of the Issues' in Bamber, G. and Spremann, K. (eds.) *Agency Theory, Information and Incentives*, Springer-Verlag, Berlin.

Binks, M. R. and Coyne, J. (1983) *The Birth of Enterprise*, IEA Hobart Paper, No. 98.

Binks, M. R. and Vale, P. A. (1990) *Entrepreneurship and Economic Change*, McGraw Hill, London.

Binks, M. R., Ennew, C. T. and Reed, G. V. (1988) 'The Survey by the Forum of Private Business on Banks and Small Firms', in Bannock, G. and Morgan, E. V. (eds.) *Banks and Small Businesses: A Two Nation Perspective*, Forum of Private Business/National Federation of Small Business.

Binks, M. R., Ennew, C. T. and Reed, G. V. (1989a) 'The Differentiation of Banking Services to Small Firms', *International Journal of Bank Marketing*, Vol. 7(4) pp. 10–16.

Binks, M. R., Ennew, C. T. and Reed, G. V. (1989b) The single European act and the relationship between small firms and their banks, *Managerial Finance*, Vol. 16, no. 5, pp. 7–13.

Binks, M. R., Ennew, C. T. and Reed, G. V. (1990) 'What Corporate Customers will need in the 1990s', in Chartered Institute of Bankers *Retail Banking in the 1990s: The Opportunities and Threats*, CIB, London.

Bolton Report (1971) *Report of the Committee of Inquiry on Small Firms*, chaired by J. E. Bolton, Cmnd. 4811, HMSO, London.

Carey, T. P. A. (1989) Strategy formulation by banks, *International Journal of Bank Marketing* Vol. 7, no. 3, Special issue.

Charkham, J. (1989) 'Corporate governance and the market for control of companies', *Bank of England Panel Paper*, No. 25.

Clarke, P. D., Edward, P. M. Gardner, E. R. F. (1988) The genesis of strategic market-ing control in British retail banking, *International Journal of Bank Marketing*, Vol. 6, no. 2, pp. 5–19.

de Meza, D. and Webb, D. C. (1987) 'Too much investment: a problem of asymmetric information', *Quarterly Journal of Economics*, Vol. 102 pp. 281–292.

Hakim, C. (1989) *Identifying Fast Growth Small Firms*, Department of Employment, January.

Hall, G. (1989) 'Lack of finance as a constraint on the expansion of innovatory small firms', in Barber, J., Metcalfe, J. S. and Porteous, M. (eds.) *Barriers to Growth in Small Firms*, Routledge, London.

Harrison, R. T. and Mason, C. M (1990) 'The role of the business expansion scheme in the UK', *Omega*, Vol. 17(2) pp. 147–157.

Macmillan, H. (1931) *Report of the Committee on Finance and Industry*, HMSO, Cmnd 3897.

McKibbin, G. and Guttman, J. (1986) The marketing of financial services to the small business sector – A research based approach, *Marketing Intelligence and Planning*, Vol. 4, no. 3, pp. 46–56.

Newman, K. (1984) *Financial Marketing and Communications*, London, Holt, Reinhardt and Winston.

Reed, G. V., Binks, M. R., Ennew, C. T. (1990) Matching the characteristics of a service to the preferences of customers, *Managerial and Decision Economics*, Vol. 12, pp. 231–240.

Roach, C. (1989) 'Segmentation of the small business market on the basis of banking requirements', *International Journal of Bank Marketing* Vol. 7(2) pp. 10–16.

Stiglitz, J. and Weiss, A. (1981) 'Credit rationing in markets with imperfect informa-tion', *American Economic Review*, Vol. 71 pp. 393–410.

Vittas, D. (1986) 'Banks' relations with industry: an international survey', *National Westminster Bank Review*, February, pp. 2–14.

Wilson, H. (1979) *The Financing of Small Firms*, Report of the Committee to Review the Functioning of Financial Institutions, HMSO Cmnd 7503.

Yao-Su Hu (1984) *Industrial Banking and Special Credit Institutions: a Comparative Study*, Policy Studies Institute.

Chapter 5

Bannock, G. (1989) *Taxation in the European Community: the Small Business Per-spective*, Paul Chapman Publishing.

Barr, N. A., James, S. R. and Prest, A. R. (1977) *Self-Assessment for Income Tax*, Heinemann Educational Books, London.

Budd, A. (1991) The 1991 budget in its historical context, *Fiscal Studies*, Vol. 12, No. 2, May 1991.

BZW Property Sector Report, 1989.

Chittenden, F. C., Risner, C. and McConnell, J. (1989) The role of the accounting profession in the development and growth of small firms, The Chartered Association of Certified Accountants, *Research Report 17*.

Devereux, M. (1988) Corporation tax: the effect of the 1984 reforms on the incentive to invest, *Fiscal Studies*, Vol. 9 (1).

Domar, E. D. and Musgrave, R. E. (1944) Proportional income taxation and risk taking, *Quarterly Economic Journal*.

Gower, L. C. B (1981). Professor Gower was a member of the committee established to review the workings of company law in the U.K. He wrote an appendix to this report suggesting a new form of incorporation for small firms which became known as the Gower Report. See, for example, *A New Form of Incorporation for Small Firms*, Department of Trade Consultative Document Cmnd. 8171, London, HMSO.

Inland Revenue Annual Report 1989/90.

Kay, J. A. (1990) Tax policy: a survey, *Economic Journal*, 100, March.

Keith, Lord (1984) *The Enforcement Powers of the Inland Revenue*, HMSO.

King, J. and Wookey, C. (1987) Inflation: the Achilles heel of corporation tax, Chartered Association of Certified Accountants, *Research Report 9*.

Pointon, J. and Sprately, D. (1988) *Principles of Business Taxation*, Clarendon Press, Oxford.

Research Report 17 (1970) Committee's Questionnaire Survey.

Sandford, C. T., Godwin, M. R., Hardwick, P. J. W. and Butterworth, M. I. (1981) *Costs and Benefits of VAT*, Heinemann Educational Books.

Sandford, C. T., Godwin, M. R. and Hardwick, P. J. W. (1989) *Administrative and Compliance Costs of Taxation*, Fiscal Publications.

Scott, M. and Bruce, R. (1987) Five stages of growth in small business, *Long Range Planning*, Vol. 20.

Watson, R. (1990) Employment change, profits and directors' remuneration in small and closely held UK companies, *Journal of Political Economy*, February 1990.

Wilson, H. (1979) *The Financing of Small Firms*, Report of the Committee to Review the Functioning of Financial Institutions, HMSO Cmnd 7503.

Chapter 6

Advisory Council on Science and Technology (ACOST) (1990) *The Enterprise Challenge: Overcoming Barriers to Growth in Small Firms*, HMSO, London.

Bank of England (1983) The Unlisted Securities Market, *Bank of England Quarterly*, 23, pp. 227–231.

Bannock, G. and Doran, A. (1987) *Going Public*, Paul Chapman Publishing.

Batchelor, C. (1988) Private financing: money and time to offer, *Financial Times*, 19 July, p. 9.

Batchelor, C. (1989a) Private investors: not just a wing and a prayer, *Financial Times*, 24 January, p. 17.

Batchelor, C. (1989b) Business angels: an investment of time and money, *Financial Times*, 21 November.

Best, M. H. (1989) Sector strategies and industry policy: the furniture industry and the Greater London Enterprise Board. In Hirst, P. and Zeitlin, J. (eds.) *Reversing Industrial Decline?* Berg, Oxford pp. 191–222.

Binder Hamlyn (1986) *Going to the Market: A Survey of Businessmen's Experience of the USM*, Binder Hamlyn, London.

Binks, M. (1979) Finance for expansion in the small firm, *Lloyds Bank Review*, 134, pp. 33–45.

Binks, M. R. and Coyne, J. (1983) *The Birth of Enterprise*, IEA Hobart Paper, No. 98.

Binks, M. and Vale, P. (1984) Finance and the small firm, Nottingham University Small Firms Unit, *Discussion Paper* No. 2.

Birley, S. and Westhead, P. (1989) *Private advertised sales in the United Kingdom*, Cranfield Entrepreneurship Research Centre, Cranfield Institute of Technology, Cranfield, mimeo.

British Venture Capital Association (1989) *The need to stimulate seed capital*, BVCA, London, mimeo.

British Venture Capital Association (1990) *1989 Report on Investment Activity*, BVCA, London.

British Venture Capital Association (1991) *1990 Report on Investment Activity*, BVCA, London.

Buckland, R. and Davis, E. W. (1989) *The Unlisted Securities Market*, Clarendon Press, Oxford.

Burns, P. and Dewhurst, J. (eds.) (1986) *Small Business in Europe*, Macmillan.

Cary, L. (1991) *The Venture Capital Report Guide to Venture Capital in Europe*, Pitman, London, 5th edition.

Clark, R. (1987) *Venture Capital in Britain, America and Japan*, Croom Helm, Beckenham, Kent.

Cohen, R. (1989) Invitation to a careful dance, *Weekend Financial Times*, 18 March, p. IX.

Cooke, P. (1980) Discretionary intervention and the Welsh Development Agency, *Area*, 12, pp. 269–278.

Cooke, P. (1987) Wales. In P. Damesick and P. Wood (eds.) *Regional Problems, Problem Regions, and Public Policy in the United Kingdom*, Clarendon Press, Oxford, pp. 191–217.

Dickson, T. (1984) Venture capital: lending that helping hand, *Financial Times*, Venture Capital Survey, 28 November, pp. I–II.

Dixon, R. (1989) Venture capitalists and investment appraisal, *National Westminster Bank Quarterly Review*, November, pp. 2–21.

Financial Times (1989) The USM and Third Market, 6 February, p. 25.

Financial Times (1991) Seven in ten venture capitalists prefer manufacturing, 15 January, p. 11.

Freear, J. and Wetzel, W. (1988) Equity financing for new technology-based firms in B. A. Kirchhoff, W. A. Long, W. E. McMullen, K. H. Vesper and W. E. Wetzel (eds.) *Frontiers of Entrepreneurship Research 1988*, Babson College, Wellesley, MA, pp. 347–367.

Gaston, R. J. (1989) *Finding Private Venture Capital For Your Firm: a Complete Guide*, Wiley, New York.

Grant, W. (1982) *The Political Economy of Industrial Policy*, Butterworth, London.

HM Government (1931) Report of the Committee on Finance and Industry (Macmillan Report), Cmnd. 3897, HMSO, London.

HM Government (1959) Report of the Committee on the Working of the Monetary System (Radcliffe Report), Cmnd. 827, HMSO, London.

HM Government (1971) Bolton Report (1971) *Report of the Committee of Inquiry on Small Firms*, chaired by J. E. Bolton, Cmnd. 4811, HMSO, London.

HM Government (1979) Wilson, H. (1979) *The Financing of Small Firms*, Report of the Committee to Review the Functioning of Financial Institutions, HMSO Cmnd. 7503.

Hall, G. (1989) Lack of finance as a constraint on the expansion of innovatory small firms. In Barber, J. Metcalfe, J. S. and Porteous, M. (eds.) *Barriers to Growth in Small Firms*, Routledge, London pp. 39–57.

Hall, G. and Hutchinson, P. J. (1988) *Changes in the financial characteristics of newly quoted small firms 1970–73 and 1980–83*, Manchester Business School, Manchester, mimeo.

Hall, G. and Lewis, P. (1988) *The need for, and effectiveness of, development banking by regional agencies*, Manchester Business School, Manchester, mimeo.

Harrison, R. T. (1990) Industrial development in Northern Ireland: the Industrial Development Board. In Loughlan, J. and Connolly, M. (eds.) *Public Policy in Northern Ireland*, Policy Research Institute, Belfast.

Harrison, R. T. and Mason, C. M. (1989) The role of the Business Expansion Scheme in the United Kingdom, *Omega*, 17, pp. 147–157.

Hayton, K. (1989) The implications of the Local Government and Housing Bill for local economic development, *Local Economy*, 4, pp. 3–16.

Industry Department for Scotland (1987) *1986 Review of the Scottish Development Agency: Report of Review Group to Secretary of State for Scotland*, Industry Department for Scotland, Edinburgh.

Inland Revenue (1990) *Inland Revenue Statistics 1990*, HMSO, London.

Jack, A. (1990) Death threat that mars birthday celebration, *Financial Times*, 10 November, p. 9.

Lawless, P. (1988) Enterprise boards: evolution and evaluation, *Planning Outlook*, 31, pp. 13–18.

Marshall, M. and Mawson, J. (1987) The West Midlands. In P. Damesick and P. Wood (eds.) *Regional Problems, Problem Regions, and Public Policy in the United Kingdom*, Clarendon Press, Oxford, pp. 95–124.

Mason, C. M. (1989) Explaining recent trends in new firm formation in the UK: some evidence from South Hampshire, *Regional Studies*, 23, pp. 331–346.

Mason, C. M. and Harrison, R. T. (1989) Small firms policy and the 'North–South divide' in the United Kingdom: the case of the Business Expansion Scheme, *Transactions*, Institute of British Geographers, 14, pp. 37–58.

Mason, C. M. and Harrison, R. T. (1990) Informal risk capital: a review of US and UK evidence, *Venture Finance Research Project Working Paper* No. 1, University of Southampton (Urban Policy Research Unit) and University of Ulster (Ulster Business School).

Mason, C. M. and Harrison, R. T. (1991a) A strategy for closing the small firm equity gap, *Venture Finance Research Project Working Paper* No. 3, University of Southampton (Urban Policy Research Unit)/University of Ulster (Ulster Business School).

Mason, C. M. and Harrison, R. T. (1991b) Venture capital, the equity gap and the north-south divide in the UK. In Green, M. (ed.) *Venture Capital: International Comparisons*, Routledge, London, pp. 202–247.

Mason, C. M. and Harrison, R. T. (1991c) Informal investors, *CBI Smaller Firms' Economic Report*, CBI, London, January, pp. 12–18.

Mason, C. M, Harrison, R. T. and Chaloner, J. (1991) Informal risk capital in the United Kingdom: a study of investor characteristics, investment preferences and decision-making, *Venture Finance Research Project Working Paper* No. 2, University of Southampton (Urban Policy Research Unit)/University of Ulster (Ulster Business School).

Mason, C. M., Harrison, J. and Harrison, R. T. (1988) *Closing the Equity Gap? An Assessment of the Business Expansion Scheme*, Small Business Research Trust, London.

Mawson, J. and Miller, D. (1986) Interventionist approaches in local employment and economic development: the experience of Labour local authorities. In Hausner, V. A. (ed.) *Critical Issues in Urban Economic Development: Volume 1*, Clarendon Press, Oxford, pp. 145–199.

McKean, B. and Coulson, A. (1987) Enterprise Boards and some issues raised by taking equity and loan stock in major companies, *Regional Studies*, 21, pp. 373–384.

Merchant, K. (1990) Only a poor cousin, *Financial Times Venture Capital Survey*, 26 November, p. 2.

Monck, C. P. S., Porter, R. B., Quintas, P. R., Storey, D. J. and Wynarczyk, P. (1988) *Science Parks and the Growth of High Technology Firms*, Croom Helm, Beckenham.

Murray, G. (1990) *Summary findings of the British Venture Capital Association/ Warwick Business School 1990 Venture Capital Survey*, Warwick Business School, Coventry, mimeo.

National Economic Development Committee (1986) *External Capital for Small Firms*, National Economic Development Office, London.

National Economic Development Committee (1987) *Corporate Venturing: A Strategy for Innovation and Growth*, National Economic Development Office, London.

Oakey, R. (1985) *High Technology Small Firms: Regional Development in Britain and the United States*, Frances Pinter, London.

Oakley, P. G. (1987) External corporate venturing: the experience to date. In Rothwell, R. and Bessan, J. (eds.) *Innovation: Adaptation and Growth*, Elsevier, Amsterdam, pp. 287–296.

Ormerod, J. and Burns, I. (1988) *Raising Venture Capital in the UK*, Butterworth, London.

Peters, I. (1989) *Small Business Growth: Spatial and Non-Spatial Aspects of Development*, unpublished Ph.D. Thesis, University of Southampton.

Pratt, G. (1990) Venture capital in the United Kingdom, *Bank of England Quarterly Review*, 30, pp. 78–83.

Reid, G. C. and Jacobsen, L. R. jr (1988) *The Small Entrepreneurial Firm*, Aberdeen University Press, Aberdeen.

Rich, D. C. (1983) The Scottish Development Agency and the industrial regeneration of Scotland, *Geographical Review*, 73, pp. 271–286.

Robson Rhodes (1984) *A Study of Businesses Financed Under the Small Firms Loan Guarantee Scheme*, Department of Trade and Industry, London.

Shilson, D. (1984) Venture capital in the United Kingdom, *Bank of England Quarterly Bulletin*, 24, pp. 207–211.

Turok, I. and Richardson, P. (1989) Supporting the start-up and growth of small firms: a study in West Lothian, *Strathclyde Papers on Planning*, University of Strathclyde, Glasgow.

Turok, I. and Richardson, P. (1991) New firms and local economic development: evidence from West Lothian, *Regional Studies*, 25, pp. 71–83.

Vickery, L. (1989) Equity financing in small firms. In Burns, P. and Dewhurst, J. (eds.) *Small Business and Entrepreneurship*, Macmillan, London, pp. 204–236.

Wetzel, W. E. jr (1986a) Entrepreneurs, angels and economic renaissance, in Hisrich, R. J. (ed.) *Entrepreneurship, Intrapreneurship and Venture Capital*, Lexington Books, Lexington, MA, pp. 119–139.

Wetzel, W. E. jr (1986b) Informal risk capital: knowns and unknowns. In Sexton, D. L. and Smilor, R. W. (eds.) *The Art and Science of Entrepreneurship*, Ballinger, Cambridge, MA, pp. 85–108.

Chapter 7

Aldrich, H., Jones, T. and Zimmer, C. (1986) Small business still speaks with the same voice: a replication of 'the voice of small business and the politics of survival', *Sociological Review*, Vol. 34.

Amabile, T. M. (1990) Within you, without you: the social psychology of creativity, and beyond. In M. A. Runco and R. S. Albert (eds.) *Theories of Creativity*. London: Sage.

Ambler, M. and Kennett, S. (1985) *The Small Workshops Scheme*, London: Department of Trade and Industry.

Beesley, M. and Hamilton, R. (1986) Births and deaths of manufacturing firms in the Scottish Regions, *Regional Studies*, Vol. 20.

Begley, T. M. and Boyd, D. P. (1986) Psychological characteristics associated with entrepreneurial performance, in R. Ronstadt, J. A. Hornaday, R. Peterson and K. H. Vesper (eds.) *Frontiers of Entrepreneurship Research*, Wellesley, Mass.: Babson College, Centre for Entrepreneurial Studies: 146–165.

Binks, M. and Vale, P. (1990) *Entrepreneurship and Economic Change*, London: McGraw-Hill.

Blanchflower, D. and Oswald, A. (1991) Self-employment and Mrs Thatcher's enterprise culture, in *British Social Attitudes: the 1990 Report*, Aldershot: Gower.

Bolton Report (1971) *Report of the Committee of Inquiry on Small Firms*, chaired by J. E. Bolton, Cmnd. 4811, HMSO, London.

Boswell, J. (1973) *The Rise and Decline of Small Firms*, London. George Allen & Unwin.

Brockhaus, R. H. (1980a) Psychological and environmental factors which distinguish the successful from the unsuccessful entrepreneur: a longitudinal study, Academy of Management Meeting.

Brockhaus, R. H. (1980b) Risk taking propensity of entrepreneurs, *Academy of Management Journal*, 23, 3: 509–520.

Brockhaus, R. H. (1982) The psychology of the entrepreneur, in C. A. Kent, D. L. Sexton and K. H. Vesper, (eds.) *Encyclopedia of Entrepreneurship*, Englewood-Cliffs, N.J.: Prentice-Hall.

Brockhaus, R. H. and Horwitz, P. S. (1986) The psychology of the entrepreneur, in D. L. Sexton and R. W. Smilor, (eds.) *The Art and Science of Entrepreneurship*, Cambridge, Mass.: Ballinger: 25–48.

Brockhaus, R. H. and Nord, W. R. (1979) An exploration of factors affecting the entrepreneurial decision: personal characteristics vs. environmental conditions, *Proceedings of the National Academy of Management*.

Burrows, R. (1991a) A socio-economic anatomy of the British petty bourgeoisie: a multivariate analysis, in R. Burrows (ed.) *Deciphering the Enterprise Culture: Entrepreneurship, Petty Capitalism and the Restructuring of Britain*, London. Routledge.

Burrows, R. (ed.) (1991b) *Deciphering the Enterprise Culture: Entrepreneurship, Petty Capitalism and the Restructuring of Britain*, London. Routledge.

Burrows, R. and Curran, J. (1989) Sociological research on service sector small businesses: some conceptual considerations, *Work, Employment and Society*, Vol. 3.

Burrows, R. and Curran, J. (1991) Not such a small business: reflections on the rhetoric, the reality and the future of the enterprise culture, in M. Cross and G. Payne (eds.) *Work and the Enterprise Culture*, London, Falmer Press.

Caird, S. (1989) A review of methods of measuring enterprise attributes, Durham: DUBS *Occasional Paper* 8914.

Caird, S. (1990) What does it mean to be enterprising? *British Journal of Management*, 1, 3, 137–145.

Cantillon, R. (1931) *Essai sur la nature du commerce en général*, edited and translated by H. Higgs, London: Macmillan.

Carland, J. W., Hoy, F., Boulton, W. R., Carland, J. A. C. (1984) Differentiating entrepreneurs from small business owners: a conceptualization, *Academy of Management Review*, 9, 2: 354–359.

Carsrud, A. L., Olm, K. W. and Eddy, G. G. (1986) Entrepreneurship: research in quest of a paradigm, in D. L. Sexton and R. W. Smilor (eds.) *The Art and Science of Entrepreneurship*, Cambridge, Mass.: Ballinger: 367–378.

Casey, B. and Creigh, S. (1988) Self-employment in Great Britain: its definition in the LFS, in tax and social security law and in labour law, *Work, Employment and Society*, Vol.2.

Casson, M. (1982) *The Entrepreneur – An Economic Theory*, Oxford: Martin Robertson.

Checkland, S. (1981) *The Upas Tree: Glasgow 1875–1975 and After . . . 1975–89* (2nd ed) Glasgow: Glasgow University Press.

Chell, E. (1985) The entrepreneurial personality: a few ghosts laid to rest?, *International Small Business Journal*, 3, 3: 43–54.

Chell, E. and Haworth, J. M. (1988) Entrepreneurship and entrepreneurial management: the need for a paradigm, *Graduate Management Research*, 4, 1: 16–33.

Chell, E. and Haworth, J. M. (1990) Profiling entrepreneurs: multiple perspectives and consequent methodological problems. Paper presented at the Fourth Workshop on Recent Research in Entrepreneurship, E.I.A.S.M./E.C.S.B., Cologne, 29–30 November (in press).

Chell, E., Haworth, J. M. and Brearley, S. A. (1991) *The Entrepreneurial Personality: Concepts, Cases and Categories*. London and New York, Routledge.

Collins, O. F., Moore, D. G. and Unwalla, D. B. (1964) *The Enterprising Man*, East Lansing: Graduate School of Business, Michigan State University.

Collins, O. F. and Moore, D. G. (1970) *The Organisation Makers*. New York: Appleton-Century-Crofts.

Cooper, A. C. (1973) Technical entrepreneurship: what do we know? *R & D Management*, Vol. 3.

Cooper, A. C. (1986) Entrepreneurship and high technology. In D. L. Sexton and R. W. Smilor (eds.) *The Art and Science of Entrepreneurship*, Cambridge, Massachusetts: Ballinger.

Cromie, S., Callaghan, I. and Jansen, M. (1990) The entrepreneurial tendencies of entrepreneurs. Paper presented to the E.I.A.S.M. Seminar, *Research in Entrepreneurship, 4th Workshop*, November, Köln.

Cromie, S. and Johns, S. (1983), Irish entrepreneurs – some personal characteristics. *Journal of Occupational Behaviour*, 4, 317–324.

Cross, M. and Payne, G. (eds.) (1991) *Work and the Enterprise Culture*, London, Falmer Press.

Curran, J. and Blackburn, R. (eds.) (1991) *Paths of Enterprise: the Future of the Small Business*, Routledge.

Curran, J., Blackburn, R. and Woods, A. (1991) Profiles of the small enterprise in the service sector. Paper presented to a meeting of the ESRC Small Business Research Initiative at the University of Warwick, April 1991.

Curran, J. and Burrows, R. (1988a) *Enterprise in Britain: A National Profile of Small Business Owners and the Self-Employed*, London. Small Business Research Trust.

Curran, J. and Burrows, R. (1988b) Ethnicity and enterprise: a national profile. Paper presented at the 11th Small Firms Policy and Research Conference, Cardiff Business School, November.

Dale, A. (1986) Social class and the self-employed, *Sociology*, Vol. 20.

Dale, A. (1991) Self-employment and entrepreneurship: notes on two problematic concepts, in R. Burrows (ed.) *Deciphering the Enterprise Culture: Entrepreneurship, Petty Capitalism and the Restructuring of Britain*, London, Routledge.

Drucker, P. F. (1985) *Innovation and Entrepreneurship: Practice and Principles*, London, Heinemann.

Economists Advisory Group (1981) *Enterprise West: A Study of Small Businesses in the West of England*, London, Shell UK.

Employment Gazette (1988) November.

Filion, L. J. (1990) Vision and relations: elements of an entrepreneurial metamodel, *International Small Business Journal*, 9, 2, 26–40.

Flamholtz, E. G. (1986) *How to Make the Transition from an Entrepreneurship to a Professionally Managed Firm*, San Francisco, Jossey-Bass.

Fothergill, S. and Gudgin, G. (1982) *Unequal Growth: Urban and Regional Employment Growth in the UK*, London, Heinemann.

Gibb, A. and Quince, T. (1980) Effects on small firms of industrial change in a development area, in A. Gibb and T. Webb (eds.) *Policy Issues in Small Business Research*, Farnborough, Saxon House.

Ginsberg, A. and Buchholtz, A. (1989), Are entrepreneurs a breed apart? A look at the evidence, *Journal of General Management*, 15, 2: 32–40.

Goffee, R. and Scase, R. (1985) *Women in Charge: The Experience of Female Entrepreneurs*, London: Allen & Unwin.

Goldthorpe, J. with Llewellyn, C. and Payne, C. (1987) *Social Mobility and the Class Structure in Modern Britain* (2nd ed), Oxford: Clarendon Press.

Goss, D. (1991) *Small Business and Society*, London. Routledge.

Gould, A. and Keeble, D. (1984) New firms and rural industrialisation in East Anglia, *Regional Studies*, Vol. 18.

Gudgin, G. and Fothergill, S. (1984) Geographical variation in the rate of formation of new manufacturing firms, *Regional Studies*, Vol.18.

Hakim, C. (1988) Self-employment in Britain: a review of recent trends and current issues, *Work, Employment and Society*, Vol. 2.

Hamnett, C. (1989) Consumption and class in contemporary Britain, in C. Hamnett, L. McDowell and P. Sarre (eds.) *The Changing Social Structure*, London: Sage.

Hampson, S. E. (1982) *The Construction of Personality*, London: Routledge & Kegan Paul.

Hampson, S. E. (1988) *The Construction of Personality* 2nd ed. London: Routledge.

Haworth, J. M. (1988) *An Investigation of Entrepreneurial Characteristics using Latent Class Analysis*, unpublished Ph.D. thesis, Department of Business and Management Studies, University of Salford.

Hebert, R. F. and Link, A. N. (1988) *The Entrepreneur – Mainstream Views and Radical Critiques*, 2nd ed. New York: Praeger.

Hisrich, R. D. (1986) The woman entrepreneur: characteristics, skills, problems, and prescriptions for success, in D. L. Sexton and R. W. Smilor (eds.) *The Art and Science of Entrepreneurship*, Cambridge, Massachusetts. Ballinger.

Hobbs, D. (1988) *Doing the Business: Entrepreneurship, the Working Class and Detectives in the East End of London*, Oxford, Oxford University Press.

Hornaday, R. W. (1990) Dropping the E-words from small business research. *Journal of Small Business Management*, 28, 4 (October), 22–33.

Johnson, P. (1983) New manufacturing firms in the UK Regions, *Scottish Journal of Political Economy*, Vol. 30.

Johnson, P. (1986) *New Firms: an Economic Perspective*, London: Allen & Unwin.

Kanter, R. M. (1983) *The Change Masters*, New York, Simon & Schuster.

Keat, R. and Abercrombie, N. (1991) *Enterprise Culture*, London, Routledge.

Kets de Vries, M. F. R. (1977) The entrepreneurial personality: a person at the crossroads, *Journal of Management Studies*, (Feb.): 34–57.

Kilby, P. M. (ed.) (1971) *Entrepreneurship and Economic Development*, New York, Macmillan.

Knight, F. H. (1921) *Risk, Uncertainty and Profit*, New York, Houghton Mifflin.

Lloyd, P. and Mason, C. (1984) Spatial variations in new firm formation in the UK: comparative evidence from Merseyside, Greater Manchester and South Hampshire, *Regional Studies*, Vol. 18.

MacDonald, R. and Coffield, F. (1991) *Risky Business? Youth and the Enterprise Culture*, London: Falmer Press.

McClelland, D. C. (1961) *The Achieving Society*, Princeton, N.J., Van Nostrand.

McClelland, D. C. (1987) Characteristics of successful entrepreneurs, *Journal of Creative Behavior*, 21, 3: 219–233.

McClelland, D. C. and Winter, D. G. (1971) *Motivating Economic Achievement*, New York: Free Press.

Marshall, A. (1920) *Principles of Economics*, 8th ed. London: Macmillan.

Mason, C. (1991) Spatial variations in enterprise: the geography of new firm formation, in R. Burrows (ed.) *Deciphering the Enterprise Culture: Entrepreneurship, Petty Capitalism and the Restructuring of Britain*, London, Routledge.

Maya, N. (1987) Small business and social mobility in France, in R. Scase and R. Goffee (eds.) *Entrepreneurship in Europe: the Social Processes*, London: Croom Helm.

Meager, N. (1989) Who are the self-employed? *Anglo-German Self-Employment Project: Working Paper No.1*, Brighton, Institute of Manpower Studies.

Meredith, G. G. Nelson, R. E. and Neck, P. A. (1982) *The Practice of Entrepreneurship*, Geneva, International Labour Office.

Miller, D. and Friesen, P. H. (1982), Innovation in conservative and entrepreneurial firms: two models of strategic momentum. *Strategic Management Journal*, 3, 1–25.

Miron, D. and McClelland, D. C. (1979) The impact of achievement motivation training on small business performance, *California Management Review*, 21, 4: 13–28.

Mischel, W. (1973) Towards a cognitive social learning reconceptualisation of personality, *Psychological Review*, 80, 4: 252–283.

Morgan, K. and Sayer, A. (1985) A 'modern' industry in a mature region: the remaking of management–labour relations, *International Journal of Urban and Regional Research*, Vol. 9.

Moyes, A. and Westhead, P. (1988) Does location matter? County-scale variations in new firm formation rates in Great Britain, Paper presented to the 11th National Small Firms Policy and Research Conference, Cardiff Business School.

Nicholson, N. (1990) Organizational innovation in context: culture, interpretation and application. In M. A. West and J. L. Farr (eds.) *Innovation and Creativity at Work*, Chichester, Wiley.

Oakley, A. and Oakley, R. (1979) Sexism in official statistics, in J. Irvine, I. Miles and J. Evans (eds.) *Demystifying Social Statistics*, London, Pluto Press.

Quinn, J. B. (1980) *Strategies for Change: Logical Incrementalism*, Homewood, Illinois. Irwin.

Rosch, E., Mervis, C. B., Gray, W. D., Johnson, D. M. and Boyes-Bream, P. (1976) Basic objects in natural categories, *Cognitive Psychology*, i: 332–439.

Rotter, J. B. (1966) Generalised expectancies for internal versus external control of reinforcement, *Psychological Monographs, Whole No. 609*, 80, 1.

Schumpeter, J. A. (1934) *The Theory of Economic Development*, Cambridge, Mass. Harvard University Press.

Sexton, D. L. (1987) Advancing small business research: utilising research from other areas, *American Journal of Small Business*, Vol. 11, no. 3, pp. 25–30.

Smith, N. R. (1967) *The Entrepreneur and His Firm: The Relationship Between Type of Man and Type of Company*, East Lansing, Michigan, Michigan State University Press.

Stanworth, J., Blythe, S., Granger, B. and Stanworth, C. (1989) Who becomes an entrepreneur? *International Small Business Journal*, Vol. 8.

Stevenson, H. H. and Sahlman, W. A. (1989) The entrepreneurial process, in P. Burns and J. Dewhurst (eds.) *Small Business and Entrepreneurship*, ch. 5: 94 –157.

Storey, D. and Johnson, S. (1987a) Regional variations in entrepreneurship in the UK, *Scottish Journal of Political Economy*, Vol. 34.

Storey, D. and Johnson, S. (1987b) *Job Generation and the Labour Market*, London: Macmillan.

STRATOS (1990) *Strategic Orientations of Small European Businesses*, Aldershot: Avebury.

Sweeney, G. (1987) *Innovation, Entrepreneurs and Regional Development*, London: Frances Pinter.

Timmons, J. A. (1989) *The Entrepreneurial Mind*, Andover, Mass: Brick House Publishing.

Timmons, J. A., Smollen, L. E. and Dingee, A. L. M. (1977) *New Venture Creation*, 1st ed. Homewood, Ill.: Irwin.

Timmons, J. A., Smollen, L. E. and Dingee, A. L. M. (1985) *New Venture Creation*, 2nd ed. Homewood, Ill.: Irwin.

Ward, R. (1991) Economic development and ethnic business, in J. Curran and R. Blackburn (eds.) *Paths of Enterprise: the Future of the Small Business*, London: Routledge.

Watkins, D. and Watkins, J. (1984) The female entrepreneur: background and determinants of business choice, *International Small Business Journal*, Vol. 2.

West M. A. and Farr, J. L. (1990) Innovation at work. In M. A. West and J. L. Farr (eds.) *Innovation and Creativity at Work*. Chichester: Wiley.

Whittington, R. (1984) Regional bias in new firm formation in the UK, *Regional Studies*, Vol. 18.

Woo *et. al.* (1988) Entrepreneurial typologies: definitions and implications, *Frontiers of Entrepreneurship Research*, Wellesey, Mass., Boston College Centre for Entrepreneurial studies.

Wortman, M. S. (1986) A unified framework, research typologies, and research prospectuses for the interface between entrepreneurship and small business, *The Art and Science of Entrepreneurship*, Cambridge, Mass.: Ballinger, 273–331.

Zaltman, G., Duncan, R. and Holbek, J. (1973) *Innovations and Organisations*, London, Wiley.

Chapter 8

Atkin, R. and Gibb, A. A. (1984) The Management Extension Programme. Paper presented to the Seventh National Small Firms Policy and Research Conference, Nottingham, Trent Polytechnic.

Batchelor, C. (1991) Business schools drop courses, *Financial Times*, 12 June, p. 8.

Binks, M. and Jennings, A. (1986) Small firms as a source of economic rejuvenation, in Curran, J., Stanworth, J. and Watkins, D. (eds.) *The Survival of the Small Firm*, Aldershot, Gower Publishing.

Bolton Report (1971) *Report of the Committee of Inquiry on Small Firms*, chaired by J. E. Bolton, Cmnd. 4811, HMSO, London.

Brown, R., (1990) Encouraging enterprise: Britain's graduate enterprise programme, *Journal of Small Business Management*, Vol. 28, No. 4, pp. 71–77.

Business in the Community (undated) Small firms: survival and job creation. The contribution of the enterprise agencies London, Business in the Community.

Coopers and Lybrand Associates (1985) *A Challenge to Complacency: Changing Attitudes to Training*. A report to the Manpower Services Commission and the National Economic Development Office.

Curran, J. (1988) Training and research strategies for small firms, *Journal of General Management*, Vol. 13, No. 3, pp. 24–37.

Department of Trade and Industry (1988) *DTI – The Department for Enterprise*, Cm 278, London, HMSO.

Gibb, A. A. (1986) United Kingdom, in Haskins, G., Gibb, A. A. and Hubert, T. (eds.) *A Guide to Small Firm Assistance in Europe*, Aldershot, Gower Publishing.

Gibb, A. A. (1988) *A Strategy for Improving the Demand for, and Supply of, Small Business and Enterprise Training*, Durham, Durham University Business School.

Gray, C. (1991) Self-employment and the importance of personal independence. Paper presented to fifth European Congress of Psychology of Work and Organization, Rouen, France.

Handy, C. (1987) *The Making of Managers*, London, NEDO.

HMSO (1988) *Releasing Enterprise*, Cm 512, London, HMSO.

Hyde, G. C. (1986) The relationship between policy and research. Paper presented at the Ninth Annual Small Firms Policy and Research Conference, Gleneagles, Scotland.

Kirby, D. A. (1984) Training for the small retail business: results of a British experiment, *International Journal of Small Business*, Vol. 2, No. 3, pp. 28–41.

Kirby, D. A. (1990) Management education and small business development: an explanatory study of small firms, *UK Journal of Small Business Management*, Vol. 28, No. 4, pp. 78–87.

National Audit Office (1988) *Department of Employment/Training Commission: Assistance to Small Firms*, London, HMSO.

Segal Quince Wicksteed (1989) *Evaluation of the Consultancy Initiatives*, London, HMSO.

Segal Quince Wicksteed (1991) *Evaluation of the Consultancy Initiatives – Second Stage*, London, HMSO.

Smith, A. D. (1971) *Small Retailers: Prospects and Policies*, Research Report No. 15, London, HMSO.

Stanworth, J. and Curran, J. (1973) *Management Motivation in the Smaller Business*, Aldershot, Gower Publishing.

Stanworth, J. and Gray, C. (1991) Entrepreneurship and education: action-based research with training policy implications in Britain. Paper presented at the ENDEC Conference on Entrepreneurship and Innovative Change, Singapore.

Storey, D. (1986) Entrepreneurship and the new firm, in Curran, J., Stanworth, J. and Watkins, D. (eds.) *The Survival of the Small Firm*, Aldershsot, Gower Publishing.

Sym, L. A. and Lewis, J. W. (1986) Small business start-up teaching in Scotland – a qualitative review. Paper presented to the Ninth National Small Firms Policy and Research Conference, Gleneagles, Scotland.

Tait, E. (1988) Researching small business owner-managers' perceived management education needs: an integrated framework. Paper presented to the Eleventh National Small Firms Policy and Research Conference, Cardiff, Wales.

Watkins, D. (1983) Development training and education for the small firm: a European perspective, *European Small Business Journal*, Vol. 1, No. 3, pp. 29–44.

Chapter 9

Acton Society Trust (1953) *Size and Morale: a Preliminary Study of Attendance at Work in Large and Small Units*, London, Acton Society Trust.

Acton Society Trust (1957) *A Further Study of Attendance at Work in Large and Small Units*, London, Acton Society Trust.

Allen, J. and Massey, D. (eds.) (1988) *The Economy in Question*, London, Sage in association with The Open University Press.

Annual Abstract of Statistics 1973 (1973), London, HMSO.

Atkinson, J. (1985) Flexibility: planning for an uncertain future, *Manpower Policy and Practice*, 1, Summer, 26–29.

Atkinson, J. and Gregory, D. (1986) A flexible future: Britain's dual labour force, *Marxism Today*, April, 12–17.

Ball, M., Gray, F. and McDowell, L. (1989) *The Transformation of Britain, Contemporary Social and Economic Change*, London, Fontana.

Bannock, G. and Daly, M. (1990) Size distribution of UK firms, *Employment Gazette*, 98, 5, 256–58.

Batstone, E. V. (1969) *Aspects of Stratification in a Community Context: A Study of Class Attitudes and the Size Effect*, Ph.D. thesis, University of Wales.

Bolton Report (1971) *Report of the Committee of Inquiry on Small Firms*, chaired by J. E. Bolton, Cmnd. 4811, HMSO, London.

Burgess, R. (1984) *In the Field, An Introduction to Field Research*, London, George Allen & Unwin.

Burrows, R. and Curran, J. (1989) Sociological research on service sector small enterprises: some conceptual considerations, *Work, Employment and Society*, 3, 4, 527–539.

Curran, J. (1987) *Small Firms and Their Environments, A Report*, Kingston upon Thames, Kingston Polytechnic Small Business Research Unit.

Curran, J. (1988) Employment and employment relations in the small enterprise: a review, *London Business School Small Business Bibliography*, London, London Business School Library.

Curran, J. (1990) Rethinking economic structure: exploring the role of the small firm and self-employment in the British economy, *Work, Employment and Society*, special ed., May, 125–146.

Curran, J. and Burrows, R. (1988) *Enterprise in Britain: A National Profile of Small Business Owners and the Self-Employed*, London, Small Business Research Trust.

Curran, J. and Stanworth, J. (1979a) Self-selection and the small firm worker – a critique and an alternative view, *Sociology*, 13, 3, 427–444.

Curran, J. and Stanworth, J. (1979b) Worker involvement and social relations in the small firm, *Sociological Review*, 27, 2, 317–342.

Curran, J. and Stanworth, J. (1981a) Size of workplace and attitudes to industrial relations in the printing and electronics industries, *British Journal of Industrial Relations*, 19, 1, 14–25.

Curran, J. and Stanworth, J. (1981b) A new look at job satisfaction in the small firm, *Human Relations*, 34, 5, 343–365.

Daniel, W. and Millward, W. (1983) *Workplace Industrial Relations in Britain*, London, Heinemann.

Department of Employment (1991) *Small Firms in Britain, 1991*, London, HMSO.

Dickens, L., Hart, M., Jones, B. and Weekes, D. (1984) The British experience under a statute prohibiting unfair dismissal, *Industrial and Labour Relations Journal*, 37, 4, 497–514.

Doyle, J. R. and Gallagher, C. (1986) *The Size-Distribution Potential for Growth and Contribution to Job Generation of Firms in the UK, 1982–1984*, Newcastle upon Tyne, Department of Industrial Management, University of Newcastle.

Employment Gazette (1991) 1990 Labour Force Survey preliminary results, *Employment Gazette*, 99, 4, 175–196.

Filby, M. (1990) The figures, the personality and the bums, service work and sexuality in the retail betting industry, Mimeo, Department of Sociology and Applied Studies, Birmingham Polytechnic.

Gallagher, C. and Doyle, J. (1987) Size-distribution, growth potential and job generational contribution of UK firms, 1982–1984, *International Small Business Journal*, 6, 1, 31–55.

Gallagher, C. and Stewart, H. (1986) Jobs and the business lifecycle, *Applied Economics*, Vol. 18, no. 8, August.

Goffee, R. and Scase, R. (1982) Fraternalism and paternalism as employer strategies in small firms, in Day, G. (ed.) *Diversity and Decomposition in the Labour Market*, Aldershot, Gower.

Goss, D. (1986) *The Social Structure of the Small Firm*, Ph.D. thesis, University of Kent.

Goss, D. (1991) *Small Business and Society*, London, Routledge.

Graham, N., Beatson, M. and Wells, W. (1989) 1977 to 1987: a decade of service, *Employment Gazette*, 97, 1, 45–54.

Hakim, A. (1987) Trends in the flexible workforce, *Employment Gazette*, 95, 11, 549–560.

Hartley, K. and Hooper, N. (1990) Industry and policy, in Curwen, P. (ed.) *Understanding the UK Economy*, Basingstoke, Macmillan Education.

Henderson, J. and Johnson, R. (1974) Labour relations in the small firm, *Personnel Management*, December, 28–34.

Hochschild, A. (1983) *The Managed Heart*, Berkeley, University of California Press.

Ingham, G. K. (1970) *Size of Industrial Organisation and Worker Behaviour*, London, Cambridge University Press.

Joseph, G. (1983) *Women at Work, The British Experience*, London, Philip Allan.

Kitching, J. (1991) Abstract on M. Scott *et. al.* Management relations in small firms, Department of Employment, Research Paper no. 7, in *International Small Business Journal*, Vol. 9, no. 2, pp. 71–74.

Kitching, J., Blackburn, R. A. and Curran, J. (1990) Some theoretical and conceptual issues in the study of employment relations in the small service sector firm, Paper presented to the 13th Small Firms Policy and Research Conference, Harrogate, November.

Labour Market Quarterly Report (1991) Small Firms and Enterprise, May, 6–7.

Mars, G. and Nicod, M. (1984) *The World of Waiters*, London, George Allen & Unwin.

Murray, R. (1989) Fordism and post-Fordism, in Hall, S. and Jaques, M. (eds.) *New Times, the Face of Politics in the 1990s*, London, Laurence and Wishart.

Newby, H. (1977) *The Deferential Worker*, Harmondsworth, Penguin Books.

Piore, M. and Sabel, S. (1984) *The Second Industrial Divide: Possibilities for Prosperity*, New York, Basic Books.

Prais, S. (1978) The strike proneness of large plants in Britain, *Journal of the Royal Statistical Society*, 141, 3, 368–384.

Rainnie, A. (1989) *Industrial Relations in Small Firms, Small Isn't Beautiful*, London, Routledge.

Rainnie, A. and Scott, M. (1986) Industrial relations in small firms, in Curran, J. *et al.* (eds.) *The Survival of the Small Firm, Employment, Growth, Technology and Politics*, Aldershot, Gower, Vol. 2.

Revans, R. (1956) Industrial morale and size of unit, *Political Quarterly*, 27, 3, 303–310.

Revans, R. (1958) Human relations, management and size, in Hugh-Jones, E. M. (ed.) *Human Relations and Modern Management*, Amsterdam, North Holland Publishing Co.

Robson, D., Gallagher, C. C. and Daly, M. (1991) Job generation by size of firm, *Employment Gazette*, in press.

Roy, D. (1952) Quota restricting and goldbricking in a machine shop, *American Journal of Sociology*, 57, March, 427–42.

Roy, D. (1954) Efficiency and the fix, *American Journal of Sociology*, 60, January, 255–66.

Scase, R. and Goffee, R. (1982) *The Entrepreneurial Middle Class*, London, Croom Helm.

Scott, M., Roberts, I., Holroyd, G. and Sawbridge, D. (1989) *Management and Industrial Relations in Small Firms*, London, Department of Employment, Research Paper No. 70.

Shutt, J. and Whittington, K. (1984) Large firms and the rise of small units, Paper presented to the National Small Firms Policy and Research Conference, Trent Polytechnic, November.

Smith, C. T., Clifton, P., Makeham, P., Creigh, S. W. and Burn R. V. (1979) *Strikes in Britain, A Research Study of Industrial Stoppages in the United Kingdom*, London, HMSO.

Taylor, R. (1978) *The Fifth Estate, Britain's Unions in the Modern World*, London, Pan Books.

Wright, E. O. (1978) *Class, Crisis and the State*, London, New Left Books.

Wright, E. O. (1985) *Classes*, London, Verso.

Chapter 10

ACOST (1990) *The Enterprise Challenge: Overcoming Barriers to Growth in Small Firms*, HMSO, London.

Bannock, G. and Daly, M. (1990) Size distribution of UK firms, *Employment Gazette*, May.

Bolton Report (1971) *Report of the Committee of Inquiry on Small Firms*, chaired by J. E. Bolton, Cmnd. 4811, HMSO, London.

Bragard, L., Donckles, R. and Michel, P. (1985) *New Entrepreneurship*, University of Liege, Belgium.

Chell, E. (1985) The entrepreneurial personality: a few ghosts laid to rest?, *International Small Business Journal*, Vol. 3. No. 3.

Covin, J. G. and Slevin, D. P. (1989) Strategic management of small firms in hostile and benign environments, *Strategic Management Journal*, Vol. 10, pp. 75–87.

Curran, J. (1986) *Bolton Fifteen Years On: a Review and Analysis of Small Business Research in Britain 1971–1986*, Small Business Research Trust, London.

Deeks, J. (1972) Educational and occupational histories of owner managers and managers, *Journal of Management Studies*, No. 9, May, pp. 123–149.

Feeser, H. R. and Willard, G. E. (1990) Founding strategy and performance: a comparison of high and low growth high tech firms, *Strategic Management Journal*, Vol. 11, pp. 87–98.

Grieve Smith, A. and Fleck, V. (1987) Business strategies in small high technology companies, *Long Range Planning*, Vol. 20, No. 2, pp. 61–68.

Handy, C. *et al* (1988) *Making Managers*, Pitman, London.

Lafuente, A. and Salas, V. (1989) Types of entrepreneurs and firms, *Strategic Management Journal*, Vol. 10, pp. 17–30.

Monck, C. S. P. *et al* (1988) *Science Parks and the Growth of High Technology Firms*, Croom Helm, London.

Nicholson, N. and West, M. (1988) *Managerial Job Change*, Cambridge University Press, Cambridge.

Penrose, E. T. (1959) *The Theory of the Growth of the Firm*, Basil Blackwell, Oxford.

Stanworth, J. and Curran, J. (1973) *Management Motivation in the Smaller Business*, Gower Press, Epping.

Storey, D. J. (1982) *Entrepreneurship and the New Firm*, Croom Helm, London.

Storey, D. J. *et al* (1987) *The Performance of Small Firms*, Croom Helm, London.

Storey, D. J. (1990) The managerial labour market in fast growth firms, in Joubert, P. and Moss, M. (eds.) *The Birth and Death of Companies: an Historic Perspective*, Parthenon, Carnforth, Lancs.

Watkins, D. S. (1983) Development, training and education for the small firm: a European perspective, *European Small Business Journal*, Vol. 1, No. 3, pp. 29–44.

Chapter 11

Aglietta, M. (1979) *A Theory of Capitalist Regulation: The US Experience*, New Left Books, London.

Alexander, N. (1990) Retailing post-1992, *The Services Industries Journal*, 10, 1, January, 172–187.

Allen, J. (1988) Towards a post-industrial economy? in Allen, J. and Massey, D. (eds.) *The Economy in Question*, Sage, London.

Allen, J. and Massey, D. (eds.) (1988) *Restructuring Britain: The Economy in Question*, Sage, London.

Allen, S. and Truman, C. (1991) Prospects for women's business and self-employment in the year 2000, in Curran, J. and Blackburn, R. A. (1991) (eds.) *Paths of Enterprise, The Future of the Small Business*, Routledge, London.

Amin, A. (1989) Flexible specialisation and small firms in Italy: myths and realities, *Antipode*, 21, 1, 13–34.

Amin, A. and Robins, K. (1990) *Not Marshallian Times*, Centre for Urban and Regional Development Studies, University of Newcastle upon Tyne.

Atkinson, J. and Meager, D. (1986) Is flexibility just a flash in the pan?, *Personnel Management*, September.

Atkinson, J., Meager, N. and Wilson, A. (1990) The small firm and the local labour market: some preliminary findings. Paper presented to the Fifth ESRC Small Business Initiative Meeting, University of Warwick.

Bannock, G. (1990) *Britain in the 1990s: Enterprise Under Threat?*, 3i, Investors in Industry, London.

Bannock, G. (1991) *3i Enterprise Barometer, Report no. 14*, Graham Bannock & Partners Ltd., London.

Bannock, G. and Daly, M. (1990) Size distribution of UK firms, *Employment Gazette*, 98, 5, 256–58.

Bannock, G. and Stanworth, J. (1990) *The Making of Entrepreneurs*, Small Business Research Trust, London.

Batchelor, C. (1991) Big Brother looms into view, *Financial Times*, 28 May, p. 14.

Binks, M. and Jennings, A. (1986) Small firms as a source of economic rejuvenation, in Curran, J. *et al* (eds.) *The Survival of the Small Firm.*, Vol. 1, Gower, Aldershot.

Binks, M. (1991) Small businesses and their banks in the year 2000, in Curran, J. and Blackburn, R. A. (1991) (eds.) *Paths of Enterprise*, Routledge, London.

Blackburn, R. A. (1991) Small firms and sub-contracting: what is it and where?, in Felstead, A. and Leighton, P. (forthcoming) *Self-Employment and the Small Business in Europe: Evolution and Practice*, Kogan Page, London.

Blanchflower, D. G. and Oswald, A. J. (1990) Self-employment and the enterprise culture, in Jowell, R., Witherspoon, S. and Brook, L. *British Social Attitudes: the 7th Report*, Social and Community Planning Research, Gower, Aldershot.

Bogenhold, D. and Staber, U. (1991) The decline and rise of self-employment, *Work, Employment and Society*, 5, 2, 223–239.

Bolton Report (1971) *Report of the Committee of Inquiry on Small Firms*, chaired by J. E. Bolton, Cmnd. 4811, HMSO, London.

Brummer, A. (1991) Unemployment will stay high after recession warns report, *The Guardian*, 28 May, p. 10.

Brusco, S. and Sabel, C. (1981) Artisan production and economic growth, in Wilkinson, F. (ed.) *The Dynamics of Labour Market Segmentation*, Academic Press, London and New York.

Burrows, R. (1991a) The discourse of the enterprise culture and the restructuring of Britain: a polemical contribution, in Curran, J. and Blackburn, R. A. (1991) (eds.) *Paths of Enterprise*, Routledge, London.

Burrows, R. (ed.) (1991b) *Deciphering the Enterprise Culture: Entrepreneurship, Petty Capitalism and the Restructuring of Britain*, London, Routledge.

Burrows R. and Curran J. (1991) Not such a small business: reflections on the rhetoric, the reality and the future of the enterprise culture, in Cross, M. and Payne, G. (eds.) *Work and the Enterprise Culture*, Falmer Press, Brighton.

Cecchini, P. with Catinat, M. and Jacquemin, A. (1988) *The European Challenge*, Gower/Commission of the European Communities, Aldershot.

Clarke, S. (1990) What in the F-s name is Fordism?, paper presented at British Sociological Association Conference, April, University of Surrey.

Curran, J. (1986) *Bolton Fifteen Years On: A Review and Analysis of Small Business Research in Britain 1971–1986*, Small Business Research Trust, London.

Curran, J. (1987) Small firms and their environments: a report, Small Business Research Unit, Kingston Polytechnic.

Curran, J. (1990) Rethinking economic structure: exploring the role of the small firm and self-employment in the British economy, *Work, Employment and Society*, May, 125–146.

Curran, J. and Blackburn, R. A. (1990) Youth and the enterprise culture, *British Journal of Education and Work*, 4, 1, 31–46.

Curran, J. and Blackburn, R. A. (1991) (eds.) *Paths of Enterprise, The Future of the Small Business*, Routledge, London.

Curran, J., Blackburn, R. A. and Woods, A. (1991a) *Profiles of the Small Enterprise in the Service Sector*, May, ESRC Centre for Research on Small Service Sector Enterprises, Kingston Polytechnic.

Curran, J., Blackburn, R. A. and Woods, A. (1991b) *Profiles of Small Businesses in the Services Sector*, June, ESRC Centre for Research on Small Service Sector Enterprises, Kingston Polytechnic.

Curran, J. and Burrows, R. (1987) The social analysis of small business: some emerging themes, in Goffee, R. and Scase, R. (eds.) *Entrepreneurship in Europe: The Social Processes*, Croom Helm, London.

Curran, J. and Burrows, R. (1988) *Enterprise in Britain: A National Profile of Small Business Owners and the Self Employed*, Small Business Research Trust, London.

Daly, M. (1990) The 1980s – a decade of growth in enterprise: data on VAT registrations and deregistrations, *Employment Gazette*, November, 553–565.

Daly, M. (1991) The 1980s – a decade of growth in enterprise: self-employment data from the Labour Force Survey, *Employment Gazette*, March, 109–134.

Daniels, P. (1988) Producer services and the post-industrial space economy, in Massey, D. and Allen, J. (eds.) (1988) *Uneven Redevelopment: Cities and Regions in Transition*, Hodder and Stoughton/The Open University Press, London.

Department of Employment (1991a) *Small Firms in Britain*, London, Department of Employment.

Department of Employment (1991b) Press Notice: Preliminary Results from the 1990 Labour Force Survey for Great Britain and Revised Employment Estimates Incorporating Those Results, March 14, London.

Department of Trade and Industry (1988) *The Department for Enterprise*, Cmnd. 278, HMSO, London.

Economist Intelligence Unit (1990) The single market: threat or opportunity for smaller companies, *EIU European Trends*, No. 2, 90–94.

Edmonds, T. (1986) Small firms, background paper, House of Commons Library Research Division, June.

Employment Gazette (1991a) 1990 Labour Force Survey preliminary results, April, 175–196.

Employment Gazette (1991b) Labour trends: the next decade, May, 269–280.

Felstead, A. (1991) Facing up to the fragility of minding your own business as a franchise, in Curran, J. and Blackburn, R. A. (1991) (eds.) *Paths of Enterprise*, Routledge, London.

Foreman-Peck, J. S. (1985) Seedcorn or chaff? New firm formation and the performance of the interwar economy, *The Economic History Review*, Second series, 38, 3, August, 402–422.

Friedman, A. L. (1977) *Industry and Labour*, Macmillan, London.

Goldthorpe, J. with Llewellyn, C. and Payne, C. (1987) *Social Mobility and Class Structure in Modern Britain*, Clarendon Press, Oxford.

Goodman, E., Bamford, J. with Saynor, P. (eds.) (1989) *Small Firms and Industrial Districts in Italy*, Routledge, London.

Goss, D. (1991) *Small Business and Society*, Routledge, London.

Graham, N., Beatson, M. and Wells, W. (1989) 1977 to 1987: a decade of service, *Employment Gazette*, January, 45–54.

Hakim, C. (1988) Self-employment in Britain: recent trends and current issues, *Work, Employment and Society*, 2, 4, 421–450.

Hakim, C. (1989) New recruits to self-employment in the 1980s, *Employment Gazette*, June, 286–297.

Hallet, S. (1990) The future of estate agency: some consequences of the recent acquisition boom in South West England, *Services Industries Journal*, 10, 4, October, 759–767.

Hamilton, R. T. (1989) Unemployment and business formation rates: reconciling time-series and cross-section evidence, *Environment and Planning A*, 21, 249–255.

Henley Centre for Forecasting (1991) Leisure futures, Henley Centre for Forecasting, London.

Hirschhorn, L. (1988) The post-industrial economy: labour, skills and the new mode of production, *The Service Industries Journal*, 8, 1, 19–38.

Hirst, P. and Zeitlin, J. (1989) *Reversing Industrial Decline? Industrial Structure and Policy in Britain and Her Competitors*, Berg, Oxford.

Imrie, R. and Morris, J. L. (1988) Large firm-small firm links: the changing nature of subcontracting in Wales. Paper to the Eleventh National Small Firms Policy and Research Conference, University College Cardiff, Wales.

International Labour Office (1990) The promotion of self-employment, *International Labour Conference, 77th Session, Report VII*, ILO, Geneva.

Johnson, S. (1991) Small firms and the UK labour market: prospects for the 1990s, in Curran, J. and Blackburn, R. A. (1991) (eds.) *Paths of Enterprise*, Routledge, London.

Johnson, S., Lindley, R. and Bourlakis, C. (1988) *An Exploratory Time-series Analysis of Self-employment in Great Britain*, Project Report, DE Programme, Institute for Employment Research, University of Warwick.

Keynote Report (1990a) *New Trends in Retailing, 2nd ed.*, Key Note Publications, Hampton.

Keynote Report (1990b) *Contract Cleaning, 5th ed.*, Key Note Publications, Hampton.

Labour Party (1991) *Opportunity Britain: Labour's Better Way for the 1990s*, The Labour Party, London.

Lash, S. and Urry, J. (1987) *The End of Organised Capitalism*, Polity Press, Cambridge.

London Business School (1991) *International Economic Outlook*, London Business School.

Lorenz, E. H. (1989) The search for flexibility: sub-contracting networks in French and British engineering, in Hirst, P. and Zeitlin, J. (1989) *Reversing Industrial Decline? Industrial Structure and Policy in Britain and Her Competitors*, Berg, Oxford.

MacDonald, R. and Coffield, F. (1991) *Risky Business*, Falmer Press, Brighton.

Marginson, P., Edwards, P., Martin, R., Sisson, K. and Purcell, J. (1988) *Beyond the Workplace*, Basil Blackwell, Oxford.

Marsh, P. (1991) Warning of prolonged recession, *Financial Times*, 30 May, p. 9.

Marshall, A. (1961) *Principles of Economics*, Macmillan, London.

Marshall, J. N. (1989) Corporate re-organisation and the geography of services: evidence from the motor vehicles aftermarket in the West Midlands region of the UK, *Regional Studies*, 23, 2, 139–150.

Massey, D. and Allen, J. (eds.) (1988) *Uneven Redevelopment: Cities and Regions in Transition*. Hodder and Stoughton/The Open University Press, London.

Meager, N. (1991) *Self Employment in the United Kingdom*, IMS Report No. 205, University of Sussex.

Meegan, R. (1988) A crisis of mass production?, in Allen, J. and Massey, D. (eds.) (1988) *Restructuring Britain: the Economy in Question*, Sage, London.

Milne, S. (1991) The UK whiteware industry: Fordism, flexibility or somewhere in between?, *Regional Studies*, 25, 3, June, 239–254.

Naylor, P. (1988) In praise of older workers, *Personnel Management*, November, 44–48.

NEDO (1986) *Changing Working Patterns*. Report prepared for NEDO in association with the Department of Employment, NEDO, London.

NEDO (1991) *The Experience of Nissan Suppliers: Lessons for the UK Engineering Industry*, NEDO, London.

Oakey, R. (1991) Government policy towards high technology: small firms beyond the year 2000, in Curran, J. and Blackburn, R. A. (1991) (eds.) *Paths of Enterprise*, Routledge, London.

OECD (1989) *Employment Outlook*, July, OECD, Paris.

Pahl, R. E. (1984) *Divisions of Labour*, Basil Blackwell, Oxford.

Piore, M. and Sabel, C. (1984) *The Second Industrial Divide: Possibilities for Prosperity*, Basic Books, New York.

Pollert, A. (1988) The flexible firm: fixation or fact?, *Work, Employment and Society*, 2, 3, 281–316.

Pollert, A. (1991) (ed.) *Farewell to Flexibility?*, Basil Blackwell, Oxford.

Project North East (1989) *Young Entrepreneurs Report*, Project North East, Newcastle, June.

Rainnie, A. (1989) *Industrial Relations in Small firms, Small Isn't Beautiful*, Routledge, London.

Rainnie, A. (1991) Flexibility and small firms: prospects for the 1990s, Hatfield Polytechnic Business School Working Paper 1991/2.

Rajan, A. (1987) Jobs and the service sector: a down-to-earth look at the promised land, *Personnel Management*, April, 40–44.

Ritchie, J. (1991) Enterprise cultures: a frame analysis, in Burrows, R. (ed.) (1991) *Deciphering the Enterprise Culture*, Routledge, London.

Sabel, C. (1989) Flexible specialisation and the re-emergence of regional economies, in Hirst, P. and Zeitlin, J. (1989) (eds.) *Reversing Industrial Decline*, Berg, Oxford.

Sako, M. (1989) Sub-contracting relationships in Britain: progress towards global localisation. Paper for the Globalisation of Japanese Economy, a Symposium for the Fortieth Anniversary of the Department of Economics, Komazawa University, Tokyo, 25–26 November.

Shutt, J. and Whittington, R. (1987) Fragmentation strategies and the rise of small units: cases from the North West, *Regional Studies*, 21, 1, 13–23.

Stanworth, J. and Stanworth, C. (1991) *Work 2000, The Future for Industry, Employment and Society*, Paul Chapman Publishing, London.

Stanworth, J., Blythe, S., Granger, B. and Stanworth, C. (1989) Who becomes an entrepreneur?, *International Small Business Journal*, 8, 1, 11–22.

Steinmetz, G. and Wright, E. O. (1989) The fall and rise of the petty bourgeoisie: changing patterns of self-employment in post-war United States, *American Journal of Sociology*, 94, 5, March, 973–1018.

Storey, D. J. and Johnson, S. (1987) *Job Generation and Labour Market Change*, Macmillan, Basingstoke.

The Economist (1991) Survey: Business in Europe, June.

Trevor, M. and Christie, I. (1988) *Manufacturers and Suppliers in Britain and Japan*, Policy Studies Institute, London.

Ward, R. (1991) Economic development and ethnic business, in Curran, J. and Blackburn, R. A. (eds.) *Paths of Enterprise*, Routledge, London.

Wood, D. and Smith, P. (1989) Employers labour use strategies, First Report on the 1987 Survey. Department of Employment Research Paper No. 63, London.

Wood, P. A. (1988) Employment change and the role of the producer service sector, in Massey, D. and Allen, J. (eds.) (1988) *Uneven Redevelopment: Cities and Regions in Transition*, Hodder and Stoughton/The Open University Press, London.

Appendix A

PROBLEMS OF SMALL BUSINESSES: INTERNAL AND EXTERNAL

INTERNAL PROBLEMS

Production/R & D

Ensure capacity/throughput

Maintenance

Product development

Sales/marketing

Order book/estimates	Sales management	Marketing	Stock	Quality
Value order book/est Value by line/prod **Order book:** *region* *customer* *direct sales* *agent* *delivery period* **Estimate:** *region* *customer* *direct sales* *agent* *delivery period* **Conversion:** *region* *customer* *direct sales* *agent* *delivery period* Order acknowledgement Price Quality Delivery period Delivery Pay terms Terms and conditions Determine growth Advert policy/exp **Advert by line/prod:** *region* *customer* *direct sale* *agent*	National and export Number of salesmen Territory management Salesman commission **Recruitment/selection:** *Advertisements* *Tel/letter* *CVs* *Interview* *References* *Appointment* *Introduction* Measure/control sales Performance Salesman cars Export finance Export documentation Goods despatch Goods delivery Vehicles	**Evaluation of competition and comparison with own:** *price* *quality* *delivery* *product* *service* **Evaluation of present customer and what the market wants:** *price* *quality* *delivery* *product* *after-sales service* Establish logo/company image **Method of selling:** *direct exchange* *agent advertisements* *shop layout* *sales literature* *price lists* *salesman samples* *selling aids* **Price policy:** *what market will bear* *competitors' prices* *cost plan basis* Attitude of sales staff	Value of all stock, finished and raw Stock turnover per sales day per stock by product **Work in progress:** *value* *by product* *by job*	Number of complaints Response to complaints Percentage Measure of scrap

Financial management

Gross Income	Debtors	Bank	Gross expenditure	Book-keeping	Creditors
Income	**Debt control**	Bank relationship/ supply of info.	Expenditure	Sales ledger	**Credit control:**
Cash	**customer – vet:**	Cheque books	Cheque	Purchase ledger	*agreed payment period*
Cheque	*Written payment terms*	Statements	Cash	**O/H Central:**	*authorization of invoices*
Discounts	*Discount terms*	O/D facility	**Expenditure by function of business:**	*Telephone*	
Income by:	*Prompt invoices*	Paying in book	*capital*	*Electricity*	Credits
line/product	*Prompt statements*	Collateral	*type of material*	*Gas*	**Credit by:**
region	*Written/tel follow up*	Signing authority	*type of product/ line*	*Water*	*week*
customer	*Stop supply date*	Loans	Discounts	*Product cost:*	*customer*
Direct sales force	*Legal action date*	Interest	Number of days paid late	*labour*	*product*
Agent	*Write-off date*	Charges		*material*	
Sale of assets		Deposits		*O/h*	
Bad cheques	**Debtors:**	Credit cards		Credit control	
Factoring decision	*by week*			Debt control	
No. of days late	*by customer*	**Cash/bank balance:**		Inventory costs	
	by product			Company law a/c	
		Book figure		A/c file	
		Bank reconciliation		Stock control	
				Management central info	
				cashflow	
				Control of profit by P/L	
				Ensure liquidity	
				Ensure budget control	

Administration

Implementation of law	Premises	Mail in and out	Personnel	Security	Purchase
Ins – 3rd party	Leases/deeds	Signatories	Number	Key holders	Raw materials
Fire Cert content	Building insurance	Filing	House of work	Door/lock/ alarm system	O/h
Licences			Employment T/O		
CosHH			Employ productivity		
Data Protection	Maintenance	Typing	**Record:**	Theft inside	Capital
SSP			*late*	Theft outside	
SMP	Size, now and future		*holiday*		Quote: value for money
Employment:		Printing and stationery	*absence*	Vandalism	
toilets	Rent review		Trade unions	Fraud	Terms and conditions
first aid	Cleaning		Wage/salary review		
washing water			Working conditions	Street crime	Purchase authorization
drinking water			Overtime		
notice board			Staff selection		Order procedure
anti-discrim.			Training		
sex			Retirement age		Goods inward
race			Shortage of skills		
Attachment of order					
Temp/ventilation					**Computers: software and other equip**
Space/employee					
Contracts:					
discipline					
grievance					**fax**
Tax Corp Sched D					
VAT/PAYE/NI					
Wage envelopes					
Capital gain					**photocopier**
Death duty					
Stamp duty					
P11D					
Training boards					

EXTERNAL PROBLEMS

Lack of sales

Unfair competition

Late payment of debt

Other:

Anti-competitive practices	Government practice	Black economy	Big business	Cost and availability of finance	
				Cost	**Availability**
Full range forcing	Govt mainly deals with plc	Under pricing	Discriminatory discount	Exchange rates	Short term loans
Predatory pricing	Govt agency offers predatory price			Interest rates	Long term loans
Failure to supply	Govt agency offers cheap finance		Dominate in market	O/D rates	Mortgages
Discriminatory discounts	Subsidized imports			Bank charges	O/D
	Post out			VAT	Equity share
	Faxes			PAYE	Hire purchase/leasing
	Tel Printer			Schedule D	
				Death duty	Factoring
				Capital gains	

Burden of government

Ignorance is no defence	Penalties	Infrastructure	Compliance	Monopolies
Owner has to learn and keep up to date	Employment law	Street cleaning	Inspectors of Taxes/DHSS	Electricity
Employment law	Tax	Rail	**H&S at Work Act:**	Gas
VAT	H&S at Work Act	Pedestrian	*Local*	Water
Rates	Data protection	Waste disposal	*Fire*	Telephone
Tax law				Transport
H&S at Work Act				
Licence requirem't				
Data Protection Act				
Local authority				
Town planning				

Index